# COPING

# COPING
## MALADAPTATION IN PRISONS

**Hans Toch**
**and**
**Kenneth Adams**

*With*

**J. Douglas Grant**

Transaction Publishers
New Brunswick (U.S.A.) and London (U.K.)

Library of Congress Catalog Number: 88-19972
ISBN: 0-88738-240-1 (cloth); 0-88738-877-9 (paper)
Printed in the United States of America

Library of Congress Cataloging-in-Publication Data

Toch, Hans.
  Coping, maladaption in prisons / Hans Toch and Kenneth Adams
with J. Douglas Grant.
    p.  cm.
  Includes bibliographies.
  ISBN 0-88738-240-1
  1. Prisoners—New York (State)—Psychology—Longitudinal studies.
2. Adjustment (Psychology) 3. Deviant behavior. I. Adams,
Kenneth, 1953–    II. Grant, James Douglas, 1917–    III. Title.
HV9475.N7T64 1988                                        88-19972
365'.6'019—dc19                                              CIP

*The Observer of Peoples has to be a Classifier, a Deducer, a Generalizer, a Psychologizer; and, first and last, a Thinker. He has to be all of these, and when he is at home, observing his own folk, he is often able to prove competency. But history has shown that when he is abroad observing unfamiliar peoples the chances are heavily against him. He is then a naturalist observing a bug, with no more than a naturalist's chance of being able to tell the bug anything new about itself, and no more than a naturalist's chance of being able to teach it any new ways which it will prefer to its own.*

Mark Twain
(''What Paul Bourget Thinks of Us''
in *How to Tell a Story and other Essays,* 1897.)

# Contents

# Preface

The authors of this book share an esteemed friend who is a repository of wise sayings, and these include dicta about consumers of social science writings. "Some read numbers," the sage tells us, "others, narratives. No one likes both."

The hypothesis that readers may be inhibited by parochial predilections can be differently framed, but the caution remains essentially similar: We are warned that should we combine different approaches and modes of discourse, we risk antagonizing successive cohorts of readers.

In defiance of prophecy, this book presents varieties of data, ranging from statistical trends to intimate portraits, because we feel that we need multiple sources to make full sense of our problem. One way of stating this assumption is that one must ask "what," "who," "when" and "how" questions before one asks "why" questions. Another version of the premise would be that one must map a terrain before one can study its highlights.

Readers who accept our rationale may still find, of course, that we strain its implications. Conventional prison studies, for example, are not customarily as large scale as the one we shall present, nor are case illustrations in most books as detailed as ours. Our justifications have to do with our aims, which include ensuring that we frame unrepresentative behavior in representative contexts. We center on persons with chronic problems, for example, but must first know how the lives of such persons deviate from more prevalent and less checkered careers. Such knowledge sets limits when we consider needs, responses to needs, and reforms.

Our case studies are detailed because they are designed to provide flavor as well as facts. We feel that some details help where readers are unfamiliar with the world of prisons and prisoners, and want a sense of what this world and its inhabitants are like. Moreover, we feel that "understanding" human experience partly rests on intuition or empathy, which feeds on nuances and detail. This doubly matters where impressions we convey are derivative, requiring that we assess observers and their perspectives, as well as those of the persons observed.

Our bias is primarily (but not exclusively) psychological. This means that we are interested in individuals and their reactions to a common environment—in our case, the prison. Our concern is also clinical, in that we center on men who do not function well, hoping to improve their functioning. We have other concerns, however, which fit into criminological and prison literature, which has established sociological roots. If ours is not a "mainline" contribution, we at least hope for hospitable tolerance.

The work reported in this book is exploratory; this means that we seek shapes of unfolding things, and precategorize as sparingly as we can. We follow this course, not out of modesty, but because we feel that conventional modes of judgment (such as those that divide conduct into mad or bad) disguise and distort realities. In this sense, some of the information that follows aspires to highlight and illustrate underrated complexity.

The book reflects experience accumulated in a research enterprise that has spanned several years. This enterprise was underwritten by a grant (R01-MH39573) from the Center for Studies of Antisocial and Violent Behavior of the National Institute of Mental Health. Our hosts—who extended themselves to permit the work to be done—were the New York State Department of Correctional Services and the New York Office of Mental Health. We owe particular debts of gratitude in this connection to Dr. Raymond Broaddus and to Frank Tracy of the Department of Correctional Services, and to Dr. Joel Dvoskin and Dr. Ronald Greene of the Office of Mental Health.

We are most grateful to our associates, Gail Flint and Mary Finn, for long hours organizing data collection, coding records and supervising research assistants. We also owe thanks to many persons, including Dr. Timothy Flanagan, Dr. Cornelius Stockman and Dr. Alan Lizotte, for helpful suggestions, and we could not have operated without repeated accommodations made by Donna Mackay and her staff to allow for our protracted searches through inmate records. Lastly, we are indebted to Sally Spring, who worked many months transcribing case histories and typing and retyping text. Her patience, sense of humor and attention to detail eased the more onerous aspects of our conjoint effort.

# Introduction

The content of this book can be described with varying degrees of pretentiousness. At worst, we can claim to present highlights of a research study in which we explore the seamier side of prisons, and those who inhabit it. A feature which is unusual in this study is that we follow our subjects over a period of years, with attention to the sequence in which their problems arise. We also record a variety of behavior, focusing on mental health as well as behavioral problems, and on combinations of the two.

A more generous view of the contents of this volume is that it explores in some depth the process of coping and adaptation, or rather, of noncoping and maladaptation. Viewed in this way, we track maladaptive persons who happen to be offenders through an environment that happens to be prison, and what we find has something to say beyond corrections and criminal justice.[1] Our concern with these more general implications will become obvious as we proceed. It is implicit in the premises that underlie our choice of approach, with commonalities we see in our data, and with the inferences (transcending prisoners and prisons) we draw from our analysis.

We study inmates over time because we are interested in personal change. As we shall see (chapter 1), we can presume that being in prison represents a phase of a *career,* in the same sense as does a term in school or a period of employment. And just as scholastic averages often increase or decrease and work performance improves or declines, we expect change to occur among persons who happen to be sequestered and confined. This notion may seem obvious, but it is not, in that most citizens see prisons as warehouses.[2] As for prisoners, their goal of "doing time" implies survival is an occupation, with a concomitant suspension of development. This perspective is unfortunate given the relative youthfulness of most prison inmates, and the fact that much of the conduct for which offenders are imprisoned suggests that they could usefully acknowledge that there is room for personal improvement.

Putting aside the question of whether prisons can be designed to reha- bilitate, there is the far-from-hypothetical question of whether any envi- ronment can *avoid* contributing to changes among persons who are ex- posed to it. And if we assume that prisons must contribute to positive or negative changes among inmates whether one likes it or not,[3] it follows that inventories of prison impact can help in the rational running of prisons. In fact, only an ostrich like stance would deny that knowledge about prison effects would be irrelevant to what civilized prisons by definition should do, which includes supporting the efforts of inmates who want to grow and learn and avoiding damaging the personalities of inmates who are disturbed. These goals have been increasingly recognized by observers of prison, who spell out an obligation for prison administrators to ameliorate mental health problems and advance rehabilitative ends even where the avowed purpose of prison remains that of punishment.[4]

The idea of studying change in prisoners during their terms of incarcer- ation is by no means novel. Studies involving opinion inventories admin- istered to inmates at varying stages of their sentence once enjoyed consid- erable popularity, and the results of such surveys reinforced the concern with "prisonization" which long dominated the prison literature. This concept came to refer to a presumed process whereby prisoners increas- ingly hold anti-social, anti-staff or anti-authoritarian values, which were said to peak midway during prison sentences and to decrease in salience (in an inverted "U" curve) with the proximity of release.[5] In explaining this process, its authors assumed that heavy peer influence (the "inmate culture") always subverts the influence of prison staff. The same experts, under the spell of what became known as "functional analysis" in sociol- ogy, argued that prisoners' recalcitrance in prison represents a compensa- tory adjustment to confinement. This view of prisoner behavior originated with Richard Sykes and with Donald Clemmer, who coined the term prisonization. Clemmer's version of prisonization, however, is not that now prevalent in the literature, where the process is described as "mixed," meaning that it occurs differently for offenders who bring different out- looks and attitudes into the prison. This differentiated conception began with later studies of prisonization, which reported variations from the inverted "U" curve registered by disturbed inmates (dings), inmate poli- ticians, and prisoners who hold persistently anti-social views.[6]

Our view differs from the prisonization approach in several respects. One difference is that we do not regard the prison as a world unto itself. To the confinee, we feel, prison is a life situation (admittedly, onerous) which, like other life situations, comprises threats and opportunities that must be negotiated for a time.

We suspect that no environments—even imprisoning environments—ordain what people do, even if the uniformity of their behavior suggests this. Where people behave similarly we infer that they arrive at similar solutions to similar problems, which is a far cry from following prescriptions for adaptation. Most environments in which people spend time can statistically yield "modal" careers, and this fact holds for the academic settings in which functional sociologists (and other professors) reside. Careers—including academic careers—must run their course. This means that they must offer apprenticeship, struggle, stasis and disengagement—variations on U-shaped curves, which reflect averaged change over time.

But few social settings—including prisons and universities—constrain passive compliance. Most of us (inmates, professors and others) try to govern the directions and rates of our progress in pursuit of valued goals, interests and concerns, given the opportunities we have available. Such efforts cannot be understood by centering on settings in which our careers unfold or reducing us as to bundles of responses. Disaggregating the careers of inhabitants of an environment (as in "mixed" prisonization studies) helps, but there is no substitute for following the same persons through successive stages of adaptation. In applying this approach to prisons, we join other students of prison adjustment who have noted that

> conceptually, it makes little sense to search for the psychological effects of imprisonment without acknowledging that these effects may vary considerably across individuals . . . Individual differences in coping have been ignored by studies that have sought to measure psychological effects of imprisonment. Consequently, such studies have failed to increase our understanding of how imprisonment affects individuals. It is clear . . . that an attempt to study changes in coping behavior in prison must use a longitudinal design.[7]

In our inquiry we shall rely on incidents of behavior rather than measures of attitudes. This emphasis has advantages—it is more lifelike and reflective of reality—but it also has limitations, in that we must use prison records that describe behavior that strikes staff as noteworthy. In this sense we must see inmates through the eyes of staff, though we know that staff are not only observers of prison life but participants and actors in inmate-staff encounters. There is some virtue to this contamination, however, given the staff's responsibility to act as custodians of the prison environment, whose perspective governs official reactions to behavior. This fact helps us because our goal is to map and understand the adjustment of prisoners to prisons, which includes the prison regime they must accept.

We can thus regard prison staff judgments as a criterion measure of "good" (effective) and "bad" (ineffective) adjustment by recognizing that staff are sources of feedback and of favorable and unfavorable consequences from the setting to which inmates must adjust. This means, among other things, that an unfavorable assessment by staff brings an adverse reaction of staff, representing unwelcome feedback from the environment to the inmate's behavior. This does not imply, of course, that the inmate's acts are intrinsically unhealthy or noxious or undesirable, but does mean that the inmate who has invited problems has at minimum not advanced the cause of his getting along in the setting in which he must function.

At extremes, a relativistic approach to adaptation is obviously untenable, in that it adjudges as maladaptive whatever "sane" (or legitimately rebellious) behavior we find in "insane" (or illegitimately authoritarian) places.[8] However, we can independently assess whether a setting—such as a civilized prison system—is either insane or illegitimate, and we can reject as implausible the notion that a penchant for getting into trouble in a setting such as the prison can in any sense be equated with a pattern of heroic, principled resistance to arbitrary exercises of authority. Moreover, where destructive transactions between an inhabitant and a custodian of an environment occur (as they do where an inmate and a guard both lose their equanimity and escalate a minor confrontation), we would not adjudge the result to be an example of effective coping by anyone, but rather to be an instance of compounded maladaptiveness.

We do not deny that there are junctures at which prison inmates are cavalierly dealt with, unfairly punished, individually discriminated against or even harassed. But our presumption is that, first, such instances are circumscribed and are unlikely to underlie trends in behavior rates and patterns of incidents, with which our study deals, and second, we do not see that it follows that if one is a victim one must be a good coping victim, in that some reactions to being victimized are more constructive or effective than others. We also know that in the absence of "objective" information about staff-inmate confrontations a prisoner's self-portrait can be adjudged no less self-serving than the staff's view of the inmate.

Ultimately, however, all such arguments are academic, in that coping and adaptation are not processes that can be assessed *sub specie aeternitate*. Persons must cope *with* something and adjust *to* something, and this means that we must stipulate weaknesses, limitations and liabilities of settings in which people must function. If we ask whether a student adjusts to a school, we must be concerned with his or her academic performance, and we must use criteria such as level of attendance or truancy and the presence or absence of behavior problems. In viewing adjustment in this way we may know that the school's grading methods are imperfect, that the educational experiences it provides may be less-than-inspiring, and that "real learning" is a rare (if attainable) commodity. The need to compromise is ineluctable because the only way in which we can pose the question, how well (or poorly) does a person adapt? is with regard to the imperfect world in which the person, and the rest of us, must function.

This does not mean that experienced difficulties must be equated with maladaptiveness. One way of placing behavior in perspective is that we can compare individuals and groups who operate in the same setting, and can compare a person's behavior at one point in time with his behavior at another. Such comparisons, as we shall see, will be crucial to our concern, which has to do with patterns of adaptation, and changes in such patterns over time.

### Patterns of Maladaptation

It is not easy to define the relationship between patterns of maladaptation and patterns of adaptation or successful coping. The latter are the converse of the former, of course, but the range of nonmaladaptive behavior includes marginal adjustment and rock-bottom survival as well as mastery of environmental demands.

The dictionary defines "to cope" as "to deal with and attempt to overcome problems and difficulties." The definition is congruent with social science usage, which sees coping as taking place wherever the environment presents the person with a problem, and the person attempts to solve the problem. An attempt to solve a problem is something that can be defined by default. It is different from trying to escape from a situation or persevering in the use of familiar but inapplicable solutions.[9]

If we define coping as an effort at problem solving, one link between coping and maladaptation is that maladaptation can interfere with coping. In schools, for example, habitual truants and miscreants can reduce their chances of responding to educational challenges by making themselves unavailable to learning experiences. Only extraordinary compartmentalization of time and energy can permit a person who is maladaptive in some ways to effectively cope in other ways, and even this option becomes foreclosed where responses to the person's maladaptation (such as suspension from school) remove available coping options.

If coping is more than an absence of maladaptation, we infer that maladaptation must be more than non-coping or not bothering to cope. The dictionary is ambivalent in this regard, however, since it defines maladaptation as "poor or inadequate adaptation" but includes "not conducive to adaptation" as a definition of "maladaptive." "Poor or inadequate" does not tell us much, but "not conducive to" is expanded in the definition of "maladapted" as "unsuited or poorly suited (as to a particular use, purpose or situation.)"

It is clear that maladaptive behavior, thus defined, includes efforts at coping which are clumsy or unsuccessful, and that the dysfunctional consistency such behavior implies has to do with its unsuitability to the environment in which the person operates. This definition helps us in thinking about patterns of maladaptation, because it implies that the patterning refers to a specifiable disjuncture between behavior trends and environmental demands. In other words, when we describe a pattern of maladaptation, we expect to see a person or a group who is consistently running into difficulties in a given setting because the behavior it engages in within the setting conflicts with requirements, demands or challenges of the setting.

We assume that a single "maladaptive act" would be hard to come by if we use this definition because of the inference of "unsuitability," which requires a sample of behavior large enough for us to speak of a trend, and a correspondingly adequate sample of environmental challenges or demands. By the same token, generalizing beyond given persons in given settings is not provided for in the concept of maladaptation: if we take the issue of "unsuitability" seriously, we cannot talk of "maladaptive persons" but must think in terms of "persons whose behavior is maladaptive to a setting." However, we might acknowledge that maladaptiveness can generalize to the extent to which settings make comparable demands, and the person's behavior remains consistent.

## What, Exactly, is Maladaptative?

The definitions we have reviewed thus far do not provide criteria we need to adjudge "unsuitability" or ineffectiveness of coping. We must supply our own criteria. The four criteria that are customarily used when people classify some behavior as maladaptive imply notions of the person consistently failing to accomplish goals, the person arranging for self-destructive or self-injurious contingencies, the person demonstrating deficits of perceptiveness, skill, or acumen and finally, the person creating problems for the environment and/or other persons in the environment.[10] It is reasonable to assume that any and all of these criteria could denote maladaptation, with the proviso that "all" is better than "any," and that "more" is better, in adjudging behavior maladaptive.

If we take our four criteria in combination, it means that persons who manifest patterned maladaptation must demonstrate consistent failures of accomplishment or self-defeating behavior, manifest clumsiness and other deficits in efforts to negotiate their environment, and produce problems for other persons in the environment.

Combinations that fall short of this formula might be considered less serious or very specialized. A disturbed student who is disruptive and academically deficient might thus be considered a more serious problem than a student who is disruptive but who academically excells; however, a student who regularly assaults vulnerable classmates could qualify as a very serious problem even if he is academically proficient and gets an exemplary bill of mental health.

Seriousness of maladaptiveness has to do with the level, frequency or patterning of maladaptive behavior. We have already implied that when we ourselves speak of maladaptiveness we shall require sufficiently large samples of behavior to speak of patterns or trends. We shall review samples of behavior in the aggregate, defining clusters of maladaptation for the population, with particular regard to who manifests these clusters, and at what juncture they manifest them. We shall later describe the maladaptive careers of individual persons, regarding each as a large sample of incidents to which we can apply our four criteria of maladaptation.

### Maladaptive Behavior in the Prison

The most obvious criterion of maladaptation in the prison is that of disciplinary infractions. Infractions are charges lodged by guards (and on occasion, by other staff) against inmates that bring penalties which range from the suspension of minor privileges to extended periods of segregation and the loss of good-time credit which shortens an inmate's sentence.[11] Infractions are thus acts that are deemed objectionable to setting-custodians, and which result in adverse repercussions to the actor.

We have said that we are concerned with *patterns* of behavior, and it follows that occasional prison infractions can be accorded no significance, in that patterning implies respectable behavior samples. In the case of infractions there is another reason for requiring numbers, of course, because one must allow for the sometimes imperfect exercise of discretion by prison staff who are the observers and judges of behavior.

High infractions rates carry advantages as measures of behavior. Used in the aggregate, infractions are a reliable measure first because records of infraction are exhaustively maintained, second, sources of judgments are spread among many staff functioning in a variety of settings, and third, behavior descriptions are tangible and are governed by definitions in prison rule books. Validity of infraction measures is in turn enhanced by the requirement that charges be documented, particularly where a charge is serious, and by the fact that the level of visibility of behavior for which inmates are apprehended is usually high. None of this, of course, bears on whether the behavior is maladaptive, beyond the fact that we can define acts as maladaptive if they reliably invite repercussions which are aversive and reduce the person's availability for coping opportunities.

The issue of whether prison violations can be classed as maladaptive arises because prison rules at first glance gratuitously circumscribe behavior. Prison rules cover a great deal of ground and are very restrictive if we compare them to criminal codes and other strictures imposed on citizens in the free world. To place this difference in context we must keep in mind that not only are prisons by definition freedom-reducing places, but a prison is also a closed and intimate social milieu in which people face twenty-four-hour-a-day enforced contact and cohabitation. One attribute that is thus shared by the prison and other similar environments—such as military installations, boarding schools, monasteries and hospitals—is that each person's behavior can significantly affect the experience of other persons, and can enhance or contaminate their quality of life. Prisons are thus settings that test the capacity of persons to constructively (or nondestructively) coexist with other persons and to deal with the adversities of enforced cohabitation.

Prison guards are monitors and arbiters of this human pressure-cooking arrangement. Guards are also, of course, wielders of power, and it is this fact which has impressed most observers of prisons.[12] The view of these observers gains credence from the fact that the jurisdiction of guards is substantial—one might even say, absolute and pervasive—in that it permits guards to control almost any aspect of the lives of inmates.[13] Moreover, disobeying guards' orders and showing them disrespect places inmates at risk of being penalized, though the penalties for such offenses (unless aggravated) are modest.

More important is the fact that power-in-use differs from power-in-theory, in that in most prisons guards claim that they have little, if any, actual power, and that they are subject to more circumscription than the inmates they supervise.[14] Setting this somewhat overblown claim aside, we know that guard power is sharply limited by the need to secure inmate cooperation, which means that there must be considerable give and take. Observers have also noted that most guards want to be seen as "good joes," or at least as fair and dispassionate.[15] Many guards maintain that the respect of inmates must be earned by the way authority is exercised, rather than by entitlement.[16] Most importantly, guards know that full enforcement of prison rules is impossible, and that a routine of "writing up" every inmate who could be charged would paralyze the prison disciplinary system, and that disciplining many inmates would make guards, rather than inmates, be adjudged maladaptive.[17]

The discretionary element in rule enforcement varies, to be sure, with attributes of the inmate's offense. Acts that are committed in private are less apt to bring sanctions than those that are designed for ostentatious display, and persistent offenses that follow repeated admonitions (sessions of "counseling") reliably invite formal dispositions. Violations that are nondiscretionary per se include assaultive, predatory and violent behavior, the destruction of prison property (for which repayment is exacted), drug and alcohol involvement, and threats to order maintenance, which covers behavior ranging from arson to the instigation of prison riots.

A fact of relevance is that the least leeway for discretion and the heaviest penalties accrue to acts of physical violence which are obviously acts that threaten the personal safety of persons in the prison, which in most instances means other inmates. What this implies is that pejorative characterizations of the codified disciplinary system (as arbitrarily regulating behavior in subservience to order-as-an-end-in-itself or as a manifestation of paranoia or nitpicking) apply with lesser cogency to the system in practice. It reserves its most consistent and serious attention to protecting members of the community from other members of the community. In such instances the rules may be said to penalize a minority while at the same time benefitting the majority of inmates, and in particular those who stand most in need of protection by the system.

Another point that is not obvious is that prison regulations are heavily publicized and are subject to universal cognizance, so that violations in ignorance or by happinstance are rare. Every inmate who arrives in prison is handed a rule book, whose content is the core of the induction process. Prisons are also legalistically oriented, particularly in processing serious violations which carry serious penalties.[18]

The point of belaboring such facts is to show that rule-violating in the prison—and particularly, persistent rule-violating—can indeed serve as a measure of maladaptation, despite the fact that prisons are probably more authoritarian than they need be and rely excessively on the enforcement of proliferating disciplinary codes, which regulate inmate behavior in excessive detail. The reason why one need not be deterred by these considerations is first that rule violations by an inmate require that the inmate ignore or defy a set of norms one presumes him to know and understand; second, formal charges by staff imply that their preferred informal control process has failed, which suggests that the inmate may be unable to relate constructively to persons in authority; or third, that the informal process has been transcended by the seriousness of the inmate's violation, which suggests that the inmate has manifested a disregard for community norms or a deficit of adjustment; and finally, at worst, the inmate may harm or threaten others, which makes him a danger to his environment. Such considerations must be added to those we have mentioned (self-destructive consequences) which have to do with the penalties that prison infractions invite, and the options they foreclose.

### The Disturbed-Disruptive Syndrome and Other Illogical Patterns

So far the doubts we have addressed focus on infractions as behavior-descriptions; the other side of the coin is that one's image of infractors does not resemble one's stereotype of maladaptiveness, which evokes a person who demonstrates ineptness and nonresilience rather than malevolence and disruptiveness.

Contrasting images are reinforced by the literature, which describes chronic prison infractors as young, criminally sophisticated offenders who serve short sentences but arrive with extensive apprenticeships in jungle warfare from exposure to juvenile facilities and other prisonlike settings.[19] By contrast, the inmates who have trouble surviving in prison are depicted as personally nonresilient and disadvantaged individuals with subculturally unsophisticated backgrounds and histories of mental health problems, who follow a retreatist path in the prison and are victimized by more sophisticated peers.[20]

The contrast between these two types is inviting on several grounds: first, it helps us make a distinction between mad and bad persons which is conceptually reassuring, particularly because "madness" can be attributed to personal limitations while "badness" can be blamed on exercises of volition; second, the two types of persons appear to call for different institutional responses, which in one case means punitive (or at best, corrective) measures, and in the other consists of protective, supportive and therapeutic services; and finally, the two types of persons are ideal-type participants in stereotyped transactions in which transgressors are victimizers and the "weak" provide a pool of invitingly helpless victims.[21]

Considerations such as these account for the fact that the literature contains little information that points to the possible evanescence of the distinction it likes to draw between intransigence and nonresilience. This failure to consider mad (weak)/bad (tough) combinations holds particularly for offender populations, who consequently bluff us (despite evidence of neuroticism, for instance) with well-rehearsed veneers of toughness, or regale us with rosters of symptoms in mitigation of shamelessly predatory behavior.

Occasional indicators exist, to be sure, that raise questions for us about the airtightness of customary dichotomies, particularly in settings (such as prison) where we have client behavior under close scrutiny. Settings created for particularly troublesome inmates, for example, find physicians responding to obvious mental health problems,[22] while diagnosed inmate-patients (when they are not medicated into a stupor) are often troublesome to their keepers. The latter fact has enabled us to describe a subpopulation of "disturbed-disruptive inmates" (DDIs) which does a great deal of shuttling between disciplinary segregation and mental health settings.[23] This group is instructive, because it causes conflicts in the prison around the question of who is a "legitimate mental health problem" as opposed to a management problem masquerading as a patient.[24]

The presumption we test in the study we shall report below is that the "disturbed disruptive" combination is the tip of an iceberg whose dimensions may be substantial. We postulate that an unknown proportion of persons who *are* problems (prove troublesome to settings in which they function) also *have* problems (demonstrate psychological and social deficits when they are subjected to closer scrutiny). In ventilating this assumption we recognize that lines are hard to draw and definitional problems are overwhelming. The latter consideration particularly applies to nonresilience, which lacks criterion measures that are agreed upon and reliable.

We should like to define personal nonresilience or mental nonhealth as generously as possible. We do not wish to be limited by epidemiological estimates of diagnosable conditions, nor by the proportion of inmates entitled to clinical services. However, in the absence of impressions about the psychological condition of individual inmates, we shall be forced to rely (at least for the purposes of the statistical picture we draw in the first part of this volume) on mental health contacts of inmates as an indicator of the presence or absence of difficulties. And as in the case of disruptiveness, we must invoke behavior descriptions by staff—in this case, mental health staff—to describe mental health-related problems of inmates.

Our concern is with the overlap, if any, between behavior that results in disciplinary infractions, and problems that bring inmates to the attention of mental health staff. With respect to the latter, the delivery system available in the prison is obviously a critical variable, and we are fortunate that the mental health services available to our inmates (which we shall describe in chapter 1) are extensive, though we think that an even more comprehensive system could be devised, which could accommodate a wider range of problems than those addressed in conventional clinical taxonomies. (We shall return to this issue in our last chapter.)

It stands to reason that most prisoners have no mental health or disciplinary involvements to speak of, while some will be substantial infractors, mental health clients, or both. Over time we also expect that inmates will move from one category of adaptation or maladaptation to another. This is the type of shift that is referred to by Seymour Halleck when he writes that

> If we observe the oppressed person longitudinally, we find that at any given moment in his life he employs one or more of the adaptational alternatives (normality, illness and criminality) we have listed. He either passively accepts his plight or actively tries to change it through socially acceptable channels, through illness or through criminal activities.
>
> These adaptations are neither static nor exclusive of one another. Often, two or three adaptations will characterize the person within a brief span of time. The "choice" of adaptation will be primarily influenced by two factors, the advantages provided by an adaptation plus its availability.[25]

We expect to speak of maladaptive phases of a person's career, and we expect maladaptive behavior to change in level or quality over time. In scrutinizing career phases we expect that we shall find variations as well as consistency in the quality of maladaptation.

Given the source from which we draw the careers that we shall review, we expect to find some persons who are long-term maladapters. This is not so much because we shall deal with offenders but because we shall deal with prison inmates. Though it is true that prisons contain persons convicted of crimes, prisons are also repositories of rejects from settings designed to deal with persons rejected by other settings. In other words, the behavior of which the offender stands convicted and which sends him to prison may be a less blatant indicator of his problems than his behavior in the community and in the prison. In some cases (such as with a psychotic who occasionally pulls himself together and commits a routine burglary) a person's crime may mark the high point of his resilience. Elsewhere, a crime may be more representative of a person's difficulties, and carry these to extremes.[26]

We must again stress that we shall think of patterns of adaptive or maladaptive behavior rather than of persons who are fated to demonstrate maladaptation in perpetuity. Being sensitive to change particularly assists those who must eventually address the question of what to do about persons whose maladaptiveness is consistent and persistent.

### Contaminated and Uncontaminated Patterns

The clearest instance of maladaptive prison behavior is that of the inmate who violates prison rules because he is limited, confused, self-destructive, incompetent or emotionally disturbed. Such a person meets every criterion of maladaptiveness, because his behavior is undesirable from his own vantage point, as well as that of the setting in which he must function. Persons about whom we only know that they are disruptive are a less clearcut group, because they can argue that they do what they choose to do, and that their only problem is an unjust system that keeps them from doing it. The extent to which we accept or question this position and variations of this position defines the complexity that we see in the person's pattern of behavior.

Mental health staff are divided in their position on this key issue. There are some staff who contend that chronicity of misbehavior denotes complexity of motive, and that the persistent infractor has implicit mental health problems.[27] A more conservative view presumes that most infractors are of no interest to clinical professionals in that they at worst suffer from a characterological defect which is unresponsive to therapeutic ministrations.[28]

Disciplinary personnel hold a more differentiated view, in which they share the inmate's perspective (at least, of his own motives), but sometimes question it. When staff pose questions about inmate motivation, they may do so by raising the issue of whether the inmate is disturbed or nondisturbed; however, the question is broader and more sophisticated. The issue has to do with the appropriateness, congruence, or fit between the inmate's behavior and the prison's response to the behavior. This question arises because the prison's response—which is mostly punitive—presupposes that the inmate's behavior is volitional and, they hope, susceptible to deterrence. This means that disciplinary sanctions are most appropriate where the inmate does what he does because he wants to (and would do it again), and less appropriate where the inmate's motives are complex and his basic problem or disposition remains unaddressed by the sanctions to which he must be subjected.

The point was well captured by Vernon Fox thirty years ago. Fox wrote that

> The traditional prison summary court, which places prisoners in solitary confinement for misconduct, operates on the assumption that the offender is a free moral agent who chooses to violate rules and can be "conditioned" to behave otherwise. . . . The increased demand on the emotionally immature individual or the psychopath actually intensifies his problem, setting up the recidivism cycles and resulting in repeated misconduct of the same general type without the ability to appraise himself.

> For those people, there is a need for a moratorium on the system of rewards and punishments to permit emotional maturation to occur in a controlled environment. . . . Consequently, the custodial personnel who attempt to maintain discipline in a prison must be prepared to understand human behavior, rather than trying to judge the amount of pressure necessary to keep a man in line.[29]

It appears obvious that when prison staff themselves react by raising questions, or when they contend that questions relating to the inmate's motivation or limitations could be raised if a forum for raising such questions existed, we ought to assume that the inmate's pattern of maladaptation is probably complex, even though mental health staff maintain that the inmate is clinically nondisturbed.

This does not mean that the line between "routine" chronic misbehavior and more complex patterns of maladaptiveness is easy to draw; it does mean, however, that any attempt to draw this line by exploring the complexity of inmate motives can render a service both to the inmate and those who must deal with him.

The issue we are raising is not confined to prisons and their inmates. Disruptive students in school settings raise similar questions, and keep raising them as they move from classrooms to alternative classroooms to reformatories, jails and prisons. In the case of some such unimpressive careers, the answers to definitional questions pour in, in confusing fashion. Dossiers contain diagnoses such as "childhood schizophrenia," "extreme learning disability" and "antisocial personality disorder." At the same time they describe the person with characterizations such as "hedonistic," "callous," "predatory," "explosive" and "manipulative," and abound with references to low self-esteem, bouts of anxiety and traumatic injuries sustained by falling off trees.

Confusing biographies not only reflect checkered careers, but reveal unsuccessful efforts by observers to make sense of them. To help solve this situation and to improve understanding we would have to accommodate added complexity by recognizing that conceptually disparate traits (including vulnerabilities and antisocial propensities) can coexist, and different labels can address different features of the same person, or traits that emerge at different points in time. We would also have to acknowledge that observers will talk past each other as long as they reflect different concerns (a concern with disruptiveness, for instance, or a concern with pathology) and are unwilling to relinquish these concerns. It is obvious, moreover, that some concepts (such as speculations about neurological dysfunctions) are inhospitable to integrated perspectives because they preempt the field, while at the same time they maintain distance from the data to be explained, which are the person's specific acts. It may be sophisticated to postulate that a person's misbehavior has neurological origins, for instance, but this hypothesis does not help us to understand why he does what he does.

The word *understand,* in this context is crucial. In trying to explain maladaptations to any setting, we need information that persons who run the setting can use in making sense of behavior. We also need concepts the maladaptive person himself can use in trying to get a handle on his behavior, which excludes concepts that are needlessly pejorative, intangible, or obtuse.

Concepts that are most useful must describe patterns of behavior; they must accommodate change, while acknowledging continuity. Problems thus arise where characterizations follow individuals beyond their point of applicability, or presuppose qualitative shifts where change is gradual. The phrase "schizophrenia, recovered, in remission," for example, sounds as if it describes a person who was ill but is now well; but what matters most about many persons described in this way is that they are neither ill nor well, and that they have a great deal of difficulty adjusting to life situations and can be driven over the edge by overstimulating demands.

It is important to be aware of where the person stands in relation to his short-term and long-term career, as is a sense of how the person relates to his environment. In this regard it is crucial that clinicians and others who deal with a person have intimate knowledge of the setting in which he functions (a school psychologist, for example, is advantaged in dealing with a maladaptive student), and this includes researchers who are concerned with studying adaptation. In this sense, a study of prison adaptation must be based on knowledge of the prison, and the reader of such a study will probably encounter more detail than he wishes to about life in the prison.

Research about adaptation must eventually cumulate, as does any other research. As we add portraits of career segments that describe the adjustment of different persons to different settings, the specifics that have to do with attributes of persons and settings (and the transactions between them) will no doubt merge into more general descriptions of behavior.[30]

Our study is thus a building block. It also has a related limitation that we must mention. We shall describe maladaptation of inmates to the prison, and this means that we provide a picture of prison adjustment which is one sided and incomplete. Human adjustment must be described as a combined portrait of adaptive and maladaptive behavior, which requires that we inventory adaptive as well as maladaptive acts. In the case of prisons, this presupposes that we include in narratives a running account of inmate involvements in programs, constructive extracurricular pursuits, and links to significant others.

One reason we have not provided accounts of this kind is that we could not provide them. Prisons keep the most careful track of inmate behavior that is risky and objectionable, but to date maintain no equivalently systematic records of the constructive involvements of inmates. This circumstance does not hold across all prisons, of course, and the situation may improve as prisons become uncongested and program-related concerns regain salience.[31] In the interim we glean that we can, and we shall touch on some benefits of positive prison involvements.

This report is divided into sections which explore different aspects of the problem we have outlined. We begin with a statistical section which describes comprehensive samples of behavior incidents, moving from cross-sectional pictures to sequential ones, and from unidimensional to multidimensional views. We next turn to examine detailed accounts of the behavior of some prisoners over time, grouped in terms of the content of their behavior. Finally, we outline a regenerative enterprise that we believe uses some of our methods and findings.

## Notes

1.  A comparable claim is made by Zamble, Porporino and Kalotay, who write that "since prison represents one particular environment, rather more uniform than most, knowledge of how inmates respond to the situations they experience in prison would be a significant step toward a more general understanding of how people cope with their environments. It would therefore be a theoretical problem of some general interest" (E. Zamble, F. Porporino and J. Kalotay, *An Analysis of Coping Behaviour in Prison Inmates*. Toronto, Canada: Ministry of the Solicitor General of Canada, Programs Branch, 1984, 3).

2.  This statement holds to the extent to which the public gives the matter any thought, though to be fair, the public is more concerned about keeping offenders off the street than about the content of prison programs. What public sentiment does is to impel legislators to lengthen prison terms, and the deemphasis of programming occurs as a result of prison congestion (See H. Toch, "Warehouses for people?" *Annals, American Academy of Political and Social Science,* 1985, *478,* 58–72). Warehousing has also been furthered by critics who have contended that rehabilitative programs do not work (e.g., R. Martinson, "What works?—Questions and answers about prison reform," *The Public Interest,* Spring 1974, 22–55), or that inmate involvement in prison programs responds to the blackmail that is inherent in parole decisions in indeterminate sentencing (D. Fogel, . . . *We are the Living Proof . . . The Justice Model for Corrections.* Cincinnati: Anderson, 1975).

3.  We noted elsewhere that "we can, of course, carelessly leave the environment's impact to chance by running warehouses where we unwittingly let negative influences predominate. Or, we can consciously try to maximize constructive and positive forces available to us even in the last-resort prisons. . . . Cognizance of prison impact and its management takes us into the treatment area, whether we like it or not" (H. Toch, "Classification for programming and survival," D. A. Ward and K. F. Schoen, eds., *Confinement in Maximum Custody.* Lexington: D. C. Heath Lexington Books, 1981, 40). See also R. Johnson, *Hard Time.* Monterey, CA: Brooks/Cole, 1987.

4.  This distinction is explicitly drawn by Norval Morris, who writes that " 'rehabilitation,' whatever it means and whatever the programs that allegedly give it meaning, must cease to be the purpose of the prison sanction. This does *not* mean that the various developed prison programs within the prison need to be abandoned; quite the contrary, they need expansion. But it does mean that they must not be seen as *purposive* in the sense that criminals are to be sent to prison *for* treatment" (N. Morris, *The Future of Imprisonment.* Chicago: University of Chicago Press, 1974, pp. 14–15). According to this position,

rehabilitative programs can be justified because the prison can thus meet the urgent needs of large proportions of disadvantaged persons in prisons who stand in need of remedial services (N. Morris and G. Hawkins, *Letter to the President on Crime Control*. Chicago: University of Chicago Press, 1977), or because the alternative is to let people actually deteriorate in confinement. In the words of another author, "Rehabilitation in this sense means a state effort to prevent and neutralize the unwanted harmful side effects of its own punitive intervention, as well as to respond to the human challenge posed by the extremely socially deprived offenders" (E. Rotman, "Do criminal offenders have a constitutional right to rehabilitation?" *Journal of Criminal Law and Criminology*, 1986, *77*, 1023–1068, p. 1028).

5. The first of the questionnaire studies that showed the inverted "U" curve was reported by Stanton Wheeler ("Socialization in correctional communities," *American Sociological Review*, 1961, *26*, 697–712). Wheeler's is a cross-sectional study, but he suggests reinterviewing inmates in future studies. Wheeler also anticipates that the liberalization of prison conditions "may be able to strengthen tendencies toward positive change in attitude during the late phases of imprisonment." Wheeler's study has been repeatedly replicated. One successful large-scale replication is that of Peter Garabedian ("Social role and processes of socialization in the prison community," *Social Problems*, 1963, *11*, 140–152).

6. Garabedian, note 5, supra. Donald Clemmer writes, "we may use the term *prisonization* to indicate the taking on in greater or less degree of the folkways, mores, customs, and general culture of the penitentiary. Prisonization is similar to assimilation" (D. Clemmer, *The Prison Community*. New York: Holt, Rinehart and Winston, 1965, p. 299). Clemmer distinguishes between "universal factors of prisonization," which have to do with inmates accepting their inmate status and making a home of the prison, and long-term prisonization, which embues inmates with "the criminalistic ideology in the prison community." Clemmer's scheme suggests that the longer the inmate stays in the prison, the more antisocial he will become.

7. Zamble, Porporino and Kalotay (note 1, supra,) p. 21.

8. D. Rosenhan, "On being sane in insane places," *Science*, 1973, *179*, 250–258; *180*, 365–369.

9. Robert W. White writes that "it is clear that we tend to speak of coping when we have in mind a fairly drastic change or problem that defies a familiar way of behaving, requires the production of new behavior, and very likely gives rise to uncomfortable affects like anxiety, despair, guilt, shame, or grief, the relief of which forms part of the needed adaptation. Coping refers to adaptation under relatively difficult conditions." ("Strategies of adaptation: An attempt at systematic description," in A. Monat and R. S. Lazarus, *Stress and Coping*. New York: Columbia University Press, 1985, p. 123). If an organism is to successfully adapt, according to White, it must "keep securing adequate information about the environment; (2) maintain satisfactory internal conditions both for action and for processing information; and (3) maintain its autonomy or freedom of movement, freedom to use its repertoire in a flexible fashion" (p. 130). A more detailed prescription is provided by Bramson, who suggests that "underlying the coping process are six fundamental steps that will help you to cope successfully, no matter what Difficult Person you need to deal with. (1) Assess the situation. (2) Stop wishing the Difficult Person were

different. (3) Get some distance between you and the difficult behavior. (4) Formulate a coping plan. (5) Implement the plan. (6) Monitor the effectiveness of your coping strategy, modifying it where appropriate" (R. M. Bramson, "Toward effective coping: The basic steps," in Monat and Lazarus, *Stress and Coping*, 24. Howard and Scott define effective coping as consisting of "assertive" responses, "in which the organism meets the problem directly and attempts a solution" (A. Howard and R. A. Scott, "A proposed formula for the analysis of stress in the human organism," *Behavioral Science*, 1965, *10*, 141–160, p. 147). Alternative (maladaptive) responses include withdrawing from the problem (denying the problem or retreating from it), blind aggression, panic and inertia. These types of responses are sometimes called "fight/flight reactions," and are contrasted with "problem solving," which is adaptive.

10. In most maladaptation there is also a tendency for the ineffective behavior to persist or to escalate despite feedback of ineffectiveness. In discussing the careers of chronic disciplinary violators in the prison, for example, Vernon Fox speaks of a "recidivism cycle," which he describes as follows: "The progression begins with (1) the situation in the institution with which the prisoner cannot cope, (2) failure to solve the problem, followed by (3) replacement of realistic efforts by substitute regressive behavior, (4) an intensification of the original problem by failure of substitute methods, (5) repeatedly grasping for an answer, any answer and, finally (6) the compulsive repetition of the one answer he has found whether it works or not" (V. Fox, "Analysis of prison disciplinary problems," *Journal of Criminal Law, Criminology and Police Science*, 1958, *49*, 321–326, p. 325).

    Another point made in the literature is that maladaptive persons seek reinforcement from other maladaptive persons, whereas good copers have recourse to persons who can assist them in trying to solve their problems (D. Mechanic, *Students Under Stress: A Study in the Social Psychology of Adaptation*. New York: Free Press, 1962).

11. Good time credit is subject to restoration if the inmate's behavior improves and the improvement is sustained over time.

12. For a comprehensive discussion of the exercise of power by correction officers, see G. M. Sykes, *The Society of Captives: A Study of a Maximum Security Prison*. Princeton: Princeton University Press, 1958.

13. This relationship between custodians and inmates has been described by Erving Goffman, whose observations, however, derive from contacts between hospital attendants and psychiatric patients. See E. Goffman, "On the characteristics of total institutions," in *Asylums: Essays on the Social Situation of Mental Patients and Other Inmates*. Garden City, N.Y.: Doubleday (Anchor), 1961.

14. Among the studies which describe the feeling of powerlessness of guards are E. D. Poole and R. M. Regoli, "Alienation in prison: An examination of the work relations of prison guards," *Criminology*, 1981, *19*, 251–270; and H. Toch and J. Klofas, "Alienation and desire for job enrichment among correction officers," *Federal Probation*, 1982, *46*, 35–44.

15. Sykes, *Society of Captives* (note 12 supra). Also see T. Mathiesen, *The Defences of the Weak: A Sociological Study of a Norwegian Correctional Institution*. London: Tavistock, 1965.

16. L. X. Lombardo, *Guards Imprisoned: Correctional Officers at Work*. New York: Elsevier, 1981.

17. Sykes, *Society of Captives* (note 12, supra); Lombardo, *Guards Imprisoned* (note 16).

18. Due process in disciplinary hearings has resulted from court interventions and the threat of further interventions, and it includes such elements as the disclosing of charges, the calling of witnesses at the inmate's request, expeditious processing, the availability of appeals, the maintenance of stenographic records, and the presence of a staff member representing the inmate's interests.

19. Two reviews cover publications that provide data about chronic prison offenders; they are W. Chapman, "Adjustment to prison: A review of inmate characteristics associated with misconduct, victimization and self-injury in confinement." *Classification Improvement Project, Working Paper*. Albany, New York: New York State Department of Correctional Services, 1981; and T. Flanagan, "Correlates of institutional misconduct among state prisoners," *Criminology*, 1983, *21*, 29–39.

20. D. A. Jones, *The Health Risks of Imprisonment*. Lexington, MA: D. C. Heath, (Lexington), 1976; H. Toch, *Men in Crisis: Human Breakdowns in Confinement*. Chicago: Aldine, 1975. Among inmates, those who experience crises include an overrepresentation of young inmates and of men with past violence involvements, though other demographic variables (e.g., ethnicity) differentiate the vulnerable and disruptive prisoner subpopulations.

21. L. H. Bowker, *Prison Victimization*. New York: Elsevier, 1980; D. Lockwood, *Prison Sexual Violence*. New York: Elsevier, 1980; C. Bartollas, S. Miller and S. Dinitz, *Juvenile Victimization, The Institutional Paradox*. New York: Wiley, 1976.

22. For instance, the Mecklenberg Correctional Center, the specialized institution of the Virginia Department of Corrections, which contains inmates deemed seriously disruptive, records that "twenty seven percent (of disruptive inmates) have been previously committed to a mental health facility for treatment. Of these with prior psychiatric commitments, the average inmate has been committed on 2.12 occasions" *Mecklenberg Treatment Program, Mecklenberg Correctional Center*. Boydton, Virginia: Mecklenberg Correctional Center, December, 1981 (mimeo). Another case in point is provided by an Ohio study of intractable inmates, intractability being defined as "a chronic disciplinary and adjustment problem within the prison" (L. B. Myers and G. W. Levy, "The description and prediction of the intractable inmate," Columbus, Ohio: Battelle, 1973, p. 11). Myers and Levy find that "the intractable group had a higher frequency of sick calls (about twice as high), with tension as the primary complaint (22%), and tranquilizers as the primary prescribed medication (44%)" (p. 15). They also note that "psychometric test results show that the intractable group scored lower on all IQ, grade level, and psychometric aptitude tests," and that "the intractable group had higher scores on the MMPI (Depression) Scale" (p. 16). The psychometric data are particularly revealing. In the distribution of composite IQ scores (Optic and WAIS), the range of scores for the intractable group extended to a bottom score of 52 (compared to low scores of 72 and 77 for the "tractable" group), and the range for revised Beta scores is 47 to 112 for "intractable" inmates and 70 to 121 for the "tractable" group.

   Studies of disruptiveness in mental hospitals also show that chronic patterns are heavily concentrated among a minority of patients. One study cited by Smith found that "2 percent of patients accounted for 55 percent of all violent incidents" (A. C. Smith, "Violence," *British Journal of Psychiatry*, 1979, *134*, 524, 529, p. 529). A Canadian team surveyed 198 patient assaults, and discovered that "13% (N = 18) of the patients committed 61% of the assaults" (V. L. Quinsey, "Studies in the reduction of assaults in a maximum security psychiatric institution," *Canada's Mental Health*, 1977, *25*, 21–23, p. 21).

23. H. Toch, "The disturbed disruptive inmate: Where does the bus stop?" *Journal of Psychiatry and Law*, 1982, *10*, 327–349. The shuttling procedure is called "bus therapy," and it reveals pressures to make the "bus stops" as brief as decency permits. Wilson notes that "administrators from mental health and corrections agencies will each maintain in theory that they are best qualified to handle the 'mad and bad.' But in practice, neither wants to deal with him. The frequent result is a brutalizing series of transfers. . . . 'There are,' says Rowen (of the AMA) 'problems in both camps. Correctional administrators, wanting to get rid of their bad apples, will slip them off to mental health. And the mental health administrators don't want to monkey around with acting-out clients, so they send them back.' " R. Wilson, "Who will care for the 'mad and bad'? "*Corrections Magazine*, 1980, *6*, 5–17, p. 8.

Freeman, Dinitz and Conrad conclude that "neither mental hospitals nor prisons welcome the disturbed and dangerous inmate. . . . The resulting 'bus therapy' expresses the reluctance which both kinds of institutions feel in contemplation of the burden of this kind of inmate. Until courts and administrators can establish rules to govern the disposition of such inmates their programming will be punctuated by bus movements which are clearly not intended for their benefit"(R. A. Freeman, S. Dinitz and J. P. Conrad, "A look at the dangerous offender and society's efforts to control him," *American Journal of Correction*, January-February, 1977, 25–31, p. 30).

24. Wilson, "Mad and Bad" (note 23, supra) points out that "a common criticism by psychiatrists of prison administrators is that they want the doctors to handle the problem cases, which are not always psychiatric problems" (p. 14). Vicki Agee, by contrast, recalls that "we drove our disturbed delinquents there—they beat us back—with the diagnosis of 'manipulation'. . . . (We) tried to outplay Mental Health at the 'Name Game.' They won, of course—you can't help but win when you hold all the cards. . . . Most of the games revolve around the Psychotic versus Character Disorder (diagnoses). . . . Character disorders (which I think means anybody who intimidates, messes over, or hurts people) particulary do not belong in hospitals, because they are untreatable" (V. L. Agee, "The closed adolescent treatment center: Utah Correctional Association Annual Conference," September 10, 1981, p. 2).

25. S. L. Halleck, *Psychiatry and the Dilemmas of Crime.* New York: Harper and Row, 1967, p. 73.

26. Zamble, Porporino and Kalotay, note 1, supra; Johnson, note 3, supra.

27. This is the position reflected by Vernon Fox (note 10, supra. One forensic clinician suggests a delivery modality he calls "The Bum of the Month Club" to which wardens would be invited to send obstreperous inmates (Joel Dvoskin, personal communication).

28. See D. Reveron, "Mentally ill—And behind bars." *APA Monitor*, March, 1982, 10–11. The "characterological defect" view is often expressed by diagnosing inmates as suffering from "antisocial personality disturbance." This category, as defined in the *Diagnostic and Statistical Manual* (third edition) could be applied to most inmates, but is in practice reserved for those who manifest behavior problems.

29. Fox, *Prison Disciplinary Problems* (note 10, supra), p. 326.

30. Examples of studies in widely different settings are Mechanic's classic observations of graduate students who must cope with comprehensive examinations (note 10, supra), and the famous study by Janis of patients who face impending operations (I. L. Janis, *Stress and Frustration*. New York: Harcourt, Brace Jovanovich, 1969). As an example of cross-application, Janis's findings could be used by prison administrators to design a meaningful orientation experience for inmates. Compilations of stress/adaptation case materials such as the Monat and Lazarus reader (note 9, supra) frequently draw their illustrations from a large variety of life situations, but integrative concepts that link such diverse experiences and the responses to them remain to be developed.

31. The advent of prison information systems is a mixed blessing, because such systems permit systematic tracking of prisoner involvements, but are built around forms that discourage the detailed entries which are needed to reconstruct inmate experiences and responses to programming.

# Part I

# Aggregate Patterns

# 1

# Data Collection and Analysis

In this chapter, we will describe our research site, introduce our approaches to the use of aggregate statistics, review the data collection procedures and discuss several of the problems we encounter in a project of this type.

As of September 1986, the New York prisons in which we conducted our research housed 38,000 inmates in fifty correctional institutions that employed 21,000 prison staff.[1] The system is not only cosmopolitan and substantial (the third largest in the country) but the administrators of the system have identified our subject matter as an area of concern to them, as have the providers of mental health services to the system. This interest matters because the cooperation of agency officials proved to be critical in gaining access to the large number and variety of prison and mental health records we needed.

Strong support of our project can be partly traced to a tradition of concern in New York State for locating inmates with "special needs" and providing services for such inmates. New York's top correctional official recently declared,

During my tenure as Commissioner, DOCS (the Department of Correctional Services, New York's prison system) has steadily expanded and improved the programs available to inmates with developmental disabilities and other handicapping conditions. I also recognize that we need to do more. And, we are willing to do more.

At reception, inmates who are identified as being most in need of special services are referred to the extended classification program. Here, a more in-depth evaluation is performed and the individual's behavior will continue to be observed and assessed. Special assessment instruments are administered to these inmates. These instruments are then scored and evaluated.

Inmates who go through extended classification will be held at reception until an appropriate placement can be made, taking into consideration . . . the safety and individual needs of the inmate. . . . In order to establish appropriate work and treatment programs for such inmates, it is absolutely necessary that DOCS be able to identify and fully assess all inmates suspected of having handicapping conditions.[2]

New York also has a longstanding tradition of care for inmates who need formal mental health services. The system once contained two large hybrid institutions (prison hospitals), which had widely recognized progressive features, but retained individual inmates for protracted periods of time. This latter problem led to a series of court decisions on commitment and discharge procedures and treatment resources.[3] The state eventually responded to this situation by completely overhauling the prison mental health system. Along with the organizational transfer of responsibility for the treatment of mentally ill inmates to a different agency (the Office of Mental Health), a new service delivery system was set in place including an accredited acute care hospital facility—Central New York Psychiatric Center (CNYPC).

The new system was organized around a community mental health model which has as one of its goals reducing the time patients spend in hospital settings.[4] Administrators assumed that if mentally ill inmates are to spend more time in their "community" (i.e., prison), they would have to be provided with a variety of supportive services. Recognition of this fact led to the development of a network of prison outpatient clinics. These clinics, described as "satellites units" of the hospital, are located at major prisons scattered throughout the state. Each satellite unit is staffed by psychiatrists, psychologists, social workers and nurses, and comes equipped with provisions for short-term observation and residential treatment. Several satellite units offer longer term residential programs (Intermediate Care Units), operated jointly with the prison system. These programs are designed to house inmates who do not require hospitalization but who have serious difficulties adjusting to prison life.

Inmates come to the attention of mental health staff in a variety of ways. During the reception and classification process, inmates may be referred immediately to mental health staff or they may be assigned to a prison with a satellite unit and placed on caseload. In the correctional system, moreover, any staff member can refer an inmate to the mental health unit. Many, if not most, referrals come from security staff, who by virtue of their position observe the inmate's daily behavior in a variety of social settings. Finally, inmates have the option of making a self-referral to mental health staff.

These recent developments in the prison mental health system have held a number of implications for our project. Most significantly, the involvement of the Office of Mental Health in prisons created a division of responsibilities across agency lines and issues surfaced where lines proved difficult to draw clearly. One such issue has to do with the sorts of inmates who are of interest to us, and particularly the mentally disordered inmates who disrupt prison routines.

Especially promising was the fact that the involvement of the Office of Mental Health led to a substantial improvement in clinical recordkeeping and the fact that the emphasis on outpatient treatment meant that mentally ill inmates would be spending as much time as possible in the prison, where prison records could track their careers. From a research point of view, these developments suggested the existence of relatively reliable and complete data sources about inmate mental health problems in the prison.

As we have noted, we are interested in manifestations of symptomatic and disruptive behavior over the course of an inmate's prison term, and we are especially interested in the more extreme ends of these behavioral spectrums. This agenda poses a number of methodological issues relating to sampling, sources and coding of data, and the description of sequences of events over time.

### Sampling

Inmates who are highly disruptive or who are seriously emotionally disturbed admittedly constitute a minority within prison populations. The relatively small number of inmates who are the primary focus of this study poses the first research design problem. In order to insure reliability in statistical analyses, one needs an adequate number of subjects. When simple random sampling procedures are applied to the study of infrequent events large sample sizes with correspondingly large expenditures of resources are necessary to meet this requirement. A way of dealing with this problem is to make sampling procedures more efficient by using a stratified design. This design involves a two-step procedure that first divides the population into strata or groups and then randomly samples at different ratios across strata. The advantage of a stratified design is that it allows one to "oversample" subjects of greatest interest and "undersample" subjects of least interest.[5] This is the procedure we chose to employ.

Our sampling frame, or the population from which we select our sample, is a cohort of inmates released from the New York State prison system between July 30, 1982 and September 1, 1983. During this fifteen-month period a total of 10,534 inmates were released to the community. Prison mental health experience and rate of disciplinary infractions are the strata we use in our sampling procedures.[6]

In New York, inmate disciplinary records are stored at the last facility of confinement so there is no central source to tap for this information. This meant that before we could stratify the cohort we had to collect the disciplinary record of each inmate from the prison from which he was released. With the cooperation of the Department of Corrections we were able to collect disciplinary records for 9,103 inmates. We then tabulated the number of disciplinary incidents and used this information in conjunction with admission and release dates to identify inmates with high and low infraction rates.

Our next step was to cross-reference the names and birthdates of inmates in our release cohort against computerized client records maintained by the Office of Mental Health. This matching procedure allowed us to identify inmates who were hospitalized during incarceration or who had received outpatient services.

The two steps allowed us to cross-classify the cohort of inmates in terms of mental health experience and disciplinary history. We could then proceed to oversample inmates with histories of serious mental health problems and inmates with extensive disciplinary records. The stratification categories and the sampling ratios we employed are displayed in Table 1. As this table shows, we included in the sample all inmates who were hospitalized during their prison term as well as all inmates with disciplinary rates above the 95th percentile.

To compensate for the selection biases introduced through stratification, an inverse weighting procedure must be used in the statistical analyses. For example, cases from strata with a sampling ratio of one-half are multiplied by two during statistical analyses, cases with a sampling ratio of one-eighth are multiplied by eight and so on. Cases with a sampling ratio of one (i.e., hospitalized inmates) are unaffected by inverse weighting. The weighting procedure yields estimates for the release cohort, and

**TABLE 1.1**
**Details of stratified random sampling design**

| DISCIPLINARY EXPERIENCE | | | PRISON MENTAL HEALTH EXPERIENCE | | | | | |
|---|---|---|---|---|---|---|---|---|
| | | | NO SERVICE (n = 7565) | | OUTPATIENT (n = 1368) | | HOSPITALIZED (n = 170) | |
| Group name | Annual rate | Percentile range | Sampling ratio | N of cases | Sampling ratio | N of cases | Sampling ratio | N of cases |
| Low | 0–2.5 | 0–50 | 1:10 | 480 | 1:2 | 328 | 1:1 | 56 |
| Medium | 2.6–4.9 | 51–75 | 1:8 | 209 | 1:2 | 163 | 1:1 | 48 |
| High | 5.0–9.9 | 76–92 | 1:5 | 188 | 1:1 | 218 | 1:1 | 26 |
| Special interest | 10.0+ | 93–100 | 1:1 | 565 | 1:1 | 174 | 1:1 | 41 |

for this reason the number of cases reported in tables exceeds the number of cases we sampled.

### Sources of data

Our primary source for disciplinary information is the warden's record card. This document follows an inmate as he moves through the correctional system and lists the date, charges and disposition of each prison rule violation. The warden's card also serves as a record of institutional transfers. Our major source of information for mental health-related behavior was the treatment files maintained by mental health staff. These files also follow inmates through the correctional system and contain all clinically relevant information.

Prison and mental health files can be seen as documenting a series of events over the course of a prison term, and we approached the coding task from this framework. For each relevant entry in an inmate's record, we would code the date of the event and the associated event descriptions. For example, when reviewing disciplinary records we would code the date of the infraction, the disciplinary behavior and the disposition. Similarly, when reviewing mental health files we would code the date of the observation and the observed behavior that was described. Although we developed separate coding schemes for disruptive and symptomatic behavior, use of behavioral codes was not constrained by the source of information. Thus, if disruptive acts were noted in the mental health files they were coded along with symptoms that were described. In addition to observations of the inmate's behavior, we coded dates and destinations of prison transfers, including commitments to the hospital and placement in special therapeutic correctional programs.

The event framework allows us to combine prison and mental health information into a single file and to arrange the data in chronological order. This means that we can locate incidents in time over the course of an inmate's prison term and describe temporal sequences of events.

The Department of Correctional Services tapped their computerized recordkeeping system to provide us with background information on inmates in the sample. Additional information—including preprison mental health experience—was collected from the inmate's central office folder. Our main sources for this information were the presentence report which accompanies an inmate into prison and his prison classification documents. We also used central office files to supplement the warden's card in situations where disciplinary information was missing or incomplete.

Mental health files are retained at the last treatment facility, and the Office of Mental Health arranged for our access to these records by having them shipped to their central office. Despite such cooperation, we were unable to locate files for 256 outpatients in our sample after canvassing all prison treatment facilities.[7] These inmates were admitted to outpatient service but no record could be found concerning the nature of their problems. We were, however, able to consult computerized service delivery records. We found that service delivery contacts for these inmates were very infrequent and in many cases limited to only one contact. While we cannot be certain about the precise nature of these inmates' problems, it appears unlikely that the problems at issue were serious.

### Prison careers

We have indicated that we approach the description and analysis of an inmate's prison experiences as a delimited portion of a career. The dictionary defines a "career," among other things, as a "course" or "passage," and more specifically as a "course of continued progress as in the life of a person." Our use of the term "career" is more or less consistent with this definition which does not require that the term refer to occupational or professional advancement. Within the social sciences there is well-established precedent for using the career concept quite broadly. Career studies have included descriptions of the socialization of medical students[8] and of the lives of drug addicts over time.[9] Studied in this way, a career involves "an activity or sequence of activities with a natural history that is seen without particular regard to high or low points but rather to changes over time that are common to participants. In this sense careers such as pool hustler, felon, hippie, mental patient, and alcoholic can be approached in the same way as those of lawyer, doctor, businessman, pop star, and so forth."[10]

More recently, the career framework has been applied to the study of the difficulties and successes of mental patients as they move from hospital to community.[11] In these studies, as in the present study, one focus is on sequences of experiences marked by significant transitions from one social context to the next. Since we are interested in prison experiences we circumscribe an inmate's career as time spent between admission and release, and, when we find it useful to refer to parts of an inmate's prison career, we will speak of such periods as career segments or stages.

Our descriptions of inmate careers in the aggregate focus on changes in rates of behavior. Since a rate is defined in terms of a number of observations per unit of time (such as a year), we need to select an appropriate time unit before we can calculate rates. The selection of the rate denominator can be a critical choice since it can influence the way we perceive changes in rates over time. In general, given a fixed observation period, as the time unit for computing rates becomes smaller more data points will be generated and there will be more "noise" in the time curve. Conversely, as the time unit becomes larger fewer data points are generated and the time curve appears smoother.

In a related fashion, we need to deal with the fact that inmates serve widely varying amounts of time in prison, from as little as one year to as many as ten or more years. Time plots have to be made comparable across inmates with different prison terms if the data are to be analyzed in aggregate form. Prison terms can be divided on the basis of absolute time units (such as days, weeks, months) or proportional time units (such as halves, thirds, quarters). As we pointed out in the introduction, early prisonization studies generally trisected the inmate's career, dividing the prison term into the first six months, a variable middle phase, and the last six months.[12] More recent research on inmate behavior has used proportional time measures. For example, one study investigated disciplinary infraction rates over time by dividing an inmate's prison terms into four equal units (quarters).[13]

A proportional time model has the virtue of simplicity since each inmate, regardless of length of prison term, has the same number of time-served units. However, under a proportional model the amount of time represented by each unit becomes smaller or larger as the prison term becomes shorter or longer. For example, one-quarter of an eight-year prison term represents twice as much time as one-quarter of a four-year term. Differences across time units can be important because, as we have already noted, the size of the denominator used in computing rates influences the picture of time curves. The absolute time model avoids this problem but produces unequal numbers of time units across prison terms of varying lengths. If we elect to compute rates over successive three-month periods, an inmate serving eighteen months will have six data points, an inmate serving twenty-one months will have seven data points, and so on. Since we can only combine inmates with the same number of data points into an aggregate time curve, this would mean that we would have to present separately as many analyses as there are unique numbers of data points.

The following example based on hypothetical data illustrates some of the issues that are involved. Let us assume that we have three inmates serving prison terms of 15, 21 and 27 months. Let us also assume that the monthly number of disciplinary involvements for each inmate remains at 1 for the first 3 months, increases by 1 each month for the next 3 months, remains constant at 4 for the next 3 months, declines by 1 each month for the next three months and remains constant at 1 until the end of the prison term. These data are displayed in Figure 1.1. We can see that the infraction pattern is essentially the same for all three inmates, and the distinguishing

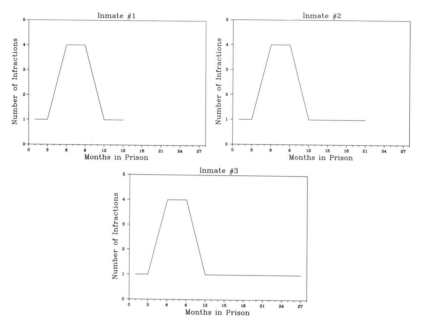

**FIGURE 1.1**
**Monthly rate of disciplinary infractions for three hypothetical inmates.**

factor among the curves is the length of the "tail" or the segment representing the period beyond 12 months.

Figure 1.2 displays the infraction rates for the same three hypothetical inmates when the prison term is divided into thirds. We find that for the first inmate the curve shows a sharp rise and fall consistent with the pattern in figure 1.1. In contrast, the curve for the second inmate indicates steady disciplinary involvement followed by a decline, while the curve for the third inmate shows a consistent decline in disciplinary involvement. The reason why the proportional model produces such different patterns becomes clear if we divide the curves in Figure 1.1 into three equal segments. Since the proportional time segments for each inmate vary in length (i.e., 5, 7, and 9 months) they intersect the monthly plots at different points, thereby obscuring common features of the original curves.

The curves we have presented are hypothetical and therefore present a neater picture than we might expect to find in the real world. However, the data illustrate a plausible scenario of prison adjustment which may be characterized by a sharp period of transition taking place early in the sentence and covering a relatively fixed period of time (that is, the length of the transition period may be independent of the length of the prison

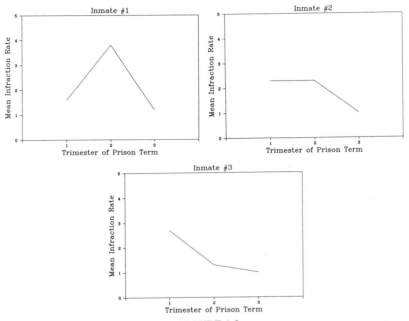

**FIGURE 1.2**
**Mean rate of disciplinary infractions by time-served trimester for three hypothetical inmates.**

term). An absolute time model would confirm this hypothesis, but a proportional time model would lead us to the opposite conclusion.

In sum, when computing rates over time we need to keep in mind the following: first, the base period should be small enough so as to be sensitive to important short-term variations but not so small as to highlight fluctuations that contribute little to our understanding of the problem, and second, base periods should be comparable across inmates so as to allow for aggregate analyses, and should not vary greatly in absolute amount of time.

We approached the problem of selecting a rate denominator inductively and began with a trial and error process. After computing rates over a number of time periods, it appeared that a three-month interval captured the important features of the distribution while reducing excessive noise in temporal fluctuations. This decision, however, leaves unresolved issues relating to proportional and absolute time models. Our strategy was to develop a hybrid model that retained the advantages of each pure model. We first divided the sample into time-served groups and then divided the prison terms for each group into equal segments. The number of segments was selected so as to yield an average value of approximately three months across inmates within a group. This produced a model in which the number of segments was the same within but different across time-served groups.

The four time-served groups we created are short-term (8 to 18 month), low average-term (19 to 30 months), high average-term (31 to 48 months), and long-term (49 months and more). Descriptive statistics on the distribution of cases and on the length of time segments across groups are displayed in Table 1.2. This table shows that 27% of the sample falls in group 1, 41% in group 2, 19% in group 3 and 13% in group 4. We also note that the mean career segment length is 84 days for group 1, 79 days for group 2, 93 days for group 3, and 92 days for group 4.

Given that the number of segments varies by time-served groups, data will be presented separately for each group when necessary. In addition, since the length of time segments is similar but not identical across inmates we must standardize rates to avoid introducing error into the statistical analyses. We therefore present annual or yearly rates throughout.

TABLE 1.2
Number and length of prison term segments by time served.

| Time-served group | Number of segments | Length of segments | |
|---|---|---|---|
| | | Mean | Std. dev. |
| Short-term 8–18 months (n = 2,379) | 6 | 84 days | 15 days |
| Low-average term 19–30 months (n = 3,653) | 9 | 79 days | 11 days |
| High-average term 31–48 months (n = 1,665) | 12 | 93 days | 12 days |
| Long-term 49+ months (n = 1,206) | 24 | 92 days | 34 days |

## Notes

1. NYS Department of Correctional Services, "Annual Report—1986" (mimeographed) Albany, September, 1986.
2. Testimony of Thomas A. Coughlin before Assembly Standing Committees on Correction and Mental Health, Mental Retardation and Developmental Disabilities, December 9, 1987, *Public Hearing on Persons with Developmental Disabilities and the Criminal Justice System,* pp. 1–3.
3. For a discussion of the early history of inmate mental health services in New York, see Association of the Bar of New York City, *Mental Illness Due Process*

*and the Criminal Defendant.* New York: Fordham University Press, 1968. For a commentary on the legal issues that resulted in changes in the NYS forensic system, see G. Morris, "The confusion of confinement syndrome: An analysis of the confinement of mentally ill criminals and ex-criminals by the Department of Corrections of the State of New York," *Buffalo Law Review,* 1968, *17,* 561–99.

4. An outline of concepts underlying the organization of NYS prison mental health services can be found in New York State Office of Mental Health, CNYPC—Psychiatric Services for Convicted Persons: A "Community" Approach, Albany (mimeographed).

5. A discussion of the technical aspects of stratified sampling designs can be found in R. Ackoff, *The Design of Social Research.* Chicago: University of Chicago Press, 1953.

6. For practical reasons, we limited our sample to males. Among inmates for whom we were able to locate disciplinary records, only 4% (n = 367) are women. This low proportion reflects the fact that relatively few women are sent to prison. In addition, we found that female inmates are less likely to exhibit the types of behavior of interest to us. Female inmates had a lower (about 30%) mean infraction rate and only two women were hospitalized, although a substantial proportion (37%) were placed on outpatient caseloads.

7. Demographic comparisons between outpatients for whom we were able to locate treatment files and other outpatients reveal the following differences: Outpatients with treatment files are less likely to be high school graduates (23% v. 29%), less likely to be employed at conviction (64% v. 75%) and more likely to admit to drug use (65% v. 58%). On the average, outpatients are also younger (25.4 years v. 27.0 years), are first arrested at an earlier age (17.3 years v. 18.3 years), and are first institutionalized at an earlier age (20.2 years v. 21.7 years). There are no statistically significant differences between the two groups on mental health history variables.

8. O. Hall, "The stages of a medical career," *American Journal of Sociology,* 1948, *53,* 327–36.

9. D. Waldorf, *Careers in Dope.* Englewood Cliffs, NJ: Prentice Hall, 1973.

10. Waldorf (note 9, supra) p. 10. Similarly, Goffman (Intro., note 13) writes "(t)raditionally the term 'career' has been reserved for those who expect to enjoy the rises laid out within a respectable profession. The term is coming to be used, however, in a broadened sense to refer to any social strand of any person's course through life. The perspective of natural history is taken: unique outcomes are neglected in favor of such changes over time as are basic and common to the members of a social category, although occurring independently to each of them. Such a career is not a thing that can be brilliant or disappointing; it can no more be a success than a failure (p. 125)."

11. H. Steadman and J. Cocozza, *Careers of the Criminally Insane.* Lexington, Ma: DC Health and Co., 1974.

12. See Wheeler (Intro., note 5) and Garabedian (Intro., note 5).

13. T. Flanagan, "Time served and institutional misconduct: Patterns of involvement in disciplinary infractions among long-term and short-term inmates," *Journal of Criminal Justice,* 1980, *8,* 357–67.

# 2

# Patterns of Prison Misbehavior

In this chapter we are concerned with the distribution of disciplinary infraction rates across types of inmates and prison terms. We will identify the social and criminal correlates of prison misbehavior and describe patterns of disruptiveness over the course of institutional life. Finally, we will develop a career typology that distinguishes patterns of highly disruptive behaviors and we will investigate the characteristics of inmates who display different patterns.

We begin by looking at the overall infraction rate for inmates in our sample. Among the entire release cohort, the average disciplinary rate is 3.6 infractions per year. Infraction rates do not vary much across time-served groups with the exception of long-term inmates who have a substantially lower rate than do other inmates (2.6 per annum).

Table 2.1 summarizes the results of a multiple regression analysis exploring the relationship of criminal and social history variables to overall infraction rates. The analysis indicates that age and pre-conviction employment status are the variables most predictive of disciplinary rates. In general, younger inmates and unemployed inmates are likely to have higher levels of disciplinary involvement. We also find other variables to be modestly predictive of infraction rates. A history of prior arrest for violent crime and race (low in the case of whites, high for nonwhites) shows a positive correlation, while education level shows a negative correlation. We also find that type of offense is a very weak predictor of infraction rates. In the analysis, dummy variables were created for each crime type with the exception of robbery, and results are to be interpreted in relation to this crime category. We find that persons convicted of murder, rape, assault and drug offenses have lower infraction rates, while persons convicted of burglary have higher infraction rates. The strongest relationship is for murder, although taken as a whole conviction offense information increases the amount of explained variance only by about one percent.

TABLE 2.1
Results of stepwise multiple regression analysis of disciplinary infraction rates.

| Step | Variable | Beta | Sig. | R Square |
|---|---|---|---|---|
| 1 | Age[a] | −.26 | .000 | .170 |
| 2 | Employment[b] | −.20 | .000 | .213 |
| 3 | Prior violent offense | .09 | .000 | .225 |
| 4 | Education[c] | −.07 | .000 | .231 |
| 5 | Marital Status[d] | −.08 | .000 | .235 |
| 6 | Race[e] | .07 | .000 | .239 |
| 7 | Murder[f] | −.07 | .000 | .243 |
| 8 | Burglary[f] | .03 | .000 | .244 |
| 9 | Rape[f] | −.04 | .000 | .245 |
| 10 | Assault[f] | −.03 | .001 | .246 |
| 11 | Drug[f] | −.03 | .001 | .247 |

a—at prison entry
b—not employed (low), employed (high) at conviction
c—high school graduate—no (low), yes (high)
d—single (low), married (high)
e—white (low), nonwhite (high)
f—conviction offense

Prior research shows age to be a consistent correlate of prison infractions, and our data reconfirm that young inmates are much more prone to engage in prison misbehavior than older inmates. Previous research has also shown marital status and work history to be fairly consistently associated with infraction rates, and we find similar associations. Although we did not find strong effects for conviction offense, murderers have been reported to have lower prison infraction rates, and our data are consistent with this finding. We find that employment history is associated with infraction rates, while most other studies do not report this relationship. However, our results, which indicate that single, unemployed, uneducated inmates have higher infraction rates, demonstrate a consistent pattern, in that these data suggest that offenders with marginal lifestyles in the community have greater difficulty adjusting to prison. Race has shown very mixed associations with infraction rates, and this means that our findings may not be generalizable to all correctional systems. The fact the prior violence emerges as an important correlate of prison infractions suggests continuity of misbehavior from community to institution. However, the influence of preinstitutional behavior appears to be at work only at extremes, since prior criminal record did not emerge as significant in the analysis.[1]

## Timing of Disciplinary Infractions

We now examine issues regarding the timing of disciplinary involvement. In general, we find that the greater the delay in onset, the lower the overall infraction rate. For example, inmates who commit their first violation within thirty days of admission show a rate of 7.3 infractions as compared to a rate of 1.8 infractions for inmates who commit their first violation more than 150 days into their sentence. Inmates who begin violating rules early in their prison sentence tend to accumulate more substantial disciplinary records than other inmates.

Mean annual infraction rates over career segments are displayed in Figure 2.1. In general, we see that the overall pattern is relatively similar across time-served groups. Infraction rates are highest at the beginning of prison terms and lowest at their end. Early portions of sentences are characterized by a sharp rise and fall in disciplinary rates, after which disciplinary rates show a consistent downward trend. The rate of decline is related to the length of the sentence, with short-term inmates showing the steepest drop and long-term inmates displaying the most gradual decline.

This statistical pattern pertains to the "average" inmate, and we might expect that the picture is more appropriate for some inmates than others. We have seen that criminal and social history variables are related to infraction rates, and this leads us to ask whether these variables influence the pattern of infraction rates over time. Age is of particular interest, since

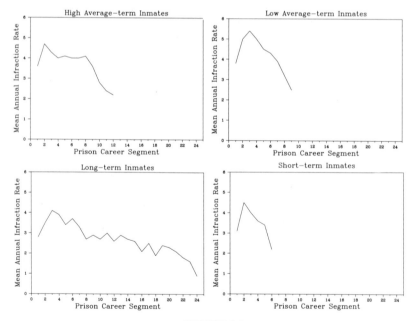

**FIGURE 2.1**
**Mean annual disciplinary infraction rates by time served.**

this variable has been often reported as a strong correlate of antisocial behavior. Figure 2.2 displays mean infraction rates over career segments by age categories.

The data indicate that young inmates consistently have higher infraction rates at all points in a prison term. We also observe that young inmates exhibit the most dramatic changes in misbehavior rates over time. The infraction rates of these inmates rise sharply in the early stages of the prison career and then steadily decline over the remainder of the sentence. In contrast, we find that older inmates have lower infraction rates that remain fairly stable from admission to release. Thus, the infraction rate curve for older inmates appears relatively flat and fails to exhibit any substantial fluctuations over time. These age-related patterns hold across all time-served categories. Finally, we point out that young, long-term inmates exhibit the highest infraction rate of any inmate group.

In sum, we find that a consistent pattern characterizes inmate disciplinary rates over the course of prison terms. Rates of disciplinary involvement exhibit a sharp rise and fall early in the sentence and then continue to decline until release to the community. The overall pattern maintains across time-served groups but varies dramatically by age, being most characteristic of younger inmates. Younger inmates exhibit the sharpest

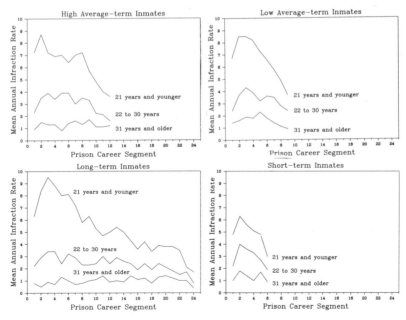

**FIGURE 2.2**
**Mean annual disciplinary infraction rates by age and time served.**

changes in misbehavior rates, while rates for older inmates are relatively constant over time. In addition, we find that younger inmates reliably demonstrate higher infraction rates at all points in their sentence. This finding tells us that overall higher infraction rates for young inmates are not just the result of short periods of intense disciplinary involvement. Rather, a greater propensity for disruptiveness maintains across the entire prison sentence of these inmates.

A strong inverse relationship between age and rates of antisocial behavior ranks as the most consistent finding in criminological research. Explaining this association, however, has not been a popular pastime since "when attention shifts to the meaning or implications of the relationship between age and crime, that relation easily qualifies as the most difficult fact in the field."[2]

In an attempt to explain the age-crime relationship, some scholars have emphasized the variety of social and psychological changes that accompany the aging process.[3] These changes can include developments in areas of marriage, family and employment that lead to greater attachments to others and stronger community ties. Changes can also include the broad psychological developments we shall discuss in chapter 13, such as replacement of hedonistic values with more abstract and principled normative systems, and shifts in time perspectives from a concern with immediate to one with longer term consequences of behavior. Recently, some have argued that age per se should be viewed as a cause of criminal or antisocial behavior.[4] The argument is based on the fact that the age-crime relationship appears to be both universal (that is, it maintains across cultures and across institutional and noninstitutional settings) and constant (that is, it persists across historical periods). From this point of view, chronological age and not the concomitant changes of growing older constitute the basis of the age-crime relationship.

The data we have presented contain an aging effect, since as inmates become more prosocial over time they also grow older (or vice versa), which raises the possibility that changes in disciplinary involvement may simply be the result of increasing chronological age. By implication, however, if chronological age is the operative factor, prison experiences should contribute little to the decline in infraction rates. We therefore can expect to find equivalent infraction rates across inmates of the same age at different points in their sentences. In order to address this issue, we computed infraction rates for age equivalent groups at various points in the prison term. We especially examined the time surrounding admission and release, because these periods encompass the greatest difference in behavior.

The data in table 2.2 suggest that prison experiences *do* temper inmate

TABLE 2.2

**Mean annual disciplinary infraction rates during early and late segments of prison terms for inmates of the same age.**

| Age | First 6 months | Last 6 months | First 9 months | Last 9 months |
|-----|------|------|------|------|
| 18 | 9.0 | 5.6 | 9.1 | 9.0 |
| 19 | 7.6 | 5.6 | 8.4 | 7.2 |
| 20 | 6.2 | 4.4 | 6.8 | 5.5 |
| 21 | 5.6 | 4.8 | 6.3 | 5.3 |
| 22 | 4.6 | 4.0 | 4.8 | 4.4 |
| 23 | 4.0 | 3.2 | 4.4 | 3.5 |
| 24 | 4.6 | 2.8 | 4.7 | 3.5 |
| 25 | 3.0 | 2.6 | 3.0 | 2.9 |
| 26 | 2.8 | 2.8 | 2.8 | 2.8 |
| 27 | 2.2 | 2.4 | 2.5 | 2.4 |
| 28 | 2.8 | 2.6 | 3.1 | 2.4 |
| 29 | 2.0 | 1.8 | 2.1 | 1.9 |
| 30 | 2.2 | 1.8 | 2.1 | 2.3 |
| 31 | 3.0 | 1.8 | 3.2 | 2.3 |
| 32 | 1.4 | 2.0 | 1.3 | 1.7 |
| 33 | 2.0 | 2.0 | 2.5 | 1.6 |
| 34 | 1.0 | 1.4 | 0.9 | 1.6 |
| 35 | 1.8 | 0.6 | 2.1 | 0.8 |

*Note: Age categories are based on age at admission for early prison segments and age at release for late prison segments.*

misbehavior. Infraction rates are lower at the end of prison sentences than at the beginning, allowing for the fact that inmates grow older while incarcerated. The effect, however, is conditioned upon chronological age such that *only* inmates under twenty-five years of age show a decrease. We also notice that chronological age has a stronger effect on infraction rates than stage of sentence, in that reductions are more substantial across age categories holding location in sentence constant.

These data support the argument that age per se does not provide a complete explanation of why misbehavior decreases as inmates complete their sentences. Although chronological age is strongly related to rates of disruptive behavior, experiential factors emerge as important added considerations, particularly for young offenders. The simple passing of time may serve to reduce antisocial propensities, but what happens while time passes is not completely irrelevant.

The experience-based changes we infer from the data are interesting because of where and for whom they occur. Prisons stand outside the context of normal social arrangements. They provide a highly structured environment with opportunities for education and job training more assertively available than in the community. Young inmates, who are presumably more rambunctious and less mature than older inmates, appear to derive some benefit from this forced choice environment. We must assume that learning, the association of positive and negative consequences with behaviors, plays a role in fostering changes. We shall also show (in chapter 12) that meaningful participation in conventional activities can turn attitudes in a prosocial direction, and we shall argue that maturational advances at the lower end of the spectrum can have substantial influence on behavior. It is perhaps both surprising and encouraging to find that prison inmates who are initially most resistant to restrictions on their personal liberty demonstrate increasing levels of conformity over time.

Given that antistaff values find expression in prison rules violations, our data hold implications for theories of prisonization.[5] We recall that early perspectives implied that prisonization might be an adjustment to confinement, which means that it would increase as a function of time served. This framework is clearly not supported by the data.[6] Not only do infraction rates show a consistent nonlinear pattern early in the prison term, but the overall direction of change is opposite of that predicted.

We have also noted that more recent perspectives view prisonization as a nonlinear function of time, and often describe this in terms of an inverted-u pattern.[7] This framework predicts that degree of prisonization will rise and then fall over the course of a sentence and be greatest in the middle of the sentence where inmates are most removed in time from community influences.[8] The data indicate that disciplinary rates rise and then fall as predicted, but the fit of the inverted-u pattern appears to vary by sentence length. The careers of short-term inmates fit the pattern best, but inflection points for longer term inmates occur much earlier than at midsentence. We might be inclined to interpret the curves as evidence for the differential appropriateness of the inverted-u pattern by sentence length except that disciplinary rates for all sentenced groups peak during the second or third career segment. It seems to us that the more important finding is that disciplinary rates peak for all inmates somewhere between the first six to nine months of incarceration. That this point happens to be closer to midsentence for short-termers than for other inmates can distract us from the consistency in the data.

We also do not find strong evidence for an "anticipatory resocialization" effect, which is an important part of the inverted-u theory of prisonization.[9] Rates of antisocial behavior do not decrease just prior to release, but instead seem to reflect a steadied decline. Since this conclusion is based on visual inspection of the graphs, we attempted to investigate the "anticipatory resocialization" issue more directly. The concept predicts that levels of conformity increase in preparation for return to the community, and key factors in this equation are proximity and certainty of release date. Events that clearly signal impending return to the community should therefore produce noticeable changes in behavior. We examined infraction rates at one- and two-month intervals before and after the last parole hearing, in which the inmate learns of his impending release and found rates to be nearly identical. We also compared disciplinary rates between penultimate and release facilities, and we found no difference.

We interpret the pattern of changes in disciplinary rates as evidence that prison entry marks a difficult period of adjustment. Being incarcerated seems to involve a period of "transition shock" as represented by a consistent rise in disciplinary rates early in the sentence. Adjustment difficulties are most substantial among the young, in that young inmates have the highest infraction rates and show dramatic changes in behavior. In contrast, disciplinary rates for older inmates are low to begin with and fail to show any remarkable changes. However, we find that early periods of incarceration generally stand out as a critical stage given that they are characterized by the highest levels of nonconformity. We also find that young inmates continue to have the greatest problems adjusting, but that following initial adjustment difficulties the overall trend is that of consistent improvement in behavior over time.

Our findings bear on issues regarding differences in adjustment patterns between short-term and long-term inmates. Prior research reports that long-term inmates consistently have lower infraction rates than other inmates, even across age categories.[10] We have not found this observation to be replicable. In fact, we find that among the young, infraction rates for long-term inmates peak higher than for other inmate groups. Changes in sentencing practices, producing corresponding shifts in inmate populations, may help to account for the different findings. In recent years, prison administrators have observed that changes in laws dealing with violent and repeat felons have created a new breed of long-term inmate who is more difficult to manage.[11] It is possible that our data reflect this development among inmates serving long sentences.

Prior studies also find that infraction rates of long-term inmates are fairly stable over time, leading to the conclusion that unlike other inmates, long-termers do not undergo critical stages of adjustment. In contrast, we find that differences in adjustment patterns are more a function of age than of sentence length. The adjustment patterns of long-term inmates resemble those of other inmates across comparable age groups. Some researchers have also observed that compared to other prisoners, long-term inmates demonstrate a more settled and mature attitude, are more accepting of their situation, are more likely to recognize the need to get along with prison staff and peers, and tend to view their prison activities in the context of more extended time perspectives. It would appear that these perspectives are typical of older inmates, a group that is overrepresented among long-termers.

## Types of infractions

A variety of rules, ranging in degree of seriousness and in purpose, govern inmate behavior. Some prison rules find analogues in the outside community, other rules are common to institutional settings, and yet still other rules are unique to the prisons. We can now examine the frequency of rule violations across categories. We will then investigate differences in types of infractions across inmates.

Overall, we find that the most common disciplinary charge is refusing orders (45 percent), followed by failure to follow posted facility rules (35 percent).[12] Other frequent charges relate to inmate movement (28 percent) and interference with or harassment of prison staff (23 percent). The incidence of violence is relatively high (17 percent) and is on par with charges of creating a disturbance (17 percent) and contraband violations (14 percent). Violations involving the destruction of property are relatively infrequent (6 percent), as are violations of fire, health and safety rules (4 percent), riots, strikes or escapes (2 percent) and sexual misbehavior (0.5 percent). Self-injuries (0.2 percent) and victimizations (0.2 percent) written up as disciplinary incidents characterize a very small proportion of violations.

When we examine types of violations by age of inmate, modest differences surface. Young (21 years or below) inmates are more likely to be charged with violent behavior than older (over 30 years of age) inmates (18 percent versus 13 percent). In contrast, older inmates are more likely to be involved with contraband violations (18 percent versus 11 percent) and riots, strikes or escapes (4 percent versus 2 percent).

Violent behavior is of particular interest since normative prohibitions against such acts transcend institutional settings. We find rates of violent and nonviolent infractions to be correlated at about the .50 level. This association carries several implications. On the one hand, we can infer that violent inmates are not highly specialized and lead relatively extensive and checkered disciplinary careers. In addition, we can infer that highly disruptive inmates show a greater propensity towards violence. This suggests that rules peculiar to prison settings are not the exclusive source of problems for inmates with serious adjustment difficulties.

When we examine rates of violent infractions over time, we find that the general pattern parallels that of overall infraction rates. For all time-served groups, rates of violence peak in the early stages of the prison term and then rapidly fall off. Violence rates show more oscillation than overall disciplinary rates, but this may be a function of scale and of low base rates.

The next question we examine deals with consistency of disciplinary behavior over time. In order to facilitate this analysis, we coded disciplinary incidents into a single description based on an ordinal set of categories. In hierarchical order, the categories we used are violent behavior, creating a disturbance, refusing orders, inmate movement violations, property or contraband violations, and other violations.

Table 2.3 presents a matrix showing correlations between types of antecedent and subsequent infractions. Given the large number of cases involved, nearly all of the correlations are statistically significant at the .001 level. Looking at the matrix, we find that the strongest relationships are consistently found along the diagonal although size of correlations is not large (around .07). These data indicate that inmates demonstrate some degree of consistency in the types of violations they engage in over time. This tendency holds true for even relatively infrequent behaviors such as violence and contraband offenses. While these findings do not suggest a high degree of specialization, they stand in contrast to studies that fail to find any consistency in offense behavior.[13]

### Career typology

Up to this point, our analyses have focused on central tendencies (that is, mean infraction rates) and on differences between groups of inmates (that is, young and old, short-term and long-term). Patterns of human behavior that encompass a great deal of variation at the aggregate level can not be taken for granted at the individual level. We now turn our attention to the individual level of analysis and develop a typology of inmate disciplinary careers. One purpose of the typology is to describe the individual patterns of adaptation that occur in prisons. In addition, the typology will lay the groundwork for investigating questions relating to chronic disciplinary violators.

Our typology is constructed around sequences of highly disruptive behavior throughout the course of prison sentences. We begin with our basic framework of career segments and designate segments as "disruptive" if the annualized rate of infractions is greater than twelve. This criterion corresponds to the 95th percentile in the distribution of overall infraction rates.

After classifying career segments as disruptive or nondisruptive, we have to devise a method for organizing combinations into similar patterns. Problems we need to face are that inmates have different numbers of career segments across time-served groups and that the number of possible

TABLE 2.3
**Pearson correlations between type of preceeding and subsequent disciplinary infractions.**

| Type of preceeding infraction | TYPE OF SUBSEQUENT INFRACTION (n = 70,906) | | | | | |
|---|---|---|---|---|---|---|
| | Violence | Disturbance | Refuse orders | Movement | Property/ contraband | Other |
| Violence | .07*** | −.01 | −.03*** | −.04*** | .00 | .00 |
| Disturbance | .00 | .07*** | −.03*** | −.01*** | −.01*** | −.01 |
| Refuse orders | −.02*** | −.01*** | −.07*** | −.02*** | −.03*** | −.02*** |
| Movement | −.04*** | −.03*** | −.01 | .09*** | −.01* | .01 |
| Property/contraband | −.01* | −.01** | −.03*** | .00 | .07*** | −.01*** |
| Other | −.02*** | −.01 | −.01*** | .00 | .00 | .05*** |

*p. less than .05
**p. less than .01
***p. less than .001

patterns is extremely large. By simply designating career segments as disruptive or nondisruptive, we can identify 64 different patterns for short-term inmates and 16,777,216 different patterns for long-termers. It is unlikely, of course, that every pattern will be represented in our data, but the need for organization and simplification should be obvious. We therefore labelled career segments as part of early, middle or late career stages, with particular designations contingent on sentence length. Short-term inmates would have only early and late career stages, while high-average term would have only one middle stage and long-term inmates have two middle career stages.[14] These divisions are based on our data, which indicate that infraction rates of short-term inmates are in abrupt decline over most of the sentence, while rates of long-term inmates show a much more gradual decline.

As the next step in constructing our typology, we designated career stages as either disruptive or nondisruptive. To screen out unusually brief periods of disruptive activity, we require that at least two-thirds of the career segments in a given career stage be labelled disruptive in order for the career stage to be classified as disruptive. This requirement insures chronicity in the identification of disruptive career stages. In sum, our classification scheme is built around three career stages (early, middle, late) which are characterized as disruptive or nondisruptive. This scheme leads to a total of eight adjustment patterns. We describe the patterns as follows: conforming (low, low, low), late-bloomer (low, low, high), inverted u-shape (low, high, low), mid-bloomer (low, high, high), early starter (high, low, low), u-shaped (high, low, high), late reformer (high, high, low) and chronic (high, high, high).[15]

Table 2.4 contains the overall distribution of disciplinary careers and the distribution by time-served group. We find that three-quarters of the inmates (75.3 percent) can be classified as "conformers" in that they fail to exhibit any period of highly disruptive behavior. Thus, the majority of inmates are relatively well-behaved and do not encounter substantial problems adjusting to prison rules.[16]

The most common pattern of disruptiveness is the early starter (6.9 percent). This pattern is followed in frequency by inverted u-shape (4.6 percent) and late reformer (3.5 percent) careers. Less frequent career patterns are chronic (3.0 percent), u-shape (2.5 percent) and mid-bloomer (1.5 percent). The distribution of patterns varies across time-served groups and, in particular, chronic patterns are less frequent among long-term inmates. This finding is consistent with the fact that long-termers have a lower overall infraction rate and probably reflects the difficulty of maintaining a high level of antisocial behavior over a very long period of time.

The career typology we have developed is an individual-level classifica-

TABLE 2.4
Distribution of disciplinary career patterns by time served.

| Disciplinary career pattern | Total (n = 9,428) | TIME-SERVED GROUP | | | |
| --- | --- | --- | --- | --- | --- |
| | | Short term (n = 2,914) | Low-average term (n = 3,653) | High-average term (n = 1,655) | Long term (n = 1,206) |
| Nondisruptive (low, low, low) | 75.3% | 78.0% | 72.0% | 69.7% | 86.6% |
| Early starter (high, low, low) | 6.9 | 10.9 | 5.6 | 4.3 | 4.6 |
| Inverted U (low, high, low) | 4.6 | XXXX | 6.6 | 9.5 | 3.2 |
| Late bloomer (low, low, high) | 2.8 | 5.4 | 2.1 | 1.5 | 0.2 |
| Late reformer (high, high, low) | 3.5 | XXXX | 4.4 | 7.4 | 3.5 |
| U-shape (high, low, high) | 2.5 | XXXX | 1.1 | 0.9 | 0.6 |
| Mid-bloomer (low, high, high) | 1.5 | XXXX | 2.4 | 3.0 | 0.4 |
| Chronic (high, high, high) | 3.0 | 5.8 | 5.8 | 3.6 | 0.9 |

tion that illustrates the variety of ways in which inmates adjust or fail to adjust to their environment. In this respect, the career typology takes us beyond aggregate descriptions of adjustment patterns. Yet, we find that the "early starter," a pattern reflected in the overall distribution of infraction rates, is the most frequent of the disruptive types. We also note the low proportion of chronic infractors. This finding indicates that relatively few inmates present serious disciplinary problems over most of their sentence.

Our typology comprises all the logical combinations of patterns within the definitions we have set, and intuitively we might suspect that some disruptive patterns are more significant or important than others. One way of approaching this issue is to examine the relative frequency of each subtype as we just have done. From this perspective, subtypes that rarely occur can be viewed as relatively inconsequential elements of the typological scheme. Another strategy is to examine whether subtypes differ in terms of features that are not constituent parts of the typology. The latter approach moves us beyond consideration of typologies as a useful tool for describing behavior patterns and leads us to ask if patterns of behaviors correspond with personal attributes. Subtypes that simply describe behavior tend to be less useful than subtypes that also distinguish types of people. This is so because relationships between personal attributes and behavior patterns can provide insight into motivations which in turn can lead to explanations. Thus, having described the *what* of our typology, we now try to identify the corresponding *who* which will put us in a position to speculate about the *why*.

We begin our investigation with a discriminant function analysis. As the name suggests, this technique allows us to determine whether we can "discriminate" across career types.[17] Independent variables are grouped into functions, and the results tell us how the functions relate to categories of the dependent variable. If the functions are discriminating, our ability to correctly classify individuals by career type should be high.

At the outset we attempted to distinguish across the career patterns, and we imposed no restriction on the number of functions. After several trials it became obvious that only a few functions are statistically significant, and that we could classify accurately only three career types. These patterns are the nondisruptive, the early starter and the chronic. On the basis of these first findings, the remaining career types were then combined into a single category, and the analysis was repeated.

The final analysis generated three statistically significant functions which are displayed in Table 2.5 The asterisk identifies the function for which the loading of a variable is largest. The first function describes inmates with the following characteristics: older at admission, did not receive mental health services in prison, high school graduates, and no prior record of criminal hospitalization. The second function describes employed, nonwhite, drug offenders with longer prison terms and with prior prison experience who are younger when first arrested and older when first institutionalized. The third function describes inmates with no prior record of violent offense, with varied conviction offenses (assault, rape, burglary, robbery, and murder),[18] who are unmarried, admitted drug users, and without a record of civil hospitalization. In general, the first function describes older inmates with no record of mental health involvement, the second function describes criminalized minority group drug offenders, and the third function describes the majority of the inmate population (at least in terms of commitment offense).

The proportional contribution of each function to the total amount of explained variance in the variables is 90 percent for the first function, 7 percent for the second function and 3.0 percent for the third function. After performing a varimax rotation, which optimizes the fit of the functions to the variables, the percentages for each function become 48 percent, 47 percent and 5 percent respectively. The first two functions share most of the explained variance while the last function contributes

**TABLE 2.5**
**Description of functions produced by discriminant analysis.**

| Variable | Function 1 | Function 2 | Function 3 |
|---|---|---|---|
| Age at prison entry | .82* | −.20 | −.11 |
| Prison mental health experience | .32* | .00 | .17 |
| Education (H.S. grad.) | .19* | .05 | −.09 |
| Prior criminal hospitalization | −.14* | .07 | .01 |
| Employment (at conviction) | .08 | .54* | .25 |
| Age at first institutionalization | −.37 | .48* | .44 |
| Time served | −.28 | .45* | −.11 |
| Prior prison experience | −.30 | .43* | .07 |
| Age at first arrest | .30 | −.36* | .32 |
| Race (nonwhite) | −.02 | −.25* | .09 |
| Drug use | −.15 | .23* | .05 |
| Prior violent offense | .04 | .17 | .64* |
| Assault[a] | .01 | .02 | .52* |
| Rape[a] | .13 | −.10 | .51* |
| Burglary[a] | .04 | −.13 | .47* |
| Robbery[a] | −.03 | .13 | .26* |
| Murder[a] | .17 | .02 | .24* |
| Marital status (married) | .19 | .09 | −.23* |
| Prior civil hospitalization | −.04 | .05 | −.16* |
| Drug offender[a] | .04 | .03 | .14* |
| Percent of explained variance in variables | | | |
| Before rotation | 90 | 7 | 3 |
| After rotation | 48 | 47 | 5 |

*—highest factor loading
a—conviction offense

very little. This finding indicates that the third function is relatively unimportant, which is not surprising given the variables that compose this function.

Table 2.6 displays the relationships of the functions to career categories. Function 1 shows a positive relationship to the nondisruptive group and negative relationships to the other groups, the strongest of which is for the chronic career type. Function 2 shows relationships that are very similar to function 1, while function 3 is positively related to the early starter pattern and marginally related to the other groups. The strongest relationships in the table indicate that nondisruptive inmates are more likely to resemble older inmates with no mental health involvement or criminalized drug offenders while chronic career types are less likely to resemble these

**TABLE 2.6**
**Relationship of discriminant functions to career categories.**

| Career category | Function 1 | Function 2 | Function 3 |
|---|---|---|---|
| Nondisruptive | .48 | .41 | − .03 |
| Catchall[a] | − 1.36 | − .87 | − .06 |
| Early starter | − 1.34 | − 1.47 | .47 |
| Chronic | − 1.98 | − 1.94 | − .04 |

a—includes inverted U, late bloomer, late reformer, U-shape and mid-bloomer.

inmate groups. To a lesser extent, we find·that the early starters resemble the typical offender at least in terms of commitment offense.

Perhaps the findings of greatest interest that derive from the discriminant analysis are the classification results displayed in Table 2.7. Overall, we are able to classify correctly 65 percent of the inmates, which represents a significant achievement. The proportion of correct classifications is adjusted for the actual distribution of the data, thereby imposing a more stringent criterion. Accuracy of classification varies across career types and is greatest for the nondisruptive pattern. We are able to classify correctly 77 percent of the nondisruptives, with misclassifications distributed evenly across remaining categories. Classification results for the chronic career type are good in that we can accurately classify 51.5 percent of these inmates. Errors in classification for the chronic pattern concentrate in the nondisruptive group.

The discriminant analysis performs less well in predicting the early starter pattern or the catchall group of patterns. Among the early-starter

**TABLE 2.7**
**Classification results from discriminant analysis.**

| Actual Group Membership | PREDICTED GROUP MEMBERSHIP | | | |
|---|---|---|---|---|
| | Nondisruptive | Catchall[a] | Early starter | Chronic |
| Nondisruptive | 77% | 8% | 6% | 9% |
| | (5146) | (559) | (381) | (592) |
| Catchall[a] | 41 | 24 | 7 | 28 |
| | (471) | (274) | (84) | (320) |
| Early starter | 33 | 11 | 23 | 33 |
| | (202) | (66) | (139) | (203) |
| Chronic | 26 | 12 | 10 | 52 |
| | (129) | (57) | (50) | (251) |
| Percent of "grouped" cases correctly classified = 65% | | | | |

a—includes inverted U, late bloomer, late reformer, U-shape and mid-bloomer.

inmates, 23 percent are correctly classified, with errors evenly balanced between nondisruptive and chronic patterns. The classification results for the catchall group are very similar, although more classification errors involve the nondisruptive group.

Discriminant analysis examines relationships of independent variables grouped as functions across all categories of the dependent variable. The format interposes an intermediary element in the interpretation of effects (i.e., a function) and does not allow us to examine differences between some categories, excluding consideration of other categories. The technique, for example, does not readily lend itself to answering questions such as how do early starters differ from chronics? More sophisticated questions such as how differences between nondisruptives and early starters compare to differences between nondisruptives and chronics are even more awkward to address.

In order to investigate these questions, logistic regression analysis was performed between pairs of the career types that emerged as significant from the discriminate analysis. Logistic regression operates on a modification of standard regression procedures to provide estimates of how independent variables affect the log-likelihood that a given case will fall into either category of the dependent variables.[19] The results of the analyses are presented in Table 2.8. The interpretation of effects derives from the direction and relative magnitude of coefficients.

We find that in comparison to nondisruptive inmates the early starters are younger, less educated, more likely to be nonwhite, single and unemployed and less likely to have been in prison before. The early starters are also less likely to require mental health services in prison, serve shorter prison terms and have greater chances of being sentenced for assault, rape and burglary. Most of these differences emerge in a comparison of chronics to nondisruptives, but the magnitude of effects tends to be greater. Additional differences are that chronic disruptives start their criminal careers later but are institutionalized earlier. This paradox may be partly explained by the finding that chronic disruptives are more likely to have a history of violent crime, since early institutionalization may reflect shorter, more serious criminal careers. Chronic disruptives are also more likely to have a history of civil psychiatric hospitalization and less likely to be sentenced for murder, assault, and rape in their current prison term. When we compare early starters to chronics we find that only a few personal characteristics distinguish between career types, including age of first institutionalization, employment, violent offense history and mental health experience.

In summary, the data indicate that we can distinguish three career types—nondisruptive, early starter and chronic—in terms of inmate attrib-

TABLE 2.8
Results of logistic regression analyses between types of disciplinary careers.

| | Nondisruptive v. Early starter | Nondisruptive v. Chronic | Early starter v. Chronic |
|---|---|---|---|
| **Social history** | | | |
| Age at prison entry | − .66 | − 1.04 | |
| Age at first arrest | | .96 | |
| Age at first institutionalization | | − 1.44 | − 1.17 |
| Race (nonwhite) | .69 | .73 | |
| Education (H.S. grad.) | − .55 | − .69 | |
| Employment (at conviction) | − .56 | − 1.07 | − .59 |
| Marital status (married) | − .86 | − .39 | |
| **Criminal history** | | | |
| Prior prison experience | − .49 | − .59 | |
| Prior violent offense | | .95 | .85 |
| **Mental health history** | | | |
| Prior civil hospitalization | | .71 | .60 |
| Prior criminal hospitalization | .52 | .93 | .40 |
| **Conviction offense** | | | |
| Murder | | − 2.01 | − 2.34 |
| Assault | .72 | .80 | − 1.52 |
| Rape | 1.02 | − 2.06 | − .36 |
| Burglary | .75 | | − .72 |
| Robbery | | | − .49 |
| Time served | − .34 | .14 | .23 |
| Constant | 1.44 | .08 * | 1.91 * |
| Goodness of fit $X^2$ | 1035 | 1244* | 599* |
| d.f. | 1006 * | 586 * | 243 |
| Hosmer statistic | 25* | 35* | 8 |
| d.f. | 8 | 8 | 8 |

*p. less than .00

utes. We also find that our ability to classify inmate behavior patterns on the basis of personal attributes is greatest at the extremes and otherwise relatively weak. The discriminant analysis classifies best the nondisruptives and the chronics and the logistic regression equation fits best (as indicated by the Hosmer statistic) when we compare these two groups. These findings lead us to conclude that nondisruptive and chronically disruptive careers involve very different inmates, while other careers encompass a relatively homogeneous inmate group.

Chronic disruptives differ from nondisruptives in a number of ways that not surprisingly includes being younger. We also note that inmates who present chronic disciplinary problems are relative newcomers to crime as evidenced by tendencies to begin criminal involvement at a later age and to arrive at prison with no prior incarceration experience. However, against this relatively modest framework of criminal achievement, we find that the chronics are more likely to have a track record of violence and their chances of having been in a civil psychiatric hospital are greater. The salience of civil as opposed to criminal hospitalizations is noteworthy because of differences in the reasons for commitment. Criminal hospitalizations are predicated on manifestations of pathology and antisocial behavior, leaving open the possibility that one may be interpreted as the other. Civil hospitalizations present a less ambiguous symptomatic picture, which makes a stronger argument for a link between a history of pathology and prison disruptiveness. Our ability to predict with a fair degree of accuracy which inmates will become chronic violators, coupled with their brief but violent and pathologically tinged community track record, suggests the viability and utility of targeting these inmates for intensive therapeutic interventions. The multivariate analyses confirm that chronically disruptive inmates differ from other inmates in ways that transcend the behavior at issue. Differences in background characteristics can provide clues as to the nature of the maladaptive process, and the fact that psychiatric hospitalization is a predictor of chronic disruptiveness suggests that serious psychological deficits may be at work. The modal pattern of increasing conformity over time indicates that initially high rates of prison misbehavior do not signal impending chronicity. This means that inmates must be given the opportunity to work out transitional adjustment problems and only when misbehavior persists beyond the point when most inmates begin to adapt to their situation should remedial intervention strategies be considered.

Murderers, assaulters and rapists are more likely to be nondisruptive than chronically disruptive, while assaulters, rapists and burglars are more likely to be early starters than nondisruptive. Common offense behaviors (such as assault and burglary) thus seem to be associated with typical disruptiveness patterns. The tendency for murderers to be well-behaved inmates has been noted by others, and our results confirm this finding.

Prior violence discriminates between nondisruptives and chronics as well as between early starters and chronics, representing a continuity of serious antisocial behavior. Most of the factors that distinguish between nondisruptive and typically disruptive inmates (such as the early starters) distinguish even better between nondisruptives and chronic inmates. These findings suggest that as we move across degrees of disruptiveness the same factors discriminate between groups of inmates with few new variables entering the picture, and contrasts become increasingly sharper as we approach extremes. Differences between early starters and chronics relate mostly to prior violence and to mental-health experiences, again suggesting that extreme disruptiveness is presaged by serious antisocial behavior and may be influenced by pathology.

## System Costs Associated with Chronic Disruptiveness

We have suggested that therapeutic programs targeted at chronically disruptive inmates may be both appropriate and advantageous. This suggestion is based on our findings that chronic disruptives tend to have histories of emotional disorder and violent behavior. Another consideration that enters the equation is the disproportionate amount of prison resources that chronically disruptive inmates consume. These resources involve the administrative processing of infractions as well as the imposition of punitive measures. We have seen that chronically disruptive inmates constitute 3 percent of our release cohort, but this small group accounts for 12 percent of adjudicated disciplinary infractions, 13 percent of time spent in keeplock and 9 percent of time spent in special housing disciplinary units. If we include the semichronic disruptive inmates (midbloomer, u-shape and late reformer) we find that 12.5 percent of the inmate population accounts for 34 percent of disciplinary infraction, 35 percent of time in keeplock and 32 percent of time in special housing disciplinary units. Our data confirm what most prison administrators have probably come to suspect through experience, which is that a small group of recalcitrantly disruptive inmates consumes a disproportionately large share of prison resources. This small group represents a substantial portion of the workload of disciplinary committees, and more frequently requires placement in high security disciplinary settings. These facts suggest that there is payoff in developing intervention programs that can intercept cycles of chronic misbehavior for inmates who are unresponsive to disciplinary actions based on traditional notions of punishment and deterrence.

### Notes

1. See Intro., note 19 for some sources that provide a review of research on disciplinary infractions.
2. T. Hirschi and M. Gottfredson, "Age and the Explanation of Crime," *American Journal of Sociology*, 1983, *83*, 552–84, p. 552.
3. J. Wilson and R. Hernstein, *Crime and Human Behavior*. New York: Simon and Schuster, 1986.
4. Hirschi and Gottfredson, note 2 supra.

5. Prisonization involves a complex socialization process that includes, but is not limited to, the adoption of anti-staff values. Wheeler (Intro., note 5) writes ". . . conformity to staff expectations obviously taps only part of the phenomena referred to as prisonization by Clemmer and others. It does seem to get at a central core: the acceptance or rejection of norms and role definitions applied to inmates by the prison staff" (p. 700). Since prison rules represent a formal normative code of staff expectations of inmate behaviors, we can expect that as antistaff values increase, behaviors that indicate a rejection of this code will also increase.

6. Clemmer (Intro., note 6) suggested that length of exposure to prison was directly related to degree of prisonization. In other words, Clemmer viewed prisonization as a linear function of time-served.

7. Wheeler (Intro., note 5) emphasized the importance of inmate time perspectives relative to prison admission and release, leading him to develop a model of prison careers with early, middle and late stages. Wheeler also emphasized the competition between the value systems of prison and society. His research led him to conclude that "inmates who have been in the broader community and inmates who are to return to that community are more frequently oriented in terms of conventional value systems. Inmates conform least to conventional standards during the middle phase of their institutional career. These inmates appear to shed the prison culture before they leave it, such that there are almost as many conforming inmates at the time of release as at the time of entrance into the system" (p. 706). This pattern of prisonization is often described as an inverted-u (low, high, low), implying that prisonization is a nonlinear function of time-served.

8. Wheeler (Intro., note 5) states that "we might expect that the (prison) culture would exert its major impact on inmates during the middle of their stay, at the point in time where an inmate is farthest removed from the outside world" (p. 709).

9. Wheeler (Intro., note 5) describes the concept of "anticipatory resocialization" as "the preparatory responses that frequently precede an actual change in group membership, such as the movement from prison to the broader community" (p. 698). He goes on to elaborate that "as time for release approaches, the problems deriving from imprisonment recede relative to prospective adjustment problems on parole. Such a shift in reference should also give rise to a resocialization process beginning just prior to release" (p. 709).

10. Although Flanagan (chap. 1, note 13) found strong effects for age, he also found that long-term inmates have lower infraction rates across all age categories and across amount of sentence served.

11. See, for example, National Institute of Justice, U.S. Department of Justice. Criminal justice research solicitation: Improving the handling of long-term offenders. Washington, D.C.: April, 1982.

12. Since a disciplinary incident (estimated N = 79,435) can involve more that one rule violation, percentages sum to greater than 100.

13. The issue of offense specialization has received much attention in the criminological literature (see, for example, M. Wolfgang, R. Figlio and T. Sellin, *Delinquency in a Birth Cohort.* Chicago: University of Chicago Press, 1972). Our statistical analyses resemble prior research in that we examine consistency between pairs of sequential events, and we define similar behaviors in terms of quasi-legal offense categories. This approach has several limitations since first,

degree of consistency may increase if we view events from a broader time perspective (for example, entire careers), second, gross categories of behavior may fail to reveal consistency operating at a different level (such as motivational or situational consistency) and, finally, aggregate analyses can mask consistency at the individual level, especially if most offenders are jacks of all (criminal) trades and only a small proportion of offenders are specialized.

14. We designated time-served segments (1 up to 24) in terms of career stages (early, middle, late) as follows. Short-term inmates: early—1 to 3, late—4 to 6; low average-term inmates: early—1 to 3, middle—4 to 6, late—7 to 9; high average-term inmates: early—1 to 4, middle—5 to 8, late—9 to 12; long-term inmates: early—1 to 6, early middle—7 to 12, late middle—13 to 18, late—19 to 24.

15. Our classification of disciplinary patterns builds upon the fourfold scheme—accidental, early-starter, late-bloomer and chronic—developed by Freeman and his colleagues (R. Freeman, J. P. Conrad, S. Dinitz, and I. Barak, *Out of Circulation: The Dangerous Offender in Prison*. Lexington, Ma: D. C. Heath (Lexington), in press).

16. An issue we might pursue is whether the observed distribution of career types differs from that which can be expected to occur by chance. Our major interests, however, lie not in the proportion of inmates with a given career type, but in identifying differences in personal attributes among groups of inmates with various patterns of maladjustment. The typology of disciplinary careers is a vehicle that moves us toward this end by allowing us to disaggregate patterns of disruptiveness, and later on we will use multivariate statistical techniques to examine differences between groups of inmates.

17. For a technical discussion of discriminant analysis see J. Johnston, *Econometric Methods*, 2nd Edition. New York: McGraw-Hill, 1972, and R. Bibb and D. Roncek, "Investigating group differences: An explication of the sociological potential of discriminant analysis," *Sociological Methods and Research,* 1976, *4*, pp. 349–379. Discriminant analysis is a statistical technique that appears to be uniquely suited to our investigation. Bibb and Roncek note that a useful application of the technique is that of "testing preexisting typologies for empirical adequacy." They go on to say that "(o)nce data are grouped into cells of the typology, discriminant analysis can be used to measure the power of the schema. . . . it is also possible to identify precisely those variables which are most crucial in contributing to differences among cells (p. 372)." Discriminant analysis assumes interval level data, statistically independent and normally distributed variables and equal variance-covariance matrices between groups (Ibid, p. 364). Although the technique is fairly robust with regard to violations of these assumptions, particularly with large samples, we will use logistic regression analysis (which does not require these assumptions) to confirm our results.

18. Sodomy, larceny, drug and "other" are the only offense categories not included in this function.

19. For a technical discussion of log-linear techniques see Y. E. Bishop, S. E. Feinberg and P. W. Holland, *Discrete Multivariate Analysis: Theory and Practice*. Cambridge, Ma: MIT Press, 1975. In logistic regression analysis, the chi-square statistic is used to judge the fit of the model to the data. A low chi-square value (with a correspondingly probability value) indicates small differences between observed and predicted values. By this criterion, our logistic

# 3

# Patterns of Pathology

In the preceding chapter, we examined one manifestation of maladaptive behavior—repeated violations of prison rules. In this chapter, we examine behavior that suggests another form of maladaptation—that produced by emotional disorder. We will describe the personal attributes that are associated with emotional problems and ascertain the timing of symptomatic events. We will particularly focus our attention on inmates who require hospitalization, since these inmates are the most seriously disturbed mental health clients.

We begin by examining the background characteristics of inmates who require mental health services. Looking at Table 3.1, which displays social and criminal history information, we find that hospitalized inmates are older at admission to prison, less likely to be married, more likely to have been living alone at time of conviction and disproportionately fall into the lower IQ range. These inmates are also more likely to stand convicted of murder, rape and assault, to have a record of violent criminal behavior prior to their current conviction and to have been in prison before. These differences help to account for the fact that hospitalized inmates serve longer prison terms, nearly twice as long, compared to inmates who do not require mental health services.

We also find that outpatients comprise the highest proportion of white inmates, are younger at admission to prison and show lower levels of educational achievement. They are also least likely to have held a job at conviction, and most likely to have a history of drug abuse. In addition, they are most likely to stand convicted of burglary, and they begin their criminal involvement at an earlier age.

Inmates who did not receive mental health services are more likely to be convicted of drug offenses. They also demonstrate a lower probability of having been in prison before and of having a record of violent crime prior to their last offense.

TABLE 3.1
Social and criminal history by prison mental health experience.

| | No Service (n = 8012) | Outpatient (n = 682) | Hospitalized (n = 145) |
|---|---|---|---|
| **Social history** | | | |
| Race (nonwhite) | 73% | 62% | 71% |
| Education (H.S. grad.) | 26 | 23 | 28 |
| Employment (at conviction) | 67 | 64 | 77 |
| Drug use | 61 | 65 | 50 |
| Marital status (married) | 32 | 31 | 15 |
| Living arrangements at conviction (alone, institution) | 14 | 18 | 39 |
| Age at prison admission[a] | 26.2 | 25.4 | 28.6 |
| **Criminal History** | | | |
| Prior prison experience | 26 | 29 | 38 |
| Prior violent offense | 53 | 62 | 72 |
| Age at first arrest[a] | 18.2 | 17.3 | 18.7 |
| Age at first institutionalization[a] | 21.4 | 20.2 | 21.7 |
| **Conviction Offense** | | | |
| Murder | 6 | 10 | 11 |
| Rape | 2 | 5 | 7 |
| Sodomy | 2 | 6 | 6 |
| Robbery | 35 | 33 | 37 |
| Assault | 6 | 7 | 9 |
| Burglary | 19 | 21 | 15 |
| Larceny | 3 | 2 | 3 |
| Drug | 19 | 9 | 6 |
| Other | 9 | 9 | 6 |
| **Time Served** (months)[a] | 28.2 | 35.1 | 51.0 |

a—mean value

Table 3.2 compares the preprison mental health experiences of patients and nonpatients. We find that inmates who were hospitalized during their current prison term are substantially more likely to have a record of prior hospitalization. Overall, 61 percent of hospitalized inmates show a history of psychiatric commitment upon admission to prison. Experiences of forensic hospitalization are more common, although the difference in the incidence of criminal and civil commitments is not large (42 percent versus 33 percent). We also find that the proportion of outpatients with a preprison history of psychiatric hospitalization is more than twice that of inmates who do not receive mental health services (16 percent versus 7 percent).

When we examine inmates with a preprison history of psychiatric commitment, we find that the mean time between the last hospitalization and prison admission is shortest for inmates who are subsequently hospi-

TABLE 3.2
Preprison mental health history by prison mental health experience.

| Mental health history | PRISON MENTAL HEALTH EXPERIENCE | | |
|---|---|---|---|
| | No Service (n = 8012) | Outpatient (n = 682) | Hospitalized (n = 145) |
| I.Q. at prison admission[a] | 99.3 | 96.8 | 89.3 |
| Prior psychiatric hospitalization | 7% | 16% | 61% |
| Prior civil hospitalization | 4% | 10% | 33% |
| Prior criminal hospitalization | 4% | 10% | 42% |
| Years between last hospitalization and prison admission[a] | 8.6 | 5.8 | 3.9 |

a—mean value

talized (3.9 years) and longest for inmates who do not receive mental health services (8.6 years).

The picture that emerges of hospitalized inmates is that of persons with multiple social and psychological deficits. These inmates are unlikely to have established significant interpersonal attachments or stable domestic arrangements prior to entering prison. The majority have already spent time in psychiatric hospitals, both criminal and civil, and their measured intellectual ability is below that of other inmates. Both the experience and recency of preincarceration psychiatric commitment emerge as major risk factors in prison hospitalization. Inmates who are unsuccessful at negotiating the prison environment are likely to have demonstrated similar coping problems in the community. These findings point to a continuity of psychiatric disability from one setting to the next, at least within a limited time frame. Finally, hospitalized inmates evidence a propensity towards violence both in terms of current and prior offenses which makes it unsurprising that many of these inmates have been in prison before, and that as a group they serve prison terms that are much longer than average.

The average demographic profile of outpatients is that of a social dropout who turns to crime possibly as a "vocation." These inmates, who tend to be disproportionately white, find it difficult to stay in high school or to hold a job, and they begin their criminal careers early in life. Burglary and drug abuse are favored activities pointing to a combination of economic and escapist motivations to crime. These inmates also show preincarceration involvement with the mental health system. Although the findings are more dramatic for hospitalized inmates, these data are consistent with the argument that a history of emotional disorder predicts future emotional disorder.

## Descriptions of Inmate Behavior

Having described the characteristics of inmates who receive mental health services, we can now describe the nature of their emotional problems. We begin by examining the behavior of inmate patients in table 3.3. For hospitalized inmates, we list hospital and prison experiences separately. We also note that the data are presented in a multiple response format which indicates the proportion of observations that contain descriptions of various behaviors. Since more than one piece of behavior may be

### TABLE 3.3
Percent of mental health observations by categories of behaviors.

|  | HOSPITAL PATIENT | | OUTPATIENT |
|  | Hospital (n = 10258) | Prison (n = 8554) | (n = 3379) |
|---|---|---|---|
| **Thought Disturbance** | | | |
| Delusions, hallucinations | 32% | 41% | 13% |
| Disoriented (time, place, or person) | 2 | 3 | 0.6 |
| Confused, disorganized | 19 | 24 | 10 |
| No insight, poor judgment | 13 | 4 | 4 |
| Other | 4 | 8 | 4 |
| **Self Injury** | 4 | 9 | 6 |
| **Affect, mood disturbance** | | | |
| Flat, inappropriate effect | 13 | 12 | 7 |
| Depressed | 9 | 16 | 18 |
| Anxious, excited | 16 | 27 | 39 |
| Angry, hostile, suspicious | 17 | 13 | 8 |
| Other | 2 | 2 | 1 |
| **Social Behavior** | | | |
| Withdrawn behaviors | 26 | 30 | 19 |
| Refusing medication | 12 | 12 | 5 |
| Poor hygiene | 4 | 6 | 2 |
| Maingering, manipulative | 4 | 2 | 3 |
| Other | 0.2 | 0.3 | 0 |
| **Psychomotor Behaviors** | | | |
| Sleep disturbance | 5 | 4 | 15 |
| Hyperactive | 11 | 12 | 5 |
| Hypoactive | 7 | 4 | 2 |
| Motor tension | 1 | 2 | 2 |
| Somatic complaints | 16 | 6 | 4 |
| Eating disorder | 2 | 4 | 2 |
| Other | 2 | 12 | 5 |

*Note:* Since a symptomatic observation can involve more than one behavior, percentages sum to greater than 100.

described in a single observation, the percentages sum to greater than unity.

The most frequently reported symptoms for hospital patients are thought disturbances typical of psychoses—hallucinations and delusions—appearing in at least one of three observation reports. The second most frequent symptomatic behavior, also characteristic of psychotic disorders, is confused, disorganized and irrelevant speech. Other common observations describe anxious or excited moods, withdrawn behavior, and hyperactivity. As we might anticipate, the symptomatic picture for outpatients differs substantially from that of hospital patients. Clinical notes for outpatients are most likely to describe anxious and depressed moods and sleep disturbances. Yet we note a substantial reporting of withdrawn behavior and of serious thought disturbances among the outpatients, although levels do not reach those of hospitalized inmates.

Differences in symptomatic behavior are observed for hospitalized inmates across settings. Reports of hallucinations, delusions, self-injury, and anxious or depressed moods are more common in prison. In contrast, notations that patients lack insight or adequate judgement and that patients appear to be manipulative or are malingering are more likely to appear in hospital records. Patients are also more likely to voice somatic complaints while hospitalized, a finding which may be related to changes in medication regimens or which may reflect greater attentiveness to physical maladies by patient and clinician. Finally, we note that medication refusal does not vary between prison and hospital, even though forced medication is an option that is available in hospital settings, and we assume that patients must be aware of this fact.

In general, the data confirm the obvious fact that most observation of hospitalized inmates describe serious psychiatric disorders. Outpatients are much less likely to demonstrate serious symptomatology, and those who do exhibit serious symptoms demonstrate that at least some serious disorders can be accommodated in prison settings. These findings suggest that levels of intervention are geared to problem seriousness and are consistent with the community mental health model we described in chapter 1.

We find that the symptomatic picture becomes less serious as the same patients move from prison to hospital. This difference is important because it indicates that clinicians do not always see the same problem as the treatment responsibility transfers from one staff member to the next. In this case, differences in symptomatic behavior may result from environmental changes as patients move from prison to hospital. However, the fact that hospital staff are more likely to characterize patients as malingering or manipulative indicates that these differences may be perceptual, which can create friction between prison and hospital treatment staff.

### Symptom Rates Over Time

Having described the overall distribution of symptomatic behavior, we can now turn to changes in the rates of these behaviors over time. Figure 3.1 displays mean annual symptom rates for hospitalized inmates over the course of their prison term. The data includes observations made during hospitalization and therefore represent a comprehensive picture of inmate experiences.

Looking at the graph, we find that short-term inmates show a dramatic oscillation in symptom rates. Symptomatology is very high at admission, drops substantially about half-way through the sentence, and then rises sharply just prior to release. In addition, we find that short-term inmates display the highest level of symptomatology, peaking at a mean rate of 65 per year. The trend for both low-average- and high-average-term inmates is very similar. Symptom rates reach their highest point early in the prison term and show a relatively steady decline over time. The situation for very long-term inmates, however, is substantially different. For this inmate

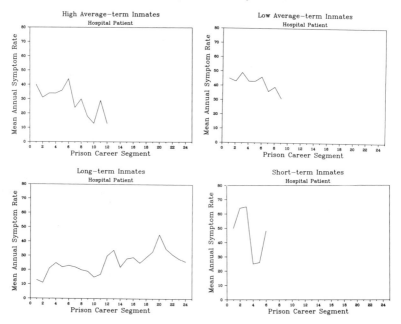

**FIGURE 3.1**
**Mean annual symptom rates for hospital patients by time served.**

group, symptom rates start off at a relatively low level and increase steadily throughout the prison term.

A common feature across time-served groups of hospitalized inmates is that symptom rates briefly increase toward the end of the prison term. Both the high-average and the long-term inmates show a small "spike" in symptom rates in roughly the last quarter of the prison term. The increase, however, is most noticeable for short-term inmates who enter and leave the prison with nearly equal rates of symptomatic behavior.

Figure 3.2 charts rates of symptomatic behavior for outpatients. The first item we notice is that compared to hospitalized inmates outpatient symptom rates are relatively low, reaching a high of only 6.7 per year. Looking at the overall trends, we find that inmates serving shorter sentences enter prison with relatively high levels of symptomatic behavior that drop off very sharply over time. In comparison, symptom rates for longer term inmates show less variability. However, high-average term inmates evidence mildly declining symptom rates while long-term inmates show an opposite trend. For outpatients, displays of symptomatology tend to be brief. If we divide the prison term into early, middle and late stages, we find that only one fourth (23.2 percent) of outpatients display symptomatic behaviors at a nonzero rate for more than one career stage.

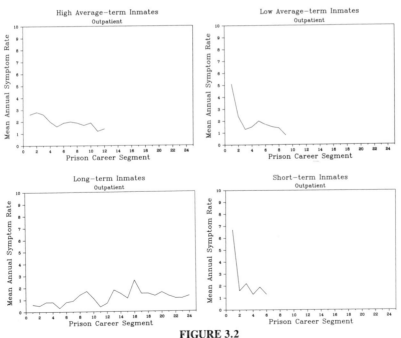

**FIGURE 3.2**
**Mean annual symptom rates for outpatients by time served.**

Symptom rate patterns reveal fair consistency between hospitalized inmates and outpatients, but differ substantially across time-served groups. Short-term inmates consistently show the most unstable levels of pathology. However, hospital inmates demonstrate a cyclic rise and fall pattern, while outpatients evidence a declining trend. For both classes of patients, decreasing levels of pathology are characteristic of average-term inmates, while long-term inmates show steadily increasing pathology levels. In general, it seems that symptomatic behavior tends to subside over time for most inmates. The exception is the long-term inmates, who appear to demonstrate increasing pathology levels.[1]

The observation that symptom rates for hospital patients show a brief increase prior to discharge from prison is interesting, since the pattern suggests that pathology levels for severely disturbed inmates rise in anticipation of return to the community. The findings thus suggest an "anticipatory release" phenomenon, the nature of which is quite different from that discussed in the prisonization literature. Severely disturbed inmates may view the transition from prison to community as a stressful experience, thereby engendering a rise in symptomatology. This scenario implies the utility of prerelease preparation programs and the coordination of treatment plans between prison and community for inmates with serious emotional disorders.

## Timing of Hospitalizations

Figure 3.3 displays the cumulative percent distribution of days between prison admission and initial hospitalization. We see that first commitments occur very early in the prison term and that inmates with a preprison psychiatric history are hospitalized earlier than other inmates. Among hospitalized inmates, half of the inmates with a prior record of hospitalization and almost two-fifths of other inmates were committed within six months of prison entry. These data suggest that early portions of a prison term represent a "critical period" during which there is a tendency for serious symptomatology to make an initial appearance. This tendency is exacerbated if an inmate has a preincarceration history of psychiatric hospitalization.

There are several factors, which may be working together, that can help to account for our findings. One possibility is that early hospitalizations reflect situations wherein inmates who are seriously emotionally disturbed at sentencing continue the course of their illness upon admission to prison. We can add to this the facts that the activities of prison inmates are scrutinized daily, thereby lessening the chances that eccentric behavior will go unnoticed, and that prisons generally have ready access to mental

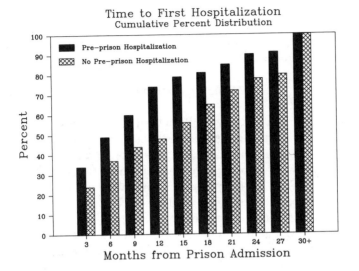

**FIGURE 3.3**
Cumulative percent distribution of time to first hospitalization by
preprison mental health experience.

health staff, which affords greater opportunities for diagnosis. This interpretation receives some support from the data in that 8.3 percent of the
hospitalized inmates, as compared to less than one half of one percent of
other inmates, were found incompetent to stand trial prior to conviction
on their current offense. While incompetency findings are predicated on
criteria that go beyond the simple presence of mental disorder, the data
confirm that at least some inmates who require hospitalization in prison
were suspected of being seriously emotionally disordered following arrest.[2]

Another possibility is that prison admission is a stressful experience that
can strain coping resources to debilitating levels for some inmates, and
this effect becomes amplified for inmates with a history of emotional
problems. We have already discussed the notion of "transition shock"
with regard to our analysis of disciplinary rates, and the data on psychiatric
hospitalization provide additional evidence for this type of process.[3] We
find the confluence of findings to be significant on several accounts. The
early months of incarceration appear to be a critical transition period
during which problems of adjustment are greatest and maladaptive behaviors come to the fore. Although inmates can manifest their coping difficulties in a variety of ways, we find that personal characteristics increase the
likelihood that certain maladaptive behavior will manifest itself. Young

inmates are more likely to "act-out" or rebel against institutional rules, while inmates with a history of emotional problems are more likely to decompensate to a point where hospitalization becomes necessary. In this regard, our data confirm that there are risk factors associated with various avenues of maladaptation.

### Multiple Hospitalizations

Thus far, our analysis has only dealt with initial hospitalizations. We can expect that some inmates will end their careers as hospital patients after one commitment and that others will go on to recidivate. This leads us to examine the issue of multiple hospitalizations. In our sample, nearly half (49 percent) of the hospitalized inmates were committed once, one quarter (25 percent) were committed twice, and over one quarter (26 percent were committed three or more times.

In Table 3.4 we find the proportion of multiply hospitalized inmates by time to first hospitalization and by length of incarceration. The data indicate that the timing of the initial hospitalization does not affect the chances of rehospitalization. Inmates who are first hospitalized very early in their prison term have the same probability of being rehospitalized as

**TABLE 3.4A**

**Percent of hospitalized inmates with multiple hospitalizations by time to first hospitalization.**

| Time to first (single) hospitalization | | TYPE OF HOSPITAL PATIENT | |
| --- | --- | --- | --- |
| | | Single | Multiple hospitalization |
| 2 months or less | (n = 40) | 50% | 50% |
| 3 to 8 months | (n = 37) | 57 | 43 |
| 8 to 16 months | (n = 30) | 37 | 63 |
| 17 months or more | (n = 40) | 50 | 50 |

**TABLE 3.4B**

**Percent of hospitalized inmates with multiple hospitalizations by time served.**

| Time served on current sentence | | TYPE OF HOSPITAL PATIENT | |
| --- | --- | --- | --- |
| | | Single | Multiple hospitalization |
| 18 months or less | (n = 14) | 64%* | 36%* |
| 19 to 30 months | (n = 45) | 62* | 38* |
| 31 to 48 months | (n = 35) | 51* | 49* |
| 49 months or more | (n = 53) | 32* | 68* |

*—p. less than 0.05

inmates who are first hospitalized later in their sentence. In contrast, we notice that length of incarceration is related to the chances of rehospitalization, in that inmates serving long prison terms are more likely to be hospitalized more than once. Specifically, the probability of rehospitalization among long-term inmates is more than double that of short-term inmates.

Juxtaposed against this relationship, we find that the proportion of time inmates spend in hospitals relative to length of prison term is fairly constant across time-served groups. The proportions are 19.5 percent for short-term inmates, 18.2 percent for low-average term inmates, 14.9 percent for high-average term inmates and 17.6 percent for long-term inmates. This finding indicates that while long-term inmates are hospitalized more often, their relative amount of hospital time is comparable to that of inmates with shorter sentences.

As we already noted, hospitalized inmates in our sample have a fifty-fifty chance of rehospitalization. However, the probability of recommitment is related to the number of prior commitments. Conditional probabilities for second thru sixth hospitalizations are . 51, .51, .58. .64, and .71. By the time an inmate has been hospitalized seven times, the chances are four out of five (.80) that rehospitalization will be necessary. Thus, the probability of recommitment increases as the number of prior commitments increases.

We have identified two factors that play an important role in rehospitalization. The first is the length of time that an inmate is in custody of the system. In general, the longer disturbed inmates are incarcerated, the greater the chances they will require rehospitalization. This relationship may be interpreted simply as a reflection of time at risk, since the length of an inmate's sentence circumscribes the prison's responsibility for providing treatment. A competing explanation derives from the assumption that prison environments aggravate psychiatric disorders among highly vulnerable inmates. Thus, our findings can be interpreted as supporting the principle that continued exposure to pathogenic stimuli increases the probability of rehospitalization.

By extending our investigation into the community, we could evaluate competing explanations by asking whether short-term inmates have comparable rates of rehospitalization over a standardized followup period. In so doing, however, we would have to allow for differences between prisons and the community in both formal and informal commitment practices. On the basis of the available data, we feel that our findings on multiple hospitalization are best interpreted taking a "time at risk" perspective. The fact that the proportion of time inmates spend hospitalized is the same across time-served groups suggests that need for hospitalization is relatively constant adjusting for sentence length. Furthermore, although long-term inmates do show higher symptom rates over time, the increase is very modest.

We have also seen that the chances of rehospitalization increase as an inmate builds up a track record of psychiatric commitments, and that beyond a certain point the probability of recommitment begins to approach certainty. This finding indicates that a small number of inmates have emotional problems that are both serious and chronic, raising the question of whether periodic hospitalization supplemented by outpatient services is the most appropriate treatment model for this group. Repeated ''shuttling'' of patients between prison and hospital can aggravate an inmate's condition, and can unduly strain working relationships between custody and treatment staff.

Our findings on rehospitalization hold several implications for mental health service delivery. The most obvious implication is that treatment planning should allow for length of incarceration. An inmate's availability for services, which is fundamentally related to the likelihood of achieving treatment goals, is circumscribed by legal decisions made at sentencing. By definition, inmates with short prison terms can not be long-term clients of a prison mental health system. In the case of such inmates, service delivery must be geared towards reaching shorter term objectives, and treatment plans need to be organized around the coordination of services between prisons and community agencies. In contrast, inmates with extended prison terms have the opportunity to become longer term clients of a prison mental health system. Clinicians therefore have the opportunity to work towards more enduring or difficult-to-achieve treatment goals, and are also in a better position to take advantage of prison resources by coordinating therapeutic and correctional programs.

## Notes

1. A possible explanation for the increasing symptom rates of long-term inmates changes in record keeping. In chapter 1 we noted that in 1975, the Office of Mental Health assumed responsibility for treatment services leading to improvements in clinical records. This transition occurred seven to eight years prior to the time period that defines our release cohort, and some inmate patients in our sample had served prison terms that span this period. For inmates serving ten years in prison, the first five to seven career segments would fall under the old system. While we did find and code mental-health-related information prior to 1975 in both correctional and mental health files, our impression is that the frequency of observation notes, particularly in hospital settings, is greater under the new system.
2. One large-scale study of defendants found incompetent to stand trial reports

that 41% of these defendants were eventually sentenced to incarceration. (H. Steadman, *Beating a Rap?* Chicago: University of Chicago Press, 1979).

3. Zamble, Proporino and Kalotay (note 1, Intro.) reach a similar conclusion. They report that "most behavioral measures show again that the effects of imprisonment seem to be minimal and mostly limited to the beginning of the term" (p. 135). Similarly, they write that "the initial traumatic effects of imprisonment were greatly alleviated over time, and by the end of the study only a few still showed evidence of serious emotional distress" (p. 133).

# 4

# Disturbed-Disruptive Patterns

Up to this point we have separately examined patterns of misbehavior and emotional problems, and we have seen two different pictures emerge. Disruptive behavior reveals a consistency that cuts across sentences of varying lengths. Rates of infractions peak shortly after admission to prison and then steadily decline. The manifestation of symptoms, in contrast, shows greater variety, but the general pattern, especially among outpatients, is one of declining rates over time. There are also indications that for hospitalized inmates prison admission and release are junctures that coincide with increased levels of personal difficulty.

We now explore how disturbed and disruptive behavior relate to each other, and we will focus on the coincidence and sequencing of these two types of behavior. After investigating these issues, we will examine how prisons attempt to manage multifaceted behavior problems.

A number of prior studies report that mentally ill inmates have higher-than-average disciplinary rates.[1] Our data indicate that hospital patients have a mean annual rate of 5.1 infractions, while outpatients have a rate of 5.9 infractions, and no service inmates have a rate of 3.7 infractions. The rate for hospital patients is adjusted for time spent outside of prison and the outpatient group represents only those inmates who we could verify had received services. These differences in disciplinary rates are consistent with other research and suggest that within prison settings emotional disorder and disruptive behavior are interrelated. We also found that outpatients have higher infraction rates than hospital patients. We will have more to say about this finding at a later point.[2]

Disciplinary records list incidents officially handled as violations of prison rules, and mental health files likewise record observations that are relevant to the diagnosis and treatment of emotional disorders. Types of records overlap with types of behavior, but the correspondence is not perfect. Disruptive acts can be described as an aspect of a mental health problem while displays of symptoms can be noted as part of a disciplinary incident.

We found that 130 disciplinary incidents included descriptions of emotional problems, and that of these incidents, 112 involved reports of self-injury. Descriptions of disruptive acts in mental health files present a very different situation. Among hospitalized inmates, we find that 3.5 percent of symptomatic observations include assaultive behavior, 4.6 percent describe a serious disturbance (such as yelling, screaming, shouting), 2.8 percent list refusing an order (for example, won't come out of cell), 11.2 percent report refusing medication and 7.4 percent characterize the patient as hostile, angry or belligerent. Overall, 27.2 percent of prison incidents (18.4 percent if we exclude refusing medication) involve disruptive behavior. Outpatients' records reveal similar findings with 1.5 percent of prison mental health observations involving assaultive behavior, 1.5 percent describing a serious disturbance, 9.9 percent including refusing orders, 5.7 percent noting medication refusal, and 5.7 percent describing the patient as angry, hostile or belligerent. Among symptom descriptions for outpatients 25.9 percent (21.2 percent if we exclude refusing medication) report disruptive behavior.[3]

These data indicate that, while descriptions of disturbed behavior rarely find their way into official disciplinary records, disruptive behavior is likely to be frequently listed in mental health files. For both hospital patients and outpatients, about one quarter of clinical observations include descriptions of disruptive behavior. These findings show that disruptiveness is often part of the presenting symptomatic picture considered by clinicians, and the frequency of such notations in treatment files confirms that mental health staff view the appearance of disruptive behavior as clinically relevant.

To a large extent, the one-sided overlap we observe between reports of disruptive and disturbed behaviors can be attributed to differences in the ways disciplinary and mental health files are kept. Most descriptions of disciplinary incidents are terse, usually listing the rules that are violated or giving a shorthand description of the person's behavior (such as out of place, refused an order). While we coded as much detail as the records offered, the mental health files contained more narrative accounts and provided more extensive descriptions of incidents. For these reasons, our data do not permit conclusions as to whether disciplinary committees are aware of behavior which suggests that an inmate is emotionally disordered, though at a later point we will examine evidence that indicates that disciplinary committees are sensitive to the possible presence of mental illness among disruptive inmates.

The act of designating specific acts as symptoms of illness, or as sanctionable violations of prison rules or as both depends in part on judgments about an inmate's mental health status and about the relationship of this status to the person's behavior in a given situation. In general, we might expect that the chances of disruptive behavior being referred for disciplinary action diminish in the presence of flagrant emotional problems. This would appear to be especially true for situations that combine minor infractions with evidence of serious pathology. Figure 4.1 examines this issue by comparing the proportion of inmates written up for disciplinary incidents to the proportion who exhibited disruptive symptoms of mental illness before and after hospitalization. The disruptive symptoms we refer to represent pieces of behavior that are listed as prison rules violations and therefore present an opportunity for disciplinary action. The data clearly indicate that as hospitalization approaches, the reports of disciplinary violations go down while reports of disruptive symptoms go up. We also find that rates of both disciplinary incidents and disruptive symptoms are lower after hospitalization.

These findings suggest that a redefinition of disruptive behavior occurs in the presence of serious psychopathology. Behavior that otherwise might be regarded as a violation of prison rules becomes viewed as part of the

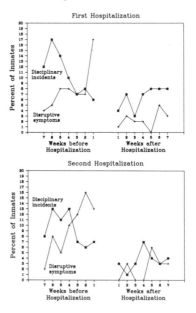

**FIGURE 4.1**
**Percent of inmates with disciplinary incidents and disruptive symptoms before and after hospitalization.**

overall symptomatic picture, and punitive responses come to be seen as less appropriate in light of impending hospitalization. One of the factors that helps to account for this change in perspective is that inmates who are suspected of being seriously mentally ill are usually placed in specialized therapeutic settings. One consequence of sequestering emotionally disordered inmates is to minimize the impact of disruptive behavior on institutional order. In this regard, therapeutic interventions that become appropriate given displays of symptomatic behavior can help to reduce the pressure on custodial staff to react to the person's disruptive behavior. Placement in therapeutic settings also represents a professional judgment that an inmate may be mentally ill, thereby reinforcing the notion that unusual behaviors should be interpreted as manifestations of symptomatology.

### Disciplinary careers of inmate patients

Do patterns of disciplinary involvement differ for inmates with and without emotional difficulties? Table 4.1 displays the distribution of disciplinary career types by mental health status. We find that nondisruptive

**TABLE 4.1**
**Distribution of disciplinary career patterns by prison mental health experience.**

| | PRISON MENTAL HEALTH EXPERIENCE | | |
|---|---|---|---|
| | No service (n = 7634) | Outpatient (n = 435) | Hospitalized (n = 141) |
| **Disciplinary career pattern** | | | |
| Nondisruptive (low, low, low) | 77.8% | 63.0% | 68.1% |
| Early starter (high, low, low) | 6.3 | 13.6 | 7.1 |
| Inverted-U (low, high, low) | 4.2 | 6.7 | 7.8 |
| Late bloomer (low, low, high) | 2.4 | 3.4 | 5.0 |
| Late reformer (high, high, low) | 3.0 | 4.4 | 2.8 |
| U-shape (high, low, high) | 2.3 | 2.1 | 2.8 |
| Mid-bloomer (low, high, high) | 1.4 | 1.6 | 2.8 |
| Chronic (high, high, high) | 2.5 | 5.3 | 3.5 |

careers are less frequent among mentally ill inmates. Overall, 67.6 percent of hospitalized inmates, 60.1 percent of outpatients and 77.1 percent of no service inmates fail to show periods of substantial disciplinary involvement. Looking at the distribution of other career types, we observe that hospitalized inmates are more likely to demonstrate late bloomer (low, low, high) and mid-bloomer (low, high, low) patterns and are less likely to show early starter (high, low, low), late reformer (high, high, low) and chronic patterns (high, high, high). In contract, outpatients are overrepresented in late reformer (high, high, low) and chronic patterns (high, high, high) and underrepresented in the early starter (high, low, low) pattern.

In general, hospitalized inmates are less likely to show disruptiveness patterns that encompass early portions of the sentence while outpatients are more likely to demonstrate patterns that span more than one career stage (i.e., semichronic and chronic patterns). Given that hospitalization tends to occur early in the prison term and that inmates are not at risk for disciplinary write-ups while hospitalized, disciplinary patterns for hospitalized inmates appear to be influenced by the timing of commitments. Hospitalization thus intersects disciplinary careers in such ways that common patterns of disruptiveness (i.e., early starter) occur less often. In addition, the disciplinary careers of hospital patients suggest that a transition occurs from serious psychopathology to high levels of antisocial behavior. At a later point we will investigate the issue of behavior transitions more directly.

Career patterns for outpatients allow us to be more specific with regard to our finding that these inmates exhibit high infraction rates. Higher infraction rates do not result from brief periods of unusually intense disciplinary involvement but rather can be attributed to fairly chronic disruptiveness. Thus, outpatients generally accumulate substantial disciplinary records by persisting in rules violations over long periods of time.

### Combined Disturbed and Disruptive Patterns

We now turn to examine questions regarding the coincidence of symptom-related and disruptive behaviors. One of the simplest analytic strategies to suggest itself involves a straightforward investigation of the relationship between rates of disciplinary incidents and symptomatology. In light of the findings reported in earlier chapters, however, we can find several problems with this approach. We have already noted that patients are not at risk for disciplinary actions while they are hospitalized. This means that there can be no relationship between symptom rates and infraction rates during hospital stays, and we have just seen how these gaps influence disciplinary patterns so that characterizing disturbed-disruptive patterns over entire prison careers is difficult for hospital patients. Among outpatients, we have also seen that rates of symptomatic behavior are low and that individual manifestations of pathology tend to be relatively brief. In contrast, outpatient disciplinary rates are relatively high, and these individuals exhibit fairly chronic disruptiveness. On the basis of these findings we can anticipate that periods of overlap between disturbed and disruptive behavior for outpatients will be relatively infrequent and brief.

Our analysis of disturbed-disruptive patterns builds on the concept of "episode" which can be defined as a series of incidents that are proximate in time. The episode as a framework for analysis offers several advantages in that we can use the number and types of behaviors to describe and classify episodes. We can also examine transitions from one type of episode to the next as well as locate episodes within career segments.

A key item in the definition of an episode is the maximum time between successive incidents. While selection of this criterion is in a sense arbitrary, choices can be guided by several considerations. In our case, the time frame should be such that we can view the pieces of behavior as related manifestations of an inmate's coping difficulties. Our time requirement for defining incidents as part of the same episode is ten days. Thus, two behaviors that occur within ten days of each other represent the start of an episode, while a hiatus of at least eleven days between successive incidents signals the end of an episode. Given this criterion, we find that an average episode for hospitalized inmates lasts 13.4 days and contains 6.7 incidents while outpatient episodes last 8.0 days and include 3.0 incidents. We also find that hospital patients average 7.3 episodes over the course of their prison term while outpatients average 4.5 episodes.

We characterize episodes as either disturbed, disruptive or disturbed-disruptive based on the presence of symptomatic and disciplinary behavior. For hospitalized inmates, 44.1 percent of episodes are classified as disturbed, 22.5 percent as disruptive and 33.4 percent as disturbed-disruptive. If we describe episodes in terms of seriousness of behavior, we find that 47 percent are nonviolent-nonpsychotic, 35 percent are psychotic-nonviolent, 13 percent are nonpsychotic-violent and 4 percent are psychotic-violent. The distribution of episode classifications for outpatients is 13.3 percent disturbed, 64.9 disruptive and 21.8 disturbed-disruptive. Alternatively, outpatient episodes can be described as 68.4 percent nonpsychotic-nonviolent, 5.0 percent psychotic-nonviolent, 25.6 percent nonpsychotic-violent and 0.9% psychotic-violent.

Looking more closely at the various types of episodes, we find that, on the average, disturbed-disruptive episodes for hospitalized inmates last longest (18.5 days) and comprise the largest number of incidents (9.2). In contrast, disruptive episodes are shortest (6.8 days) and have the fewest number of incidents (2.6). Disturbed episodes fall in between, with an average length of 13.0 days and 8.4 incidents.

It is not surprising that disturbed episodes are the most common type of episode for hospitalized inmates, given the nature of this group. Yet, it is significant that we find disturbed-disruptive episodes (33.4 percent) are more common than disruptive episodes (22.5 percent). This finding indicates that more often than not periods of high disciplinary involvement overlap with symptomatic behavior for seriously disturbed inmates. We also note that the most serious type of incident, violent-psychotic episodes, is extremely infrequent (4 percent) much more so in fact that the prevalence of nonpsychotic-violent episodes (13 percent). Our analysis identified fifty such episodes over the combined prison terms of 145 seriously disturbed inmates. The rarity of violent psychotic episodes is significant because this combination of behavior is central to stereotypic views of the "criminally insane."[4]

In contrast, we find that among outpatients disruptive episodes (64.9 percent) are most common, followed by disturbed-disruptive episodes (21.8 percent). Consistent with these findings we note that outpatients are more prone to violent episodes than hospital patients (35.5 percent). Finally, we see that among outpatients pure disturbed episodes are relatively rare (13.3 percent). These data indicate that disruptiveness is the central feature of maladaptive patterns among outpatients. Though sometimes disruptiveness is linked with symptomatology, unadulterated manifestations of emotional disorder are unlikely to occur.

Table 4.2 examines transitions between types of episodes for hospitalized inmates. The data depict the distribution of classifications from preceding to subsequent episodes. In looking at the table, we notice a strong consistency between successive episodes, as indicated by the high

**TABLE 4.2**
**Distribution of transitions from prior to subsequent episodes for hospital patients.**

| Prior episode | SUBSEQUENT EPISODE | | | |
|---|---|---|---|---|
| | Disturbed | Disruptive | Disturbed-disruptive | Hospital |
| Disturbed | 42.7% | 2.5% | 18.8% | 36.0% |
| | (n = 206) | (n = 12) | (n = 91) | (n = 483) |
| Disruptive | 12.5 | 58.5 | 21.8 | 7.3 |
| | (n = 31) | (n = 145) | (n = 54) | (n = 248) |
| Disturbed-disruptive | 27.6 | 8.0 | 40.5 | 23.9 |
| | (n = 103) | (n = 30) | (n = 151) | (n = 89) |
| Hospital | 50.2 | 16.1 | 25.5 | 8.2 |
| | (n = 134) | (n = 43) | (n = 68) | (n = 22) |

percentages along the diagonal. This means that our best prediction of the next type of episode is that it will be the same as the preceding one. Beyond this general observation, we find that disturbed episodes are likely both to precede and follow hospitalization. Disturbed-disruptive episodes show an equal chance of being followed by a hospitalization or by a disturbed episode, while disruptive episodes are more likely to be followed by disturbed-disruptive episodes than by disturbed episodes. We also find that four out of ten hospitalizations (41.6 percent) are followed by episodes that involve disruptive behavior. Finally, we note that transitions from purely disturbed to purely disruptive episodes and vice versa are infrequent.

Data on transitions between episodes for outpatients are presented in table 4.3. Again we find that transitions between episodes of the same type are common. However, unlike the pattern for hospitalized inmates, we find that transitions to purely disruptive episodes are more likely across the board. We also find that transitions to disturbed-disruptive episodes are less likely. These results are consistent with the statistical picture of lower symptom rates and higher infraction rates of outpatients.

We now consider the characteristics that differentiate between types of episodes, including inmate attributes and characteristics of preceding episodes. Table 4.4 contains the results of logistic regression analyses comparing one type of episode to all others from hospitalized inmates. Because we are interested in the influence of prior episodes, the first episode in a series is not included as part of the dependent variable.

The results indicate that disturbed episodes are unlikely to be preceded by disruptive episodes or by disturbed-disruptive episodes. We also find that disturbed episodes occur later in the prison term and are more likely to involve inmates convicted of sodomy. In comparison, disruptive episodes occur earlier in the prison term, and they tend to be preceded by a

**TABLE 4.3**

**Percent distribution of transitions between preceeding and subsequent episodes for outpatients.**

| Preceeding episode | SUBSEQUENT EPISODE | | |
|---|---|---|---|
| | Disturbed | Disruptive | Disturbed-disruptive |
| Disturbed | 45.9% | 23.2% | 30.9% |
| | (n = 83) | (n = 42) | (n = 56) |
| Disruptive | 3.8 | 81.0 | 15.2 |
| | (n = 42) | (n = 893) | (n = 167) |
| Disturbed-disruptive | 17.9 | 42.8 | 39.3 |
| | (n = 62) | (n = 148) | (n = 136) |

TABLE 4.4
Results of logistic regression analyses comparing one type of episode to all others.

| | TYPE OF EPISODE | | | |
| | Disturbed | Disruptive | Disturbed-disruptive | Hospital |
|---|---|---|---|---|
| **Social history** | | | | |
| Drug use | | | 1.88 | |
| **Criminal history** | | | | |
| Prior prison experience | | | | 1.05 |
| **Current prison experience** | | | | |
| Time-served (months) | − .003 | | | |
| Time-served (proportion) | 1.14 | | | |
| Sodomy conviction | .71 | | | |
| **Prior episode** | | | | |
| Disruptive type | − 2.41 | 2.15 | | |
| Disturbed-disruptive type | − .78 | | | |
| Duration | | − .08 | − .01 | − .06 |
| Num. of discip. infract. | | | | − .30 |
| Num. of symptoms | | | | .12 |
| Num. of psychotic symptoms | | | | .14 |
| **Current episode** | | | | |
| Timing | | | | |
| #1 to #10 | | 1.60 | | |
| #11 to #20 | | .77 | | |
| Duration | | − .80 | | |
| Constant | − .42 | − 2.35 | − .73 | − 4.62 |
| Goodness of fit X² | 1078* | 728 | 1133 | 369 |
| d.f. | 822 | 873 | 874 | 946 |
| Hosmer statistic | 3 | 10 | 5 | 26 |
| d.f. | 8 | 8 | 8 | 8 |

* p. less than .05

disruptive episode shorter than the current episode. Disturbed-disruptive episodes are also likely to follow in sequence, and they tend to involve inmates who admit that they are drug users. It comes as no surprise that the number of symptoms in an episode that precedes hospitalization, especially psychotic symptoms, is positively related to hospitalization, while the number of disciplinary infractions is negatively related to hospital commitment. In addition, the extent of prior prison experience shows a positive relationship to hospitalization.

In general, the results of the multivariate analyses confirm what we observed in the transition matrix. There is continuity in maladaptation in that as inmates move from one episode to the next, they tend to repeat similar types of behavior. This tendency is akin to the consistency we observed in transitions between one disciplinary incident and the next as discussed in chapter 2. An interesting aspect of this continuity is what we do not find to be significant. With the exception of hospitalization, the number and types of behavior in the preceding episode are unrelated to the type of subsequent episode. These negative findings suggest that a general pattern of escalation or de-escalation of behavior is not characteristic of episode transitions.

With regard to admixtures of behavior we find that simple transitions from disturbed to disruptive or vice versa are rare. Instead we find a tendency to move to or persist in "combination" episodes. The timing of episodes reveals that disruptive episodes occur early in the prison term and disturbed episodes occur late.

In general, the findings suggest that disturbed-disruptive inmates present a complex behavioral picture that remains fairly constant over time. When changes are observed the short-term trend (between episodes) is that of moving from simple to complex patterns, while the general long-term trend (across prison terms) is that of moving from disruptive to disturbed behavior. In other words, inmates rarely oscillate between disturbed and disruptive behavior. Rather, they tend to specialize in one behavior or the other, or they repeatedly manifest both types of behavior at about the same time.

These findings point to some encouraging and some difficult aspects of dealing with inmates who have serious adjustment problems. General types of maladaptation tend to be consistent over time, suggesting that individual patterns can be identified and that appropriate interventions can be generated. Yet, we see that maladaptation can not always be described neatly since inmates often display compound adjustment problems. Furthermore, when unidimensional problems change direction they tend to take on new features, retaining the old. Thus, many seriously maladjusted inmates present a complex behavioral picture and changes in maladaptive patterns tend to add complexity. The challenge then is to develop interventions that accommodate behavioral complexity and to interrupt cycles of development early when problems are neater and possibly easier to address.

Our findings for hospital inmates underscore the limitations of viewing custodial and mental health problems as separate and discrete. Temporal coincidence does not necessarily imply causation in the sense that disciplinary problems are always the result of emotional disorders, but it does suggest that at some level different manifestations of coping problems are interrelated. An integrated framework that posits relationships between emotional and interpersonal deficits would appear to be more useful than a paradigm that insists on artificially drawn boundaries. Human service professionals may gravitate towards neat definitions of their clientele, but our data suggest that problems of maladaptation are often more complex, in that they include more than one problem area.

## Administrative Responses

Disciplinary infractions for hospitalized inmates are roughly equally distributed across disruptive episodes, disturbed-disruptive episodes and nonepisodic situations (31 percent, 31 percent and 38 percent respectively). For this group of inmates, infractions that are part of a disruptive episode are treated more seriously than are other infractions. About 15 percent of infractions in disruptive episodes result in a superintendent's hearings, an administrative procedure that often leads to the imposition of severe penalties, compared to about 10 percent of other infractions. On the other hand, we find that about 15 percent of infractions in disturbed-disruptive episodes result in a mental health referral by the disciplinary committee compared to about 5 percent of other infractions. Thus, infractions that are part of a series of misbehaviors tend to be handled more seriously than other infractions, while infractions that coincide with symptom-related behavior are more likely to be viewed as possible manifestations of emotional disorder.[5]

Rates of disciplinary behaviors can be affected by therapeutic interventions. For hospitalized inmates, the mean annual rate prior to commitment is 8.3 infractions.[6] In the post-hospitalization phase the comparable rate drops to 3.5 infractions. However, transfers to other therapeutic settings do not show similar effects. Prior to admission into special prison programs (such as APPU, Merle Cooper and ICP), the mean annual infraction rate is 4.3 infractions. During program enrollment, the rate rises to 5.5 infractions, and after leaving the program, the rate drops back to 4.2 infractions. The increase in disciplinary violations while inmates are enrolled in these programs is curious and may result from greater surveillance that accompanies participation in these programs.

In reviewing correctional folders, we found that disruptiveness is often cited as a reason for institutional transfers, and many times a notation indicating that the inmate requires a more secure custodial setting is added. For chronically disruptive inmates, who spend most of their prison careers in maximum security facilities, justification for transfer occasionally invoked the argument, We've had him long enough. Now it's some one else's turn. What we found to be most interesting were rationales postulating that inmate behavior may improve as a result of transfer.[7] A simple version of this rationale is based on the premise that changes in prison environment are disequilibrating and can interrupt the momentum of disruptive behavior. A more sophisticated version highlights situations where interpersonal relationships have degenerated to a point where improvement is effectively foreclosed. The opportunity for a "fresh start" at another institution may allow an inmate to extricate himself from what has become an entrenched cycle of disruptiveness. A still more sophisticated version of this strategy attempts to match inmates to environments in such a way as to turn the tide of disruptive tendencies. For example, inmate behavior may improve from transfer to a prison that has a different population mix. Transfer to prisons with specialized programming that can address an inmate's personal deficiencies or that might capture and sustain his interest are another version of this strategy.

Use of transfers as a means of curbing disruptive behavior implies a positive relationship between disciplinary and transfer rates. We therefore examined these correlations and found different patterns across time-served categories. For short-term inmates, disciplinary and transfer rates show negative correlations. (in the order of $-.07$) toward the end (last three career segments) of prison careers. For inmates with low-average prison terms we find few statistically significant correlations. High-average term inmates show positive correlations (between .04 and .09) toward the end of their prison term, and long-term inmates shows relatively strong negative correlations (between $-.08$ and $-.17$) during the first half, and equally strong positive correlations (between .11 and .20) during the second half of their sentence.

These findings do not provide a straightforward confirmation of the hypothesis that inmates are transferred in response to behavior probems. The data point in opposite directions across prison terms of inmates with different sentence lengths. It is difficult to make sense of contradictory findings, and with this caveat in mind our interpretation of the data is as follows: For short-term inmates there appears to be a preference for dealing with problems at the institution where problems become manifest. This preference may develop in response to the fact that short-term inmates enter and leave the prison system very quickly, so there is less opportunity to solicit transfers. Long-term inmates present more opportunities for transfers. Yet, we find relationships in opposite directions between the beginning and end of long prison terms. This finding suggests an initial preference to deal with problems where they occur even for long-term inmates. It is only later in the sentence, perhaps after local attempts to deal with problems have failed, that the strategy of interrupting disruptive behavior through institutional transfers becomes deployed.

An example of a transfer predicated on the assumption that a change in population mix can reduce disruptive behavior is that of moving an inmate from a youth facility to an adult institution. The rationale is that older inmates are less inclined to act in ways that reinforce immature behavior and can serve as positive role models for young inmates. We find that such transfers are rare, but they do appear to have the effect of reducing misbehavior. Inmates transferred from youth facilities to mainline correctional settings show an average annual rate of 11.6 pretransfer infractions compared to a rate of 7.9 infractions after transfer. In comparison, the mean infraction rates before and after transfers between maximum security institutions are almost identical (5.5 pre; 5.4 post). It is of course possible that changes in disciplinary rates are the result of different disciplining thresholds between staff of different institutions.[8] Although we are not in a position to test this alternative explanation, the data do not require us to reject the hypothesis that actual changes in inmate behavior take place.

Disciplinary committees face a difficult situation when dealing with emotionally disordered inmates. On the one hand, legalistic concerns dictate standardized case processing with equivalent punishments assigned to similar infractions. Yet, mentally ill inmates are often involved in nonroutine violations, and if disciplinary committees are to fulfill their "correctional" function, a more flexible, individualized posture seems warranted.

Our data indicate that disciplinary dispositions for seriously emotionally disturbed inmates often involve requests for mental health services, which shows that officers who assign penalties are concerned about their effects. Among hospitalized inmates, one out of ten disciplinary incidents result in referrals to clinicians as compared to a rate of about one in fifty incidents for other inmates. We also find that when a request for therapeutic services is made, disciplinary committees are less inclined to see a need for punitive action. Among incidents involving mental health referrals, 43.1 percent were given nonpunitive dispositions (such as counselling, suspended sentence) compared to 26.5 percent of other infractions. This tendency, to be sure, is affected by an inmate's status as patient, as evidenced by the finding that among hospitalized inmates 55 percent of incidents involving mental health referrals were unaccompanied by punitive sanctions.

When we compare disciplinary outcomes between inmate clients and other inmates, we find the overall distributions to be nearly identical. If we disaggregate outcomes by type of incident, some differences emerge for violent infractions. Table 4.5 shows that violent infractions by hospitalized inmates are more likely to result in nonpunitive dispositions (such as counseling), and the proportion of such dispositions is almost twice as great for the hospitalized group as it is for the no-service group (16 percent versus 9 percent). At the same time, however, we find that violent infractions by hospitalized inmates disproportionately invite the most serious

**TABLE 4.5**
**Percent distribution of disciplinary dispositions by type of infraction and prison mental health experience.**

| Disposition | PRISON MENTAL HEALTH EXPERIENCE | | |
| --- | --- | --- | --- |
| | Hospital | Outpatient | No Service |
| **Nonviolent infractions** | | | |
| Counseled | 29.9% | 26.7% | 28.2% |
| Loss of privleges | 25.3 | 26.9 | 28.5 |
| Keeplock | 37.5 | 37.5 | 35.3 |
| Special housing/ loss of good time | 4.0 | 4.0 | 3.4 |
| Other | 3.3 | 4.9 | 4.6 |
| **Violent infractions** | | | |
| Counseled | 15.7 | 11.2 | 8.8 |
| Loss of privleges | 9.1 | 11.5 | 13.9 |
| Keeplock | 46.2 | 52.9 | 57.1 |
| Special housing/ loss of good time | 28.0 | 23.2 | 19.4 |
| Other | 1.0 | 1.2 | 0.8 |

penalties (28 percent versus 19 percent) such as loss of good time or placement in special housing units. Before discussing the implications of these findings, we turn to examine disciplinary responses to other mental health-related behavior.

Some infractions can be described as peculiar or eccentric in that they lead us to ask questions about an inmate's emotional condition. These infractions stand out not just because they are relatively infrequent, but because the standard presumption of a rationally motivated offender seems inappropriate. How do disciplinary committees respond to such situations? In order to investigate this question, we classified infractions as "peculiar" if they suggested that the inmate manifested a highly unusual state of mind. Infractions such as self-injury, throwing feces, setting fire to one's cell and poor personal hygiene were included in this category. Supporting our assumption that these behaviors are suggestive of unusual emotional states, we found that 12 percent of infractions for hospital patients fell in this category compared to 4 percent for outpatients and 3 percent for nonpatients.

We find that in general "peculiar" infractions are dealt with less severely than other infractions. For example, such incidents more commonly result in loss of privileges (33 percent versus 27 percent) than in keeplock (29 percent versus 38 percent). When we examine the dispositions of these infractions by level of seriousness (violent versus nonviolent), however, we find that assaultive acts combined with behavior suggestive of emotional disorder are dealt with more seriously than other assaults. Among peculiar assaults, 35.8 percent thus resulted in loss of good time or placement in special housing compared to 20.3 percent of other assaultive infractions.

Some of our findings demonstrate the willingness of disciplinary committees to invoke the assistance of mental health professionals. To be sure, the attractiveness of the mental health option varies with the type of inmate and the type of behavior under consideration, yet, among seriously disturbed inmates, one out of ten disciplinary incidents leads to a request for clinical assistance. Such outreach efforts are important because they represent attempts by disciplinary committees to understand reasons for infractions and to consider underlying causes of disruptiveness. They are also important because they imply that disciplinary committees worry about the impact of what they do, and they implicitly acknowledge a need to have available options that might ameliorate or supplement the usual punitive measures.

Our findings also highlight some of the tensions administrators face when dealing with problem inmates and choosing between competing models of prison discipline. A "flexible rules" model, which proposes that disciplinary responses be custom-tailored to individuals, holds out the possibility that underlying causes of antisocial behavior can be considerately or constructively addressed. In contrast, a legalistic model, which emphasizes consistency and fairness in procedures and outcomes, is a cornerstone of general deterrence strategies for maintaining institutional order.[9] The conflict is that actions that are beneficial to the person may be viewed as counterproductive from an institutional perspective and vice versa.

Given that over one quarter of all infractions involve non-punitive or relatively minor dispositions, disciplinary committees can not be accused of taking the position that every violation of prison rules should result in punishment. Additionally, the fact that about half the incidents in which hospitalized inmates are referred for mental health services are unaccompanied by sanctions indicates that disciplinary committees feel comfortable about suspending or mitigating punishment where they feel that it would serve no purpose. The other side of the coin is that in the remaining half of the incidents disciplinary committees saw a need to combine punishment with treatment. These situations suggest that multiple goals are sometimes pursued by incorporating aspects of a "flexible rules" approach into a legalistic model.[10] The differences we reported in how assaultive acts are responded to are relevant to this issue. Not all violent behavior is viewed as a serious threat to institutional order. However, assaultive acts coupled with disturbed behavior are punished more harshly than other assaults, indicating that these "mixed" incidents, which are often spontaneous and unpredictable, are viewed as more serious threats to the task of maintaining prison order. For us, this finding illustrates how issues pertaining to behavioral complexity, including assumptions about rationality and the effect of punishment on behavior, can become secondary considerations in situations where perceived threat to institutional order is great, and the option of sanctioning is the only one available.

## Notes

1. K. Adams, "Former mental patients in a prison and parole system: A study of socially disruptive behavior," *Criminal Justice and Behavior*, 1983, *10*, 358–84. K. Adams, "The disciplinary experiences of emotionally disordered inmates," *Criminal Justice and Behavior*, 1986, *13*, 297–316. H. Toch and K. Adams, "Pathology and disruptiveness among prison inmates," *Journal of Research in Crime and Delinquency*, 1986, *23*, 7–21.
2. Earlier (Toch and Adams, note 1 supra) we reported that outpatients had lower infraction rates than hospitalized inmates. This finding was based on an analysis that included outpatients for whom we subsequently were unable to locate treatment files.
3. Since mental health observations can include more than one disruptive behavior, the totals we report are less than the sum of individual behavior categories.
4. The term "criminally insane" variously refers to persons with combined criminal justice and mental health involvement. The major categories are (1) inmates found incompetent to stand trial; (2) inmates adjudicated not guilty by reason of insanity; (3) mentally ill prison inmates; and (4) civil mental patients legally classified as dangerous. Both clinicians (see T. Thornberry and J. Jacoby, *The Criminally Insane*. Chicago: University of Chicago Press, 1979) and the general public (see H. Steadman and J. Cocozza, "Selective reporting and the public's misconception of the criminally insane," *Public Opinion Quarterly*, 1977, *41*, 523–33) view this group as being highly unpredictable and dangerous.
5. A possible explanation for this finding is that types of disciplinary infractions differ between single and episodic incidents. Another possible explanation is that evaluations of infractions as either serious or symptomatic are contingent upon the context of other recent behaviors.
6. Disciplinary rates throughout the analysis of transfer effects are based on the entire period spent at sending and receiving institutions.
7. This perspective contrasts with others that view prison transfers as an unregulated form of punishment (see J. Broude, "The use of involuntary interprison transfer as sanction." *American Journal of Criminal Law*, 1974, *3*, 117–64).
8. Another consideration is a statistical "regression effect," which refers to the fact that when persons are selected on the basis of extreme scores, subsequent scores will gravitate back towards the mean score. Although we did not specifically choose inmates with high infraction rates for this analysis, the scenario we are investigating assumes that disproportionate disciplinary involvement is one reason behind transfers from youth facilities to maximum-security adult facilities.

9. D. Glaser (*The effectiveness of a prison and parole system.* Indianapolis: Bobbs-Merrill, 1964) is probably the leading proponent of the flexible rules model. He writes "(t)he flexible-rule and constructive-penalty approach . . . is more concerned with giving the deviant inmate new hope than with giving him new fears. . . . . It follows from any conception of rehabilitation as a change in a man's inner values that discipline rehabilitates inmates most in the long run of their lifetimes, and probably improves their behavior in prison as well, if the rules become internalized as their personal moral opinions. If rules are accepted only as part of the restrictions of the immediate environment to which one must learn to adjust in order to avoid penalties, there is no interest in following them when the environment changes, or whenever the risk of being caught and punished is considered negligible" (p. 181). In contrast, D. Fogel (". . . *We are the living proof.* . . ." Cincinnati, OH: Anderson, 1975) was among the first to argue for a legalistic model of prison discipline. He writes "(I)n the context of prison, justice-as-fairness means having clear rules, insuring their promulgation, and following a procedure for determining and punishing rules infractions rooted in due process safeguards. (p. 228)."

10. See Adams (note 1, supra, 1986) for additional evidence on this subject.

# Part II

# INDIVIDUAL PATTERNS

# 5

# A Taxonomy of Maladaptation

To derive a better picture of maladaptation in the prison we reviewed the careers of some of the men in our cohort in as much detail as possible.

Our review covered the careers of 239 men. We selected as candidates for review four types of inmates: inmates with dense disciplinary dossiers that contained descriptions of eccentric violations; inmates on mental health caseloads with high disciplinary infraction rates; inmates with high infraction rates who had been clients of special programs; inmates with low measured intelligence and high disciplinary infraction rates.

We screened the folders of all inmates drawn from these sources and discarded those that contained no detailed behavior descriptions. Since we don't know what factors influence data availability, we record no claim of representativeness for our cases. What we claim is that the inmates we reviewed fall within the high range of maladaptive behavior which is of interest to us.

We extracted all behavior descriptions that the folders contained, arranged the data in chronological order, and prepared synopses or summaries of them. In each case we began by listing the inmate's offense and characterizing his official record of misbehavior. We then entered a step-by-step narrative of the inmate's career over time, starting with his first prison sentence and ending with his reconfinement where it occurred. We followed this narrative with a short analytic statement, characterizing the behavior pattern with as much specificity as possible.

After the case histories were prepared, we reviewed a subsample of the accounts and drafted a roster of themes (with definitions) to cover the principal features of the behavior patterns. This roster was subsequently reorganized and shortened by consolidating themes.

## Nature of the Pattern Analytic Scheme

The taxonomic system we shall detail evolved inductively. This means that we do not claim that the classification is theory-based. The selection of themes, however, reflects conscious and unconscious biases, and we can list some of the former as constituting underlying assumptions:

(1) *We assume that behavior is purposive, though some behavior is more purposive than other behavior.* We ask, What is the person we review trying to achieve? The question is often difficult to answer, and when we deal with maladaptive behavior we are more frequently baffled, because conventional conceptions of purpose are derived from, and associated with, adaptive behavior. This means that in defining purpose we must sometimes strain to accomodate idiosyncratic ends and improbable means-end relationships. The difficulty is most acute when we try to specify the goals of disturbed persons, but also applies to impulse-ridden individuals, whose peremptory approaches to goal-achievement distract from goals that are pursued.

(2) *We assume that behavior is guided by perspectives, and that these perspectives can be consistent across behavior.* We ask, How does the person define the situation to which he responds? The task is to reconstruct the definitional scheme, putting aside the issue of how rational or irrational it may be. We assume that the only world one is in a position to respond to is the world that one perceives, and that external definitions of stimuli are therefore not helpful. On the other hand, the difference between "objective" (externally defined) and "subjective" (individually perceived) impingements can help us to explain seemingly cryptic conduct. This is particularly the case where distortions or reinterpretations occur repeatedly in different situations, prompting consistently inappropriate reactions.

(3) *We believe that nuances matter.* We ask, What, precisely, does the person resonate to when he responds as he does? We hold that if we want to differentiate maladaptive acts from each other, we must discriminate among equivalently dysfunctional behavior in terms of the quality of the perceptions that underlie it and of the feelings with which the behavior is imbued. It matters whether a person feels pushed, crowded, overwhelmed or degraded, and whether he explodes with helpless anger, resentment, panic or rage. The stimulus for differently motivated behavior may be identical (for example, the person may be admonished), and the response may be indiscriminable (the person may lash out), but to advance understanding we center on subtle differences in the process that intervenes between stimulus and response.

(4) *We believe that effective coping is problem solving, and maladaptiveness isn't.* We ask, How does the person approach problems so as to

end up creating new problems for himself and other persons? There are two parts to this question. The first has to do with failures to achieve goals, and with ways in which these come about. The issue is that of social competence, or lack thereof. The second concern relates to interpersonal strategies and approaches to other people that end up creating resentment, disharmony, conflict and suffering. The concern is broader than the first because we assume that acceptable problem solving excludes instance in which problems are "solved" at the expense of others, even where this is done "competently."

(5) *We suspect that any failure to be instructed is in itself instructive.* We ask, To what extent is the person unable to profit from experience? The answer to this question helps us to see a link between coping failures. Most persons occasionally fail, but learn from their mistakes rather than making comparable mistakes over and over. Where a person perseveres in demonstrating conduct that has untoward consequences, we define the person's maladaptation as patterned, even when his difficulties are at first glance disparate.

(6) *On the other hand, we feel that a person's capacity for change must be acknowledged.* We ask, Where, when and how does the person improve his pattern of behavior? Behavior patterns extend over time, but rarely over lifetimes. The point of tracking careers is to define behavior in terms of its onset and decay, as well as in terms of increases and decreases in its level and quality.

Where changes in behavior are noted, we can try to assign the inception of change to the person and/or the setting. One question is whether we are witnessing a fundamental reorientation or the results of an intensification or diminution of pressures or temptations. Changes also sometimes provide clues about why the person originally behaved as he did, why he behaves differently now, and what it would take to regenerate him further.

(7) *We regard settings as limiting behavior options, but not as constraining them.* We ask, to what extent is the person's behavior forced upon him by circumstance? Many persons engage in less-than-effective behavior but describe themselves as unable to act otherwise. To the point to which they are correct they have an alibi: their behavior, though imperfect, could not be deemed maladaptive. A person cannot be adjudged to be a poor problem solver because he fails to solve an insolvable problem, or because he fails to explore unavailable (or only remotely available) options. To assess adaptation we must consider the constraints within which the person operates and gauge the quality of his solutions in terms of the adequacy of resources that are available to him. By the same token, we must recognize that perceiving behavior as constrained (assuming that a person must persist or flee, for example) is self-exonerating. One corrective to buying into this premise where it is unjustified is to compare the person's behavior to that of

others faced with comparable circumstances who have achieved different outcomes. Another strategy is to review the chronology of events, which can show that a person has helped to create the situation to which he feels "constrained" to respond. Many offenders thus cite addiction as a cause of crime, ignoring antecedent behavior (drug taking) in which they exercised options.

(8) *We see setting attributes as variations on common themes.* We ask, To what extent does the person react to a setting as he would to other settings? Adaptation can be at times setting-specific, and adapting to one setting (such as country life) can spoil us for another setting (city life.) One way to deal with this problem is to refrain from generalizing. We view the displaced farmer in the city, and adjudge him to be a lamentable coper, admitting that he might be a better coper back home. This strategy is most appropriate when we are concerned with problems of adaptation to specific settings (in this case, the asphalt jungle) but teaches us less than we ought to know about the process of adaptation. A contrasting strategy is to center on people moving across as many settings as possible. Using this approach we may conclude that our farmer is resilient (effective in coping with changes of setting) though he remains a small-town person at heart.

There is much to be learned in tracking persons from one setting to another, but there are disadvantages as well. Adaptation is always *to* something, and to appreciate what coping with a setting means, we need to know detailed facts about the setting (whether the setting is a school, hospital, factory, foreign country or prison) because these facts define the tasks with which the setting's inhabitants must deal and the difficulties they must negotiate.

It is true, of course, that *any* setting—no matter how exotic it may be—has attributes in common with other settings, but *no* setting contains shared attributes without skewing them in some fashion. In other words, there is no such thing as a *typical* setting, nor one that is *unique*.

If we need detailed knowledge of environments in which coping occurs, tracking people across environments becomes a difficult feat. A compromise is to remain with one environment or type of environment, but to view it in the context of other environments, limiting inferences to the extent of the overlap we infer. This means that caution must be exercised in characterizing anyone's overall coping capacity based on his behavior in one environment, but that we can generalize about coping if we consider attributes of the setting and think in terms of settings with comparable attributes. If a prison inmate takes unkindly to guards we may thus expect that he will do equally badly in organizations in which he encounters guard equivalents (teachers or foremen) who evoke the same resentments that prison guards evoke. By the same token, prisons do not gauge the person's capacity to negotiate some challenges (such as how to deal with persons of the opposite sex) which are not among the attributes of the setting.

## Goals of Classification

Our taxonomy is not designed as a diagnostic system, but as an aid to thinking about maladaptive behavior in the prison and (to some extent) elsewhere. The purpose of the categories is not to fit people into types but to group behavior patterns to facilitate discussion of the dispositions and motives they reflect. The scheme, in other words, is a behavior-related shorthand system. In using the system we do not ask, Is the person a type 1 or type 2 person, but, Does it make most sense to think of the person as engaging in type 1 or type 2 behavior?

Our assumption is that the *process* of using the system matters as much as its substance. We see such usage ideally as a group process, and the concern with classification as a stimulus to group thinking and as a means of expediting discourse. Instead of "going back to scratch" in a group's efforts to understand an individual, the taxonomy can help by taking the group part of the way, providing conceptual options and headings which they can try on for size.

We do not regard the themes that we propose as mutually exclusive, but as segments along continua of behavior. In drawing lines between such segments we venture hypotheses about the dynamics of behavior and about the motives that behavior subserves. Alternate headings represent alternate (but often related) hypotheses, subject to documentation and verification. The point is to find the most plausible summary for a set of behavior incidents, and the plausibility of one summary or another can be a subject to spirited and sometimes enlightening debate.

## Outline of the Classification System

We grouped patterns under five headings to describe the dominant goals the behavior patterns appeared intended to subserve. The goals we listed are those of (1) gratifying impulses, (2) seeking refuge, (3) enhancing esteem, (4) pursuing autonomy and (5) maintaining sanity. These goals are not personal portraits but dispositions we assume are pre-potent *while* the person is engaging in maladaptation.

We shall describe and illustrate our categories in the chapters that follow. At this point we offer brief, preliminary characterizations of the five headings and definitions of the themes subsumed under each:

*(1) Gratifying Impulses:*

Under this heading we describe difficulties that derive from an emphasis on immediate and short-term gratification, with limited regard for longer-term consequences or interests of others. The categories we include under this heading are the following:

- *Unlicensed Conduct:* Defines a person who operates at the level of infancy, and who engages in repeated behavior designed to satisfy his needs in direct and primitive fashion. (This category represents the "purest" type under the heading.)
- *Predatory Aggression:* The person regards others as objects of need satisfaction and uses violence or threats of violence to intimidate, extort, and expropriate or strong-arm those susceptible to intimidation.
- *Frustration to Aggression:* When such a person is disappointed or obstructed in the pursuit of his goals, he becomes disgruntled and engages in explosive aggression, which mostly consists of expressions of blind anger and rage.
- *Stress to Aggression:* When situations close in on the person, he experiences panic and anxiety, and he tends to blow up under pressure with tantrums that express a sense of helplessness.
- *Russian Roulette:* The person takes unreasonable risks in pursuit of short-term goals and excitement, and seemingly does not care that he gets into trouble, or at least does not draw lessons from the fact.
- *Jailing:* In pursuit of his definition of the "good life"—which consists of accumulating illicit amenities—the person centers on sub rosa activities (which include hustling), and participates elsewhere as a sideline.
- *Games That Turn Sour:* The person engages in nonreflective, childlike, self-serving, short-sighted and irresponsible behavior which generates adverse repercussions. When this occurs, the person indulges in self-pity rather than self-reflection.

*(2) Enhancing Esteem*

Under this heading, we describe behavior designed to cement the person's sense of self-esteem, either by trying to build a reputation, or by defending against feelings of low self-esteem through compensatory behavior. Most of the patterns described under this heading feature displays of violence or aggression.

- *Advertising Toughness:* The person engages in demonstrations of toughness in an attempt to achieve a reputation as a person to be admired by his peers.
- *Conforming:* The person is a member of a violence-prone peer group who acts with and on behalf of his group and in defense of its values.
- *Gladiating:* The person regards violence as a skill and a routine way to resolve disputes, and he engages in combat readily and casually to resolve interpersonal problems.
- *Preempting Unpopularity:* The person expects to be rejected and reacts with provocation and hostility in anticipation of rejection, thus documenting his assumptions.
- *Countering Aspersions:* The person feels easily disparaged and affronted, and reacts violently when he feels offended or slighted.
- *Standing Fast:* The person feels unable to compromise or retreat from rigidly defined positions, and equates this stance with defending his sense of worth.

### (3) Pursuing Autonomy

Under this heading we describe behavior that is concerned with one's dependence upon or independence from parental figures, such as persons in authority. For men who engage in such behavior, the issue of dependence/autonomy is emotionally charged, because it relates to definitions of adulthood which include emancipation and loss of support.

- *Dependence:* The person expects and pursues "parental" intervention to arrange a congenial environment for himself.
- *Conditional Dependence:* The person alternates between dependent and rebellious behavior, depending upon whether he feels his needs are met or frustrated.
- *Defying Authority:* The person takes a systematically rebellious, defiant and challenging stance toward those in authority.
- *Rejecting Constraints:* The person feels that no one has a right to infringe his autonomy and to tell him what to do; he reacts angrily to infringements whose rationale he cannot accept. (Apprehension and punishment are irksome to such a person because punishment is reminiscent of childhood.)

### (4) Seeking Refuge

Under this heading we describe behavior in which the person retreats from a setting because he regards it as threatening. The issue for the person is safety, and his strategy is physical retreat. (This is different from psychological retreat or escape from reality, which we cover under our next heading.)

- *Sanctuary Search:* The person has victim attributes or self-assigned victim attributes which inspire retreat into protective settings, or the need to be placed in such settings.
- *Catch 22:* The person both seeks and rejects protective settings. He feels a need for sanctuary, but protective arrangements are uncongenial to him because they are circumscribing, or he regards protective settings as nonequivalent and feels that the choice matters.
- *Sheep's Clothing:* The person seeks sanctuary, but with safety achieved, he changes his role from victim to aggressor and becomes assertive, manipulative, pugnacious or predatory.
- *Bluff Called:* The person starts with a stance of defiance and toughness, but ends up declaring himself in need of protection.
- *Turned Tables:* Exploiting others backfires, and the victimizer becomes a victim who must retreat from perceived threats.
- *Earned Rejection:* Clumsy interpersonal manipulations boomerang, and ineffective behavior invites situations that require the person to seek sanctuary.
- *Stress Avoidance:* The person seeks refuge from stress posed by the presence of others, which he cannot tolerate; he may also suffer from considerable anxiety, short of a break with reality, which causes him to retreat. (This subheading is transitional to the next heading.)

## (5) Maintaining Sanity

Under this heading we describe behavior that is engaged in by disturbed persons as they try to negotiate their social environments while grappling with the feelings, urges, and assumptions that are products of their pathology. We speak of "maintaining sanity" because such persons struggle (mostly unsuccessfully) against loss of control and of contact with reality.

- *Escaping Reality:* The person withdraws from his surroundings, lives exclusively in a private world, and at extremes neglects his self-care and hygiene.
- *Flight-Fight:* The person for the most part withdraws but on occasion explodes, attacks other persons in his environment, or attempts self-destructive acts.
- *Paranoid Aggression:* The person feels persecuted, explodes at persons who he imagines wish him ill or want to harm him, and otherwise lives with suspicion and unease.
- *Tinged Rebelliousness:* The person on occasion attacks or resists per-

sons in authority, but his protest and rebelliousness go hand in hand with feelings that are products of his disorder, such as fear, confusion, and the inability to cope with complexity.
- *Cryptic Outbursts:* The person engages in seemingly unmotivated attacks on others and/or against himself; his motives for these outbursts are private, inaccessible, and related to his mental condition, including hallucinations, delusions, accumulating tension, anxiety, resentment and self-hate.
- *Oscillating:* The person oscillates between being emotionally disturbed and nondisturbed, sometimes depending on contextual conditions, in other instances reflecting seemingly spontaneous change. Viewed over time, such a person shows contrasts between behavior deemed normal and disturbed.

### Applying the Classification

The themes we have defined were devised as shorthand language for describing maladaptive behavior patterns in the prison, and our premise was that these themes are best used by groups (not excluding the subject of discussion) as a way of thinking about a person's behavior.

Given this view of the taxonomy and its use it would make no sense for one typologist (worse, the originator of the taxonomy) to classify the 239 case histories we compiled on the presumption that his is the final judgment. On the other hand, if we constituted a small group to discuss the cases, we would lose the opportunity to assess the reliability of the hypotheses advanced as independent assessments. We compromised by having the code developer (whom we shall call "Coder 1") independently arrive at preliminary assessments, then having a second coder (Coder 2) arrive at a final classification.

We began by having Coder 2 independently classify subsamples of ten to fifteen protocols. After each subsample was completed, Coder 2's ratings were compared with those of Coder 1 and discrepancies between ratings were resolved through conference discussion. These discussions provided training in the classification system for Coder 2, and incidentally led to clarification and modification of the classification categories.

This procedure was continued until Coder 2 felt he had reasonable understanding of the categories. The subsamples covered included 103 protocols, leaving 136 protocols which were classified by Coder 2 without consultation with the initial coder. We can look at reliability of classification of these 136 cases over the major categories, over subcategories within each of the major ones, and over the entire group of thirty-one subcategories.

For the 136 protocols, Coder 1 and Coder 2 agreed on classification in one of the five major categories in ninety-one cases, or 67 percent of the time (agreement expected by chance is 20 percent). There was variation in the ease with which categories could be clearly identified, ranging from 46 percent for Seeking Refuge to 88 percent for Maintaining Sanity. The figures are

Gratifying Impulses ................................................ 59%
Defending Esteem ................................................ 67%
Pursuing Autonomy............................................... 59%
Seeking Refuge................................................... 46%
Maintaining Sanity................................................ 88%

Agreement was also calculated on classification into subcategories for those protocols in which there was agreement on the coding of the major category (disagreement on the latter would preclude agreement on the subcategory classification). For the 91 protocols on which such agreement occurred, Coder 2 agreed with Coder 1 in forty-eight cases, or 53 percent of the time (agreement expected by chance ranges from 14 to 20 percent, depending on the number of subcategories involved.) Again, there were differences in the ease of classifying subcategories across the major categories. The proportions are

Gratifying Impulses ................................................ 62%
Defending Esteem ................................................ 79%
Pursuing Autonomy............................................... 62%
Seeking Refuge .................................................. 64%
Maintaining Sanity................................................ 32%

Finally, agreement was calculated across the entire range of thirty-one subcategories. For the 136 protocols, Coder 2 agreed with Coder 1 in forty-eight cases, or 35 percent of the time (agreement expected by chance is 3 percent).

We can conclude that the classification system has sufficient reliability for its use in analysis, though it would invite further development as a typology. The classifications used in this report are somewhat more reliable than the percentages given above portray in that the conference agreement, identifying the *primary* theme in the protocol, was used to replace Coder 1 classification when there was a discrepancy between the two coders.

There is evidence that additional training of Coder 2 would have improved agreement. An analysis of the results of conference codings show that these were resolved in favor of Coder 1 in 71 percent of the cases and in favor of Coder 2 in 22 percent of the cases.[1] In the remaining cases, (7 percent) the coders agreed to use a new category.

The most exciting result of the consensus codings was the development arising from the discussion of disagreements in classification. By having each coder create a rationale for the (disagreed) code given by the other, each coder expanded his understanding of the pattern revealed in the protocol. It became clear that we were approaching consensus by integrating one another's perceptions into our own sets and biases. The result of these shared approximations was a fuller understanding of what was being suggested by the individual inmate's protocol, and this in turn enriched our understanding of the kinds of behaviors used—simultaneously or sequentially—by the inmate.

In what follows we give examples of these shared perspectives. In each case there were differences in the classification of the protocol. The indented material is taken from the protocol and is intended to support either one or the other of the classifications. The commentary summarizes the understanding that came out of the discussion of the disagreement.

*Gratifying Impulses: Russian Roulette versus Defending Esteem: Advertising Toughness*

The "Russian roulette" element has to do with going out of one's way to take chances:

> "the defendant was raised in a decent religiously oriented environment but rejected this as being 'too boring.' " This suggests that the man seeks excitement by skirting danger or at least by taking risks at every turn. He admits that he finds it exciting to drive stolen cars. He accumulates stolen razor blades in his locker and carries marijuana cigarettes through detection equipment. He displays loaded guns and throws bars of soap at officers. He finds such games exciting.

But the man also engages in demonstrations of toughness in an attempt to achieve a reputation as a person to be admired by his peers:

> he signs himself into protection after receiving threats. When he leaves protection he attacks another inmate, hitting him in the back with a broom. An officer who investigates this incident concludes, "I believe the inmate used this incident to avoid a reputation as a 'snitch.' "

It is easy to see a synthesis in which Russian roulette behavior is the dynamic used to advertise toughness in order to enhance esteem—not only in the eyes of the inmate's peers, but to handle the man's own anxieties concerning his self-image.

Toughness can projected by other than Russian roulette behavior, and Russian roulette behavior can in turn be used to handle impulse control anxieties without the need to impress peers.

There is justification in the protocol for each coder's perception of the inmate's pattern of behavior. Each coder can be considered to have some approximation to "the truth" about the inmate. Sharing of these approximations led to a new synthesis, an enhanced understanding in which the whole became more than the sum of the perceptions of the individual coders.

*Pursuing Autonomy: Rejecting Constraints versus Defending Esteem: Advertising Toughness*

Consider the following two excerpts:

> "you were given an order to move down a table and fill the last seat at supper meal in the mess hall and you refused to obey this order. At this time more inmates came to the table and they refused to move down. You then said to the other inmates 'you guys don't have to move down just because the officer says so.' The officer asked you if you were the spokesman for the group, and you replied 'yes, they are my home boys.' "

> The man is a professional alcoholic and vagrant. However, both in prison and outside the prison he is a bum with pride, and some of his conflicts with officers reflect efforts to preserve his self esteem and reputation.

This could well be an (in prison and outside prison) alcoholic who pursues autonomy through alcoholism and rejects constraints because he feels (and needs to feel with alcohol's help) that no one has a right to tell him what to do. Hence he reacts angrily to infringements on his autonomy, whose rationale he cannot understand and/or accept.

Such a pattern is at least compounded by the "bum with pride" component. Rejecting constraints becomes, for the man, a means to advertise his toughness and to achieve a reputation as a person to be admired by his peers.

Incidentally, this pattern synthesis is relevant to the finding that the pattern of defying authority—in which the offender takes a systematically rebellious, defiant and challenging stance toward any person in a position of authority—is rare and seldom simple. The stereotype of an "authority problem" as the outstanding dynamic of chronic offenders does not hold up. All authority problems are not alike, and complicated patterns underlie the stereotype.

*Seeking Refuge: Bluff Called versus Defending Esteem: Preempting Unpopularity*

One integration of patterns is sequential. In the following case, initial aggressiveness brings about bluff-calling and fearful requests for protection.

The man is transferred out of his first prison after several fights and an attempt at suicide. He complains that "the rejection of people on the outside and the many frustrations he is facing, have led to this 'blow up.' " The second prison describes the man as "definitely not an asset." His first major incident at this prison begins after he concludes that he had been insulted by a fellow inmate and enters his enemy's housing unit armed with a shovel intent on "self defense." It requires four officers to subdue the inmate, who complains that "other inmates threatened his life." After he is released from segregation the man asks for protection claiming that "he has many troubles with his peers," though a counselor suspects that he is attempting to control his outbursts by segregating himself so as to avoid rejection by the parole board.

The next incident shows that the man's losses of temper in the prison are not confined to inmates. The charge reads: "on the above date and time the officer reports that you had extra rations of sausage on your tray and that he ordered you several times to put them back but you refused . . . the officer reports that you assaulted him by hitting him in the face with a tray full of food and again assaulted him by hitting him in the face with your fist. (He) reports that you caused a disturbance in the mess hall by your actions of not following direct orders and by assaulting him while you were in line for breakfast." The inmate is not only punished for this incident but is transferred to administrative segregation (involuntary protection) "until such time as you are either released or transferred from this facility." This move is prompted by the fact that the inmate has succeeded in making a number of enemies who have taken to assaulting him whenever the opportunity arises.

The inmate is rescued from permanent segregation status through transfer to a maximum security prison which has an older population and a notoriously strict regime. In this institution the inmate spends the remainder of his time without a single disciplinary incident.

This man's difficulties are twofold. First, he has a hair trigger temper and explodes at the slightest provocation, thereby generating conflicts, punishments, and unequivocal unpopularity. Second, the man's peers regard him as a threat which must be neutralized. As a result the man becomes afraid and must be protected, which to him is a fate indistinguishable from punishment. The irony is that the man reacts the way he does because he is easily hurt and arranges for himself to be more substantially hurt.

Again, each perceived pattern catches a significant component of what the inmate is doing, but integrating the perceptions of the two coders produces a more complete understanding of the inmate's behavior.

*Seeking Refuge: Turned Tables versus Gratifying Impulses: Jailing*

Another example of enrichment through shared perceptions is the somewhat sequential merging of a pattern of exploiting others which backfires (Gratifying Impulses) and a pattern in which the victimizer becomes a victim, whose fear inspires retreat (Seeking Refuge). The shared perception begins with the inmate's pursuit of his definition of the "good life," which consists of accumulating illicit amenities through subrosa activities (including hustling), while his participation in more approved activities is only a sideline (Gratifying Impulses: Jailing).

The latter pattern misses the intrigue dynamic of the refuge seeking described below, but the refuge-seeking pattern leaves out, or at least belittles, the man's sophisticated engagement in and manipulation of correctional institution dynamics:

> The inmate is, however, not an unfortunate victim of his sexual preference, forced to spend years vegetating in the sterile backwaters of the prisons to which he is assigned. His pattern rather resembles that of a scorpion who darts out from under rocks, stings passing animals and then darts back again. He belongs to a subgroup of inmates who exploit each other for material gains and exploit others weaker than themselves, and who experience strongly felt rivalries which lead to no-hold-barred competition. This subgroup has members in every prison and outside the prison, so that their vendettas can be extended and can be carried over from one setting to another. The vendettas lead to aggressive acts which include physical altercations, threats, manipulation of others in rival cliques and the manipulation of prison staff to serve the interests of one clique at the disservice of another. In this connection a favored strategy involves informing on any illegal activities of opponents, and manufacturing details of illegal acts where necessary to supplement the facts.

> In this game prison staff are not in charge, but rather are pawns of inmate machinations, and are particularly susceptible to peremptory bids that capitalize on staff's responsibility to ensure that no inmates are harmed, to react to violation of rules and to observe inmates' civil rights. This man presses all three of these buttons with recurrent claims that he is about to be knifed or burned alive, with submissions in which he identifies inmates engage in illegal acts, and with grievances and law suits. In this case staff know what the inmate is about but are still obliged to move the inmate and/or his enemies around the chess board of the prison system until they literally run out of squares. In the meantime, the man's list of enemies cumulates, and the proportion of time he spends locked away in protection becomes increasingly substantial.

*Pursuing Autonomy: Rejecting Constraints versus Defending Esteem:*
*Countering Aspersion*

Another integration comes from the interaction of countering aspersion efforts with behavior that rejects constraints:

The man's unpredictability results from the fact that one does not know when he feels mortally affronted because one no more understands him than he understands those around him. The central issue often appears to be that the man feels himself treated like a child, and that his version of machismo holds that no man must be ordered about by another man and that it is demeaning and insulting to be told to do things, particularly when you explained why you do not wish to do them, or would have explained it if you could have.

The issue of uniforms does not enter the equation because the man sees encounters between himself and officers as personal, and perceives custodial instructions as originating in whims and expressions of disdain or disrespect. When the man feels disdained or disrespected in this way he reacts at the first available opportunity, which may not coincide with the move that sparks the offense to which he reacts.

In the first incident, for example, the officer does not know that the inmate is puzzled and enraged when the officer takes the plastic spoon the inmate thinks he will need for his meal. The officer also does not heed the inmate's expression of resentment, which consists of spitting on the floor, and the attack follows when the officer lectures the inmate about prison sanitation rules, which the inmate (who does not understand most of this lecture) perceives as adding insult to injury. In the second incident the officer is similarly oblivious to the fact that the inmate is enraged because he has ordered one brand of cigarettes and has been mistakenly given another, an act the inmate regards as deliberate and contemptuous.

When the inmate must rely on officers to obtain what he needs (or thinks he needs) such as cigarettes, a sergeant or a psychiatrist, or permission to wash his clothes, he feels that this dependency in itself is demeaning. Thus, when his requests are not immediately responded to, the humiliation becomes more serious because not only has he had to ask for something, but those who have compromised his manliness by making him a mendicant now deny his requests to show him who is boss. He also sees himself receiving arbitrary and demeaning messages when officers present him with forced choice situations (such as "submit to the frisk or return to your cell") which do not include the option (go to the yard for exercise) the inmate elects to exercise. Since the officers want what they want and the inmate wants what he wants, there is nothing further to be said as he sees it, and a fight ensues, and his subjection by (occasionally overwhelming) force reinforces his perspective. The fact that he keeps losing these fights because he is badly outnumbered has no bearing on the principle involved, which is that a man must fight when he must fight, and that it is better to fight and lose than to permit oneself to be belittled and emasculated by being ordered about like a child, having legitimate requests denied, or having somebody else's will prevail in a contest of will, which denotes childish subservience.

To be wrestled to the ground by vastly superior forces is not unmanly and is not a cause for shame, particularly if one can indicate, by spitting at one's retreating enemy or by otherwise declaring oneself inviolate ("you can't hurt me. Me tough") that suppression is not tantamount to surrender.

It can be argued that pursuing autonomy (rejecting constraints) is the means whereby the man attempts to enhance his self-esteem (countering aspersions). He feels easily disparaged and affronted, and reacts violently when he regards himself as offended or slighted, which occurs when there is infringement on his autonomy.

These of course are only illustrative examples. The point we are making is that shared perceptions, using the patterns as a relevant frame of reference, can enrich individual perception. The empirically grounded framework of incident pattern analysis can facilitate both self- and self-other understanding.

## Conclusions

There is sufficient independent coding agreement to warrant further development of the pattern analytic scheme and use of the existing scheme for heuristic purposes.

The process of sharing perceptions of patterning over incident reports is a promising procedure for building interest and competence in studying and understanding patterns. A pattern analyser projects his own biases and understandings into his perception of incidents. This can create concentration and motivation for understanding, particularly if it is your own incidents you are observing. Sharing pattern perceptions further enriches and enhances the integrity of the approximations to "pattern truth."

The objective of pattern analysis we shall outline in our last chapter is to develop an understanding of the chronic offender's repetitious behavior which will make sense to him and for which he can construct a self-management strategy. We assume that the understanding must have enough group consensus for the group to be able to provide insights and support for the offender, and to help him make sense of his behavior.

Pattern analysis requires intense study, and a group sharing of pattern analysis provides a concentrated introduction to participation in group problem solving addressed to the understanding of behavior.

## Note

1. There is reason to believe that something other than the persuasion of seniority determined the conference resolutions. Coder 1 and Coder 2 have worked together in developing classification systems over a series of correctional studies. They are very comfortable in disagreeing with one another, and in turn respect the other's opinions in resolving disagreements.

# 6

# Gratifying Impulses

The maladaptive behavior patterns which unquestionably get the worst press are those in which adults govern their encounters in childlike ways, reacting to temptations and pressures as do infants by easily yielding to short-term opportunities and exploding under stress. Though such patterns of behavior, on the face of it, reflect developmental problems, they tend mostly to be characterized by emphasizing the extent to which they reliably depart from adult (read, "civilized") standards of conduct.

This observation need not surprise us because the behavior at issue is invariably destructive, is often illegal and is persistent over time. Delinquents who manifest developmental problems are thus considered better-than-average bets for careers that begin early and end (if ever) late. These delinquents have been dubbed *unsocialized aggressive* by some observers because the key impulse that they express is aggression. Wattenberg has described the manifestation of this disposition as follows:

> Lacking any security and confronting aggression, these children carry so heavy a load of hate that they cannot master it or their other impulses except for temporary delinquent purposes. In school, they are readily recognized even in primary grades. They cannot settle down to work; they are enraged by minor setbacks; they see the world as united against them; they are cruel to other children; they are foolhardy little daredevils bereft of a sense of consequences.

> Unless something is done, these violent and aggressive boys will develop into equally dangerous men. Throughout their lives they will menace other people and themselves.[1]

The term *unsocialized* is apt because the primitive stance to life situations taken by such persons suggests failure of the process (socialization) whereby families and schools try to promote self-controlling behavior. Concepts such as "impulsivity" and its variants are useful in that they describe results of socialization failure which have to do with defects in the mechanisms which mediate between impulses and the expression of impulses, and which modulate or suppress inappropriate urges. This problem is one which most mental health professionals do not feel they can remedy.[2] Mental health workers who come into contact with impulsive clients are apt to emphasize the need for ''structure,'' which implies that the person's problems can be most appropriately addressed behind walls, with punitive, disciplinary and other behavior management options.[3] These options are routinely deployed with persons who manifest maladaptive impulse-related behavior patterns, and they can be defended as serving social control functions for the environment and having deterrent value for the person. We shall see that unfortunately the second of these goals is rarely achieved, which makes it unlikely the first goal—which derives from the second—can be served.

Gratifying one's impulses is by definition a destructive enterprise, since it takes place at the expense of other persons, who become objects of need satisfaction. Less obviously, impulse gratification can be self-destructive, not only because it places a person at loggerheads with his environments, but because the reactions he thus invites compound his problems, and can escalate into ugly, no win confrontations. Successful and remunerative careers of unlicensed conduct are rare (at least, in prisons), compared to patterns in which unhappy consequences are more salient than the behavior that produced them. Moreover, in most patterns of impulsivity, failures to profit from experience become an increasingly obvious liability. A brief example which may illustrate this observation is that of a man who arrives in prison having just turned seventeen. He has participated in four robberies committed in close succession, and some of these are perpetrated after he is placed on probation for the others. The man's prison career spans four years, during which he commits every possible prison violation, ranging from littering to assault.

The presentence report records that this man is unusually candid about his offenses. In one case, for example:

> He frankly admitted his guilt and accepted full responsibility for the offense, stating that he was the individual who pushed the complainant to the ground and snatched the envelope from his hand. He stated that his juvenile accomplice, while present, did not actively participate in the offense. He stated that he committed the offense because he wanted some money and the complainant looked like an easy mark.

With respect to another robbery he explains that ''he and some friends were coming from a party when they saw the complainant. He seemed like 'an easy mark' and they decided to rob him.'' A probation officer classifies the man as ''a violent antisocial individual who presently shows no signs of modifying his behavior,'' and concludes that ''he requires a structured setting for the protection of society and himself.''

The man is sent to a youth prison, where he does well in a vocational program but within months ''has received . . . 49 days cell confinement, mostly for being abusive, harassment, refusing direct orders, fighting and creating a disturbance.'' Later the inmate receives another thirty-day segregation sentence and is transferred to a regular prison where his deportment is excellent, which earns him a transfer to a lower security prison where his behavior almost immediately degenerates. Here he has a large number of fights and is written up for stealing, buying commissary goods ''with insufficient funds,'' disobeying orders, swearing at guards, and ''an assortment of other misbehavior.''

At the request of the parole board the man is referred to mental health staff ''for possible behavior modification therapy.'' At first, staff report that ''his attitude toward counseling has been very good.'' Months later, however, the inmate is again described as earning misbehavior reports for ''persistently defying authority and disregarding rules.'' He is caught smoking marijuana, assigned ninety days of segregation, and transferred to a regular prison where he is stabbed by a fellow inmate after serving as a ''lookout'' in another stabbing incident involving one of his friends. After this experience the inmate is involuntarily segregated and transferred to a different prison, where he is again placed in protection until he is paroled. His parole, however, is short lived in that he is caught driving a stolen car (an incident in which he also resists arrest), cashing a forged check and carrying a loaded revolver.

We observe that this man is incredibly recidivistic, both in the community and in the institution. In both settings he is a minor underworld figure who commits visible offenses which carry high risk of apprehension and sanctions. His involvement shows him closely linked to similarly inclined companions, though he also experiences difficulties because he ignores or rejects various dictates of authority. Oddly enough, the man appears more likely to take a recalcitrant and rebellious stance in a low-pressure setting than he does in a more serious prison. The contrast, in fact, is noteworthy in that the first time he is placed in a high-security setting, the man remains a model inmate for five months and on a second occasion, he records only two violations in nine months. In other words, he takes advantage of any relaxed atmosphere by testing its limits but shows evidence of being deterred by a no-nonsense custodial regime. The deterrence effect, however, does not generalize, and it does not transfer to a lower pressure regime nor to the community. One reason for this fact is that the man cannot resist temptation, which in his case consists of ''easy marks'' (that is, vulnerable victims), of congenial peers who are about to embark in mischief or conflict, and of authority figures whose injunctions and unwelcome intrusions can be defied through displays of manliness and recalcitrant autonomy. The latter behavior carries adverse consequences, of course, but the man appears insufficiently impressed by these (especially in less punitive settings), and his memory is conveniently short.

### Predatory Aggression

It is easy to overlook the self-destructiveness of a behavior pattern to whose consequences the person himself is oblivious. It is even easier to ignore consequences for the person where these seem deserved, as they are among predatory aggressors, whose unlicensed conduct includes using violence or threats of violence to intimidate or strongarm weak or susceptible victims. An example of such a pattern is that of a young man who has been convicted of a mugging. He serves a short sentence but a very variegated one in that he breaks virtually every rule in the inmate rule book.

As soon as the inmate enters the system he alerts staff to the fact that he expects a hostile reception from other inmates because he has "hurt a lot of dudes out there" who might "take revenge." He does become involved in fights but also encounters problems for writing on walls, creating disturbances, violating the dress code, being out of place, using abusive language, passing contraband, destroying property, talking, playing his music loudly, delaying counts, harassing officers, carrying weapons and other offenses. Really serious involvements have to do with a propensity the man develops to make advances to female staff members. In one institution a nurse complains that he keeps appearing requesting that his genitalia be examined because he suffers "from too much masturbating." The nurse eventually reports:

> I had informed the doctor of the problem with the inmate the previous day, and he agreed to see him and treat the problem. The inmate refused to let the doctor touch him and requested that I hold him again. The doctor asked the inmate to immediately remove himself and noted the incident on the inmate chart. Again (during the next two days) the inmate reported to the medical building and I refused to even talk with him and he was instructed by the other nurse to leave. In the interest of my safety and due to total humiliation I'm requesting that this inmate be so assigned that he will not have to associate with me.

In the next prison to which the inmate is sent a female officer reports:

> He has been harassing me for a while now. I verbally warned him about touching me. One morning during the week (I don't remember the date) he passed by me

a number of times and each time he touched me. He would either hit my arm with his arm, swing his hands back and forth, and hit my leg with his hand. When I told him about it he claimed he didn't know he was touching me. I told him from now on to walk around the table away from me but on (date) he started touching me again. He would sit at a table close by me and ask me personal questions, where I lived because he wants to see me when he gets out, what kind of car I drove, was I married, do I have any kids, did I ever go to bed with a black man, if I ever kissed a black man. I never answered any of his questions except to tell him to stop asking me about my personal life because it was none of his business. He said I was beautiful and he was in love with me.

One month after the inmate is paroled he becomes involved in a series of holdups of patrons of restaurants. As soon as the inmate is incarcerated he becomes enmeshed in a new series of transgressions. Staff whimsically observe that he "knows better, as he has served time before. Obviously, he doesn't care." During rare intermissions from segregation the inmate is assigned as a porter, and he is caught stealing from fellow inmates who are determined to exact retribution. He is locked in protective segregation, but an enemy reaches him there and throws "a mixture of hot water and hot baby oil" onto his chest, inflicting burns. The inmate promptly reveals the identity of his enemy and informs on many other inmates, who happen to be members of his gang. As a result the inmate now becomes a favored target of retribution from erstwhile companions.

In relation to his transgressions the inmate lies to staff and continues to be insubordinate. In one incident he agitates other inmates waiting for home telephone calls, informing them that "these fucking C.O.s are always fucking everybody out of everything." He also keeps flagrantly stealing, and on one occasion is apprehended wearing eyeglasses he has appropriated from another inmate.

In mid-sentence the man is not only protectively segregated but the prison system is close to running out of institutions to which he can be safely transferred, given the ill will he has by now generated.

We note that this man's code of conduct is clearly devoid of ethical norms. He is bent on illustrating the proposition that there is "no honor among thieves," and he lies and steals in the prison and out of the prison. In fact, he steals from companions and betrays them whenever it suits his short-term ends. The fact that he informs on others, however, does not make him an asset for staff because he is prone to lie and dissemble when lying and dissembling are advantageous to him. All people are objects to this man and all persons are targetted for exploitation and expropriation. Targets, of course, very much include women, and the fact that a woman may be a staff member or wearing a uniform is inconsequential as far as this predator is concerned.

It is obvious that this man plays his games casually as the mood or impulse strikes him. He is not following a serious strategy in that he is seemingly unconcerned (to the point of obliviousness) about consequences at the time that he acts. This unconcern gives his behavior the appearance of self-destructiveness in that he continues to behave as he does even when adverse consequences are certain, as they are when he visits the infirmary for the seventh time demanding sexual contact with a nurse, publicly wears eyeglasses he has stolen from a fellow inmate, or continues stealing in situations where he is the only plausible suspect. Understandably, as time goes on, the consequences of such behavior cumulate, and the man's career takes a turn for the worse. The man must now seek refuge to gain physical safety, but even this does not bring him face to face with realities he steadfastly continues to ignore. To the end he antagonizes staff on whom he depends for survival and stirs up trouble among peers, adding to his roster of enemies. The prison's assigned role is to protect this man from himself, a goal with which he steadfastly fails to cooperate.

Such are the grounds for classing the man's behavior as maladaptive, granting that he is not a candidate for compassion, nor inspires regenerative assistance. The point that is crucial is that when this man acts in what he regards as his interest (which is most of the time) he reliably defeats his ends, and he is so constituted that he is unable to profit from the experience.

### Frustration to Aggression

Not all impulsives, to be sure, blithely go through life disregarding self-generated adversities, unfazed by the obstructions and untoward circumstances they encounter. A key attribute of core impulsivity (denoted by the concept "low frustration tolerance") leads us to expect that impulsives will not only act blindly to satisfy their needs, but will react equally blindly when they do not achieve the satisfaction to which they feel entitled. Many such persons will feel affronted and outraged when they are stymied, and will express their sense of outrage through acts of physical aggression. These frustration-aggression reactions are obviously harmful to the impulsive person's environment, but are also maladaptive because they reflect a real loss of control and tend to exacerbate the adversities which prompt them.

An illustration of this pattern is furnished by a young inmate convicted of a burglary and an attempted robbery. In prison this man becomes involved in fights and horseplay and a number of incidents of fire setting. He is also repeatedly charged with lying and stealing.

It is recorded that the man has been mostly institutionalized since the age of eleven, at which time he "was diagnosed as hyperactive and sent to children's village for approximately two years." In another institution where the inmate is detained an entry notes that he "assaulted a counselor with an iron bar causing injury to his elbow. He is also accused of smashing six doors and causing damage in excess of $250." He is transferred to yet another youth institution from which he escapes one week before he becomes involved in the offenses for which he is convicted.

The inmate makes a suicide attempt in jail, but in the reception center mental health staff clear him for membership in the general population. He is sent to a youth prison where he receives high ratings as a kitchen worker, but has difficulties accomodating to the custodial regime. This combination—the fact that the inmate takes his work seriously but has trouble adjusting to supervision—produces a serious incident which earns the inmate three months of segregation, some loss of good time credit and a psychological referral. An officer involved in this incident reports:

> I went to the back sink to pick up a spatula that was needed on the serving line. As I started to walk away with the spatula, the inmate came up to me and said, "I need the spatula at the back sink to scrape the pans with." I then informed the inmate that we have a regular pan scraper for that job and that I would get it for him in about five minutes when I had someone to cover me on the line. I then walked to the serving line, set the spatula down, and turned around to walk back to my station on the line, and collided with the inmate who was directly behind me. He attempted to pick up the spatula when I again said, "no." I blocked his path of retrieval and ordered him out of the serving area. The inmate then walked out but turned and said, "don't push me no more, don't put your hands on me because I won't be fronting." The inmate was raising his hands in a menacing way the entire time that he said this. I then ordered the inmate to return to the back sink area. I again told the inmate that I would get him a pan scraper as soon as possible and ordered him to return to the area. The inmate then stated that if I came any closer that he would hurt me. I again ordered him to return to his area. In order to avoid a situation where someone could get injured I left the confrontation and returned to the serving line.

The officer reports the incident to a sergeant, who attempts to lock the inmate in his cell. The sergeant reports:

> I approached the inmate and told him that he had been keeplocked and I wanted him to come to reception with the officer and myself. The inmate refused to leave the kitchen and said, "fuck that. I'm not leaving and nobody better put their mother-fucking hands on me." He was very anxious and nervous, in a fighting position and constantly moving around. The inmate picked up a can opener (approximately 24 inches long) and stated, "don't nobody come near me. I will hit you." He continued moving and again stated, "The state considers this a deadly weapon and I am going to use it as a deadly weapon. If any of you try to take me out of here, I'm going to use this weapon on you, you, and you."

Other inmates and myself tried to talk him into putting the weapon down and coming with the officer and myself. Finally he gave the weapon to the inmate and I escorted him to reception without further incident.

The disciplinary board explains its penalty by reminding the inmate that "in your last twenty-two appearances . . . you have been extensively counseled regarding your unsatisfactory behavior." The board recalls that on occasions it has suspended the inmate's sentence to test his capacity to exert self-control. The board discusses the inmate's failure to respond to this treatment, and they add that:

hopefully he will understand that it is necessary to control his temper and not to resort to violence when frustrated by situations. The inmate is to be referred for psychological evaluation because of his fluctuation in admitting and then denying statements and charges.

When the inmate is served with the formal charges resulting from the mess hall incident he explodes, and when he is served with charges resulting from his explosion he explodes again, sets a fire and refuses to permit himself to be transferred to an observation cell. A narrative history of the entire sequence reads as follows:

At approximately 4:57 p.m. you intentionally broke your lightbulb . . . Approximately five minutes later you destroyed your cell bench and table by throwing said items around your cell and ramming your bed against your cell wall. At approximately 6:20 p.m., same date, it was discovered that you had caused your toilet bowl to separate from the wall, breaking the wall mounting section of same, and that you had dismantled your metal bed frame. At approximately 6:40 p.m. you refused to comply with orders given to you to effect your movement to an observation cell . . . You instead threatened the sergeant stating, "if you come in after me I'm going to fuck one of you up." You then positioned yourself in the left rear corner of your cell wearing a pair of cloth workgloves . . . you raised both of your hands (gloved) and started swinging them about when the officers approached you. You continued to resist by swinging your hands and kicking your feet about wildly when (the officers were) removing you from your cell to effect the cell transfer. During said movement it was discovered that you had set fire to your mattress causing a section of the mattress cover approximately eight inches in diameter to burn before being extinguished.

The inmate attributes his actions to feelings of "hostility" and explains that "he refused to come out of his cell because he was upset about being charged with another incident and receiving a superintendent proceeding." The inmate also explains that "when the officers came and grabbed me I struggled to get their arms off me. I had no intention of striking anyone." He later writes:

I realize what I did was wrong but I meant no harm. I was just frustrated because I felt I was in the right and that no one would take time out to really investigate what really happened . . . I do not normally act this way. I was also frustrated because of family and girl problems and also because I have another year to serve after this sentence and I see my second (parole) board (in a few days) and I didn't want to go being in the box . . . I promise that my behavior will improve.

Three weeks later the inmate sets fire to a large pile of shredded paper on his cell floor and is referred for psychiatric observation. The fire is described as an expression of the inmate's continued feeling of "frustration," and staff conclude that he "goes through periods of not caring what happens to him." The parole board refuse to parole the inmate, concluding that he "should continue psychotherapy . . . and utilize psychiatric services," but after six months they release the inmate with the provision that he be referred for mental health assistance.

A few months after completing his parole the inmate breaks into a luxury apartment and is apprehended by two police officers, who arrest him. The officers report that when they "start to handcuff" the man he becomes acutely disturbed and pushes one officer into the path of an approaching car which runs over the officer's foot. The inmate then escapes and is chased by the other officer who apprehends him, after which the inmate is described as "resigned to his situation."

This man among other things explodes when he feels cornered. Situations in which the man has a right to feel cornered arise frequently as a result of his own actions, which he usually views as innocent or at least as insufficiently serious to produce the consequences that they produce. In retrospect the man invariably regrets his explosions but at the time he explodes the encompassing feeling he seems to experience is panic and a sense of hopelessness and a desire to reverse the inevitable fate that looms before him. It appears as if he symbolically wants to reverse the course of history, wipe the slate clean and destroy a game that he has obviously lost. He wants desperately to escape from the situation, but at some level he knows that he can't, which makes him helplessly angry.

The man is probably correct when he claims that he does not mean to attack guards and other authority figures but sees them as menacing and as placing him in imminent physical danger. He reacts to the officer in the kitchen, for example, as if the officer was intending to beat him, and he similarly appears afraid of officers who intend to escort him to an observation cell. In both instances the guards represent unwitting consequences of actions the inmate has reflexively and unthinkingly taken, such as reclaiming a spatula or expressing his frustrations by wrecking his cell.

Incidents represent chains of junctures in which impulsivity has invited retributive consequences which the man cannot accept or assimilate. When in an appeal he writes "I meant no harm" he probably accurately describes his motives, though the owners of apartments he burglarizes might quibble. The inmate is certainly far from engaging in a calculus that includes gains and risks, which means that what an outsider might define as just desserts to the inmate represents the manifestation of an arbitrary, inhospitable fate which he finds too painful to face.

## Stress to Aggression

The flavor of frustration-induced aggression is that it expresses blind— or at best, retaliatory—rage. Other explosions, however, have a different flavor that is more evocative of panic and of a sense of helplessness. The issue for the persons involved in such explosions is still frustration, but rather than feeling crossed or offended these persons feel impotent or defeated.[4] These persons do not see their environment as hostile, but rather as overwhelming. Sensing no recourse as events inexorably close in on them, they throw tantrums that symbolize despair.

Persons who explode in this way can be described as "stressed," in that the challenges they encounter exceed their self-defined capacity to cope.[5] The reason impulsivity is also at issue (despite evidence of anxiety) is because of the helpless, out-of-control, reactive nature of the responses that stress inspires.

A case which illustrates the process is that of an inmate serving a prison sentence for burglary, who becomes involved in a strange assortment of institutional rule violations in which the most frequent charge is "destruction of state property." There are also incidents involving arson, fighting, one assault on an officer and a suicide attempt in which it is charged, "you admitted that you had inflicted these cuts to gain attention but that you never had any intention of committing suicide." The inmate is also occasionally found out of place and is written up for refusing to work or for not reporting to assignments.

The man has a history of problems. At age seven it is recorded that he "is a very immature boy and very possibly brain damaged." Seven years later complaints are registered by the school system. Among other things the boy is charged with having destroyed the car of a teacher by setting it on fire in the school parking lot. All sorts of other incidents are cited. For example, the inmate is dropped from one school program because

> his (vocation) teacher reported that he became very easily frustrated and would lash out at the equipment in his service station attendant course. He knocked

over the tire changer and the bubble machine. The other boys were frightened and soon learned to avoid him.

The inmate becomes a problem for the community by setting expensive and life-threatening fires. He burns down one building, for instance, because "he was angry at (a resident) for failure to return a hammer and a screwdriver he had borrowed a number of months before." He narrowly misses burning down an office building owned by the telephone company, claiming "that he did it because men from the telephone company teased him."

The inmate is placed in a psychiatric facility from which he escapes to the Canadian border. The staff report that:

> He was not in need of psychiatric treatment but rather of a supervised closed environment in which the chance of further incendiary acts could be precluded. Cognitive functioning is simplistic and concrete, with no evidence of major psychiatric disorder. Although constantly seeking attention and acceptance from peers and staff, the level of such interpersonal skills resulted in rejection and nonacceptance by the peer group. . . . [The inmate] stated he would elope whenever given the opportunity. . . . It became necessary to transfer him to a secure locked ward to prevent further incidents which threatened injury to self or others [including the real danger of incendiarism]. . . . A transfer agent accompanied him to a developmental center for his admission, as ordered in a family court order.

The developmental facility complains that the inmate "has frequently threatened to use physical force to attain his end." They also complain that the inmate "cut through his window screen and left the grounds." In later reports the staff point out that the inmate

> shows no respect for the other boys' property and if someone has a toy he likes, he takes it without permission and does not return it when asked. Occasionally some clients have stood up to him, attacking him. These boys he now tends to leave alone. It is the defenseless ones that he bothers.

After the inmate is discharged, he runs away from a foster home, steals a car and sets it on fire and is rotated through several other programs. A hospital setting which discharges the inmate reports that "he had phoned the police department and told them that if he wasn't released he was going to hurt someone and that he was not receiving any treatment in the hospital and that it was not fair to keep him here." The man is returned to the developmental center. Here he breaks into the administration building and sets a fire in a trash can, and it is this offense for which he is sent to prison. In the presentence report the probation officer writes:

It is the recommendation of the county probation department that the defendant be sentenced to an indeterminate term at a New York State correctional facility. This recommendation is based on the rationale that the community needs to be protected from the defendant's inappropriate behavior *and because there is no viable alternative available* [Emphasis added].

When the man enters the prison, the intake analysts note that he "makes a favorable impression, and did not appear to be a particularly resistive or hostile sort, but may be given to using rather poor judgment." The inmate almost immediately embarks on a long string of incidents which changes the "favorable impression" he has made. He does not like being locked up and makes a set of ropes out of bedsheets and when these are confiscated he cuts his arms with a piece of glass. He also "burned his blankets, sheets, and pillowcases because he wanted out of his cell" and "threw bedding out of his window." Two weeks later the inmate sets fire to his mattress, explaining that "the reason he set the fire was to kill himself" because "he had just realized how much time he had to do, and that he did not have any visits." The man also incurs other prison violations, including for refusing to come out of his cell and participate in programs. Staff explain that "this is a very disturbed resident as far as this facility is concerned, (who) is scared to death of the more mature population" and should "be transferred to a facility for younger men."

The inmate is, in fact, transferred to a youth prison, where he continues to experience difficulties. In one incident, for instance, an officer reports:

The inmate never came out of his cell when the bells rang. When I went down to see what was the matter the inmate was laying on the bed. I asked him if he was going to program. He stated, "No, I'm not going to fucking program. I'm fucking sick." The inmate was given a Notice of Report.

The inmate explains that his medicine "does not help him" and that "he refused to come out of his cell because he fears other inmates and he won't ask for help because he fears retaliation." A psychiatrist writes:

Apparently this inmate has been experiencing behavioral difficulties leading to numerous disciplinary proceedings. The inmate is on mental status observation in reception at present time because of an apparent outburst of uncontrollable aggressive behavior. He acknowledged with regret and spontaneously being in "deep trouble" and appears very distressed over his losing control of himself. However, he indicated "it wouldn't have happened if he was not provoked." He feels strongly that he will not be able to control himself and fears that he might do something "more serious" stating he will continue to fight if provoked "until I did."

By this time the inmate has been written up for a variety of offenses including fights, attempts at self-mutilation and refusals to participate in programs, and he claims that inmates and officers "pick on him." There is validity to at least some of these complaints in that he has been removed from school "due to being picked on by other students." The inmate becomes increasingly disgruntled with his situation. Early one morning an officer reports that "the inmate crushed his eyeglasses by stepping on them, then handed them over to me and stated that he likes tickets." That same evening another officer reports:

> The inmate admitted that he did not have his keeplock tray to turn in because he had thrown it out the window. The inmate was questioned about his misbehavior. His retort was, "I'm not in jail anymore. I can do whatever I want to. The fact is I threw just about everything in my cell out the window." In checking the yard under his cell is was observed that several articles of clothing, bed linens, books, etc. were there. The inmate has been acting strangely of late. He appears to not care about anything.

A counselor interviews the inmate and reports:

> He admits destruction of state property (eyeglasses) by stepping on them. Claims he had too many problems, fight in the center yard, harassment from several inmates on the company. After breaking his glasses he admitted cutting his left forearm. Later that evening he admits he threw his clothes, his coat, his books, his hat, bed linens, I.D. card, program card, church card, medication card, keeplock tray out the window. He claims he did this because he hopes to be released on appeal. He also claims he cannot take the harassment by inmates and (an officer). He claims he has not listened to the adjustment committee because he cannot take the harassment any longer.

> The next night he banged on the wall and threw his bucket against the wall and started throwing things around in his cell. He presently claims that he has been "seeing images of his family." He also claims he has been hearing voices from his family to come home. He claims he then punched the radiator and yelled at the voices.

The inmate appears before the disciplinary board and remarks, "you tell your damn officers to leave me alone or next time someone is going to get hurt." He also explains that he "tries to be cool" but when he gets upset he "just goes off."

The inmate is briefly hospitalized for anxiety but otherwise continues to regularly appear before disciplinary panels for a variety of violations. He is finally transferred to a special protective unit, where he is accused of "self inflicted wounds in the cell block" which "caused the disruption in the smooth order of the facility." He explains that "he acted out because he had many problems on his mind," but the panel penalizes him "in an effort to assist the inmate in altering his inclination toward life threatening behavior and to impress on him that this type of behavior is inappropriate and will not be tolerated in this environment."

Program staff write that the inmate "is a generally cooperative person; however, he does act impulsively." They point out that despite several misbehavior reports the man's performance "is still a vast improvement over the behavior he exhibited at his two previous facilities" and "it would appear there is some slow positive program adjustment within the (unit)."

The inmate completes his sentence in the program, and is paroled with the provision that he be referred to a mental health setting, but soon returns to prison convicted of attempted arson in satisfaction of a charge of arson, burglary and attempted rape. According to the probation officer who prepares the pre-sentence report:

> He had been upset because his sister would not let him live at her residence any longer and for about four weeks he had been living "on the streets" sleeping anywhere he could find. This consisted mainly of cardboard boxes outdoors. He also was drinking heavily and smoking marijuana every day. He further states that at the time of the crimes he didn't care what he did or what happened to him because his "life has been hell." On the day of the incident he was drinking all day in various downtown bars  He felt depressed and angry at his sister for putting him out of her home. . . . He states that there was no reason for picking (a specific) residence to start a fire. He states that he picked it because when it came over him to start the fire "it was the closest one." . . . He set the fire in a store because he was upset because there was no money there for him. As he was leaving the store by way of the fire escape he noticed a young woman walking past. He states that he followed her hoping to have sexual relations with her. After following her for a while he ran up and grabbed her from behind. . . . He states that he didn't want to hurt the woman, just have sex with her. He states further that he "doesn't care anymore what happens to me." He feels that he would rather spend the maximum amount of time on his sentence and not get out on parole.

After the inmate returns to the prison, intake analysts write that

> he had been adjusting adequately at the reception center until just recently when he reacted to a situation by punching the wall and burning himself with a cigarette. He had previously expressed to the counselor that he was doing alright, but continually had feelings of anger and "felt like going off."

The inmate returns to the protective program and "attempted suicide by overdosing with dilantin, which necessitated his being transported to a hospital." Three months later he requests protective custody because (he indicates) another inmate had "stated he was going to stab him when he got the chance since he refuses (the other inmate's) sexual demands."

This man has been placed in a succession of settings with which he cannot cope and which cannot cope with him. When a setting overtaxes the man's capacity to adjust to it, his first reaction is to try to escape, and when escape is thwarted he sometimes explodes with frustration. Ironically the inmate often discovers that the setting in which he next finds himself is even more frustrating, and this makes him nostalgic for settings in which he has failed to cope at earlier junctures. It is in this spirit that the man demands return to a developmental program from which he has eloped and where he subsequently sets a fire when the pressure again mounts. It is also in this spirit that he talks longingly (or at least resignedly) of prison when he is rejected by relatives and is relegated to living in discarded cardboard containers.

At earlier junctures in the inmate's career some of his explosions have a vindictive, retaliatory flavor and they are directed at perceived sources of frustration. Subsequently his explosions become general expressions of frustration, and even become intrapunitive, and they are sometimes symbolic expressions of disgust and despair in which the man communicates that he is helplessly angry, though he paradoxically maintains "I don't give a damn anymore."

Some of the change in the man's outlook has to do with the fact that he increasingly feels that the cards (meaning life circumstances in general) are stacked against him, that no one likes him and that everyone wishes him harm. This makes the man feel very resourceless and tense and he senses the tension in himself. The man concludes that at some juncture he must "go off," a circumstance which he—somewhat reluctantly—regards as a given. In other words, he almost sees himself as a pawn of his own runaway feelings, which he in turn ascribes to the overwhelming array of hostile forces which impinge on him. This view in part derives from the fact that he holds a low opinion of himself and that he has given up even the slightest tinge of hope of negotiating the challenges of his environment.

### Russian Roulette

Not all impulsivity reflects awareness of the repercussions that impulsivity invites. Where awareness of consequences exists, a person may regret his actions, but he may see himself as powerless to affect them. In such instances the inability to profit from experience has to do with difficulties—or at least, perceived difficulties—in maintaining a resolve to reform, or in translating this resolve into action. In other cases, however, the person may not care about the propensity he has to arrange adverse repercussions through impulsive acts.

One variant is the converse of the protestant ethic, which prescribes that we defer short-term rewards to secure long-term benefits. Any impulsive person's sights are almost by definition set on the present, or at most on the short-term future, and a more extended perspective is unattractive to him. In some cases this stance is accentuated, however, in that the person seems to go out of his way to take risks to defy probabilities of consequences and to value the defiance. The gain is not only short-term reward, but the excitement of obtaining this reward under inhospitable circumstances, which makes the enterprise a test of resilience or a game.

A case in point is a man who has returned to prison following a conviction for fraudulently obtaining Social Security cards and cashing other people's unemployment checks. In prison the man's offenses include such charges as refusing orders, loitering, creating disturbances, fighting and lying.

This man's earliest conviction follows an armed robbery in which he approaches a pedestrian with the words "give me money or I'll kill you." After this offense he is interviewed in the jail by a probation officer who finds that he is "under the influence of foreign substances." In the interview, the man himself "describes his days as filled with either 'hanging out at home' or socializing with friends from the neighborhood." Four years later he has collected $30,000 in fraudulent government funds. At this time he tells a probation officer that he is "a real dope fiend" and "then stated that he 'doesn't give a fuck.' " In a later interview he again makes an unfavorable impression. The probation officer writes:

> He was obviously under the influence of drugs. He admits that he has been abusing heroin quite heavily for the past month, ever since he took his plea. . . . He claims that he has been maintaining his habit by "wheeling and dealing, scheming and borrowing." [He] admits that he had shot heroin several hours prior to his interview.

In prison this man is first assigned to a medium-security setting from which he is evicted after inciting other inmates to a miniriot in the mess hall. In this incident the inmate, who at the time is a member of the institution's liaison committee, produces a paper alleging that "we can get all the food we want. The superintendant said so." According to a correction officer,

> He stopped at the line and demanded more food. I says, "you have to wait till almost everybody is served. If there is any left over you could possibly get more food." He started yelling and screaming in the line, "if we don't get more food, how would the cooks and officers like to be taken hostage over more food?" At that time I ordered him to go to the table. He stayed right there and kept yelling and screaming at us, "how would the officers and cooks like to be held hostage?" . . . All the inmate liasion committee paper stated is that all inmates should receive the same amount of food from the first inmate to the last inmate.

According to the inmate himself it was not he, but the officer, who had lost his cool. The inmate testifies,

> He tell me I don't know what you're talking about. What are you, crazy? He's the one that came out the side of his neck. I saw him getting all upset. I just took my tray and sat down. That was it. . . . Nobody mouthed off at him. He's the one who started mouthing off. I just sat down. I saw the way he was getting.

The inmate is assigned to another prison which recommends him for medium-security placement, but the recipient institution turns him down based on his record as a ring leader of disturbances. The prison therefore has to keep the inmate, but defends its recommendation based on the contention that "the incident was not quite as serious as officials first thought." Prison staff discover, however, that the mess hall disturbance was not an isolated event. In an incident weeks later an officer reports:

> You were in the big yard and broke company formation and ran to the big yard gate, and you were yelling, "come on, let's get the fuck out of here." At this time other inmates left the company with you but when ordered to come back, they did. The officer states you continued to run and attempted to incite others to join you.

In another disturbance the inmate prolongs a telephone conversation after having been told that his time was up, and is then cut off. The inmate remonstrates with the officer in charge, who reports:

> At this time there were approximately 15 inmates in the area and five complained that they did not have enough time. You had also told the inmates "watch your time. He'll fuck you over."

The inmate receives a thirty-day penalty for this incident but his punishment is suspended and he is paroled. Three months later he returns, having been violated "for continuing to use drugs and failure to make office reports." He serves six months additional time and is released on the expiration date of his sentence. In two months, however, he is stopped by a police officer after he drives through a red light and cannot produce a license or registration. The police further report that "a gun, fully loaded, was discovered sticking out from under the driver's seat." The man thus returns to prison where he accumulates a string of violations, all of which involve possessing marijuana, with occasional excursions into owning ten-dollar bills or storing liquids with high alcohol content. At this time the man resides in an institution for younger offenders from which he requests transfer, arguing that "I'm over the age of 18 and not an adolescent to be treated as one, and will not tolerate any harassments by the officials of this facility which are constantly disrespecting the adolescents that are in this facility."

This man appears to enjoy taking risks, or at least disregarding odds. His pattern of behavior can be described as brazen. He boasts about being a dope fiend and takes few pains to hide incriminating evidence such as being intoxicated during interviews, and having marijuana cigarettes in his cell and having loaded guns while driving unregistered cars. His lying is transparent, and it seems more designed for show than for exoneration. The man appears to be full of joy of life as he defines it. His protests are exuberant and they suggest that he gets carried away whenever the opportunity arises to make a scene, particularly when he can get others to join in the excitement.

The inmate is probably right when he argues that it is officers who lose their cool and not he, because his dominant emotion is enthusiasm rather than anger. The man uses drugs to get excitement and commits crimes that are visible and involve sufficient risk to make them exciting. He continues sensation seeking in prison through participation in the prison underworld and through the games he plays with authority figures and the prison disciplinary machinery.

Deterrence is a concept that obviously does not apply to this man because the threat of punishment appears to be an incentive to him. Taking risks, as he sees it, may be the spice of life.

### Jailing

When a person with a short-term perspective finds himself temporarily in any environment, the here-and-now setting is the one that becomes the world of consequence to him and the arena in which he seeks his rewards. In the prison, this stance is called "jailing," a term which means "to cut yourself off from the outside world and to attempt to construct a life within the prison."[6] The impulse-dominated prisoner pursues impulse satisfactions by seeking the acquisition of prized illicit amenities. Life after prison has no meaning to the person because it lies in the irrelevantly remote future; the "official" prison is only of interest to him insofar as it provides increments in privilege, and his program participation is at best perfunctory. Impulsive patterns such as "hustling" are transplanted from the community to the prison, but many prisoners "jail" as a career, and such persons have often spent their lives in institutions. The perspective of an individual of this kind, according to John Irwin, can become specialized:

> The prison world is the only world with which he is familiar. He was raised in a world where "punks" and "queens" have replaced women, "bonaroos" are

the only fashionable clothing, and cigarettes are money. This is a world where disputes are settled with a pipe or a knife, and the individual must form tight cliques for protection. His senses are attuned to iron doors banging, locks turning, shakedowns, and long lines of blue-clad convicts. He knows how to survive, in fact prosper, in this world, how to get a cell change and a good work assignment, how to score for nutmeg, cough syrup, or other narcotics. More important, he knows hundreds of youths like himself who grew up in the youth prisons and are now in the adult prisons.[7]

One example of a "jailer" is a man who has burglarized a hotel room and tried to rape its occupant. In the prison he commits unimpressive violations resulting in charges such as "the inmate went to the movies when he was supposed to be on bed rest," "wrestling with another inmate," "refused to lock in and kept talking with his friends," "carrying on a conversation with two inmates after the quiet bell," "stayed at the end of the company when his cell was opened for the evening mess," "came to my desk and said he didn't want to do his assignment, went to the men's room and did not return promptly," "during his cell frisk, I found contraband items including a tape deck belonging to another inmate," "during a frisk, I found a burnt soda can with a shoestring handle. He said he used it to heat water," "the inmate was told three times to stay away from another inmate who was taking a test," "he left the drafting class without permission, said he was looking for a cup," and "he threw a spoonful of macaroni, which hit several inmates sitting nearby."

This man has an extensive record of drug related charges but he also been convicted of promoting prostitution, disorderly conduct and petit larceny. He claims he has been "consuming alcoholic beverages" prior to his burglary and rape and therefore "considered himself intoxicated." He also claims that the burglary-rape was an impulsive act undertaken while enroute to "purchase a quantity of marijuana from a known dealer residing at the hotel."

The man enters the prison on crutches (he has had a leg amputated nine years earlier) and is fitted with a prosthesis. Thereafter he is evicted from a relatively progressive institution for disciplinary violations and is transferred to a more substantial prison where he signs himself into protection, claiming that an inmate "had slapped him around and threatened him with a knife" and "wanted to perform sex on him." The other inmate explains that he "is not a homo chaser" but the man is transferred to a protective program to separate him from the other inmate. In this program he secures his high school diploma, but is not considered an asset. Staff write that

since entering (program) the inmate appears to have continued his unsatisfactory custodial adjustment of the past. Specifically he has been the subject of eighteen misbehavior reports during his fourteen months tenure with this program. . . . The inmate seems to associate with only a few individuals at any given time.

These relationships appear to be . . . limited to manipulation on the inmate's part to obtain commissary items and use of the other's personal belongings. . . . The subject tends to avoid demonstrating this type of behavior with more aggressive inmates, which leads to the inference that he is an "opportunity predator" of sorts.

The man is released to the community and returns to prison after he has held up a taxi driver at knifepoint. In prison he "reports that he had a $1,000 a day cocaine habit at the time of arrest" which seems an exaggeration. He adjusts well to prison, however, is lauded for his "motivation, achievement, social behavior, and work habits" and is said to show "a cooperative spirit."

In fact, the man rather enjoys prison but—at least during his first term—makes it obvious that the prison world in which he operates is not the same prison which is run and monitored by the staff. The man's world consists of illicit amenities, of routines and pastimes that involve extensive socializing which includes exchanges of commodities and gossip, leading to the possibility of misunderstandings which lead to the possibility of conflicts. It also becomes obvious that the man is not above exploiting those who are exploitable, since he is a career hustler, and hustling includes using other people to obtain goods and services whenever assertiveness and glibness can influence those who are less verbally skilled.

When the man leaves prison he again commits a substantial offense which, given that he also has an impressive crime on record, nets him a very long prison sentence, and he embarks on this sentence giving every indication of becoming an experienced old con who creates a congenial home for himself in the institutional environment.

### Games turn Sour

Though inmates such as our jailer are successes in their own eyes, there are other impulsives who experience setbacks which they find difficult to ignore. Admitting failure, however, usually climaxes a long history of setbacks which are brushed off or blamed on adverse or malevolent circumstance.

The historical turning point tends not to be one of insight and self-discovery, but one of shock and self-pity. The person does not deduce that his childish games have boomeranged, but discovers with chagrin that others reject him determinately and consistently and/or that authorities throw the book at him.

A case in point is an inmate serving a long sentence for a robbery that has netted him twenty-six dollars. His incarceration includes a year in the jail and considerable good time credit lost because of prison violations, which mostly consist of fights with other inmates.

This man's childhood is described as "chaotic and traumatic." His mother is a heroin addict and his other parent, a stepfather, "drank heavily and beat both the defendant and his mother." According to the probation officer, the man, when arrested, "lived in 'the street,' associated with other idle and disorderly youths and seemed adjusted to the values and mores of a criminal subculture." The probation officer refers to the fact that the man has spent years being rounded up every few weeks for possessing marijuana, disorderly conduct, selling narcotics, promoting gambling and petit larceny.

The inmate himself admits to intake analysts in the prison that he has engaged

> in general hustling in order to support himself. He indicates that he generally sold marijuana but claimed that it was not actually marijuana but rolled up tea. He indicates that this was the familiar means of support for him and he apparently has adopted the values and mores of the streets.

After the inmate receives three misbehavior reports in rapid succession at the reception center, his security classification is upgraded, and he is assigned to a youth prison where he accumulates ten more misbehavior reports in a short time, which include three for fighting and one "for possession of a dangerous weapon (a razor blade melted into a toothbrush handle)." Six months later the total has climbed to eighteen reports, and one of these nets the man six months of segregation and twelve months loss of good time. This incident involves a fight in which the inmate assaults another inmate who he thinks has stolen one of his shirts, and he breaks the other man's jaw. In response to this disposition the inmate writes to the commissioner of corrections, complaining, "I don't think this sentence is fair because I've seen a few inmates get seven days for breaking another inmate's jaw, and the staff here pay me no mind."

A few weeks later, while the inmate is segregated, he runs into additional difficulties. An officer reports:

> At about 7PM in the special housing unit I smelled the odor of marijuana coming from the area of [the inmate's] cell. A cell frisk was conducted by [two officers]. They found a total of seven cigarettes believed to be a controlled substance of marijuana. The cigarettes were field tested by a sergeant with a field test kit and proved positive marijuana.

The inmate tells the sergeant that he has received the cigarettes from his stepfather during a visit, and the sergeant writes,

I asked the inmate how he had gotten the marijuana back to his cell and he stated he had swallowed a small bag of it in the visiting room, and after returning to his cell had coughed it back up.

The incident brings the inmate a ninety-day extension of his segregation time, and three additional months loss of good time.

The man completes his segregation sentence in another prison and does reasonably well thereafter, including putting in satisfactory performances at various vocational assignments. This gets the inmate some good time restored, and he is released. However, after six months of minor property offenses his parole officer (to whom he has not been reporting) revokes his parole. He serves the remainder of his sentence without becoming involved in conflicts, but he is referred to the psychologist because he "appears disturbed," and staff record that "the inmate has a tendency to escape by becoming drowsy, in contrast to others who may 'act out.' "

There is an indication that this man's pattern of adjustment has been unfrozen at this point, toward the end of his career, which is a mixed blessing because his mood is now one of apathy and depression. Prior to this, the man has faced adversity by leading a happy-go-lucky existence, using whatever resources he finds at hand and relying on his peer group for support and sustenance. He leads this existence both inside and outside the prison, hustling and socializing in a fashion which makes the enterprises difficult to distinguish. The man also relies on drugs for entertainment and to cheer him up, and he incurs frequent stays in jail, which to him is like a familiar motel room for a traveling salesman who spends a good deal of time on the road.

Some problems the man experiences in prison are similar to those he runs into on the street when police officers interrupt his card game or narcotics transactions, but prison disciplinary committees, unlike the courts, attend to *patterns* of minor transgressions, and penalize the inmate for chronicity. Another problem the man encounters is that he settles disputes through fights, and has the particular misfortune that one of his peers has a glass jaw, and that prison staff are therefore obligated to take at least one fight seriously, with painful consequences to the inmate.

Part of this man's pattern has been to do his best to ignore the physical presence of authorities such as teachers, police officers, guards, and parole officers, whom he regards as unwelcome facts of life who at worst have some nuisance value. It is this premise which is ultimately exploded by the fact that prison authorities segregate the man for extended periods of time and lengthen his prison stay, and by the fact that parole officers whom he ignores return him to prison for ignoring them.

## Notes

1. W. Wattenberg, "Psychologists and juvenile delinquency," in H. Toch, ed., *Legal and Criminal Psychology*, New York: Holt, Rinehart and Winston, 1961. The concept of the "unsocialized aggressive" delinquent was first delineated by L. E. Hewitt and R. L. Jenkins in *Fundamental Patterns of Maladjustment*. Springfield: State of Illinois, 1946.

   The diagnostic categories currently in use that apply most directly to such youths are Conduct Disorder, Undersocialized and Aggressive Types. Among the "associated features" the DSM (III) lists for conduct disorders is that "the child typically blames others for his or her difficulties, and feels unfairly treated and mistrustful of others. . . . Poor frustration tolerance, irritability, temper outbursts, and provocative restlessness are often present." As for "complications," the Manual notes that these "include schools suspensions, legal difficulties . . . high rate of physical injury from accidents, fights, along with retaliation from victims, and suicidal behavior" (American Psychiatric Association, *Diagnostic and Statistical Manual Third Edition*. Washington: D.C., 1980), pp. 46–47.

2. The most noteworthy exception to the prevailing pessimism is the work of Fritz Redl and David Wineman (see F. Redl and D. Wineman, *Children who Hate: The Disorganization and Breakdown of Behavior Controls*. Glencoe, Ill.: The Free Press, 1951; F. Redl and D. Wineman, *Controls from Within: Techniques for Treatment of the Aggressive Child*. Glencoe, Ill.: The Free Press, 1952. A more recent success story is provided by V. L. Agee, in *Treatment of the Violent Incorrigible Adolescent*. Lexington, Mass.: D.C. Heath (Lexington), 1979.

3. We have noted elsewhere that a "controlled" environment need not mean a custody-oriented environment: "A controlled environment is a setting in which milieu features can be systematically arranged to accomplish some impact. Such impact can range from humane to sadistic, from program-rich to sterile, from therapeutic to useless or harmful. . . . A closed institution can be authoritative but nonauthoritarian; it can permit participation and autonomy, and furnish more social interaction or 'Gemeinschaft' than the outside world. What the controlled environment eliminates is not democracy but anarchy (random contacts between clients and the world). For many dangerous delinquents, appropriate treatment requires intensive support and substantial retraining that can only be provided in a controlled setting." H. Toch, "Diagnosing Dangerousness and providing a controlled environment," in H. Kerner, ed., *Dangerous or Endangered? Arbeitspapiere aus dem Institut fuer Kriminologie*, Heidelberg, Germany: Univ. Heidelberg, 1983.

4. Both frustration-aggression and stress-aggression fall under the heading of *hostile* (impulse-related, angry, aversively stimulated, expressive, irritable) as opposed to *instrumental* aggression. In the latter sort of aggression, the victim is harmed as a means to secure some ulterior end, such as dominance or material reward, whereas in the former, the medium (aggression) is the message. The distinction between the two categories of aggression was originally drawn by A. Buss (*The Psychology of Aggression*, New York: Wiley, 1961) and S. Feshbach ("The function of aggression and the regulation of aggressive drive," *Psychological Review*, 1964, *71*, 257–272.)

   The frustration-aggression relationship as it is currently understood evolved out of psychoanalytic and learning perspectives (J. Dollard et al., *Frustration and Aggression.* New Haven: Yale University Press, 1930). Early literature includes a book written two thousand years ago by the teacher and philosopher Seneca, who notes that some persons are disproportionately angered by (among other things) exaggerating the import of trivia. (H. Toch, "The management of hostile aggression: Seneca as applied social psychologist," *American Psychologist,* 1983, *38,* 1022–1026.

Susceptibility to stress-generated aggression would have a different origin, including a limited repertoire of coping options, or of self-defined coping options. A man who feels his verbal skills are circumscribed, for example, may turn a verbal conflict into a physical confrontation because he finds the situation overwhelming. (H. Toch, *Violent Men.* Chicago: Aldine, 1969).

5. Persons who are clinically described as impulsives are presumed not to suffer from anxiety, but in practice impulsivity (including aggressive impulsivity) and pervasive anxiety often go hand in hand. See Redl and Wineman, 1951, note 2, supra.

6. J. Irwin, *The Felon.* Englewood Cliffs, N.J.: Prentice-Hall (Spectrum), 1970, p. 68.

7. Irwin (1970), note 6, supra, p. 74.

# 7

# Enhancing Esteem

Adaptive and maladaptive behavior frequently have the same basic goal, and nowhere is this fact more apparent than with behavior that is designed to build reputation or cement self-esteem. Enhancing esteem is deemed a "basic" need by personality theorists.[1] This means that the need for esteem is a universal and irreducible human motive but that specific indices used as measures of esteem vary from culture to culture.

Differences in indices of esteem can be sources of problems where criteria of esteem applicable in one culture are inappropriately imported into another. Skill at headhunting, for instance, may be valued in Australian hinterlands, but in New York or Melbourne demonstrations of headhunting skill could produce serious repercussions.

In this connection, recall that "cultures"—in the sense of nonoverlapping values—are often found in geographical juxtaposition, particularly in pluralistic societies such as ours. Definitions of valued behavior can thus vary in the same neighborhood or from classroom to classroom in the same school. Anthropologists speak of *sub*cultures in discussing such differences, to confirm that an overall culture to which groups belong unites them to some measure, while deviations from the values of this culture separate them.[2] The existence of subcultural values, however, is not *per se* a problem, because it is accomodated to achieve coexistence, as in families with children who belong to the teenage subculture. In such cases we tolerate differing criteria of esteem, such as prevailing indices of teenage popularity.

At times, subcultural differences become an asset. Business establishments that are culturally distinct, for example, may draw their clientelle from members of other cultures. A culture may even adopt subcultural criteria of esteem, as in the admiration we accord to members of the "jock" subculture. Congeniality cannot be assumed, however. Conflicts arise where subcultural criteria are not compatible with cultural criteria or those of other subcultures, though some discrepancies may be adjudged tolerable, such as the fact that some students pursue mediocrity to garner popularity. However, serious conflicts can arise when the behavior that is valued in a group is deemed noxious or harmful outside the group.

The most serious problems are created by members of groups (called "contracultures") that *make a point* of prescribing conduct that diverges from behavior that is valued in the culture at large. Where such norms are applied, they may earn an individual peer admiration but bring him a jail sentence. This helps to explain the behavior of teenage gang members.[3] A leading theorist, Albert Cohen, notes that preadolescents are invited to value themselves in terms of scholastic achievement, but that this is an enterprise at which many do not excel. The esteem needs of such youths would remain unmet if they valued school and thus accepted our usual criteria of success. Many youths consequently reject school as a proving ground and gain esteem through a group process that sees proficiency at violence as a measure of worth. This means that the youths can garner esteem through a willingness to engage in violent conduct.

Violence ranks among subcultural themes that are deemed maladaptive by society-at-large. One study of subcultures (by Wolfgang and Ferracuti) places this theme center stage by talking of "subcultures of violence," referring to youths who are subculturally linked because they prize violent solutions for a wide range of situations.[4] Violence is said to rank high among indices of esteem because the proficiency that is required in exercising physical violence is commonly available.[5]

When we examine persons who repeatedly engage in violence, esteem is an issue that frequently emerges.[6] One type of pattern is the "subculture of violence" pattern, and it has to do with the conferred obligation to behave violently in support of subcultural goals in exchange for peer admiration.[7]

Subcultural norms, of course, must be translated into motives, then into behavior. Some subculture members are more violent than others because they respond more eagerly—or over-eagerly—to prescriptions that place a premium on toughness or pugnaciousness. There are differences in the degree to which individuals seek subcultural approval and in the extent to which they are attracted to the behavior (demonstrating toughness) which brings approval. The result is that overconformity to violence norms can never be ascribed to group norms, but must always be traced to personal dispositions. Such dispositions often represent an exaggerated need for approval as a way of gaining a sense of esteem the person cannot otherwise secure. Given strong enough needs for esteem this pattern becomes counterproductive, in that it inspires resentment, uneasiness or fear rather than approval from others.

## Advertising Toughness

One reliably maladaptive pattern involves using violence to stage demonstrations of *toughness* which are designed to build or cement a reputation. This pattern may or may not secure approval, in that the audience may be real, imaginary or nonexistent. In either case, the goal of the pattern is to enhance one's sense of esteem under the impression that the criterion one uses (demonstrated toughness) would be impressive to others.[8]

An example of this pattern is provided by a young man involved in a gang war in the community in which one of his opponents is shot. The man's disciplinary record includes many fights and a good deal of resistance to authority.

The first prison incident is a gang fight, this time in the prison. In this incident the inmate finds that he is on the losing end of the fight, but refuses to be signed into protective custody. He not only defines himself as resilient but as a leader of organized resistance against staff. In one incident he rallies the troops on his cell gallery by yelling "kill the pigs" and throwing glass jars at officers. In another instance he is handed a disciplinary notice, castigates the officers and tells them that they are faggots and that they can not make him conform, and he then challenges them to "send me to the box, I don't care." He also repeatedly accuses officers of harrassment.

The man does not do better with his counselor. The counselor writes that during an interview "the resident stood up, read the bulletin board, left to get a drink of water, and informed the counselor that he would be back." The inmate does not come back. In another interview, the inmate spends time "going to the window, looking at the secretaries, checking the wall, etc." and makes fun of the counselor when asked for his plans. He tells the counselor, "I want to get involved with the blind and exercise my concerns with the field of humanity, any jobs like that, dealing with the handicapped," adding "let's get down to the dirt, this part interests you the most," referring to his disciplinary record.

The inmate routinely challenges disciplinary dispositions to which he is subjected. In the last half of his sentence he manages to have several judgments rendered in his favor, and adjustment committee decisions are expunged from his record. However, these victories do not appease him. Toward the end of his sentence there is a communication in which he ventures the conclusion that the correction officers union is running the prisons and that their goal is the systematic harrassment of inmates. He expresses his position by wearing black power jewelry. When officers show some interest in this jewelry, bitter altercations result.

In a number of instances, this inmate refuses to appear before adjustment committees or rejects the conclusions of disciplinary panels and engages in argumentative disputes after the hearings. Once, he is transferred to a lower security facility from which he is returned as unsuitable after having staged a series of disciplinary violations. However, there is also a period of progress that is associated with his attendance in a college program, and the prison sentence ends with a happy surprise in that during a substantial period it is noted that "at the present time, the inmate's institutional behavior has shown marked improvement from the past. He has been counseled to continue this improvement." Another note says: "contrary to his institutional behavior, he seems to function well in his school assignment, earned his high school diploma and is involved in the college program."

After his release the inmate is violated for failing to observe curfew and for changing his residence without permission. His first report in his new term of incarceration covers several months in which there are no disciplinary reports of any kind on file.

The inmate may have eventually reformed, but before that he has invested considerable effort to build an image designed to cement his reputation among peers. He has also gained considerable satisfaction with the rewards of being a staff resistor and a troublemaker and a defier of authority, a one-man challenge to the system. He appears to be deflected from this cause towards the end of the sentence through involvement in education, but at first continues to combine the rewards of academic success with his stance as rebel. There is therefore some indication of a graduated transfer to legitimitate opportunity structures as a means garnering esteem, neutralizing a heavy involvement in the illegitimate opportunity system that he still prizes when he operates in the community.

### West Side Story

We have noted above that in some instances, the link of the subculture to violence-related maladaptive behavior is direct, in that the person acts— or thinks that he acts—on behalf of his subculture or in defense of its interests.

A second one of our "success" stories illustrates this pattern. The man at issue arrives in prison at age sixteen, after he is involved in gang conflicts in which he has stabbed—on one occasion, fatally—members of the opposition. He has also participated in gang rapes and other assaultive offenses, lists his drugs of preference as "heroin, cocaine, marijuana, hashish, acid, pills, glue, and carbona," and confesses to "excessive" use of alcohol.

The man commits his prison violations in the early stages of his sentence. The violations include refusing to work, stealing food, intoxication, self-mutilation, fights, "destroying cell equipment" (all of it) and an assault on officers which earns the man three months of segregation and a year's loss of good time.

The assault on the officer climaxes a dramatic escalation which has relatively modest origins. An officer describes the incident as follows:

> When the inmate reported to work at approximately 9:10 AM I noticed that he had on contraband pants (ones which had been altered), and a headband (allowed only in the recreation areas), and a pair of gloves (leather) which had all of the fingers removed. I told the inmate that he was not allowed to wear these items in the laundry and then sent him by pass to the block to change his clothes. When the inmate appeared back in the laundry at approximately 9:30 AM I noticed that he was still wearing the headband and gloves. I then told him that he wouldn't be allowed to work in the laundry unless he was wearing only standard uniform items. At this point another inmate (whom he had brought back from the mess hall) appeared and told this officer that I could not tell the inmate what he could or could not wear. I then asked the other inmate who he was and what he was doing in the laundry. He stated that it was none of my business who he was and then hollered to the other inmates (in Spanish). I then asked him for his I.D. card and he stated that he didn't have one. I then went to the phone and started to call the gate to get an escort to take the inmate to his cell. The other inmate then came to the phone and tried to rip the wire from it. He then went behind this officer and grabbed me around the neck in a "yoke" hold, then hollered to the inmate, "Hit him. Do you want to hit him? Hit him. Hit him." The inmate then picked up a broom and started toward this officer. I tried to get loose from the hold and another inmate came to help hold me. The inmates pulled me against the front counter of the laundry and the inmate started swinging the broom at me . . . (Reinforcements arrived and) the inmates then let go of me and headed into the laundry corridor. . . . An unknown inmate was coming through the corridor and was carrying some broken metal chair pieces. The inmates grabbed the broken pieces of chair and headed toward us. . . . They were stopped by other officers.

In explaining this incident the inmate records that "I have been here for a while, always wore the headband and gloves. No one told me to take them off except when going into mess hall." Eight months later he again becomes indignant because he has been transferred but his property has not been expeditiously delivered to him. The explosion that is sparked by his unhappiness results in a charge which reads:

> On the above date and time an officer escorted your company to chow, but you refused to go. When the officer returned to the gallery, you had cut yourself and had broken your toilet, sink, chair and broom which were all still in your cell.

Six months later the inmate is slated for another transfer and is overheard informing a friend, "I've got to take care of business. My two crimees turned states (state's evidence) and I am going to take care of it." This remark is interpreted as a threat, and it delays the inmate's transfer and briefly places him in involuntary protective segregation. Shortly thereafter, however, the inmate undergoes a marked transmutation, after which he spends four years in confinement with a record that—with one exception—is completely incident-free. The man's reform dates almost precisely to a wedding arranged for him at the prison by the Chaplain's Corps.

After he is married the inmate is transferred to an institution where he can receive conjugal visits and take college courses. By this time he has already obtained a high school certificate in the prison and has declared that he "feels that he would like to change his previous methods of adjusting, and to change for the better."

The inmate is also referred to mental health staff when he is depressed because "his wife is having difficulty in the street," and he decides to "participate in an ongoing therapeutic program to assist him to adjust to the facility." In assessing the inmate's adjustment toward the end of this prison term, staff note his exemplary behavior, but also write that "the subject's threshold for control of anxiety appears lower than 'normal' " and that "while the subject shows progress in interpersonal skills, there still are indications that his self control needs more work."

This man enters prison as a violent gang delinquent who is, in fact, more violent than most violent gang delinquents because he explodes with indignation at the very slightest provocation. The highlight (or lowlight) of the man's prison career replicates his community violence in that he summons members of his gang—including a violent gang leader—when he feels that an officer has affronted him by asking him to take off his gang uniform, and he stages a scene from West Side Story with the officer as target. He also demonstratively explodes and lashes out at everything in sight (including himself) on another occasion in which he feels his rights have been violated, and he threatens to avenge his honor, in standard gang fashion, against erstwhile colleagues who he feels have betrayed him.

The man is transformed when he transfers his loyalty from his peer group to his new wife, and he also becomes seriously involved in prison programs, though residues of his volatility remain. In other words, the man has not changed his personality. However, whereas in the past he has engaged in assaultive acts in defense of honor, he now seeks to exert self-control in subservience to new principles and values.

### The Gladiator Syndrome

The clearest nexus between violence and esteem exists where a person prides himself in his violence proficiency and welcomes opportunities that he feels others afford him to engage in aggression which he can justify. In resolving interpersonal problems the person very often reacts because he sees himself challenged to a duel; he may also resort to violence to impress others with his physical potency.

An example (which is a third success story) is that of an adolescent incarcerated for involvement in robbing a gas station. He commits this offense while on probation for threatening a senior citizen with a knife. His prison involvements include a great deal of horseplay, a large number of fights, and conflicts with correction officers, though his record somewhat improves in the last months of his sentence.

The man's history suggests that he has a long-term propensity for involvement in confrontations. His relatives report that he "constantly picks fights with his siblings" and that he "has been acting out since he was nine years of age" and was suspended from school "for fighting." At prison intake he projects a different image, however. He is referred to mental health staff who place him on medication, and he complains that more sophisticated inmates are "bullying him." He is consequently assigned to a company of vulnerable inmates which he deeply resents, asserting that "he does not like being in a division with homosexuals." He underlines this position by breaking his sink with his bed rails, proclaiming that "if he wasn't moved to 'anywhere' he was going to break his toilet next." When compliance with this request does not follow the inmate writes to the prison's superintendent threatening that

> if you don't transfer me I'm going to fuck up somebody and break their legs and their back, so I'd appreciate it if you can please transfer me. . . . This is a pig division. I hope you know that. . . . I don't like this division, so transfer me.

The inmate's communication again does not produce the desired result so he continues to manifest his disgruntlement, mostly targetted at custodial interventions and those responsible for them. In a typical sequence the inmate exhorts other inmates in his unit to engage in loud conversation, and when instructed to be quiet he threatens to fight the correction officers. This interaction produces a major disciplinary report, which increases the inmate's displeasure, and two hours later he is charged as follows:

> While an officer was releasing you from your cell for keeplock exercise you approached the officer with your right fist clenched and verbally indicated you wanted to fight the officer. At this time you attempted to strike the officer in the face with your fist. In response the officer deflected your blow and physically restrained you while forcing you into your cell. . . . Once in your cell you armed yourself with a pen and commenced to attack (another officer.) In response he closed your cell door before you could make contact and stab him.

The inmate spends much time in segregation where he writes letters to the superintendent of the prison alleging that he is "going crazy" and being starved. The superintendent and other prison staff conclude that the inmate is "a nagging problem at this facility" and suggest that he be transferred. The transfer request is not honored, though, and the inmate becomes involved in a confrontation with a fellow inmate who lays claim to a chair in which the inmate has been sitting. In the course of this argument the inmate chases his opponent with a board hitting him in the back of the neck, claiming, in justification, proprietory rights to the chair under dispute.

As it happens the chair incident marks a turning point in the inmate's history, and thereafter his custodial record improves. He becomes voluntarily involved in group counseling and receives good evaluations from work supervisors. The institution rescinds its transfer requests and the inmate spends three months without disciplinary involvements before he is released.

This man is a gladiator who stands ready to do combat at the drop of a pin, and he defines fighting as something you do when someone has impugned your honor or challenged you or downgraded you or subjected you to an affront. The man never feels that he is outclassed, as evidenced by the fact that he tackles correction officers in pugilistic encounters as readily as he does an inmate who dares to lay claim to his chair.

Given the man's outlook it is doubly humiliating to him to confess that he is being helplessly victimized as he enters prison and to receive a living assignment which stigmatizes him as weak. The intense experience of wounded pride fills the man with rage, but the reaction is short term, and in any event he soons solves the problem by earning a reputation as prison troublemaker. The story ends happily when this campaign subsides. As the inmate settles down he responds to regular and intensive group counseling and to work assignments he finds congenial, showing maturation including a tempering of his tendency to fly off the handle when he sees himself as aggrieved.

### Countering Aspersions

Frequently, the link between esteem and aggression is a different one and has to do with low rather than high self-esteem, or at least with self-esteem that is laced with doubts, questions or misgivings. These self-doubts make esteem issues potentially explosive because the person feels that others may disapprove of him, and becomes upset when he senses evidence of disapproval. In other words, the person easily feels slighted, degraded or disrespected, which provokes him to expressions of outrage.

This pattern of oversensitivity to affront is illustrated by a man who burglarizes a furniture warehouse while he is on probation for a mugging. His prison problems include fights and assaults, threats against officers, weapons charges, fire settings, and miscellaneous violations such as "refused to return his spoon with his tray," "tampered with his radiator," "had a large amount of garbage in his toilet," "refused to move ahead to keep up with his line in the mess hall," and "failed to obtain a new I.D. card after changing his appearance."

In preparing a presentence report following the man's first conviction, his probation officer writes that "he seems to be held back due to obvious feelings of inadequacy, due to his limited skills and ability to speak English." The next presentence report records:

> He asked his probation officer for help about his drinking problem and was referred to an alcoholism program. . . . Probation records verify that the defendant did attend the program. . . . He appears to be an inadequate individual who has a great deal of difficulty coping with life.

Several months after the man arrives in prison he gains visibility by reacting explosively when officers do not expeditiously attend to his wants. He enters the infirmary one morning, for example, suffering from effects of smoke inhalation because he has set his mattress on fire, and presents hand injuries sustained while he "ripped a wooden clothes rack from the wall of his room." He explains to the nurse that "he had informed officers that his ear hurt, and felt it necessary to underline that he 'needed attention for my ear.' " Ten days later the inmate returns with scratches on his forearms, having "cut his arms with a broken lightbulb." The next day the inmate sports innumerable abrasions after "an unsuccessful attempt to assault correction officers."

Later, a progress report notes that the inmate is "currently in special housing serving 200 days, 180 on a superintendent's proceeding and 20 added on for reports since . . . for arson, destruction of state property, health and safety hazard, refusing orders and loud and boisterous conduct. He appears to be in conflict with authority figures." In this report it is also noted that "although there was no indication of psychiatric problems initially, his recent behavior seems to indicate a need for psychiatric help."

The man is transferred to a more substantial prison, where he files a suit in which he avers that officers "kicked and punched me without provocation . . . smashed my head in against the floor and beat me. . . . I vomited blood for approximately two weeks. I suffered bruises and scars over my body, and intense physical and emotional pain." Shortly thereafter he has a fight with another inmate in which he "resisted officers who were attempting to restrain him." He reports that the other inmate "disrespected him and he had to fight." He also explains that he "was extremely angry and did not intentionally break away from the officers or disregard their orders."

The inmate is transferred to a third prison, where another inmate has to be protected from his attentions. This other inmate "has been threatened by the inmate who has attempted to get inside his cell, to rape him." The other inmate also "is afraid that the inmate will have his friends help rape him." Six months later the man is released from prison, but his parole is rescinded, in that he "used cocaine, failed to participate in Alcoholics Anonymous meetings, and failed to participate in a residential drug program."

Early in his career the man defined as a self-confessed inadequate youth who admits that he has "a serious drinking problem" for which he is ready to accept assistance. He returns to prison having rejected mandated treatment for his addictions, which suggests a change in his self-definition. Within the prison the man also undergoes a change in that he starts out defining himself as a person in need of, and "entitled to" services, and ends up victimizing vulnerable inmates. Victimizing others, however, is not the man's principal mode of aggression. He is mostly aroused by persons who he thinks have provoked him by somehow injuring his pride, and his reaction includes angry resentment at not being attended to when he feels he needs something, such as attention to a cyst in his ear.

As far as the man is concerned, his exploding is justifiable because he has asked for something (which is demeaning) and has had his request ignored (which is even more demeaning,) but the childlike and tantrumlike quality of his angry demonstrations, including inflicted injuries, raise some possibility in the minds of custodial staff that he is emotionally disturbed. Since the man regards his explosions as natural reactions to provocation, he himself dismisses them, and centers on the consequences, which he defines as "being beaten up without provocation." This stance (and the man's habit of sullenly disregarding instructions he finds uncongenial) create a communication problem between himself and the prison system.

It is conceivable that the man's limited command of English is somehow related to the fact that he feels the need for physical demonstrations to make himself understood. However, it is equally probable that the man's preferred mode of response when he feels slighted is to express his indignation physically because a verbal response does not adequately communicate the magnitude of the injury he feels.

Disciplinary committees send the man to prison psychiatrists after tantrums, but teachers have already referred him for assistance at age nine under similar circumstances. Throughout, the man's perspective has continuity. He says of his early fights that they were products of his "temper." What "temper" means in the man's scheme is that he permits himself unrestrained, impulsive aggressivity in the face of perceived injury—which he calls "disrespect."

### Preempting Unpopularity

Repeated confirmation of low self-esteem produces a related pattern, which is particularly troublesome because it is self-confirming. What the pattern expresses is the expectation of future rejection based on experiences of past rejections. The person reacts to protect what is left of his self-esteem rejecting anticipated rejectors by treating them with hostility, and he thereby provokes the precise reaction he expects, that is, rejection. The dubious achievement is a world-view in which the reaction of others to one's behavior documents the assumptions that underlie it.

This complex pattern is illustrated in an inmate convicted of stealing a truck, whose prison transgressions range from minor to major. Minor violations have to do with such things as taking extra cake or an extra pillow, being unclean, being out of place and arguing. Major violations involve serious fights, harassment of employees and "promotion of contraband."

The man serves a first prison sentence after he breaks into a camp and steals money, food and cigarettes. Breaking into a camp is something of a switch for the man who has broken out of camps at least on seven occasions and has also absconded from a home for children, a state hospital and other institutions. He has spent much of his life in foster homes, which for him are an advance because at age three social workers discover him living "in a filthy environment" with "skin lesions on his body" after they are reliably "informed that (the inmate and his siblings) were often tied in chairs and suspended by hooks from the ceiling of their parent's trailer."

The man's educational career is similarly unrewarding. Reportedly,

> his school problems included hollering, banging the desk, biting, spitting and hitting. His teacher resorted to spanking him for every offense, and it was learned that she had tied him in his chair earlier in the year (first grade). School problems carried over into the foster home where his behavior had been good.

Following a term in a children's home the inmate is transferred to a state hospital, where he is diagnosed as a sociopath and discharged. He is also evicted from the next institution, which reports that he "started a fire, exposed himself to female staff, showed poor peer interaction and staff rapport and his academic behavior (had) dropped.''

Problems continue after the man is arrested. According to the presentence report,

> the defendant's behavior in the jail has been terrible. He has had conflict with the other prisoners, threw an ashtray at the t.v. and flushed a magazine down the toilet, plugging the drain. He continued to flush the toilet, flooded the cell block, caused water damage to the first floor ceiling. . . . The defendant has also set a number of fires in his cell.

A prison sentence follows reviews of other options, which at this stage prove nonexistent. In sentencing the inmate the judge comments that

> your case does give me some misgivings because a lot of your trouble stems from your unfortunate family background. However . . . the mere fact that you haven't been blessed with parents that really care about you is not going to be your crutch throughout the rest of your life to excuse your criminal conduct. . . . At some point while you are still young you are going to have to learn that you're going to have to conform regardless of your background. Therefore, it is the sentence of the court that you be sentenced to (prison). . . . How long you are there will largely be governed by your own conduct. If you go with a chip on your shoulder with the idea of giving them a hard time you are going to receive that back from the authorities. A great measure of your future is going to be determined by your own compliance.

The inmate's ''compliance'' proves less than desired. Within weeks after the man enters the system an entry reads:

> The inmate, referred to psychiatrist this date, was brought from keeplock. . . . He is a very resentful, hostile young man who is reticent to talk about what happened. It was my impression from his stating ''someone made him do something he didn't want to do and he didn't want to talk about it'' that it probably was something sexual. He was trying to bum a cigarette and when told by the officer to go to his cell became verbally abusive. He remained angry, so he told his social worker if he didn't get out of here in two weeks he would get out in a pine box.

Three days later the inmate admits that ''he was subjected to sodomy and is fearful for his life'' and remains apprehensive for the next several days, pleading for a transfer out of the institution. A second mental health entry within this period reads:

> Inmate referred to psychiatrist this date . . . caused some disturbance during the night. He makes too many demands on officers and remains bitter and contentious and complains ''he takes too much stuff from everybody,'' indicat-

ing a persecution complex. It is his impression he needs to get out of this atmosphere. In the hospital he was kept isolated and says that does not bother him. Stated, "They are trying to subject me to homosexuality," and that about four or five hundred inmates are against him. It seems he is absolutely unrealistic and as a result it is my impression we are dealing with a schizophrenic individual, paranoid type.

The inmate is medicated and sent to a therapeutic milieu, where he is classified as a management problem. A sample entry reads:

Inmate, after being placed in keeplock for a misbehavior report, became agitated and abusive. He continued to bang on the door and threaten officers and staff. The duty doctor was notified (and) ordered (a tranquilizing injection.) She supervised the injection given by the duty R. N. Inmate was first asked if he would take the injection and he repeatedly refused. Doctors stated the injection must be given. Myself and officer wrestled inmate to the bed. R. N. on duty gave the first injection. While attempting to give the second injection inmate kicked the nurse in the right knee. Because of the agitated state of this inmate we withdrew from room to prevent further injury to inmate or staff.

The inmate is returned to the reception center, where intake classification staff record that "Obviously what we are dealing with here is not a boy but a byproduct of trauma. . . . One cannot be surprised by his current maladjustment." The inmate, however, does not evoke sympathy but makes a consistently unfavorable impression. Officers characterize him as "very loud, disrespectful and indiscrete" and point out that "he doesn't get along with anyone on the gallery and argues with all his peers."

A psychiatrist sees the inmate at this time, and writes that

it seems that a different tack has to be taken with this youngster, and he cannot be reprimanded each time he does something wrong. This is just a continuation of what has happened in the past where he was abused by the parents and as a result had to be in institutions and foster homes all of his life. As a consequence he is living out his resentfulness against his parents and can become hostile and has had to survive the best way he knew how. . . . This young man was brought up from keeplock for "fishing." It seems to me that these are all attention getting devices to annoy people as revenge for maltreatment he received in the past.

Though the psychiatrist recommends that the inmate should be given "the love and care which every youngster should have," staff find the prescription hard to act upon. Three days after the interview with the psychiatrist the inmate starts a fight and it is charged that "when ordered to stop you instead threw your shoes and clothing to the floor." The following day three more charges are entered. It is alleged in the morning that the inmate "did refuse to take medication and instead threatened the R. N. with bodily harm." At noon,

> you destroyed your bedside table, tore up your sheets, broke a total of nine windows, and destroyed your clothing. . . . You did attempt to inflict bodily harm on correction personnel by trying to strike them with a sixteen inch iron pipe when they entered your cell, by throwing a steel table against the cell bars and by throwing a lightbulb at the lieutenant. You also attempted to assault said officers by swinging your fists and kicking with your feet, and also by trying to bite any personnel that you could. . . . You made threatening remarks toward correction personnel, the judge who sentenced you, and police personnel who had arrested you. You stated that after you had been released you would return with a gun and kill as many people as you could.

The next day the inmate caps his previous day's performance with an incident in which it is charged that "you did destroy your state mattress and started a fire in your cell, thereby endangering the lives of other residents who were housed in the special housing unit area."

The inmate is assigned to a youth prison where he is promptly charged with planning an escape. He confesses that he and an associate had "planned to get knives from the mess hall, sharpen them and use them to take hostages" and that "they planned to hit the officer over the head, tie him up and take his keys," but had discovered that "they had no way of getting through the front gate unless the officer had left it open." By way of explanation for such plans the inmate tells the adjustment committee that "the people here don't give him a break and don't like him" and that "he is going to get out of here one way or another." He follows this threat by cutting his forearm, and is seen by a psychiatrist who reviews his unhappy childhood and concludes that "he became very bitter and hostile towards society and toward everyone. At times this includes himself. (He also) tries very seriously to gain attention from others which he needs very badly." The psychiatrist records that the inmate "was happy that he was given some attention, telling this examiner his future plans, explaining to this examiner how he will get rich by milking snakes in Florida when he gets a chance." The psychiatrist suggests that the inmate "should be placed in such a division that he will find some understanding from the officers, from other employees and even from other inmates." Instead, the inmate faces a term in the segregation unit, and reacts to the prospect with displeasure:

> The officer in charge of SHU phoned and said that the inmate was screaming, yelling and spitting at the officers in SHU. The writer attempted to quiet the inmate but he continued to scream, threatened to kill me and the officers if his gate was opened. As this time the entire SHU was in an uproar, with inmates

banging on the walls and gates. When the inmate's cell was opened he assumed a karate stance and told me to come and get him if I wanted to die.

Four days later the inmate is assessed $91.10 "because of destroying a toilet and sink." The psychiatrist who again sees the inmate acknowledges that "his adjustment to our institution remains deteriorating" and describes a catch-22 situation in which the inmate's experience with treatment to which he is subjected makes him bitter, which makes him obnoxious, which invites further maltreatment. The psychiatrist writes:

Wherever he went he is always unwanted and unaccepted because of his deep hostility, his strong desire to destroy everything, his unbearable attitude, his immaturity and his constant and limitless attention seeking behavior for his dependency needs. This inmate never really tried to receive any sincere help from anyone. I don't think he will be ready for some time to accept such services.

Institution staff finally succeed in having the inmate transferred elsewhere. Before he departs his counselor interviews him in the segregation unit where he is serving a two-month sentence, and writes that the inmate

appears to be well accustomed to segregation. He appears to be making good use of his time via discovery learning. He appears to be living a "Count of Monte Cristo" type life. . . . There is much pathos in this case when one takes a macro-view. There is no doubt that from a micro-view he has been a very trying case for the administration. He rationalizes his being confined to the special housing unit as an attempt to secure protective custody, states that he has experienced racial peer pressure on a continuing basis, feels that he would prefer protective custody for 180 days rather than a return to population, states that he does not want a transfer since these problems would surface elsewhere. . . . The case still does not appear "hopeless."

In the first report filed on the inmate in the institution to which he is sent his counselor records:

Resident was received and was immediately placed in the SHU to continue serving a sentence of 60 days. A short time after he was released from our SHU he was again held for a superintendent's proceeding for attempted assault on a group of inmates. He received 21 days SHU for that infraction, although while he was serving this 21 days SHU he was again cited for making and exploding a home-made bomb in the SHU. He was ordered to serve another 21 days in the SHU for this infraction. . . . His last report was for fighting. . . . It is doubtful if he will be able to adjust at this institution. However, he is being returned to his program at this time.

When the inmate is released from segregation he signs himself back in, asserting that he "just cannot get along with his peers." The inmate signs himself into protective segregation claiming that "his life is being threatened" by other inmates. The segregation unit counselor observes that "his personality complex is offensive to his peers, and for this reason he is a constant target of their abuse. His personal hygiene is abominable—he reeks of filth. Actually he is more to be pitied than punished." A week later the same counselor writes:

> We again find (the inmate) in the special housing unit as a result of receiving a threatening letter which he himself instigated by allegedly spitting on other residents and writing obscenities to said residents. Intermittently and continually we have endeavored to plead our case with hopes of transferring this individual to a more suitable facility. . . . Currently we have the individual again in a structured environment where he can or will gain very little. Once again we are appealing for consideration for his transfer to a more suitable facility from which he can enjoy benefits of population.

The inmate is in fact transferred, and his new counselor writes in the first report on the inmate that

> when he is angry he acts out. If he is frustrated he acts out. If he is thwarted he acts out. This leaves him few alternatives to his behavior except to become involved with authority figures. He appears to have related to me in a parent-child fashion. . . . He drops into my office regularly. He makes minor requests, asks for reassurance, reassures himself and me that he is doing well and is not getting into trouble. He tests me almost continuously to see if I really care about him. To date he is adjusting reasonably well. . . . He needs a strong parental figure upon whom he can model himself and someone who will be supportive and help him over the rough spots in his life. He will be seen again next week.

Before the week is up, however, the inmate faces a serious charge because he has been found in possession of torn strips of bedsheeting, road maps of Manhattan and a piece of pipe, which suggests that he is hatching plans of escape. The inmate claims that "he was being threatened with homosexual acts in population" and "that the contraband in his cell was for protection." A psychologist attempting to test him for the parole board reports:

> (The inmate) had become engaged in angry exchanges with several of the black inmates who were also in special housing. Apparently he had made several racial slurs. He had antagonized the other inmates. Even during the testing session they were shouting and cursing at him. In addition he himself is a difficult subject. He was constantly testing the limits of the examiner, playing with test materials, even after repeated requests to leave them alone. In general he was forcing the examiner to play the authority role.

The examiner also concludes that

(The inmate's) need for affection is so extreme that he does not even know where to begin looking for it. Almost all persons, especially authority figures, immediately become invested emotionally as love-hate objects that he has to first move towards, then reject before they reject him. During the testing he was constantly provoking the examiner, yet at the same time coming on as a "cute little boy."

At the institution's request the inmate is sent to another prison at a higher security level. Here he promptly signs himself into protection claiming that he has not only encountered an enemy but has made additional enemies by identifying the man to officers in the presence of other inmates, "so now I know I'm in trouble here for sure."

A few months later the inmate is paroled, is returned as delinquent eight weeks thereafter and completes the remainder of his term isolating himself as much as he can, declaring that "he has no interest in participating in programs available at this facility." A year later the inmate reappears having been arrested in possession of a stolen truck. Classification analysts send him to a special program, where he serves his sentence. Soon after he arrives at this unit staff record that

it would appear that there is some hostility and problems between the other inmates and this inmate. . . . Shortly after his arrival—indeed in the first several weeks—the inmate was involved in a physical altercation with another inmate, apparently over some discussion. . . . He keeps many inmates away through the use of poor hygiene and his rather obnoxious way of with people.

The inmate also antagonizes staff, to whom he conveys the impression that he "somehow is doing us a favor for being here." Staff report that he "informed one of the correction officers that he would not go to the shop at any cost. Nevertheless he reported to the shop each day since his assertion." As others before them, staff conclude that the inmate's "rather obnoxious behavior causes people to reject him, and thus he harbors some hostility toward them. This is occasionally evidenced when he choses to act out this hostility and thus causes further rejection."

The inmate illustrates the process in a sequence which begins when he is charged with failing to get up for breakfast on two consecutive mornings, and is penalized because he has ignored prior admonitions. The same afternoon, "the inmate, after receiving the adjustment committee decision went on a rampage slamming furniture, yelling, cursing, threatening and then giving me a raised finger, hollering '(blank) you.' " The inmate is transferred to a segregation cell, where he "was pounding the walls and screamed obscenities; however, he quickly settled down." He next appears before the adjustment committee to account for his reactions to the last adjustment committee hearing, and reacts in turn. The charge reads:

> After your recall before the adjustment committee you became verbally abusive toward officers creating a disturbance in the building, and when told to be quiet you refused to do so. You shut the door to your room and continued to be disruptive until you were removed from the building by the sergeant. You further caused a disturbance by banging the gate.

For a brief period staff think that they note "marginal progress" and specifically observe that "the inmate has shown an increasing ability to get along with the other inmates and has begun to show improved personal hygiene." There are no improvements in the inmate's "ability to get along" with staff, however. On one occasion he places a stick and an empty can on his cell gate to be "actuated when his room door was opened" and requests an officer to "open the door, causing the noise maker to create a loud noise." On another occasion he produces two boxes of books to be inventoried by the staff, and a guard reports that

> while talking to the inmate about where and how he got all the books he started telling (another officer) and myself that we had to do things his way. He kept returning to the desk area harassing (us.) I informed the inmate that the sergeant would be through soon and that he could talk to him about the book problem. He still insisted to argue, whereupon I gave the inmate a direct order to leave the desk area. He responded to the order, but not before defiantly looking at me and spitting on the floor in front of the desk.

The inmate also arranges for a second inmate to write a letter claiming to be a witness in possession of evidence that exonerates the inmate in a case he is preparing for appeal.

These incidents cause the inmate to be segregated, and he spends two months "adjusting well" and catching up on his reading. He then returns to his status as marginal program participant with the announcement that "he would change his behavior 'when I want to change, and right now I don't want to change.' " In line with this philosophy he "seems to become highly defensive when he is confronted in group," which does not stop him from "cross examining" inmates whose problems are under discussion.

A transmutation occurs a year before the inmate is released. A staff member writes that

> apparently the pivotal occurrence in persuading the inmate to improve his adjustment occurred when he received word that his appeal had been denied. At that time he probably had to admit to himself that he was not the penultimate jailhouse lawyer he fancied himself to be. His dream of thumbing his nose at the system by being released on appeal was shattered and he was finally left with the realization that his only chance for release short of maxing out was to improve his overall institutional adjustment. Concurrent with the improvement

in his disciplinary record he has improved his participation in group therapy, on his job assignment, in the shop, in the physical education program and on the building where he houses.

The parole board notes the improvement, but opines that "it is too early to determine whether or not you are sincere in your efforts to change your ways." This injunction impresses the inmate, who makes "a somewhat uninspired effort to maintain an acceptable level or participation in the program." But the level of involvement is not sufficient to convince the unit staff, who characterize the inmate as "your basic pain-in-the-neck, immature individual who . . . by his continuous aggravating behavior is a person you want to grab and shake some sense into."

The man is paroled but returns to prison within seven months convicted of negligent homicide for the unusual offense of causing the death of a four-month old baby by striking its head. The crime becomes publicized in the prison population, requiring the inmate to shuttle among protection units in search of sanctuary from indignant fellow inmates. This dependent condition does not deter the inmate from conflicts with staff. On one occasion he pushes an officer to obtain a set of papers the officer is holding. He is also charged with setting a fire, attempting to smuggle items out of prison and manufacturing weapons. Such violations, in combination with the inmate's unpopularity among his peers, cause him to shuttle between disciplinary and protective segregation status.

By this time there is remarkable consistency in the man's career, which spans three prison terms over ten years. The decade starts with the man living in fear after he has been sodomized by other inmates, and ends with unsuccessful efforts to find protection from peers who wish him harm. The decade begins with destructive rampages in response to custodial admonitions and ends with the inmate engaged in confrontations with officers and other acts of defiance against the custodial regime. There is also consistency in the cycles that characterize this man's interpersonal transactions, in which his confrontative and challenging moves lead to unpopularity which cements his bitterness and instructs his demeanor. Added consistency becomes obvious when one adds the man's preincarceration history into the equation, which in his case is unavoidable.

### Standing Fast

A third pattern that is based on self-doubt is of a different order, but is also compensatory, in the sense that the person overreacts so as to keep his vulnerabilities from being exposed. The pattern is one characterized by rigid positions and intransigent stands which are designed to suggest that the person can never be mistaken in judgment, that he omniscient, principled and infallible. Though the stance prevents people from discovering imperfections it offends because it impugns the judgments of others and reduces all negotiation to confrontations.

A case in point is that of a heavyset man born in Puerto Rico who has been convicted of robbing a pedestrian and who justifies his actions by claiming that his victim was a drunk who insisted on obstructing the landscape by sleeping in doorways. According to the disciplinary record, the man is loud and vociferous and has an affinity for threatening personnel, though he is occasionally also involved in fights with other inmates.

The man's brushes with the law begin at age twelve, at which time he is charged with assault and his career as a burglar begins. At age sixteen the man is forcibly robbing people, which is what he repeatedly does until he is arrested. The man also does not keep a low profile in the community in that he does things like breaking subway turnstiles and throwing garbage at store windows. He appears to carry weapons as a matter of routine. He is evicted from a school for truancy and attends an educational program associated with a psychiatric adolescent clinic. On other occasions he is seen by child psychiatrists.

The man's prison violations have to do with the fact that when he makes trouble (usually loudly) and is taken to account for his behavior, he wildly explodes. As a result he is not only in hot water for his original violation but has immersed himself so deeply that serious repercussions are inevitable. His first prison violation occurs in the intake facility. In this incident his living unit has been alerted to stand for a count and the man not only obstructs the procedure but "catches a very nasty attitude" when his transgression is brought to his attention. He is written up, and according to the report "picked up his locker and smashes it against the door and also threw other things in his cell and said 'I'm going to cut my wrists.' " By the time this demonstration is over the man's cell windows have been smashed and his footlocker is twisted and broken and the best he can do is to request reimbursement on the installment plan.

The next incident begins with a scene at the commissary window after the inmate has bought ice cream and has been notified that wooden spoons are not available. To this he reacts by yelling, "if I can't have a wooden spoon, he better take the (blank) ice cream back." An officer reports that

> I showed him our Out of Stock List which plainly states "we have no wooden spoons for ice cream." He then stated "well, he's going to take back the (blank) ice cream."

This monologue draws a sizeable group of spectators and the officer calls for help and suggests to the inmate that he return to his cell, which the inmate repeatedly refuses to do. He ends up taking off his glasses, explaining to the officer "you're not taking me anywhere," a stance which the inmate later describes as "I did refuse to lock in because I was right." The inmate also subsequently suggests that he could not accept the officer's evidence for the unavailability of spoons because he "can't read script writing." A progress report speculates that the inmate "may have a problem with the staff, or has a problem understanding his current predicament." It also concludes that "the resident has had some difficulty adjusting to an authoritarian environment and needs intensive counseling and direction."

Another prison violation is a replay of the inmate's standard scenario. On this occasion the inmate is intercepted in a school hallway with the school's copy of *Life* magazine. A teacher writes "I politely said to him to please never again take a magazine from my class without permission." He repeats this injunction as he and the inmate reenter the classroom. The inmate

> then started losing control and saying that he didn't give a (blank) about the magazine or me and that he better get out of my class to prevent any trouble, but he didn't. However, he still kept yelling and using obscene language.

The teacher notifies the inmate that he would be subjected to a disciplinary report and

> upon hearing the word "keeplock" he started threatening me with physical violence and started to take off his shirt. Some of the students in class tried to calm him down. He then started threatening me that sooner or later he would get me. Immediately I went to get an officer to get him out of class. As the officer entered the inmate was losing complete control. His face was getting red and his talking was incoherent. He kept using profanities and adding the word "homosexual."

This incident not only ends the inmate's academic career in prison but also leads to a request that he be transferred to another prison from which the inmate is eventually paroled after being involved in a number of violations.

Part of this man's difficulties lies in the fact that he does not know the meaning of the word "retreat." When he has broken a rule or committed a transgression he regards any injunction or admonition as a reflection on his manhood and a challenge to a duel. A duel, however, is unthinkable because prison staff and those of the criminal justice system outnumber the man. He is therefore limited to gestures such as taking off his shirt or his glasses, cursing, threatening and breaking footlockers.

The only question that is hard to resolve is why this individual cannot accommodate the possibility that robbing pedestrians or removing magazines from classrooms are actions that one need not bother to defend after one has been caught red-handed and after the prospect of punishment is inevitable. It is not clear what the man cannot assimilate, whether it is the concept that one can do wrong or the possibility that one might accept a sanction, or the notion that anything that one decides to do is subject to interpellation. The most plausible hypothesis is that once this man has embarked on a course of conduct he feels that it is unreviewable. He functions like a vehicle with no reverse gear and is therefore blind to information that casts doubt on premises such as "when one wants money one steals it" and "when somebody sells me ice cream he must give me a spoon" which justify the initiation of his delinquent or deviant acts. He feels that whatever he does is right because he does it, and that no man ever admits that he could have been mistaken or even listens to somebody suggesting that he might be mistaken; that it is embarassing to be told that you are wrong, that one loses face by permitting oneself to be told that one is wrong, and that it adds injury to insult when the person who has told you that you are wrong then punishes you because you object to being insulted.

## Notes

1. A. H. Maslow, *Motivation and Personality*, New York: Harper, 1954. Maslow defines as basic needs "the ultimate human goals or desires or needs" (p. 66). By "ultimate," Maslow means that behavior that subserves such needs cannot be tracked to ulterior or "more basic" motives.
2. A. McClung Lee, "Levels of culture as levels of social generalization," *American Sociological Review*, 1945, *10*, 485–495; M. M. Gordon, "The concept of the subculture and its application," *Social Forces*, 1947, 40ff.
3. For a discussion of the contraculture concept, see M. Yinger, "Contraculture and subculture," *American Sociological Review*, 1960, *25*, 625–635. The classic application to delinquency is A. K. Cohen's *Delinquent Boys*, Glencoe, Ill.: Free Press, 1955.
4. M. E. Wolfgang and F. Ferracuti, *The Subculture of Violence: Towards an Integrated Theory of Criminology*. London: Tavistock Publications, 1967.
5. A. K. Cohen, "Prison violence: A Sociological perspective," in A. K. Cohen, G. F. Cole and R. G. Bailey, eds., *Prison Violence*. Lexington, Mass: D. C. Heath (Lexington Books), 1976.
6. Toch (1969), chapter 6, note 3.
7. Ibid., pp. 148–153.
8. Unfortunately, clinical diagnoses do not distinguish between behavior problems that result from impulse-control deficits and those that are compensatorily addressed to issues of self-esteem. Among the "associated features" the DSM (III) lists for Conduct Disorders are "Self-esteem is usually low, though the

individual may present an image of 'toughness.' . . . In the Socialized types, sometimes there is membership in a gang and the antisocial behavior may be limited to gang activities," American Psychiatric Association (1980), p. 46 (chapter 6, note 1). The most explicit description of self-esteem-related behavior in the clinical literature is offered by the psychoanalyst Alfred Adler (A. Adler, *The Practice and Theory of Individual Psychology.* New York: Harcourt, 1927).

# 8

# Pursuing Autonomy

As we move from childhood to adulthood we gain autonomy because we achieve freedom from parental supervision but discover that we must use our own resources to deal with problems our parents have solved on our behalf. A number of the difficulties that are said to arise in adolescence relate to such tradeoffs, and have to do with conflicts around the issue of how fast autonomy can be (or ought to be) achieved. Some adolescents, for example, become oversensitive to infringements of their autonomy while simultaneously demanding childhood-related privileges, such as unconditional support.[1]

Problems of this kind are age-specific and tend to be evanescent, but they are susceptible to resuscitation in settings where authority is exercised in arbitrary fashion, particularly where those who exercise authority also control resources.[2] The problem of autonomy can also remain alive for some individuals and becomes a chronic concern to them. It particularly remains alive where the issue of autonomy-dependence has never been resolved, such as with persons for whom autonomy and/or support have never been available, for whom autonomy has been prematurely forced or for whom support has been oversupplied.[3]

Reactions that are evoked by autonomy-dependence concerns are maladaptive if they inspire emotionally charged and inappropriate behavior by persons who are supervised by other persons. Settings in which authority is assertively exercised invite autonomy-dependence concerns, and those who operate such settings must take care to draw distinctions between reactions that are proportionate and appropriate, or disproportionate and inappropriate, to the problems posed by their own management styles and patterns of supervision. Supervisors who run authoritarian settings are particularly unentitled to complain of "childlike" reactions of subordinates, or to cite such behavior of their subordinates to justify their authoritarian style of supervision.[4] On the other hand, there are settings (such as youth prisons) which contain larger-than-usual numbers of persons for whom authority-dependence issues have been unresolved, and who over-react to many situations in which autonomy or dependence is an issue.

### The Prodigal Son Syndrome

A maladaptive pattern that authority figures may at times find congenial (though the congeniality reaches diminishing returns) is when a person becomes overdependent on authority figures. Persons who take this stance place authorities in the role of parental figures who are prized as advice-givers, dispensers of services, and arrangers of environments.[5] The stance confers expected obligations as well as status, however, which often makes the dependent person annoying. At such junctures the neurotic quality of dependence becomes more obvious, and even the most nurturant authority figures come to see dependent behavior as a symptom of immaturity or resourcelessness, or of personal irresponsibility. Authority figures may also feel themselves manipulated by persons who make consistently illegitimate demands.

A case in point is that of a man sentenced for a burglary, whose prison misbehavior is largely nonserious. The man is charged with offenses such as "missed chow because he was in the shower room," "yelling and running around his dorm during count," "disruptive and noisy after warning," and "sleeping in the shop after order not to go to sleep." There is also one disciplinary charge of "attempted suicide by hanging."

The man has been in prison before, for another burglary, and starts his term belatedly because he has been hospitalized for ingesting hair lotion while in jail. He has also been in psychiatric settings. In fact, it is recorded that "this inmate has been chronically institutionalized since the age of 12 and has spent ten out of the last twelve years in institutions," which leads prison staff to conclude that "he has never really functioned on the outside and is severely disabled at this point."

The inmate is characterized as "manipulative." An example of his alleged manipulativeness is that during presentence interviews he "admitted to using drugs (various types) and requested placement in a drug program" but that at prison intake he "states that he only used drugs on an experimental basis and was attempting to get placed in a drug program rather than go to jail." The conclusion that is drawn is that the imate either claims or disclaims problems depending on the benefits such claims produce. However, it is also concluded that the man could be "subject to considerable abuse by other inmates" and therefore requires staff attention.

Several incidents continue casting doubts on the seriousness of the man's mental health problems. On one occasion he is suspected of "actively tactile hallucinating" but it turns out that he "is suffering from a psychosomatic dermatitis superimposed upon which was an unfortunate incident of a bug crawling on him (which) he reported to a physician." For this incident the man is treated with tranquilizers. In response to a subsequent complaint that he suffers from insomnia a nurse suggests to other staff that "we give the inmate a placebo with the positive suggestion that if this placebo is too strong for him it will be changed for one less tiring."

Two days after the inmate comes to prison on his main sentence he is hospitalized because he reports "ringing in his ears" and "appears acutely depressed," testifying that "I don't want to live. I can't be with people. My nerves are bad. I can't take it any more." Such statements are taken seriously because the man has undertaken two serious suicide attempts and is therefore possibly suicidal. Though he is retained in the hospital for two months, however, the inmate is discharged with the diagnosis "antisocial personality disorder." A week later he is assigned to a special program, where he spends the remainder of his term. Throughout this period the man vacillates between defining himself as an individual with problems and one who is mentally healthy. When he is denied temporary release consideration, for instance, based on his "history of mental instability" he writes that "I don't have a mental problem. I went to (the prison hospital) because I felt by me going to the hospital it would be a better atmosphere than prison." A month later he tries to hang himself with shoelaces and is treated in the prison psychiatric clinic, but thereafter protests that his suicide gesture was not a genuine attempt, "but that he just wanted to manipulate a relocation."

The inmate's living unit staff report that the inmate appears "slovenly dressed, withdrawn, childish, and usually resistant to most efforts to communicate with him, whether it be by staff or fellow inmates." In another report staff note that "he continues to look like a street urchin out of a Charles Dickens novel." Midway through the man's stay, staff write that

> he constantly sits in his own dream world waiting for time to pass. He shows no interest in anyone else, and by his disheveled appearance and lack of motivation has little interest in doing anything for himself. When confronted in a group he verbalizes his dream world of no problems when he is released. He is one of the more remarkable individuals (we have) encountered when it comes to blocking out the real world and the problems he will have to face. . . . He does as little as

possible to pass the day. . . . In the community he is the local hermit. . . . [He] spends the majority of time by himself in his room. Psychologically he appears to be somewhat depressed, but other than that he is nothing more than an extremely unmotivated, unrealistic individual. He . . . is probably as naive an individual as you can find.

Shortly before the inmate's release staff complain that "at five feet, six inches tall and probably 130 pounds dripping wet, he wants to be a professional football player," and conclude that "he does not possess the firmest of grasps upon reality and pursues his dreams probably as a way to avoid having to face the hard work and determination he will need to exhibit in order to remain on the street."

When we speak of people as "institutionalized" we think of an orientation that ties them to an inmate culture and its values. This man is "institutionalized" in a different sense. He is beaten down and incapable of functioning autonomously, and he regards institutional staff as arrangers of his environment and dispensers of services. He also feels that the button one must press to mobilize staff includes producing the appropriate self definition, which consists of the sort of problem or lack of problem that staff use as a criterion for dispensing services. This orientation is unfortunately overladen with the fact that the inmate feels beaten down, despondent, impotent and passive, devoid of hope, and occasionally anxious, which means that he does have a problem, though it is the sort of low-key problem which would qualify him as a classic neurotic if he was middle class. But in the prison this problem is not a pressing concern of mental health staff.

The reports that cover the later stages of the man's institutional history suggest that he has evolved a strategy for avoiding anxiety which consists of avoiding reality without resorting to a complete break. He ambles about the prison, spends long periods in the shower room, associates with others as little as he can, neglects his appearance and denies or ignores current or future problems. Of course he has no immediate problems, in the sense that the setting in which he resides permits him (reluctantly) to vegetate, but it is clear that as long as this man retains his way of adjusting to life he will feel that he must be permitted a passive and isolated existence, that no demands must be made on him, and that his needs must be provided for.

### Conditional Dependence

A pattern that is more extreme than chronic dependence is that of conditional dependence, in which the person's behavior becomes congenial or uncongenial depending on whether he is satisfied or dissatisfied with the quality of services he secures. The pattern is extreme on two counts: First, the person makes it obvious through expressed resentments that he regards dependency bids as demand bids, and feels entitled to get what he wants; and second, he redefines benefactors as tyrants when they do not comply with demands and conform with his expectations. The redefinition illustrates the double-edged nature of the dependence-autonomy issue, which makes persons in parental roles both desired and resented.

The attitude changes characteristic of the pattern are illustrated by a middle-aged inmate convicted of fraudulent use of stolen credit cards. The man starts his prison career with an incident of self-mutilation, but most of his other violations involve threats, abusive language, harassment, and occasionally assaults.

The inmate became a certified delinquent at age 13 and has a record of escaping from juvenile facilities. He (fraudulently) enlists in the navy at age 15, is court martialed at age 16 and spends a term in the stockade before he becomes a civilian at age 17 and embarks on a career of vagrancy, disturbing the peace, disorderly conduct, grand larceny, burglary, fraud, and forgery. The man serves time in youth institutions, jails, state prisons, institutions for defective delinquents, federal prisons, and mental hospitals. He is arrested for spending sprees involving stolen credit cards after raising suspicion because of munificent gratuities added to his restaurant bills.

Following his arrest the man is found mentally incompetent and sent to a hospital, escapes from a second hospital after he is found competent, is again found incompetent and is finally imprisoned after an unsuccessful insanity plea. He is at this juncture described as "a habitual criminal with extensive under-world involvements." The probation officer records that "the defendant impresses as having low average intelligence but is clever and manipulative," and writes that "the defendant can feign insanity at will" and that he is a "dangerous sociopath," who "during a recent prison interview initially appeared resentful of the intrusion, with his eyes popping frog-like out of his head, ultimately adopting an ingratiating stance."

The inmate succeeds in making an unfavorable personal impression on other professional staff. A psychiatrist describes him at age twenty-one as

an evasive, tricky, abusive, unreliable type who is verbose, untruthful, irritable, and defiant, with temper tantrums. Psychiatrically he is suspicious, argumentative, hostile, a definite chronic recidivist and alcoholic. He is a seriously disturbed psychopath who shows mental confusion and is markedly aggressive and assaultive. He has a cyclic personality which is severely warped and unstable. . . . [He is a] highly disturbed, unpredictable psychopath.

A first hospital commitment from the prison occurs at a time when commitment procedures are more relaxed than they are today. The commitment document describes the inmate's problem as

> he does not respond to discipline, impulsive, doesn't associate too well with other inmates. He is interested in only getting his own way. He is anti-social . . . cries readily, wrings hands. He states, "I need psychiatric help." Has a pathetic look to his face.

When the inmate arrives at the hospital his mother receives "a printed form in which she was requested to permit the administering of electric shock treatments." The inmate thereafter decides that he is not emotionally disturbed and his lawyer reports that during interviews "his speech was coherent, his reasoning logical, and his memory was excellent." The lawyer also reports that the inmate "has been at times confined with real lunatics who he says imagine themselves to be persons other than themselves" and records that an outside psychiatrist whom he has hired "advises that a continuance of such treatment could actually make the man insane."

The hospital staff defend the appropriateness of the inmate's commitment. The director of the institution writes that

> shortly following his admission he became very sullen, resentful, argumentative and litigious. He was under a great deal of tension and stated, "I can hardly control myself." He also expressed delusions of persecution, claiming that the correctional and psychiatric personnel with whom he came in contact were discriminating against him. He was also quite aggressive. During his hospital residence he has shown a great deal of hostility, was antagonistic and uncooperative. It has been necessary to place him in isolation at times. He also has a bad habit of teasing some of the other patients.

The inmate is discharged as recovered, however, and "continues to express ideas of a paranoid coloring, but not to a psychotic degree." Undaunted, he becomes a habitual client of psychiatrists in the prison. On one occasion he requests that the psychiatrist intercede to insure that his program assignment be left inviolate. On another occasion he requests the medication he received at the hospital, alleging that he suffers from "nightmares" and "feels tense and nervous." Later, the inmate arranges assignment to an invalid company. Despite this protective assignment he also manages to accumulate disciplinary violations. On one occasion he is charged with

> causing a disturbance by running naked on the flats of the north yard. There were about 1,100 inmates in the yard at the time. Your actions were also observed by employees in the administration building. Your actions could have

started a major disturbance in the yard. After you were apprehended by the correction officers you continued to drop your trousers in front of the yard inmates, causing further disturbance.

Before the inmate embarks on his last term of incarceration he throws a crutch at the judge during his trial (he now uses a crutch or cane) and continues to see a psychiatrist for medication he feels he needs to deal with depression and insomnia. He has a substantial physical disability but demonstrates that he retains considerable nuisance value. In one incident

the officer observed you having an apparent seizure. When placed in a wheelchair to be taken to the hospital clinic you stated to the officer, "we have our own A man. Stay the fuck off our gallery. Leave me the fuck alone, you son of a bitch." You repeated this several times before being taken from the block. . . . Due to the hospital staff being in the process of testing (inmates) for T.B. you were ordered to wait in the bullpen. You refused twice to leave and refused a third time when ordered by the sergeant. You then stated that you would return to the block. When the officer tried to push your wheelchair you grabbed the wheels and refused to move.

In another incident, one month later,

you requested from the officer emergency sick call forms. The forms were incomplete and when asked by the officer to complete them you started yelling, "Tell the officer to get me out of this fuckin' cell." The while striking the cell door with your cane, you continued yelling, "Get me out of this cell, you fucking asshole." When informed by the officer that you won't be seen by the medical staff until 9 a.m. you stated, "I know it's not your fault, it's that fucking officer. When I go to the hospital I'm going to hit the fucker with my stick." At approximately 9 a.m. on your way to the hospital you passed the console and said to the officer, "When I get back I'm going to give you a good reason to keeplock me."

The inmate has developed a propensity for threatening officers and for cursing them in vivid prose which becomes legendary in the prison. He also spends a great deal of time complaining that officers are indolent and do not adequately tend to his needs. He complains that officers assigned to his tier at nighttime are excessively noisy and interfere with his sleep. Staff conclude that the inmate's "ability to relate with staff appears to be marginal" and a counselor relays the consensus of prison personnel "that the subject behaves like a nasty cantankerous old man."

The prevailing impression that he has been imprisoned is not shared by the inmate, who regards closed institutions, in which he has spent most of his life, as multiple-service agencies, and rates them, as one does a hotel, for the quality of the service. He is a discriminating customer, insists on quality for money and becomes extremely resentful when service falls short of expectations.

The inmate expects mental health staff to furnish him with mood-modulating medication and placements in low-pressure settings. He expects custodial staff to efficiently supply transportation and logistical support and to cater to his physical needs. As for his mental condition, his diagnosis and status have changed so frequently and he has played so many roles that he finds it at times easy and at other times confusing to classify himself as ill or well and to act accordingly—particularly since his criterion of whether he is ill or well is the consequence of the status for the social welfare and quality of life it offers at the time.

## Defying Authority

A pattern that is familiar to prison authorities (as well as to school officials who deal with largely adolescent populations) is one of defiant resentment directed at persons who exercise quasi-parental authority. Persons who manifest this pattern are described as "having a chip on their shoulder," and sometimes as "troublemakers" who not only show defiance but who recruit others to resist direction and dictates of authority.

As indicated, one difficulty in reviewing this pattern lies in the need to distinguish legitimate resentment from illegitimate resentment, since only the latter qualifies as maladaptive, in the sense of being disproportionate and subjectively motivated. This especially matters because rebelliousness invites repression, which makes challenges of authority almost by definition self-destructive.

One clue to the maladaptiveness of defiance is the promiscuity and chronicity of the reaction. An illustrative case is that of a man serving a sentence for an armed robbery in which he steals a car. His disciplinary record is dense during the early years of his confinement and during a period mid-way in his sentence. Violations become infrequent later; there are no incidents in the last seven months of the sentence. All of the incidents involve conflicts with staff, and some have to do with riots, disturbances or strikes.

At intake the inmate impresses the interviewers as "a dull individual." He rapidly undergoes two transfers through no fault of his own, but the result is that he is removed from an academic program he feels he needs and is assigned to a job which he does not like. The inmate also ends up at a prison where, "because of his young age and small physical stature, he feels intimidated by other inmates in population." He is thereafter sent to a youth prison, but is almost immediately removed from this institution as "unsuitable" and "disruptive." He is then sent back to his first prison, where staff report that he "did not appear to be too upset regarding his return to this facility." This sentiment does not prevent the man's being transferred to another prison, which he decides he detests. A counselor who sees him for an unscheduled interview reports that

> he immediately began to complain about the facility, his assignment and his pay, demanding that he be transferred. On two or three previous occasions recently he has made similar complaints. . . . In today's interview he complained generally that his desires were not being met, stating that we are treating him "like all the rest of these niggers here." He insisted that he be transferred . . . when the counselor refused this request he became very arrogant and hostile. He stated that I should lock him in segregation before he "comes down on somebody."

The psychologist to whom the inmate is referred after this encounter describes him as "very uncooperative." He writes that the inmate

> is a contentious person who trusts absolutely no one. He claims everyone is watching him. . . . He is an extremely angry young man. He is isolated and somewhat paranoid. The prognosis for this man's future is that he will probably explode at a guard or another inmate with very little provocation. He needs psychotherapy, and quite soon.

Two months later the inmate explodes at his supervisors in his mess hall assignment. An officer involved at the inception of this incident reports,

> I asked the inmate to serve the bread to the population. The inmate then said, "go fuck yourself" etc., and stated that he would not serve the bread because "it gives him headaches." At this time a fellow inmate who was serving the butter offered to swap jobs to make the inmate happy. This they did. While watching behind the serving line I observed the inmate giving out large sums of butter (much more than allowed). I told the inmate to give out the proper portion and he again stated, "go fuck yourself," and stated that if I did not like it to serve it myself.

The sergeant supervising the mess hall subsequently reports:

> The mess hall officer came to me and told me he wanted the inmate locked up for passing out extra butter on the line and that he had told the officer to go fuck himself. I went to the inmate and asked him what he was doing giving out extra butter and talking to an officer that way. He said, "I told him to get out of my face." I told the inmate he was going to keeplock. He said that he wouldn't accept that, and walked out of the kitchen. . . . I walked over to the inmate and asked him why he was making it harder on himself. He said he wouldn't accept keeplock, that he wanted to go to the box (the segregation unit), where the men were. He went with no problem. When we got over to the unit he refused to bend over and spread his cheeks. He said it was against his religion.

In the segregation unit the inmate proclaims that he is going on a hunger strike. He indicates that he "is protesting his treatment here, stating that he 'will not be anybody's slave.' " The inmate reduces his food intake and "advised that he wished to be transferred out of the facility within five days, stating that he would not be alive beyond that time."

The man is indeed transferred, arriving back at his first prison, and almost immediately becomes involved in a group disturbance. At another inmate's direction, he (and four other men) "threw his lunch tray against the wall and then dumped his garbage back on the gallery floor . . . the inmates complained that the hamburger was cold at the noon meal. It was not."

Ten days later the man's possessions arrive, and while sorting them he "threatened that if any of his property was missing he would fuck up somebody and he didn't care if they wore green or blue. He also refused to sign a disbursement form and deposition of contraband form for property he is not allowed." After the incident the inmate requests "immediate transfer" but is not transferred. Instead he remains in the prison for another eight months, does well in his program assignments, and shows "improved behavioral adjustment."

At his next prison the inmate does well at work and has no disciplinary problems of consequence for several months, but at the end of this period is removed from the prison because he has become involved in "an unlawful assembly" as a member of a sect. It is reported that

> this unlawful assembly was preplanned and prearranged by the group, and their spokesman stated verbally that the assembly would be held. This direct confrontation was hoped to trigger off even a larger confrontation between employees and other ethnic factions that had been encouraged to join the affair. Fortunately, other inmates used better judgment and avoided the situation.

After the inmate is transferred he writes letters from his new location alleging that he is being threatened and discriminated against, and that his personal property has been impounded. Despite this campaign his custodial adjustment improves and he becomes eligible for an assignment to a less secure institution. Here he does well for a year, after which he is removed from his work assignment because he resists supervision. At this juncture it is noted that "his attitude and behavior has been deteriorating" and that he is "resistant to further work assignments." The standoff ends with the inmate demoted to a maximum security prison, where he objects to what he characterizes as "my mysterious transfer," and writes letters to state officials claiming that he is being subjected to dehumanization and discrimination, "perhaps because of my nationality, ethics, religious and cultural views of life.'' He also drafts appeals to the administration of the system requesting transfer to a prison closer to his home so that his wife, who has health problems, can visit him.

In the meantime the inmate does well in school and in program assignments until he decides that his transfer situation has become an emergency. To address this emergency he goes on another hunger strike which affects his performance. In response he is transferred and ends up at the prison where he started. In this institution he spends eight months without a single disciplinary incident and is released on parole.

When the man is at war with the prison system the battles he fights consist of escalating confrontations. There are two types of such confrontations. In one scenario the inmate functions as a loyal member of a religious group the leaders of which are committed to protest actions and confrontative tactics. The inmate's other campaign is more personal, and this campaign takes a variety of forms. One type of sequence unfolds when the inmate feels he is in an untenable position and has exhausted the procedural remedies for escaping from it. At such junctures he vigorously demands action and has evolved the original gambit of the hunger strike as a last resort. The man similarly engages in resistance when he finds supervision at work assignments overly oppressive. His resistance is passive, though in the early phase of his incarceration he often explodes and then follows up his explosions with other forms of protest to underline his grievance.

The man feels himself singled out and persecuted, which is not only congruent with his religious and political views but buttresses his sense of self-esteem because it implies that he is a political actor whose identity is taken seriously by a system to whom he has advertised his existence through letters and other forms of protest. He maintains his sanity by campaigning but also by settling down and conforming between acts of protest. His repeated transfers, however, make settling down difficult and the best he can do is to declare a truce whenever he is placed in a prison where he feels that the social milieu and opportunities conform to his requirements, and where social movements do not tempt him to join. Ironically the institution where the man finally settles down is the first prison in which he starts his stormy and cantankerous career, which raises the remote possibility that he might have adjusted to begin with if he had stayed put.

## Rejecting Constraints

Authority defiers illustrate the presence of live concerns about autonomy which in some cases are very reminiscent of adolescent crises. Developmentally related concerns become particularly explicit in situations that circumscribe, or that involve other persons instructing one to comply with demands. The issue in such instances is the premise that one cannot be told what to do and what not to do, and the underlying assumption is that an adult ought to be able to determine his own course of conduct. If his course of conduct has been questioned on a number of occasions the issue can become more serious, and those who object to this person's behavior cause him to react with increased resentment and bitterness.

An instance of this pattern is the career of a man serving the third of three prison terms for drug-related burglaries. The man commits many prison violations, which are mostly identical. In each case he refuses to obey instructions of an officer and punctuates his refusal with complaints, abusive language and threats which attract attention and thus create the possibility of a more widespread disturbance.

The man first arrives in prison convicted of a burglary and states that "he has been using drugs for seven years, using approximately $30. per day." The man also indicates that he has most recently supported himself "by gambling," which is an occupation he enjoys. The probation officer feels that the man is disarmingly honest in describing himself, and "seems to have a hopeless attitude about changing his life."

During his first prison stay the man accumulates a succession of violations which have a great deal in common. There are charges such as "inmate has to be woke up at least twice each morning and then he is still the last man off the gallery," and "the inmate stated he did not get up on the street and isn't going to change his ways here." There are also other conflicts with officers, such as "disobeying order to remove pasted pictures from cell wall," and

> the officers told him he wasn't entitled to commissary because he was confined to segregation. The inmate used profanity and threats directed toward the officer. He was told he would also be denied exercise due to his threats.

After one such altercation the inmate assaults an officer, and is transferred to a high-security prison. He is also occasionally referred to psychiatrists by the guards, once because they are concerned about his "acting up and destroying the contents of his cell," and on another occasion because he is pummelling a punching bag, "mumbling a name whenever he hit the bag." During this same period the inmate becomes involved in an art class, from which he is, however, removed because his behavior is "quite erratic" and because "he was becoming a negative influence on other students."

The inmate does well in other academic programs, though his "custodial adjustment remains marginal,'' a fact which is repeatedly discussed by the inmate and his counselor. The counselor writes:

> The resident admits having difficulties communicating with others and this seems to be at least a partial reason for his difficulties with the officers. Although he has a slight tendency to project responsibility for his actions he is aware of his overreaction to situations and has been willing to explore alternatives to this behavior. He is being seen on an ongoing basis to assist him regarding this.

The inmate is paroled and returns to prison, this time convicted of two burglaries. One of these is a spur of the moment affair prompted by the fact that the inmate encounters an open door while ''on his way to the coffee shop next door to have breakfast.'' A police officer intercepts the inmate with the stolen merchandise, and reports that ''when the defendant was arrested he said, 'You got me.' '' The second incident is less harmoniously resolved, and the inmate is charged with resisting arrest. According the probation officer,

> he states that he was using drugs at the time of this offense, was sick and needed money to buy narcotics. He states that he had been drinking as he could only afford to buy wine. He maintains that when he was apprehended by the arresting officer he was assaulted by the officer. He states that the officer stopped him and asked him what was in the box. He states he responded by telling the officer that it was none of his business. He maintains that at this point the officer shoved him. He states he tried to run but was caught. He states the officer then punched him.

The inmate reviews his prison experience with his probation officer and tells the officer that he was transferred between prisons ''after he had some difficulty with a guard,'' but that at the second prison he ''had no significant difficulties.'' He also tells the probation officer that ''approximately one week after he was released to the community he returned to abusing heroin, and eventually was using three to four bags daily.''

During this sentence the man's prison history is replicated, and one set of charges reads:

> At 7AM an officer awakened you for a count, at which time you told him he didn't have to wake you up in a nasty manner. At 8AM the officer returned to your cell and found you still in bed. He informed you it was time to get ready for your job assignment which was as a porter. At 8:30AM it was necessary to wake you up again. At 9AM you reported to your work assignment and stated to the officer, ''You don't have to wake me up at 7AM for no count. You are harassing me.'' When the officers gave you two copies of his Notice of Report you threw them out the door through the crack, and told the officer to ''Get the fuck away from my cell.'' After the officer ordered you keeplocked you started

yelling in front of other inmates who were standing around listening, "Go fuck yourself, you bastard." The officer has cautioned you previously about reporting to work at 8AM and not starting work until 9AM. . . . At 12:35PM when the officer went to feed you, you told him to stop pointing his finger at you and to stop looking at you like he wanted to hit you. You stated to him, "You want to do something about it, come on in my cell any time. I'll take you on, you punk."

The inmate is again transferred to a more substantial prison where he becomes involved in the art program, although he complains that the supplies are inadequate. His disciplinary behavior improves, and he tells his counselor that his problems in his last prison assignment were due to "a personality conflict with a correction officer," though he "does admit to having a poor temper at times, and in hindsight realizes that he could have handled the situation in a more mature manner." The counselor complains that the inmate "does not believe that drugs will be a problem for him in the future," which the counselor feels indicates "that he is not being realistic."

The counselor's assessment proves correct in that the inmate returns several months later, having committed another burglary. He again tells his probation officer "that he returned to drug usage soon after his release from jail, was using heroin intravenously, and drinking heavily when he could not afford drugs." The inmate also reports that he had been "trying to support himself by selling his paintings on the sidewalk," and points that "he specializes in seascapes in oils, and portraits in pastels."

During this sentence the man's difficulties begin in the reception center. The first report reads, "I counseled the inmate yesterday for sleeping through the 7AM count; today he again slept through my 7AM count." A week later another officer complains that the inmate "was sleeping during the 7AM count again. It seems with all the warnings that the inmate has received about this problem they are not helping." The next morning a report is filed which reads:

> the inmate slept through the 7AM count. I knocked on his door and gave him a special invitation to get up but he rolled over and returned to sleep. I have counseled him verbally on numerous occasions, and last week served him with an infraction slip for this very same offense. The inmate refused the Notice of Report.

Two hours later another report is filed which reads:

> While serving Notice of Report to the inmate for a previous offense, he became very abusive. He threw the notice back at me and said, "Take this fucking thing, you punk mother fucker. You mother fuckers are all punks. You better keep me locked in this fucking cell, you punk mother fucker. You are all just mother

fucking punks.'' The inmate kept babbling over and over these and other statements while he kicked and banged on the door of his cell. The inmate refused the Notice of Report.

The next day another report is filed which reads:

> While witnessing the sergeant counseling the inmate for a previous infraction slip, he became very loud and abusive, stating, ''Leave me in my fucking cell you asshole mother fuckers. All I want is to do time in my fucking cell.'' The sergeant ordered the inmate repeatedly to be seated and to stay quiet. The inmate insisted on causing a disturbance, repeating, ''All I want is to be left alone in my mother fucking cell. If you pig fuckers would leave me alone in my cell you could avoid a lot of trouble for yourselves. I was sent to do mother fucking time and I want to do it my way in my fucking cell. Can't you stupid asshole mother fuckers understand, in my cell?'' The inmate was immediately escorted to the Special Housing Unit and accommodated with a locked cell.

A report filed later on the same date reads:

> Upon escorting the above inmate to the Special Housing Unit he remained loud and abusive, stating, ''This bullshit ain't over yet. This fucking box ain't going to change a mother fucking thing. I still gotta do my time and I do my time the hard way.'' As we were waiting for the key to the SHU gate, inmates from another complex were on reception. The inmate took advantage of this opportunity and began shouting, ''We all gotta do something about this mother fucking joint. Us inmates are gonna start running this joint, you'll see, and any police who fuck with us is gonna get it.'' I ordered the inmate to cease his inciting behavior, as the other inmates were beginning to pay attention to his remarks. At this point the SHU gate was opened and the inmate was escorted to SHU without further altercation.

A similar set of events occurs several weeks later and culminates in an explosion directed at the adjustment committee. The report which describes this incident records that

> after reading charges to the inmate at the adjustment committee he started yelling at the lieutenant, saying, ''I'm not standing and putting my light on for the AM count for you and anybody else. I ain't putting up with this fucking shit. This court ain't fair anyway.'' The lieutenant gave the inmate a direct order to calm down and stop yelling, and also reminded the inmate of his whereabouts. The inmate yelled back at the lieutenant saying, ''I don't give a fuck. Put me in SHU.'' The inmate was then handcuffed and escorted to SHU.

The man ends his prison term with ''very good reports from his supervisors,'' and these reports stress that the man ''was very cooperative and did not need to be told to carry out his tasks.'' The inmate, however, also continues to be a discipline problem, and it is recorded that ''he has received numerous tickets for refusing direct orders." The counselor writes that the inmate "functions in structure, but only to a limited extent because he is abrupt and abrasive in his mannerisms. This has and will continue to be a problem for him both in the facility and in the community."

In some ways this man is a fatalist. He thinks he is predestined to be a drug user, though he occasionally toys with the notion of treatment. He also feels that he is not a morning person, and that it is unnatural for him to stand up and be counted at the crack of dawn in subservience to some arbitrary rule. He also feels that he has a "temper" which makes him understandably resistant to people in uniform who impolitely order him about.

Obeying the dictates of his nature, this man reacts with outrage when officers interfere with him trying to impose their will, and his outrage escalates when the same officers threaten him with sanctions for having expressed his justifiable resentments when imposed upon. The man feels particularly strongly that his cell is his castle and that doing time should mean that you can stay in your cell without interference until you are ready to face the day, and that, it being your cell, no one should have the right to intrude with wakeup calls that you have not placed.

Appeals to prison routine or regulations strike the man as irrelevant. Given this view he classifies exercises of authority as personal vendettas and views his confrontations with officers as "personality conflicts" or at worst as lapses in communication in which he might have reacted more politely, thereby reducing the possibility of escalation. In this connection, however, his fatalistic self-conception again enters the equation in the form of the "temper" which he feels adds unnecessary color to his language.

The man, in other words, views himself as floating on the tide of his compelling inclinations—which very much include inclinations he feels are less than admirable—and these lead him to drug use which leads him to crime which leads him to prison which leads him to conflicts with officers who are insufficiently understanding of the way he must do time if he is to be true to himself.

The man tells the probation officer who prepares his first presentence report, "ever since I can remember I didn't want to go to school." He also explains that he is responsible for having been barred from a racetrack where he has held an enjoyable job, and explains that he "received an undesirable discharge (from the military) for what he referred to as 'being irresponsible.' " The probation officer quotes the inmate as saying, "something must have gone wrong with me in the early stages of my life. . . . I need some type of treatment to overcome my addiction to drugs and to help me along with my inadequacy." The man remains philosophical about himself throughout his career, and increasingly accepts his "inade-quacy" as "built in," which means that not only must he live with his deficiences, but so must other people who deal with him.

## Rejecting Sanctions

Few experiences are as reminiscent of unwelcome connotations of childhood as the experience of being punished for transgressions. The issue is not merely that punishment is unwelcome, nor is it the presumption that punishments are unjust. A person may deny his culpability with respect to some of his transgressions as a matter of course, but such denials occur even where culpability is flagrant, and the denials are designed to salvage his pride. His concern is with the principle of being apprehended and taken to account when exercising his god-given right to do what he wants, which is an adult's presumed prerogative.

A person who exemplifies this pattern is a young man who is in prison for mugging a resident of a housing project in the elevator of his building. The man's disciplinary record is long and it lists a variety of infractions. A number of these are fights with other inmates but most have to do with nonconformity with prison routine compounded by lying, threats against officers and other hostile and defiant behavior, including physical assaults on custodial staff. Examples of chains of events that are recorded in the disciplinary file include:

> After being told not to go to class, the inmate went anyway. He refused to sit down and refused to leave when told to . . . insisted on returning to the class, and refused orders to sit on the bench and wait for his escort . . . Was belligerent and swore at the officer when the officer was escorting the inmate back to the block from the school.

> Inmate and officer bumped into each other by accident. The inmate got bellig-erent toward the officer, ripped his disposition sheet from the adjustment committee and threw it on the floor and refused to pick it up. He told another inmate he should have punched the officer in the face.

> The inmate was loitering in the hallway stopping to talk to other inmates. He was warned about this before. When given Notice of Report, the inmate said that it wasn't his. The officer had to make a call to confirm the name and number. It was his.

The inmate's record of arrests includes incidents in which he is charged with resisting arrest as well as other crimes. The first such incident occurs when the inmate is fifteen years old and the last immediately precedes his arrest. In this last incident the man is charged as follows:

Defendant did intentionally block pedestrian traffic and the entranceway to the lobby and did refuse to move when told to do so by the police officer. Defendant also became loud, using obscene language at the officer and did by said actions cause a large crowd to gather, which caused public alarm and annoyance. Furthermore the defendant did resist arrest as he pushed, shoved, and attempted to kick police officer and his brother officer. Necessary force had to be used to effect arrest.

Several months before, the man has been convicted of an assault. In this incident it is charged that

while in a public place he did become loud and boisterous, and when requested to disperse by the officer who was in uniform, did refuse to do so, and did punch the officer in the face, causing physical injury.

The man does not resist being arrested on his last offense but instead arranges for his parents to tell officers that he was not their son, which causes the officers to describe him as a "real wise ass." The probation officer characterizes him as having "a disregard for authority figures." He also records that the man had been discharged from the school system "as he kept getting into fights."

The man arrives at the prison reception center with a group of other inmates with whom he has had "a disagreement" in the jail, as a result of which he has been stabbed. His stay in reception is otherwise uneventful but in the prison to which he is assigned he immediately accumulates difficulties, one of which begins when the school librarian refers him to an officer assigned to the school for not having his identification card. The officer reports:

I asked the inmate where his I.D. card was and he said he forgot it. I told him he was going to get a ticket and asked him for his name and number. He turned away from the desk and started walking down the hall without answering me. I called to the inmate twice telling him to come back to the desk but both times he ignored me and kept on walking. I got up from the desk and went down the hall and stopped the inmate. I asked him who he thought he was that he didn't have to do what an officer told him to do. He then said "you can't talk to me like that. I'm not a kid. You should talk to me like a man." I then told the inmate to go back to the desk.

When we got back to the desk I called the chart office and asked for the area sergeant to be sent to the building. While waiting for the sergeant I again asked the inmate for his name and number and he said "I'm not going to give you my name until the sergeant gets here." The inmate started talking louder, saying "they want respect from us, but don't give us any. Treat us like kids instead of men. Give us tickets for nothing and then they want respect." I told the inmate to quiet down and sit down at the desk. The inmate refused to sit down and said to me "I'm going to write you up. If you are going to write me up, I'm going to write you up. If you're going to harass me, I'm going to harass you. I want your name and number. What's your name and number?'' I gave the inmate a piece of paper to write down my name and told him that I don't have a number.

Two weeks after this incident a search of the inmate's locker uncovers a pail containing three gallons of homemade wine, which sends the inmate back to the segregation tier. Here it is charged that

during your confinement in the detention unit you forcibly removed the baseboard molding and began beating the radiators in your room. You then refused to comply with the officer's order to stop doing this. When given a second order you still refused to comply.

One consequence of this incident is that the inmate is placed on restrictions, which he ignores. The driver of a bus who takes him on a subrosa expedition to the gymnasium discovers that he is an illegal migrant and reports:

When I called back to him he yelled ''those (blank) idiots don't know anything.'' He continued ranting and raving and I finally checked his pass. He had the wrong one and got off the bus saying ''you're all assholes and none of you know what you're talking about.'' When he came back on the bus I asked to see his I.D., he kept walking to the rear of the bus saying ''I don't have one.'' I asked him for his I.D. number, he again replied ''I don't have one.'' After the bus started moving he approached me saying that the correction officers in the gym were harassing him and he was not on any restriction. Upon checking this out I discovered he was lying to me. Throughout the bus trip to his unit he continued to complain that these ''police were no good'' and ''the prison was a white prison.'' After dropping him off at his housing unit I again asked him to get his I.D. and bring it out to me. I held up the bus and waited for his return, and he never came back out.

The prison's experience with the inmate leads to frantic requests that he be transferred to a more secure prison. The inmate joins in this campaign. An example of his contribution occurs after he has been locked up and demands to be let out of his cell because ''he is an epileptic and couldn't stay in the cell because it is too stuffy.'' When officers insist (after consulting a nurse) that there is no connection between the man's alleged epileptic condition and his condition of confinement he embarks on a string of obscenities and threatens to destroy his cell, receives a disciplinary report and tears it up, and ''said he put in a transfer to go back upstate three weeks ago and that maybe now 'they'll transfer me so I won't have to deal with suck ass police like you.' ''

The man is transferred to a maximum-security facility where he continues his involvement in disciplinary incidents. In the most serious of these incidents

> the inmate was arguing with an unknown inmate and refused orders to return to the block. The inmate became insolent and struck the officer in the chest with both his hands, pushing him through the bath house door. The inmate then again struck the officer. He returned to the block where the officer found him carrying a broom and threatening the officer with it. When ordered to place his hands on the cell bars for a pat frisk, the inmate turned and swung his fist striking the officer in the shoulder. Force had to be used to subdue him.

This is by far the most blatant incident in this man's checkered career. It is an exception to the man's usual routine which involves lying, cursing, and threatening but does not include the sort of physical resistance he displays when he is faced with impending arrest in the community.

This man acts the part of a bull, with the world as his china shop. In the community he engages in property offenses and feels wounded and victimized when the police, representing the victims (to whose fate he is oblivious) place him under arrest. In the prison the man feels that he ought to be permitted to do whatever he feels like doing. When he is caught transgressing he feels that his transgression should be ignored or that his self-exonerating lies should be accepted or that he should be able to walk away from the situation in which his transgression has come to light.

He takes all enforcement acts personally. While officers, including custodial officers, like to think of their uniforms as relevant to their functions and feel that personal involvement is irrelevant, this man takes the opposite view and interprets every enforcement act as a very personal putdown in which the enforcer plays an illegitimate paternal role and relegates him to the role of a child, which is an affront to his status as an adult male. The game becomes chronic because the man's disregard for anything except his own inclinations places him at risk, in the sense of inviting instructions and recriminations which he finds demeaning. He goes through life with his hands in every cookie jar and cannot tolerate the parental stance of those whose job it is to protect the cookies.

There is a cognitive and a motivational component to this orientation. The man cannot understand why police officers do not let him escape and why prison guards do not play along with his lies because these officials should realize that they will inconvenience him, which no one has a right to do. He simultaneously explodes with rage when he discovers that authorities can impose their will on him, which he equates with aspersions cast on his status as an adult autonomous male whose claims and actions are not subject to review.

## Notes

1. The diagnostic category that describes this behavior in children is that of "Oppositional Disorder." Part of the DSM (III)'s definition reads as follows: "The essential feature is a pattern of disobedient, negativistic, and provocative opposition to authority figures . . . the oppositional attitude is toward family members, particularly the parents, and toward teachers. The most striking feature is the persistence of the oppositional attitude even when it is destructive to the interests and well-being of the child or adolescent. For example, if there is a rule, it is usually violated; if a suggestion is made, the individual is against it; if asked to do something, the individual refuses or becomes argumentative; if asked to refrain from an act, the child or adolescent feels obliged to carry it out. The behavior may, in fact, deprive the individual of productive activity and pleasurable relationships. . . . If the individual is thwarted, temper tantrums are likely. These children or adolescents use negativism, stubbornness, dawdling, procrastination, and passive resistance to external authority.

   Usually the individual does not regard himself or herself as "oppositional," but sees the problem as arising from other people, who are making unreasonable demands. The disorder generally causes more distress to those around him or her than to the person himself or herself." American Psychiatric Association (1980), pp. 63–64 (chapter 6, note 1).
2. D. McGregor, *The Human Side of Enterprise*, New York: McGraw Hill, 1960; D. McGregor "Conditions of effective leadership in industrial organization" (1944), in T. M. Newcomb, E. L. Hartley, *et. al.*, eds., *Readings in Social Psychology*, New York: Holt and Company, 1947; C. Argyris, *Personality and Organization*, New York: Harper and Row, 1957.
3. H. Toch, *Living in Prison: The Ecology of Survival*, New York: Free Press, 1977, pp. 97–122.
4. McGregor (1960); Argyris (1957) note 2, supra.
5. T. Szasz, *The Myth of Mental Illness: Foundations of a Theory of Personal Conduct*, New York: Harper and Row, 1961; T. Szasz, *The Ethics of Psychoanalysis; The Theory and Method of Autonomous Psychotherapy*, New York: Basic Books, 1965.

# 9

# Seeking Refuge

To effectively cope you must first face the problem with which you want to cope, so that you can decide what to do about it. Reacting to challenges by running from them is a dereliction of appraisal, which is the first step in coping.[1] It can also be socially disapproved of behavior, and in some settings, such as prisons, it can be a transgression of rules that prescribe participation.

One reason why retreat from any life situation is maladaptive is that it leads to further retreat, in that the process of giving up reinforces a sense of failure and lowers self-esteem. This relationship is one that we have elsewhere described as a stress-enhancing cycle, which we have summarized as follows:

(1) Past successes and failures in dealing with life situations enhance or reduce our capacity to respond to stress and to master stress-related problems.
(2) Our successes and failures reflect our level of coping skills and the confidence we have in our coping skills. The latter variable is our self-confidence or "self-esteem."
(3) Successes in coping cement our coping skills and build our self-esteem—the confidence we have in our coping skills.
(4) Being disabled by stress reduces our self-esteem and our future capacity to cope.
(5) Mastering stress enhances our self-esteem and our future capacity to cope.
(6) Limited coping skills and low self-esteem tend to be self-perpetuating; so are successful coping skills and high self-esteem.
(7) Interventions that help people cope with stress help to break the failure/low self-esteem cycle.[2]

The dictum that prisons are stressful may be overstated in some respects (for example, prisons provide social services), but it cannot be overestimated in other respects. The most obvious prison stressor is that elements of the peer culture that surround the inmate can pose threats to him if he is susceptible to intimidation. This threat is tangible because—in male prisons, at least—fear is equated with "weakness," and "weakness" earns contempt and invites aggression. Predation is selectively aimed at those who are already intimidated and furthers their maladaptation. It means that men whose self-confidence, resilience and social skills are most limited are put to the heaviest tests, because they are most heavily subjected to harassment. Given this paradox, two results can be expected: (1) self-defined targets often retreat in anticipation of problems with their peers, or (2) such targets may react clumsily and contribute to escalation of their problems, and then retreat.

Though retreat and self-stigmatization are not synonymous, a request for sanctuary advertises an inability to handle situations which other persons (those who do not require sanctuary) can manage unassisted. The initiative places one in a dependant (almost mendicant) role with respect to providers of protection, and also implies a contemptuous (passively resistant) posture vis-à-vis those who value—or demand—participation. The combined effect is that one acquires nuisance value to authorities and becomes an object of disdain to peers who place a premium on personal resilience.

A typical career of a refuge seeker is that of a man who commits a burglary while he is on parole following imprisonment for a previous burglary. In prison the man is a nuisance offender. He frequently is not where he is supposed to be but he has also played his radio loudly in violation of rules and has been involved in fights.

The man first enters prison at age eighteen explaining that he has "committed burglaries for money to buy marijuana, which he feels should be legalized." He also claims "that his drinking problem served to accelerate his periods of wrongdoing."

The man encounters difficulties immediately upon entering the system. He is referred to a psychiatrist because he "seemed very disheveled and anxious" and reminisces about "having problems with other residents in the county jail." These problems do not lie behind him, and the psychiatrist finds that "he still appeared somewhat depressed, mainly in response to the treatment he received from other inmates, who often bully him." Counselors record that the inmate is "unable to cope with the daily pressures from his peers." He is also "considered immature" and is "counseled regarding his being 'bulldozed' by the more aggressive inmates."

The man is charitably assigned to a low-security camp, and is delighted with this assignment. Upon arrival he seemed rather comfortable with the camp placement and had to be restrained from breaking into light conversation with the (counselor). He does seem to have a high opinion of himself and his needs but probably not a commensurate amount of guts to back this up among his peers. This could make him an easy and satisfying target in camp for abuse.

The inmate gets to be a disciplinary problem despite his initial favorable reaction. He has to be transferred to a youth prison, and here he is raped at knifepoint by two fellow inmates. This experience leaves the man traumatized, but he is not sufficiently afraid to deter him from committing another burglary while on parole.

The inmate attributes his involvements to injudicious imbibing of alcohol. He ends up assigned to a substantial prison for intake classification, and immediately seeks protection, reporting that two other inmates have threatened to rape him. He is still in protection three months later, demanding transfer because he is "in constant fear of attacks and even death," and because he thinks he would like to become involved in an educational program. He has also mobilized his lawyer, who writes to the prison that "I implore you to do what you can before it is too late." The staff meanwhile describe the inmate as "a quiet and unassuming individual who stays in his cell most of the time and has very little to do with those who house in his area." They also record that the inmate "is somewhat slow, and seems naive in his interpersonal interactions. He is also oversensitive about sexual attacks, and these factors only exacerbate the problem."

The inmate is transferred to a lower security prison, but here becomes involved in disciplinary incidents. He attributes these to personal problems and is dealt with leniently and offered tranquilizing medication. However, he continues to disrupt prison routine and is sent to another low-security setting, where he is discovered involved in narcotics traffic. He is then transferred to a youth prison where he signs himself into protection after other inmates steal his possessions and threaten to do him "bodily harm." A similar fate befalls him in his next prison, where he is again threatened for sexual favors and placed in protective custody.

The inmate's security level is downgraded at the medium-security institution to which he is assigned. His new counselor notes that "he has had many disciplinary reports in various facilities during his present period of incarceration," but the inmate reports that he feels tense and apprehensive and requests "medication for my nerves through the day." The counselor gives the man a lecture on self-control which appears to raise his self-confidence, and for a while the inmate does well and reports no difficulties. He earns a high school diploma and is assigned to a college program. He also receives a large check in settlement of a civil suit arising from his prison rape and this check is promptly stolen from him by another inmate. This incident leads to another stay in protective segregation because the man has named a fellow inmate as a likely suspect. Thereafter his disciplinary record is again described as "deteriorating" and as "horrendous." Supervisors classify the inmate as "lazy" and the parole board declines to release him because he has made no effort to become involved in alcohol- or drug-related therapy.

Ultimately the man is transferred to a regular prison. Here he immediately requests protection because he sees himself surrounded by enemies whom he recognizes from a previous sojourn. In protection he "seems to have no problems with either staff or the inmate peer group," though he writes letters to the administration complaining about cockroaches and making unwelcome suggestions about needed improvement of conditions in the unit.

The man is transferred to another protection company, where he is adjudged "conforming" and "cooperative" and rated as demonstrating "favorable overall adjustment." However, he also becomes an informant in a stabbing incident, thereby adding new names to his roster of enemies. He must again be transferred, but he is eventually paroled.

The parole board complains about the man's failure to participate in alcohol-treatment programs, and this misgiving proves appropriate because he shortly returns to prison after committing burglaries which are preceded by the wholesale consumption of alcohol. The parole officer adds that the man had been "diagnosed as an alcohol dependent in remission" but that he "did not continue counseling and abstain from alcohol." This time the inmate "acknowledges a need for alcohol abuse counseling"in prison. Classification staff also conclude that he "should be seen as vulnerable."

Up to this point, the man has reacted to difficulties in his life by seeking refuge in intoxication. Many of his activities are designed to support his addiction which also provides him (as he sees it) with exoneration and exculpation. The man's self-image is otherwise passive, and he sees himself as lightly wafting on the breezes that impinge on him. In detention the breezes become turbulent because as a young unsophisticated addict he exudes an air of helplessness, dreaminess, nervousness, and he is therefore a ready-made victim in settings where the criterion of vulnerability is susceptibility to intimidation. The situation lends itself to escalation because the more the inmate is threatened the more nervous, intimidated and helpless he becomes. His fate is sealed through an extremely traumatic experience which leaves him in a perpetual state of fear in which he is primed for panic given the slightest cues of danger. These cues are mostly available where the inmate is quartered with more sophisticated peers. This leaves the man free to circulate only in the lowest pressure prison environments. In these environments, however, he gravitates in search of drugs or of associates in the addict culture except for one period when he is temporarily distracted by involvement in educational pursuits.

The man's lackadaisical pattern and his meandering about in low-security settings continuously force the system to upgrade his security classification, which returns the man to settings in which his panic button is easily pressed and where he must seek sanctuary in segregation cells. During moments of panic the man also feels that it is incumbent on him to identify the objects of his fear, which leaves him with the double stigma of being seen as a victim-prone informer.

The most mystifying feature of the man's pattern is the fact that despite the disproportionate pain and suffering he experiences in prisons, he continuously arranges for himself to be reincarcerated. One must either conclude that he is masochistic and that he enjoys his role of nervous sanctuary seeker or that his memory is blunted and his time perspective infinitessimally short or that his addiction, his need for chemical anesthesia, is overwhelming and preponderant. The best explanation probably comprises all three of these themes.

### Catch 22

One problem with a retreat strategy is that it requires making tradeoffs, in that a person not only separates himself from sources of danger and challenges, but from sources of rewards and satisfactions. Protective settings are circumscribing, in that they restrict a person's physical movement and increase the level of supervision to which he is subjected. While he is completely consumed with fear, such penalties may seem inconsequential, but with the passage of time, the circumscriptions he has earned as corollaries of refuge seeking may acquire unwelcome salience.

Some refuge seekers conclude that certain retreat options are preferable to others, depending on the level of amenities they offer, and the extent of the tradeoffs they require. The result of a tradeoff calculus may be a mixed pattern of conduct, featuring alternating demands for retreat and release from retreat, or leading to a commute between sanctuaries that variously meet personal specifications.

A case in point is that of a man convicted of bail jumping after he fails to appear in court to answer other charges. In prison the man is repeatedly caught in compromising positions with other inmates, and his sexual proclivities also color other offenses such as "had a shirt on that had been modified into a feminine garment" and "contraband—nail polish." The man is also involved in fights and commits violations reminiscent of his bail-jumping offense, such as "has been continually late for his assignment at the tailor shop since he got the job, which then necessitates an escort to bring him up," and "was not with his company when they returned, and was found in the commissary."

This inmate first arrives in prison convicted of a robbery in which "dressed as a woman he followed (a man) into the bathroom, pushed him to the ground, punched him and took his wallet with money in it." By this time the inmate has accumulated a record of convictions for soliciting and female impersonation, shoplifting, indecent dress, disorderly conduct and similar offenses. In the last offense for which the man is convicted it is charged that he "allegedly stole a pair of earrings from a display and did, with his fists, strike a police officer."

Probation staff speculate that "the defendant's father, [who] was an alcoholic, exerted a negative influence on the defendant" and they also note that "his IQ had been measured at 72." The man has been a homosexual since age sixteen, has been using drugs since age fourteen and is an epileptic. He "is a confirmed homosexual and transvestite, and feels more comfortable dressed in women's clothes (and) has had hormone injections in order to cause his breasts to mature and to make his buttocks more rounded and feminine." According to probation officers, "apparently he supported himself by shoplifting and by being a male prostitute. For the most part [he] dresses in women's clothing and considers himself to be female."

Not surprisingly, the inmate encounters difficulties when he arrives in prison, and he spends much time in protective custody. A typical interview in which he requests protection reads:

> He states he is in fear of his life. He is unable or unwilling to name names. He states that on several occasions he has come back to his cell and found notes on his bed which were unsigned. These notes stated in various forms that if he were caught in the right place he would be, as he put it, "iced." The inmate also states that on one occasion when he was on his bed some unidentified inmate threw scalding water on him.

The man's enemies mostly are individuals whose sexual advances he rejects, and there are many such individuals because the man "displays seductive non-verbal communication." The man also has difficulties with staff. He claims that "I'm being totally discriminated against because of what I am," and problems arise because staff refuse his requests to move into a housing area "to be around an inmate that we grew up together with." The man insists, over staff protests, on signing himself out of protective segregation despite warnings "that there were several inmates in population who were very protective and jealous of him." Problems do in fact arise, including a stabbing involving two rivals for the inmate's affections, and he has to return to protection after one inmate tells him he will kill him since "he was doing 'life' and had nothing to lose."

Soon the inmate is released and returns to a career of arrests for disorderly conduct, prostitution, theft and criminal possession of stolen property. The charge on which he jumps bail involves a robbery "perpetrated against an 80 year-old woman who was knocked down (by the inmate) and her pocketbook was taken from her person forcibly (and who) suffered a broken hip and was hospitalized for several weeks (after which time) she needed constant help in getting about, and physical care." The robbery charge is dismissed when the inmate is indicted on bail-jumping charges.

The man arrives in prison having experienced difficulties in jail where "another male inmate attempted to assault him" and he "indicates that he is interested in studying beautician courses." However, his IQ is now measured at 55, suggesting "a potential within the mental defective range," and staff find that "his attention span is very low." Staff also point out that "his overt homosexuality is manifested by his frequent flirtatious advances toward the general population" suggesting that the inmate "needs supervision in a structured environment."

The man is assigned to a program for victim-prone inmates, where his programming goal is listed as "dealing appropriately with sexuality in a prison setting, and academic training." Staff write:

> When this resident arrived he presented himself as a very insecure individual who was constantly seeking support from correction officers and counselors and other correctional staff. . . . The resident, although still quite insecure, has lessened his dependence and need for verbal support by correctional personnel. Although there have been gains since his arrival, the resident's overall program functioning could still be considered slightly below average. It is, therefore, felt at this time (that the) resident would best benefit by continued participation.

Despite this recommendation the inmate is transferred out of the unit, accumulates disciplinary reports "for everything from fighting to homosexual acts," which leads to the conclusion that he "will be unable to function in the mainstream of population in any facility." Soon thereafter the inmate is released from prison but his parole is violated when he is "found in possession of stolen credit cards." Classification staff report that

> the inmate was admitted to protective custody after stating he was being harassed for homosexual favors. . . . The inmate's situation, as in the past, is

complicated by his flirtations and overt activities which has always and will always cause him problems. As in the past he remains a management problem requiring a lot of attention and professional supervision. These needs will probably never change and he will require a significant amount of staff time with little or no return. The long term problem will really be how long this inmate can continue his lifestyle before severe psychiatric/psychological problems consume him. This may conceivably occur when he is sentenced as a predicate/ career criminal felony offender. Up to now the courts have indeed been lenient.

As a short-time solution the man is assigned to a victim-prone unit which comes closest to offering him some possibilities of short-term adjustment without the need for twenty-three-hour-a-day segregation. Long-term solutions, however, are unachievable given the man's insistence on a lifestyle which outside the prison invites arrests and in the prison promotes conflict. The man not only seeks homosexual partners that are congenial to him but seeks to derive profit from sexual encounters, and rejects partners who do not fit his prescriptions. Some of the aspirants for his affections, however, are predatory individuals who back strongly motivated overtures with threats of force that require the inmate to fight uneven battles or to retreat into settings in which he finds insufficient social stimulation.

Staff—particularly during the man's first sentence—are caught in his dilemma because they are responsible for assuring his physical safety. They thereby incur his displeasure because the man finds the sanctuaries that staff offer excessively confining, and therefore punitive. Throughout this inmate's career, however, experiments which increase his degrees of freedom also increase the problems which he generates. Such problems are not only a product of the man's flirtatiousness but also of the fact that his extracurricular activities are his vocation. The exclusivity of this orientation includes the disregard of such inconsequentials as court appearances and prison schedules, and this is one source of problems. Another is the fact that this man, who is viewed by many as a sex object, in turn views others as objects and (given his intellectual limitations) does not profit from experiences that suggest, among other things, that he has left the minor leagues of crime and is facing repeated long-term incarceration if he does not change his pattern of conduct.

### Sheep's Clothing

A person's resilience or "bargaining position" may vary with the setting in which he operates, which means that a person who can meet the challenges posed by one social setting may find himself disadvantaged in another social group. A person may also react with one type of coping deficit in one setting and show a different style of maladaptation in another.

A dramatic transformation occurs among some men who act as manipulators or become predators when they are surrounded by persons weaker than they are, but who see themselves as victims and seek refuge when their peer group contains stronger persons. Such men appear to be sheep among wolves, but are in fact sheep in wolves' clothing, and become wolves in sheeps' clothing in other milieus. In each setting these men resonate to power and exploitation, but the role they play with respect to these themes may vary.

A case in point is that of child molester, whose prison record consists of many inconsequential violations. The record lists offenses such as "suspicion of fighting," "did not turn in sheets," "refused to go to work," "wore civilian shirt to chow," "attempted to mail out a library book," "sleeping after mess callout," "ironing another inmate's pants," "sleeping in room while restricted from going into the room in the daytime," "did not have I.D. card with him," "refused to leave area of officer's desk," "unclean person," and "failed to attend regular gym class."

The inmate has been convicted of fondling a seven-year-old girl, which he freely admits to the police after waiving his rights. When he is asked, "Why did you give us this statement?" he answers, "Because you asked me to tell you what happened today with (the victim)." After a prior incident the man is referred to a mental health clinic as a condition of probation. He there reports (and later denies) that he has had sexual intercourse with his sister, who suffers from mental retardation. The man's mother is also retarded and he does not get along with his father, who reportedly "beat him all the time with his belt from age five to eighteen."

Prior to arriving in prison the man spends considerable time in the jail where he is "raped homosexually" by other inmates. When he arrives in prison rumors about his child-molesting offense spread in the inmate population, as a result of which he is severely beaten and placed in protective segregation. Prison intake analysts recommend that he "be placed in a less populated institution where he can receive the needed psychotherapy," and also report that he "scored in the mental defective range of the full (intelligence) scale."

The man is sent to a medium-security institution, where he is struck in the face by an inmate who objects to his crime. He also complains that "I am harassed in the mess hall at all meals. I don't feel safe anywhere now. It will be worse now that I told you who hit me. I need protection." The man is permitted to remain segregated for weeks and is medicated for depression and anxiety, and when he recovers he is assigned to a therapeutic community program. In their first report about the inmate, staff write

He began his involvement with individual therapy and recreational therapy. It was readily apparent that he did not possess the necessary coping skills required to make it in prison, especially in light of the nature of his present offense. In addition, because of his borderline mental retardation, his ability to function in the program was initially questionable. . . . He is quite immature and requires a great deal of attention. In striving for the attention, though, he is often quite ill prepared for some of the heavy stuff that goes along with it.

As an example of the "heavy stuff" referred to, the inmate complains that he is the object of sexual advances and of extortion efforts and that he is being beaten by other inmates, but investigation reveals that

he has tried to be "slick" by running to several inmates with some "bullshit" stirring things up and then playing dumb. He has also been involved in selling and/or exchanging articles with other inmates. While involving himself in these activities he thinks he is pretty sharp. However, more times than not the weight eventually falls back on him. In fact, as a result of his "games" he found himself in a bad position, and since he could no longer handle the pressures that went along with the games he requested protective custody under the guise of being sexually harassed by another inmate in his dorm. . . . His prognosis is poor, but where else would his behavior be tolerated?

After the inmate has spent a year in the program, staff write that "he has shown virtually no growth, nor has he given any indication that he really comprehends his behavior," although "the members of his therapy group, inmate counselors, and staff have devoted a great deal of time and energy into trying to get him to understand his behavior as it relates to his crime as well as his negative nonproductive behavior while incarcerated." The inmate is described as offering "the minimum degree of participation in order to avoid hassles," and there is a suggestion that the man's nonparticipation may be a blessing, given that "he'll give 'tough guy' responses, making a fool of himself when he participates."

Custodially the inmate accumulates difficulties as a result of the number of infractions he commits and their redundancy. He is repeatedly charged with entering the rooms of other inmates, though he has been admonished for violations of the same kind. He also occasionally threatens the officers who serve him with reports. In one such sequence, he is charged as follows:

Following the incident you were advised that you would receive a report of misbehavior as a result, and you then stated to another officer that you were going to take care of the officer who wrote you up. When questioned you said you would catch him unaware and take him off the count. When you appeared before the adjustment committee you admitted the threat and stated at that time that you were making plans on how you were going to do it and that you intended to get these officers.

Program staff write that the inmate "seems to be digging himself further and further into a hole. . . . It was almost as if he was deliberately putting himself in the jackpot." Staff also write that

> most of the other men are totally discouraged in their efforts to help this inmate. Nothing seems to sink into his head. This is perhaps because he rarely listens to what is being said, and why should he when he already has very concrete responses to offer?

A recurrent difficulty experienced by the inmate is that he tries to manipulate more sophisticated inmates and that these efforts "usually turn disastrous for him." However, the inmate mostly appears unaware of his difficulties, and in fact "is not concerned about the possible problems he may encounter when returned to general population confinement resulting from his interactions with other inmates, despite the efforts of group members on this topic."

The inmate solves part of his problem by gravitating toward peers who do not outclass him. Program staff describe this pattern in a report filed late in the man's sentence. They write:

> He associates solely with a group of individuals who have similar crimes and are viewed by staff and everyone else for that matter as immature, weak, manipulative and victim-prone to aggressive homosexuals. The constant conflicts within this group of individuals and with those inmates trying to take advantage of them produces the need for frequent interventions by staff to resolve these problems. Usually right in the middle of these conflicts is our subject. Despite being labeled as weak when compared with the majority of inmates within his group of associates he is seen as the manipulator and orchestrator of many of their conflicts.

The inmate extends his catalytic activities to staff and writes a letter to prison officials complaining about an officer who he alleges has subjected him to a systematic beating. In a report about the inmate, program staff write that he is "manipulative and mendacious in his relations with fellow inmates and staff." They deduce that he "sees the world as a very frightening place where he must scratch out a survival through any means available before or to avoid being taken advantage of." Elsewhere they speculate that the man "sees the world as a very frightening place where the strong take advantage of the weak," which means that the man will "take advantage of those who are weaker than himself, which is a basic description of his present crime."

The other side of the coin is that the man accumulates considerable experience as one of the "weak" who are taken advantage of in the community—where he is beaten by an alcoholic father—and in detention, where he is raped and assaulted. But the man does not define himself as resourceless because he does not see himself as weak and therefore does not draw the inferences one would expect from a lifetime of victimization experiences. In fact, the man even turns victimization experiences to advantage by claiming that he is victimized when he is not, so as to arrange for himself to be extricated from delicate inter-personal transactions. Mostly, the man draws the surprising inference that is described by his therapists, which is that there must be others weaker than himself whom he can victimize. In this connection the man is mostly wrong, including in his assessment of seven-year-old children who describe his overtures (in considerable detail) to their parents.

The limitations of intellect described for this man prominently center on his failure to digest the debacles he arranges for himself. This includes the disquieting redundancy of his disciplinary violations, which adjustment committees classify as stubborn recalcitrance. Beyond this penchant for redundant self-destructiveness lies the suspicion that the man may be unconsciously identifying with the aggressors of this world, whom he sees as the only show in town. The man frustrates his would-be therapists who want to uncover the ugliness of the victimization game (very much including child molesting) because he can conceive of no other game and can adduce a lifetime of documentation for his position. His own goal becomes one of making sure that he does not consistently lose the game, which is the only game he knows, and this means that he occasionally must play some other role than that of victim. Unfortunately, of course, he makes a very unconvincing aggressor, and as a manipulator he is a disaster.

### Having One's Bluff Called

Transformations of maladaptive strategies can result where the failure of one strategy requires recourse to another. One such juncture occurs where a stance of defiance or of toughness is tested against social reality, and the person who has billed himself as pugnacious or rebellious encounters determined opposition and find that he must seek refuge to escape it. Where this kind of transformation occurs one plausible inference is that the person's stance has all along been a facade designed to disguise a substratum of insecurity, or is a means of overcompensating where the person feels inadequate or afraid.

An example of the pattern is provided by a man who snatches a woman's purse after punching her in the neck. For this offense the mans spends a short time in prison during which he has fights, threatens and harasses correction officers, and distinguishes himself for use of loud and obscene language.

At the time he is arrested the man is a client of a counseling program and tells his probation officer that the counseling "had been helpful regarding a problem he had with fighting" and "that he had problems in the jail because others wanted to fight and he doesn't."

At prison entry the man's IQ is registered at 80, and intake analysts write that

the inmate was basically cooperative and tries very hard to make a favorable impression but appears to be very emotionally immature, easily influenced by others and shows little motivation to change his lifestyle. He can display a hostile attitude, desires his own way whenever possible, (and) finds constructive criticism hard to accept.

The man is assigned to a youth prison, where he accumulates sixteen misbehavior reports in three months, many for disobeying orders. In a sample incident he is charged as follows:

At approximately 5:10 AM you were told several times by a correction officer to stop talking from your gate and remove yourself from the gate. You ignored his orders by constantly talking louder. . . . You consistently yelled obscenities at the officer ("fuck you, you can't tell me what to do")—and (proclaimed) that you are not afraid of the officers or the lieutenant. Along with this you kept saying, "All I want is a superintendent's proceeding."

Institution staff conclude that the inmate's attitude toward authority is that of a juvenile who "will not admit he could be wrong. He is very defiant, blames others for his actions, says he will not change, and is willing to do his time." They test the inmate's resolve by changing his living assignment to "give him a chance to be away from the officers who he claims do not get along with him," but this strategy does not improve the man's deportment.

Eventually the inmate is released and commits two robberies—both involving female pedestrians—three months after he leaves prison. He explains that "he obtained his spending money by robbing women" and boasts that he "smoked marijuana as often as he could get the money to buy."

When the man reenters the prison, an interviewer notes scratch marks on his left forearm, which he "indicates was an attempt by him to change housing locations while incarcerated at the jail." The man is thereafter sent to a low-security facility, which soon demands that he be transferred because "he is very aggressive, constantly challenging authority, (and) this behavior can't be tolerated in our dormitory setting." In an incident of the kind referred to, the inmate shouts at another inmate who is taking a shower and then refuses to leave the bathroom, saying, "fuck you, I don't have to" and inviting the officer to a sexual encounter. He later writes a letter insisting that his transfer is unfair because he is not in fact "a ballbuster." The following week, however, prison staff report that the man "had in his possession a fifteen-inch metal rod which was sharpened to a point." While serving a segregation sentence for this offense the inmate is again written up for "talking through the window in the keep-lock yard," and gets into further difficulties when a search of his cell uncovers "what appeared to be a firebomb" and, three days later, "a metal rod approximately 18 inches long with one end sharpened to a point and the handle taped."

Subsequently the man is involved in two fights and requests protective custody after officers have concluded that a weapon and a fire in the inmate's cell "were a setup" engineered by enemies, who by this time have multiplied.

The man is transferred to still another prison, where he participates in a behavior modification therapy program. His behavior does improve but he must again be protected because fellow inmates attack him in the yard, inflicting "facial bruises and lacerations." Thereafter the man is classified as "victim prone," though he now "gets along well with staff" and is "respectful of rules." The man's disciplinary record becomes exemplary, except for an incident in which he is apprehended in sexual contact with another inmate, which is interpreted as illustrative of his susceptibility to victimization.

This inmate enters the system as a very young man of anti-social disposition. Vis-à-vis authority he takes a stance of adolescent rebelliousness, and he resents circumscriptions of his autonomy. He also does a lot of loud, aggressive and demonstrative socializing, which occasionally degenerates into fighting given that he wants to project the image of a tough young man who can handle himself in conflicts. Unfortunately building this image includes having weapons (which is probably routine for this man in the community.) He also does not project his image convincingly, and his problems with both authority figures and peers soon force him to discontinue his effort to project an image of toughness, particularly in a nonadolescent population in which men see through his facade and discover that he is a very young, very vulnerable and very inadequate person whose intellectual limitations make him socially inept and consequently susceptible to intimidation. The change in the man's status in this peer hierarchy changes his stance toward staff, whom he now regards as benevolent protectors, and who reciprocate by treating him with solicitude.

## Turned Tables

Other transformations occur where predatory propensities boomerang and the bully or predator must seek refuge because his bullying or predation has backfired. A combination of antisocial dispositions and maladroitness may provoke retaliatory reactions, and the person may view these repercussions as unprovoked threats. The person may eventually come to present himself as perennial victim, ignoring all contributions he has made to instigating his fate.

An example of this pattern is a man who serves a prison sentence for rape. His career is very stormy. He becomes involved in fights, which include attacks on other inmates with urine, water and more conventional weapons. He also threatens officers, and there are entries such as "threatens officer with obscene names," "threatened officer because he was not allowed to enter auditorium," and "when instructed to remove clothing from bars he threatened me and didn't move anything." In addition, he resists authority in more passive ways, and is charged with such actions as "refused to leave kitchen area when told to because he wasn't doing any work at the time," "refused to go to shop," "refused to return to area when ordered by officer," "refused to break when ordered," and "did not lock in properly when returning from school program."

In the description of the inmate's arrest it is reported that "he stated, 'You got the right guy who did it.' At this the detective asked, 'Did what?' and he replied, 'Raped those women.' " The presumption is that the man has been involved in several rapes, and he has in fact been convicted previously (in another state) of "assault with intent to ravish."

One of the first problems the man encounters in prison is that he meets the husband of one of his rape victims. Authorities reassign him to protect him, placing him in a special program from which he demands to be removed, claiming that he does not need therapy and that the unit "is causing me trouble with the other inmates." The man does not need anyone's help, as it happens, in engendering "trouble." One inmate who has a fight with him, for instance, reports:

> He called me a snitch during the community meeting. Later he opened his pants and told me to suck his dick and he said he was going to fuck my mom. I went up to him by his cube and told him to shut his fucking mouth: "I don't want to hear you say that again." He said, "Come on, punk" and took a swing at me. I ducked and swung back at him. The officer yelled, "Break" and I stopped, and he hit me in the eye.

There is a suggestion that the man goes out of his way to promote such encounters. It is reported that

> during a community meeting he stated to everyone (50 inmates, 8 staff person- nel) that he would "cut" anyone and he didn't care who he hurt. The same day he was involved in a fight with an inmate causing physical harm to the inmate. It is suggested that a sharp instrument, possibly a razor blade, was used by him to cause injuries to the other inmate. He stated on numerous occasions that he would do anything to get out of the program including hurting people.

The man not only attacks other inmates but also promotes incidents with prison personnel. One officer reports that:

> I was threatened on the gallery by the inmate. The inmate said, "I'm gonna get you. I'm gonna kill your fag ass. That's a promise." He then stated, "I got all the weapons I need to do it right here in my cell." At this point the inmate quickly flashed a metal object at me. I ordered him to give it to me and he refused. . . . The inmate's cell was frisked and one metal can crushed and formed into a weapon was removed.

Another officer reports:

> While feeding up the keeplock inmates. . . . The inmate said to me when I gave him his tray, "Why are you giving me that tray?" I then told him there was no special reason. The inmate then yelled, "Ya, I bet you, fucking fag." I then told him he just got a misbehavior report. He just said, "Good, give me one, you fucking fag. I'll make sure I get you when I get out of this cell."

The staff of the special program reciprocate the inmate's feelings about the program. In one report, staff writes:

> Although he is twenty-six years old chronologically he impresses as one to be about twelve years old mentally, which is stretching things. Although there is no hard evidence to prove homosexual tendencies, it has been rumored that he indeed made efforts to overpower weaker members of the community for sexual purposes. This writer has not been able to ascertain any feelings of remorse for past deeds committed by the inmate either while in or out of correctional facilities. The inmate has not benefitted from the therapeutic environment nor does it seem likely that he will do so if he were to remain. Since he has been one of the more disruptive participants it is felt that he should be transferred at this time.

The inmate is demoted to the introductory segment of the program, where staff write:

No matter how many times he is told something it is guaranteed that two days later he will again bring up the same question. The subject has received an inordinate amount of individual attention since being returned to phase one and the results are simply nil . . . He is demanding, childish and aggressive toward weaker inmates. It is the writer's opinion that the subject lacks sufficient capacity to understand the complexities of relating to people or to adjust successfully to different situations. . . . His former therapist has been directed to submit a transfer. Wherever the subject is transferred he should be kept in a controlled environment.

In his next prison the inmate continues to assault other inmates and to threaten staff. In one incident, for example, "the inmate had a choke hold on (another inmate) and they were separated with great difficulty." On another occasion it is reported that "the inmate caused a disturbance in the kitchen when told to put back sugar he had stolen from the line, and several times refused to obey an order to go to his cell, all the while verbally abusing and threatening the officer."

The inmate's counselor writes that he "has indicated to the writer that he finds it difficult to adjust at the facility" and "has many enemies here" and a transfer is therefore requested and effected.

In his next institution the man requests protective custody, claiming that difficulties have developed between himself and a gang to which he formerly belonged (the Five Per Centers), and that a representative of this group "is trying to establish a reputation" by assassinating him. After the inmate is released from protection an investigation shows that he is threatening other inmates, however, spreading rumors about inmates and experiencing repercussions. The investigating sergeant reports:

(One inmate) stated that the inmate keeps telling other inmates on the gallery that he is a fag and also that (another inmate) is his homo. I also received word from (a third inmate) that the inmate wants commissary for homosexual favors from him or he will stab him. . . . He has threatened several inmates and officers (and I) believe he extorts or tries to extort other inmates on a regular basis.

Several days later the inmate receives an anonymous note which tells him that "you might as well as pack your shit up, punk, because you will be leaving tomorrow" and he becomes apprehensive. An officer reports:

He said he wanted to leave the company and he wanted to leave now. I told him I would call the sergeant. When I left to use the phone, the inmate broke his sink and toilet.

The inmate is later moved and stages another demonstration, pointing out that "he had told the officers to move him because his cell was flooded."

He is transferred to another prison where he spends time in protection, and is returned to disciplinary segregation after he becomes involved in a fight in which he takes an officer's baton and swings the baton, striking the officer in the shoulder. Three months later he is released to the community but is returned as a conditional release violator to be retained to his maximum expiration date. He promptly demands protection; He claims that the entire membership of his former gang is pursuing him because "the word got out that he snitched on them." He reports that "they have been pointing fingers at him and he knows they will be coming after him." He also indicates that "he asked his paint shop teacher to lock him up for refusing program in order to get out of population."

The last entry in the file reports another incident in which

> During (my) rounds the inmate asked to speak to a sergeant. I informed the inmate he could speak to a sergeant when he comes on the unit. Approximately at 7:40 A.M. the inmate started breaking up his cell, throwing his metal locker against the bars and all walls. The inmate also broke the sink off the wall into several pieces.

The disciplinary committee notes that the inmate has admitted his actions and "seems to feel his request to see the sergeant did in itself justify his behavior." The committee adds that the inmate "refused to sign his admission of guilt and also refused to sign a disbursement request to cover the cost of the property destroyed by himself."

The fact that the inmate "seems to feel his request to see the sergeant did in itself justify his behavior" is representative and symptomatic of his perspective. The man feels he is entitled to announce that he will use violence and is justified in systematically deploying violence to get what he wants, especially from persons who are susceptible to intimidation, such as women and nonaggressive peers. Ironically prison staff fit into the vulnerable category because (1) constraints under which they labor make it impossible for them to call the man's bluff and (2) staff must maintain safe prisons, which means that they must remove individuals who are sources of problems from one prison and transfer them to another. The second fact is particularly germane to this man, because it means that he can extricate himself from difficulties he engenders by staging demonstrations of violence which force staff to get him out of corners while preserving his self-image. He sees himself as an individual who is not to be trifled with and wants to be viewed as an aggressor (which is manly) rather than as a victim (which is unmanly). The same view permeates the man's homosexual encounters in which, given the fact that he is an intimidator and aggressor, he can argue he is staging demonstrations of manliness, which makes his prison homosexual involvement and his rapes equivalent.

One fly in the ointment is that the man on occasion misdiagnoses his victims or underrates their support and now knows himself, or thinks himself, in danger, an issue to which he is extrasensitive given his familiarity with threat and violence. At junctures such as these he is not above informing on his enemies and invoking staff as protectors, but he can redeem his ego by breaking up his cell when pleas for sanctuary are not promptly attended to. This means that the man can define himself as a practitioner of violence even when he is engaged in ignominious flight or in search of protection.

Violence for this man is a tool which the strong use against the weak to secure compliance. What the man must struggle with is that he himself is susceptible to intimidation. A formula he has evolved is that he can use violence to extricate himself from the threat of violence, which, given his primitive view of the world, means that he is still being effective, meaning that he has done a lot of hollering over his shoulder as he retreats from the scene.

### Earned Rejection

Deficient social skills can translate into victimization because of the unpopularity a person can garner by subjecting others to unwanted attentions. In patterns of this kind refuge-seeking is a corollary of aversive impact rather than a social disposition. The person involved usually is well-inclined, and may in fact seek friendship or other positive reactions from peers when he earns their threatening responses. A transformation occurs, however, in that the person who unsuccessfully tries to negotiate a social milieu must then retreat from the setting and seek self-insulation.

An inmate who illustrates this pattern is seventeen years old when he arrives in prison with an unusual offense. The police have come upon him sitting in a stolen car and then chase him through the island of Manhattan, in the process of which he runs over a citizen crossing a road and seriously injures the man.

At intake into prison the inmate is described as intellectually and educationally deprived as well as emotionally unstable. The evaluation form records that "he admits attempting suicide several times while at the detention facility, claims he was sodomized there and preferred charges;" officially the man's jail status is "under close observation with suicidal precautions."

The inmate soon finds himself in protective segregation. It develops, according to a counselor, that he made the serious mistake of revealing the good fortune of an accident settlement. His "friends" have offered him their services as body guards and "what have you" for the "nominal" figure of a $100 weekly. When he expressed disinterest and disdain for their extortion, he alleges he was threatened by "his friends" that he "better comply or else."

The classifier records the impression that the inmate "is a dolt. He doesn't know 'come here, from sic em' and has a big mouth and ingratiating personality, all of which is capped by gross immaturity." This assessment leads the counselor to the conclusion that the inmate "can't function in population, and in essence just can't function. Some form of protection is therefore recommended.

It develops that the inmate cannot even cope with socially disadvantaged inmates in the protection program and he bitterly requests a transfer, a request which the staff enthusiastically endorse. In the next prison the man again requests protection, reporting that his fellow inmates

began to pressure him for goods. He refused to give in, and so these other inmates began to spread the word that he was a homo and also made threats on his life.

The staff find that there have been no real attempts at extortion nor threats, and they refuse to put the inmate in protection. Subsequently, however, staff change their minds after the man has a fight in which he attacks a would-be extortionist. He explains to the officers that

the white guys want nothing to do with me. They won't let me on the court or hang out with them because I have let this guy get over on me and I haven't done anything about it.

Unfortunately, the inmate chooses the mess hall for his preemptive fight, which from the staff's point of view is the worst place in the prison for a demonstration match to be staged because of the presence of three hundred excitable spectators. In the next transfer request staff note that the inmate is an "extremely immature and irresponsible individual who by his actions is capable of causing serious problems between himself and other inmates," and they write that the inmate not only cannot manage in general population but "of late cannot interact with the others assigned to the protection company." A later entry shows that the inmate has been successfully pressured by his fellow inmates, who have expropriated his tape player and other possessions.

There follow a series of incidents that involve correction officers. One officer accuses the inmate of having said that he was "going to cut up if I didn't get a sergeant and bring (him) to observation.'' The officer charges the inmate as follows:

> The officer stated that observation was filled up, and you then grabbed your razor blade and told the officer that you were going to cut up. The officer ordered you to put your razor blade back into your locker. You refused to comply with this order and pulled your razor down your left arm two or three times. The officer ordered you several times to stop and you refused to comply with the orders. You then took the razor handle and began digging at the cut attempting to make it bleed.

The inmate becomes desperate with his situation and with the pressures exerted on him. Having failed to secure escape from his dilemma by injuring his arm, he tries other measures such as kicking his door, throwing his food on the floor of his cell and in the hallway, and throwing toilet paper into the hallway. He also wrecks his cell and spits on passing officers, testifying that "I had to get off the tier because I was being harassed. So much pressure on me, and my life was threatened." The inmate claims that the porters are harassing him and that a fellow inmate whom he attacked has been threatening him. He next arrives in another facility where he is in a rage because he is taken to the hospital and reacts by attacking a nurse and making a scene. He also complains that he is systematically harassed by officers.

This inmate invites victimization, not only by what he is, but also by what he does. He makes enemies of even relatively weak peers, and antagonizes staff with a combination of excessive dependency and of refusal to comply with the protective measures they take. He oscillates between demands that he be protected and demands that he be extricated from protective settings. These demands are punctuated by dramatic gestures such as self-injury and destruction of physical surroundings because he lacks the ability to make his communications convincing, given his lack of verbal skills and social graces. The most extreme problem the man has is that he does not show his anxiety directly but manifests it in either fight or flight terms. The very offense for which he is in prison consists of a blind flight from a police encounter. The consequence of this flight is an example of the corners he gets into both in prison and in life outside the prison through clumsy maladaptive behavior which leads to equally clumsy retreats.

### Stress Avoidance

A special case of refuge seeking is the desire to experience less social stimulation and to seek relief in isolated settings. The issue here is not to escape danger but to diminish the pressures of ordinary living. The person seeks refuge from the physical presence of people because he does not know how to respond to them, or because he finds social situations painful because they are overwhelming and confusing to him. The person may experience fear, but fear is apprehension of people in general rather than of individuals who are concrete sources of danger.

A man who exemplifies this pattern serves a sentence for burglarizing the business of a former employer. His most serious prison infraction centers on the manufacture of wine, but his most frequent difficulties involve attempts at self-mutilation.

One factor that shortens this inmate's career is the fact that he serves as a police informant and supplies "information which has resulted in three misdemeanor convictions and one felony conviction." Otherwise the man does not do well. He ends his educational career after he "dropped three of his subjects and failed the other two that he was carrying," and his military career lasts for two weeks, after which he is discharged as "unable to adapt to military life." He also reports that he "has experimented with various drugs, and has used alcohol, sometimes heavily, and was drinking quite heavily on the night of his offense."

When the man arrives in prison he quickly incurs charges of self-mutilation, abusive language and refusing to go to chow. He explains his self-injury attempt by saying that "he was upset by pressure other inmates were giving him." He is consequently transferred to a lower security institution, where a search of his cell yields a large amount of yeast, two eggs, sugar, and assorted containers (a large jar, a pitcher and a cup) that smell of "home brew." The offense is aggravated, in that the inmate has stolen the ingredients for his concoction from the institutional bakery where he is employed. He does not deny this transgression reporting that "I was making the booze for myself and friends, mostly friends."

The man is involved in repeated self-destructive acts and is sent to an institution where mental health services are available. He stays for a while in the mental health unit, refuses to enter population and "after much discussion requested protective custody and wished to remain there until his parole release." These wishes are respected, given the "various suicide attempts whenever he has been placed in the general population," but two days later the inmate has "self inflicted lacerations to the abdominal area" which he explains by reporting, "I was depressed so I cut my stomach."

The man has sharply limited coping skills and even more limited self-confidence, and he takes the path of least resistance which includes stealing from his employers, informing on his crime partners, dropping out of school, quitting the military as soon as he joined it and resorting to chemical anesthesia as a form of escape.

The man is not ready to face the adversities of prison or any other setting and resorts to self-mutilation to signify that he is disinterested in meeting the challenges. Even the lowest pressure settings (including a minimum-security institution and a mental health unit) prove inadequate to the task of cementing the man's self-confidence. He retreats to protective isolation, but even this experience is overwhelming to the man, whose term of incarceration mercifully ends three weeks after he declares bankruptcy by larcerating his stomach. His capacity to manage outside the prison, of course, is in serious question.

### Notes

1. Coping has been defined as a process which is initiated by the appraisal of a problem and ends with an adaptive response; this view—which is sometimes called "transactional"—is the most satisfactorily comprehensive perspective in the stress-adaptation literature. See R. S. Lazarus, *Psychological Stress and the Coping Process*. New York: McGraw-Hill, 1966.
2. H. Toch, "Studying and reducing stress," in R. Johnson and H. Toch eds., *The Pains of Imprisonment*. Beverly Hills, Ca.: Sage, 1982, p. 37.

# 10

# Maintaining Sanity

Few questions are as difficult to resolve as those involved in defining the relationship between maladaptive behavior and mental disorders. Some critics assert that "mental disorder" is simply a concept we sometimes invoke to describe extreme maladaptiveness. By posing the issue in this way, the critics cast suspicion on the process of clinical diagnosis, whereby we define who is mentally ill and who is not. The critics imply that labelling persons "mentally ill" permits us to highlight behavior we find annoying, which provides justification for intrusive interventions. The same critics often argue, however, that diagnoses pinpoint conduct we wish to exculpate, because the concept of mental illness implies that behavior is nonvolitional.[1]

These risks are real, but there are probably comparable risks to *not* invoking diagnoses where one can invoke them, because this can deprive someone of services that are earmarked for persons who are diagnosed as disturbed, which are frequently unavailable to others. Moreover, where maladaptive conduct is not viewed as disturbed it is often viewed as malevolently intentioned, and can be dealt with punitively, as it is by the disciplinary process of the prison.

Another concern the labelling formula does not address is the nature of facts that are attended to when we adjudge conduct to be maladaptive or disturbed. Maladaptiveness denotes unsuccessful coping. If the term mental disorder is attached to extreme forms of maladaptiveness, one infers that a person who is classed as disturbed must be unable to cope with life problems. However, many people who cannot cope with life are not diagnosed as disturbed. Moreover the line-drawing process is more complicated, in that the facts that are used to arrive at diagnoses—which are called "symptoms"—are variegated, and some have nothing to do with how well the person adjusts to his environment. Though it is true that some of the attributes called symptoms are behavior patterns, others are psychological processes, and even physiological indices. And though diagnoses currently highlight behavioral attributes, this fact is a mixed blessing because the same trends deemphasize speculations about the dynamics of behavior. The prevailing concern is with increasing the reliability of diagnoses by relying on as much tangible evidence as one can describe. We can thus better answer what questions, but we are less able to deal with the questions how? and why?[2] In other words, the concern that is most crucial in our thinking about maladaptation (what is the person trying to accomplish, and how does he run into trouble?) is not the core concern of diagnosticians.

None of these issues have mattered to us thus far, because we have been dealing with maladaptive patterns which are not predominately characteristic of persons who are diagnosed as disturbed. Where persons whose maladaptive behavior we have discussed have also been diagnosed as disturbed, we have treated these sets of facts as independent. By ignoring the matter of whether the person had been formally diagnosed we did not mean to imply that diagnoses were irrelevant, but we did imply that we felt we could describe, and to a certain extent explain, the person's maladaptive behavior without raising the issue of his pathology.

The strategy becomes more difficult where the careers we review are of chronic mental patients who spend long periods in hospitals, and whose diagnosed pathology is an obvious and salient fact. In the case of such men it would be foolish to talk of maladaptive behavior without considering the person's diagnosed mental disorder. By the same token, we must make sure that our descriptions are not redundant, that is, not another way of summarizing the information that is used by diagnosticians.

If our subjects were confined hospital patients we might have difficulty circumventing redundancy, because patients' behavior in hospitals is inventoried in terms of whether it conforms to or deviates from symptoms of pathology, and the degree of maladaptiveness is equated with degree of pathology. Prisons, fortunately, use an independent criterion of adaptiveness which is that of conformity to the prison and its rules, and this criterion is fairly dispassionately applied to the behavior of disturbed inmates while they live in the prison. This means that we can raise *some* questions about the maladaptiveness of disturbed inmates that are not redundant, and these have to do with difficulties the person has in negotiating his environment (the prison), as perceived by those who run the environment.

In relation to the issue of mental illness, we shall assume for better or worse that diagnoses are valid (or mostly valid) and that the persons we shall describe are disturbed during portions of their career. Given this assumption, we can expect that disordered persons will encounter difficulties in relating to their environment which have some connection with their disorder. We could ask, How does maladaptive behavior make the person disturbed? but that is really an issue of diagnosis. Instead, we pose the reverse of the question, which is, How does the person, by virtue of the fact that he is disturbed, maladaptively relate to the setting in which he lives (which is the prison), and to the people who surround him (who happen to be inmates and prison staff)?

Since the prison has specific attributes, the answer to the question, How is the disturbed person's behavior maladaptive? will not apply in detail elsewhere, such as in street settings where most homeless patients reside. However, there are equivalent questions that can be posed for other living environments to help illuminate different links between mental disturbance and disruptive or maladaptive behavior.

### Flight: Escaping Reality

The distinction that stress researchers have drawn between coping efforts and fight-flight reactions describes some salient difficulties that many disturbed persons demonstrate in negotiating the world.[3] This is so because many disturbed persons find the world that surrounds them painful and hostile, inhospitable and strange, or at best irrelevant. They often feel that to the extent to which they respond to external demands and stimuli these will evoke unpleasant thoughts and feelings, or will upset some delicate internal balance on which sanity or survival depends. This sense of being threatened by external stimulation and the panic that perceived threats evoke inspires radical solutions, which include substituting a private, self-generated "reality" for stimuli one seeks to avoid. The result of this stance often appears as a refusal to participate in the "real world" as defined by those who inhabit it. As the disturbed person is then seen by others, he is self-insulating and uncommunicative, insistant on vegetating, and unwilling to care for himself. The picture is incomplete, however, in that the disturbed person may not be dead to the world but may live a fantasy life in which private connotations (often threatening connotations) are assigned to people around him.

An example is provided by an inmate who is serving a long sentence for rape and robbery. The man's disciplinary record is sparse in the first few years of his sentence and again in the last three years of his prison career. In the middle period, where a fair number of incidents occur, most violations have to do with offenses such as failure to wake up, refusing to work, not having a light on for the count, not coming out of the cell, and other offenses of omission.

The man's first psychiatric examination at age twelve results in a diagnosis of "adolescent maladjustment with rebellious reactions; neurotic traits with schizoid personality." Two years later the diagnosis has deescalated to "passive aggressive personality with neurotic reactions," and at the time of the man's offense psychiatrists feel that he is a "hedonistic malingerer who tries to create an impression of mental instability." In prison the man's symptoms are taken more seriously, however, and we find him committed to the hospital diagnosed as a schizophrenic after he has created a disturbance by laughing loudly to himself, being unclean and refusing to shower, becoming withdrawn and preoccupied, and claiming that he does not mind the fact that everybody in the world is against him. Subsequent hospital stays are scattered over the next few years, and do not register improvements in the situation.

In prison the man refuses medication, deals with his hallucinations by plugging his ears with chewing gum, claims he is perfectly healthy, and says that he has caused the hospital to be closed up. He also refuses to eat, which requires that he be recommitted to the hospital. Years later he is still being shuttled between prison and hospital, still claims that there is nothing wrong with him, reports that "he stayed so long in the hospital because he wanted to finish the Webster's Encyclopedia," and describes his hallucinations as a matter of his debating with himself.

It is during this period, mid-way in his stay, that the man develops problems in prisons, where he gets written up for disregarding various rules and regulations, mostly having to do with the fact that he wants to spend his time in his cell, does not want to participate in programs, and wants nothing to do with other aspects of institutional life. An entry reads:

> This counselor is unsure as to whether to treat him as a disciplinary case or as an inmate with an ongoing mental problem. He has been referred to the [mental health] unit, but they appear to be unable to help him at the present time with his condition. In all likelihood he will be assigned to the limited privileges program in the near future and will probably be content to remain in his cell, where he will be less of a problem to the security personnel.

There follow two commitments in quick succession, but the following year we find the inmate examined by the parole board, manifesting psychotic symptoms during the interview. In a commitment document shortly thereafter the inmate is described as hallucinating, as having disregarded his personal appearance and claiming that he is being poisoned. Psychiatrists report that "his suspiciousness extends to medication." The inmate's final commitment to the hospital occurs shortly before his release.

Though the man's psychotic disorder has become unavoidably obvious to prison authorities, the inmate himself would prefer to see himself as an eccentric scholar who periodically inspects hospital conditions and keeps himself from being poisoned by rejecting medication (and occasionally, food) in the prison. The man largely becomes eligible for classification as a disruptive inmate when he is more or less in remission, at which time his disruptiveness consists of demanding that he be left alone with his private ruminations.

The man's disciplinary record represents a period within which he experiences more protracted stays in the prison, and the incidents are almost entirely a product of his effort to insulate himself from his surroundings. In other words, he is being written up by officers for wanting to function as a vegetable in his cell. The extremity of the pattern is inferable from the fact that the man finds it painful to get out of his bed in the morning, turn on the light and have breakfast. Only the availability of a dark, quiet cell with room service would obviate most of these disciplinary involvements.

### Flight-Fight

Though disturbed persons may struggle determinedly to maintain a precarious equilibrium by withdrawing from the world, they rarely achieve anything approximating peace of mind. The most dramatic crisis points occur where flight reactions are punctuated by periodic or sporadic explosions, which may include attacks on other persons or self-directed injuries. Such behavior is motivated by fear and suspicion, by frustration, self-hate and pent-up tension, and often includes the conviction that the person is being persecuted by others in his environment.

An example of the pattern is provided by a young man serving a prison sentence for holding up two hamburger concessions, a spree which nets ten dollars. The majority of the man's disciplinary violations involve refusing to do things. Three months after he arrives in prison, there is an entry which reads "inmate refused to come out of his cell to go to work in the mess hall." The following month the man is repeatedly charged with refusing to turn on his cell light when officers need to see him during the inmate count. Two weeks later a charge reads, "the inmate refused to come out of his cell for his mandatory shower."

One week begins with the notation that "the inmate refused to come out of his cell to go to mandatory breakfast," which is followed (on the same date) with the entry "the inmate refused to come out of his cell to go to mandatory noon meal." The next day an entry reads "the inmate did not come out of his cell for his shower." There are many charges of a similar kind, such as "the inmate refused to do his work assignment and was found sleeping instead of working," "the inmate appeared very dirty and stunk and refused orders to clean his cell and take a shower," "during the live count (the inmate) refuses to acknowledge the officer," "the inmate was not awake for the morning bell" and "he refused to attend an adjustment committee panel."

There are incidents which have a tantrumlike flavor. One entry records that the man "broke his cell chair and threatened to kill anyone who came near him"; another notation describes the inmate "disrupting other inmates making phone calls by swearing and using obscene gestures and slamming down the phone," and a third notation records that "the inmate threw his tray into the inmates' serving line in the mess hall." In a series of related incidents the inmate attacks people who are connected with serving meals. These include behavior such as:

An officer observed you throwing your food tray at an unidentified inmate porter,

The inmate threw his ration of meat at the meat server and threw his tray at the mess hall worker,

and

he attempted to grab the inmate who was delivering food trays, stating that someone was trying to poison him and he was going to kill someone.

These are other entries which describe assaults, including one which refers to the inmate attacking a fellow inmate with a saw, one which describes him hitting another inmate with a broom, and a third in which he throws a bucket of water into a neighboring inmate's cell. The man also threatens officers on a number of occasions and once attempts to escape from prison.

The inmate describes conflicts with fellow inmates in prison as reactions to condescending treatment. After one of the occasions in which he throws trays at mess hall workers, he explains that "he (the worker) was talking to me like a homo so I threw a tray at him. I told him to get out of my face." He similarly explains difficulties with correction officers as resulting from the fact that the officers hold him in low esteem and persecute him. As to his refusals to participate in institutional inventory taking, he provides conflicting explanations. He points out that "he has been sleeping covered up for years" and proclaims that he has no recollection of having been told to keep his head uncovered. He also "claims he can't hear anything while he is sleeping."

Officers conclude that "the inmate appears to like keeplock status so he can lay in his cell" and the inmate sadly informs them that "there is nothing they can do for him as he would never get paroled and is only looking forward to his conditional release." This prediction proves accurate. The man is discharged on his conditional release date, fails to make his first report to the parole office and "two days later was arrested in the process of robbing a bank."

After returning to prison the man is described as "very uncooperative." He cannot be classified because he "continually refused to cooperate with custodial, medical and program staff." Later, staff record that "he has received a violation when he refused to comply with facility regulations and delayed the count by not complying with orders to uncover himself in bed."

Soon the man's mental condition again becomes a subject of concern. He is referred to mental health staff who record that:

> He admitted to hearing voices which occasionally tell him to do self destructive things. He indicated that he hears voices rather constantly, but they only bother him periodically.

The inmate is diagnosed as suffering from a "schizoaffective disorder" and mental health staff indicate that they "would like him to behave in a non-paranoid manner" and that they aspire to "the goal of having him clean and neat at all times." The inmate is introduced to a regime of therapy as well as medication and staff report that he "participated actively, deriving a certain amount of insight." Three months later they note that

> at the present time he is working in industry. He has adjusted satisfactorily, getting good reports. He seems to display no bizarre behavior on the gallery. He follows procedures as a clean and well groomed inmate and has many acquaintances.

The inmate is discharged into the general prison population where he becomes enmeshed in disciplinary incidents, including an explosion of rage in which he throws a glass jar at someone whose identity remains unclear, since his aim is poor.

Though this man tries hard to offer explanations for his aberrant behavior, his versions of incidents (except where he admits he is afraid that his food is poisoned) do not account for the redundancy and specialization of his offenses. One infers that this man's disruptiveness has something to do with efforts he makes to keep very unpleasant and fear-arousing feelings and urges in check. The man does this partly by insulating himself and staying asleep as long as he can while he views those around him with suspicion. His suspicions particularly focus on those who can tamper with his food, though on occasions he regards other persons as sources of physical danger or as irritants.

The man's efforts involve trying to "shut off" the criminal justice system in the shape of the presentence investigator and the prison intake personnel. He fails, however, and after this juncture things come to a head and he experiences hallucinations. Later, a tolerant program seems to help the inmate to regroup, but this program graduates him into a situation for which he appears insufficiently prepared, and the cycle starts afresh.

### Fight Patterns (1)

*Paranoid Aggression*

Violence that is associated with emotional problems is particularly alarming because the concerns that motivate it are idiosyncratic and private and inaccessible to others, and because the violence we observe seems disproportionate to stimuli that provoke it, which makes it hard to predict and to prevent.

Of the violent explosions that are associated with pathology, the most monothematic are those based on delusions of persecution. A person who engages in such violence lives with the continuous suspicion of others we have described, and often feels that he is the target of a pervasive conspiracy. The violence he manifests can be preemptively directed at persons he thinks plans to harm him, but it is sometimes intended in self-defense when the person feels imminently endangered or threatened. Real threats, unfortunately, can combine with subjective threats and can add documentation to an evolving perspective which is partly reality-based.

An example of the sort of perspective that informs paranoid violence is that of a man who comes to prison for participating in a robbery while on parole and incurs his first prison offense almost immediately, by refusing to participate in testing. A few months later this man is involved in altercations with an officer that degenerate into a scuffle. There follows a year in which there are only lower order problems, resulting in charges such as "under the influence of alcohol," "having his head covered for the count," "refusing to come out of his cell for a shower," and "refused to take off his jacket when told to by an officer." Later the man becomes enmeshed in another set of incidents in which he is belligerent, followed by two years in which there are no disciplinary entries. Another physical confrontation with an officer occurs, however, shortly before the inmate is released.

The man comes to prison at age thirty with a long sentence after he assaults an acquaintance, shooting him in the leg. The acquaintance, according to the inmate, is "a pusher who had failed to return a sum of money in lieu of a quantity of heroin which had not been received by him earlier," an account which is credible in that the district attorney decides that the victim would make a poor witness, "with some indication that he had a shady background." The inmate nevertheless receives a stiff prison sentence because he attempts a shootout with the police. The officers shoot back, injuring the man in the chest and arm, while he fires at the officers without hitting them.

Two years after this man enters prison he requests to see mental health staff, reporting that he is "rather upset" and that he is "feeling uneasy." Two months later he has an episode in which he experiences persecutory delusions, and the psychologist to whom he is referred writes that:

> The report is that he claims officers are talking about him, and he speaks of wanting to submit a writ so that they stop. . . . I checked and the officers that he claims are talking about him were not even on duty the days that he claims this incident.

Later, the man "indicates that the officers have stopped talking about him." He also applies for a furlough and supports his request with endorsements from prison staff. A chaplain, for instance, certifies that "I have come to know him rather well and have observed him at close range. He is a quiet, well behaved individual. . . . I would judge that he has embarked on a sincere quest for rehabilitation." A teacher rates the man's performance as "very high," writes that "his attitudes were excellent" and concludes that he "appeared to me to be quite mature and stable." A correction officer reports that "I have never had any problems with him. He is polite and courteous and always respectful to the officers and inmates." A second officer testifies that "he worked for me as a cell block porter, he appears to me a very quiet and serious person. He worked hard, and most of the time he stayed by himself. I can't remember him giving anyone trouble." Finally, the man's supervisor calls him "an asset to the department to which he is assigned."

The man is nevertheless turned down because of his long sentence and serious offense, and he expresses considerable bitterness. Three months later he has a second episode of feeling persecuted, he is hospitalized after he "threw a glass through the bars at an officer, injuring the officer, cutting his face and eyes." The man explains that he "believes that a bunch of officers is following the inmates and calling him names and teasing him," and "spoke of everyone's calling him a faggot or homosexual (and) claimed that when he would be in his cell at night, officers would stand in front of his cell talking about him, claiming he was a faggot."

After the man returns from the hospital he becomes "rather upset" because he discovers that his work assignment, which he likes, has been given to another inmate. He also feels that he is targetted in other respects, and he "makes references to being harassed or hustled unfairly by the administration." He later breaks down, and on this occasion feels persecuted by a fellow inmate. A psychologist reports that

> he was referred by the security department because he had a fight. The account I received was that he was overtly paranoid and accused (the other inmate) of various activities and actions, which incidentally (the other inmate) denies. . . . When I saw him he had passed through his paranoid phase and was quiet, seething with anger and rather upset. He was even angry with me who, at other times, he sees as his friend.

A few days later the inmate promises that "he would try again to get along," socially isolates himself, and "spends considerable time polishing, waxing, and mopping the floor." He is, however, transferred to another prison, in that by this time the staff and other inmates "see him as crazy."

In his next prison the inmate's counselor reports that "he shows no initiative and displays very little interest in his work," that he has received some disciplinary reports, and that "although these are not serious violations, in conjunction with his work record and attitude they indicate an overall inability to accept the rules and regulations of this facility." A supervisor echoes these complaints, writing that the inmate

> doesn't seem to associate with hardly any of his coworkers, and whenever he converses with me it is to complain about slave wages, poor food in the mess hall, etc. . . . He is frequently complaining that he doesn't feel good and would like to return to his cell. Also he is one of the last men in the shop and one of the first to line up to leave at the end of the shift.

At this time the man is paroled with a long parole period hanging over his head (given the length of his sentence), and he becomes involved in a robbery. The robbery nets him two dollars, several subway tokens and a prison sentence added to his parole period, which in theory implies a term of imprisonment of up to thirty years. He embarks on this sentence visibly irritable, which affects his prison behavior. In one incident an officer who is attached to the prison bathhouse reports:

> I called him, telling him to come in and pick up a bag of laundry. He said in front of approximately 85 inmates, "you get some of those young boys to carry those bags." I went out into the corridor and ordered him several times to get in the laundry and get the last bag. He became loud and boisterous, talking in a belligerent voice. "You talk to me like a man, not an animal." He made the

statement in front of approximately 85 inmates, (but) he finally went in and picked up the last bag.

Later, the officer's supervisor reports:

The officer called the inmate to the front of the gallery to advise him that he was submitting a report on him for an incident which had occurred in the bathhouse corridor. At this time the inmate reached out and pushed the officer against the wall and ripped the pocket of his shirt. The officer grabbed the inmate around the chest to subdue him. (Two other officers) immediately came to the assistance of the officer. (One) grabbed the inmate by the arms, (the second) grabbed him by both of his legs and the inmate was wrestled to the floor face down, was held there until handcuffs were brought to the area and applied to the inmate's arms. The inmate was then escorted without further incident to the facility hospital . . . seen by (a psychiatrist) who ordered that he be admitted to the hospital for mental observation.

After the inmate is segregated, another serious incident occurs in the segregation housing unit. According to the report:

A correction officer informed his sergeant that the inmate appeared to be depressed and did not take his breakfast. The sergeant went down and talked to the inmate but he would not speak. When the sergeant returned to the officer, the officer informed him that the inmate was going to court tomorrow and would have to go through his personal property to get his legal work, to take with him. The sergeant returned to the inmate's cell and told him he would have to come out of his cell to go through his property for his legal work but (the inmate) would not answer the sergeant. Instead he took a piece of paper and wrote on it that he wanted to see his lawyer at his cell. He was informed by the sergeant that this would not be possible, but that he would see his lawyer when he went to court. He again wrote a note asking where his lawyer was. Seeing the state of depression the inmate was in, the sergeant filed an observation report to the psychiatrist for observation. The sergeant notified a deputy superintendent who recommended the sergeant have a psychologist go to the special housing unit and interview the inmate. . . . (The psychologist) left the special housing unit and said she would talk to the psychiatrist about her findings and notify the special housing officers if the inmate would have to be moved to hospital observation [The psychiatrist determines that the inmate must be moved to the observation tier, and officers are so instructed.] . . . The sergeant went to the inmate's cell and told him he had an interview at the hospital and the inmate ignored him.

The incident ends with the inmate having to be tear gassed and "carried by the arms and legs to the shower area, where he was put under the shower for decontamination."

Shortly thereafter the inmate is hospitalized. Psychiatrists report at this time that he has stopped eating because he believes that prison authorities are adding embalming fluid to his food.

There follow two quiescent years with only minor incidents. This period ends when an officer in the mess hall insists that the inmate cannot wear a shirt on which he has written his name in large letters, and the inmate (for whom the monogram has special significance) ignores the officer's request. After the inmate sees the disciplinary panel they charge that

> You did threaten the committee by stating that if you weren't locked up you would take them off the count. You also threatened and harassed the committee by stating no one could take your name away and it didn't make any difference if you did 30 years in your cell or six feet under, and that we could kiss your ass, that you were not going to take any more harassment. You also refused direct orders to stand still and place your hands behind your back.

Three days later the inmate is transferred to a psychiatric observation wing, and two weeks later he is hospitalized. A psychiatrist reports:

> There was a definite delusional assumption that everybody in prison was against him, especially the officers who had elected him for harassment, for what reason he did not know. He also recognized in other prisoners his brother, and stated his determination to kill these inmates because of these inmates being against his brother. He also included me in his delusional ideation in stating that I am harassing him in observation and therefore joining the crowd who was after him.

Another lull (lasting some eighteen months) follows, after which the inmate again becomes irritable, possibly because time he has lost as a result of disciplinary proceedings is not restored to him. One officer reports, "the inmate was let out of his cell by mistake and became very belligerent—was not going to return to his cell." On another occasion, "the inmate was screaming and hollering about his cell not being opened. He gave the officer a hard time, using obscene language."

Thereafter the inmate is rehospitalized because he refuses ophthalmic treatment, "based on a delusional system with very heavy religious overtones in which he believes he is a direct descendant from Cain (while) everyone else is a descendant from a weak maternal object consisting of diads and triads." The inmate also at this time is "screaming and hollering at people passing his cell."

Later the man returns to prison, his disciplinary record again becomes very good, and work supervisors are delighted with his performance in his prison assignment. A psychiatrist who interviews the man for the parole board, however, finds him argumentative, in that he

> was offended by the idea that the interviewer is asked to provide a psychiatric report, and that it may have some influence on the parole decision. He did not

think it would be possible for anyone to give an opinion on a matter concerning him, as he felt he knew what had happened.

The psychiatrist concludes that the inmate is "very defensive and suspicious of the system." The parole board releases the inmate, however, stipulating that "a mental hygiene referral and evaluation are mandatory."

The man experiences a downhill progression in his career. He starts out as a delinquent, operating on the fringes of a gang, plays pool and raises pigeons. He incurs his first prison sentence for a relatively minor offense and emerges from prison to renew a relatively unimpressive pattern in which he sustains a drug habit by modestly dealing in drugs. At this stage he demonstrates some eccentricity (his uniform consists of dark glasses and a peaked hat) but is otherwise unremarkable until he panics following an altercation with a drug dealer who has sold him contaminated drugs, and seeks to evade arrest by shooting police officers, which converts him from an overaged delinquent into a long-term prisoner.

The man embarks on his career as a long-term prison resident by being a model inmate, but a brief and sudden lapse into delusions suggests that at some level he has difficulties assimilating the awesome sentence which hangs over his head. He is even more seriously traumatized when his failure to earn a furlough underlines the extremity of his fate, and his problems are next compounded because he discovers that insult has been added to injury in that he has lost a prized work assignment through transfer to the hospital. This is one of several disappointments which convey to the man the feeling that he is subjected to an inhospitable fate, which (in the process of assigning blame or responsibility) sets the stage for a frame of mind which oscillates between chronic bitterness and episodes of paranoid delusions. In his delusions the man mostly targets correction officers, but on at least one occasion he focuses on a fellow inmate. Between such episodes, he copes by segregating himself and manifesting his displeasure through a solemn demeanor and the stance of a chronic malcontent.

Through an irony of fate this man, who already feels that the cards are stacked against him, returns to prison facing an even more substantial sentence on the strength of a robbery which nets him almost nothing, and the irony escapes the man, whose resentment and fear of the future are understandably substantial. These feelings place the man in an unreceptive frame of mind when he enters prison, and his attitude contributes to an explosion when he feels himself unjustly disciplined for a demonstration of irritability. When the man is in turn penalized for exploding, he is severely traumatized. He retreats into a shell of dazed despondency from which he is extricated by a dose of tear gas, only to lapse into a psychotic episode which requires his hospitalization.

Other psychotic episodes follow, and invariably result from conditions of extremity, such as when the man feels himself pushed by unreasonable demands and penalties and when he resists these demands, generally by ignoring them. In the interim the man presents no problems, though when he is pressed (such as by a psychiatrist who interviews him for the parole board), he makes it obvious that he feels put upon and unfairly treated. If one sets aside his own contribution to his fate it is, in fact, obvious that he has been dealt heavy blows, which means that in his case the line between paranoia and life is evanescent. This is particularly the case with circumstances that immediately precede the onset of his symptoms, which typically include a seemingly arbitrary action by someone in authority, such as an officer who insists on converting a technical violation into a disciplinary charge or a group who turns him down for furlough on seemingly unjust grounds, followed by punishment for a manifestation of disgruntlement.

Such experiences plausibly translate for the man into the assumption that he is helplessly subjected to an overwhelmingly inhospitable fate with no recourse and no escape, which no doubt contributes to his feelings that hostile forces are personally invested in a conspiracy that is directed against him. In other words, beyond whatever susceptibilities the man brings to life situations that predispose him to illness, he encounters catch-22 situations which would tax anyone, since they validate the message of the man's tattoo which reads "born to loose." Feeling persecuted is the closest the man can come to answering the question of why this should be the case.

### Fight Patterns (2)

*Tinged Rebelliousness*

A different form of violence is of most concern to persons in authority (such as prison staff), because it consistently is directed toward them. Given its choice of target, the anti-authority violence of disturbed persons appears to resemble explosions that are sparked by autonomy-dependence concerns (see above). But the motives that are often at issue are more complex, in that they run deeper and are accompanied by feelings (such as fear), assumptions (such as delusions) and distortions of perception that are products of a confusion and unhappy obsessions. The behavior, in other words, is "overdetermined," meaning that it reflects private as well as public concerns.

An example of the pattern is provided by a man serving a long sentence for a bank robbery. The man's disciplinary record is unusually checkered.

There are arguments and fights, threats and attacks against officers, and there is a great deal of eccentric behavior, which ranges from sedate that is, "sleeping under his bed in a corner of his cell") to extremely nonsedate that is, "threw human defecation on walls").

The man enters prison at nineteen, but first comes to the attention of authorities at nine for a variety of offenses, and soon spends time in reform schools, where his intelligence is classed as "borderline."

When the man reenters prison five years later his IQ registers in the average range, but psychologists report that he has emotional problems. They write that

> he admitted to jumping out of a window, to overdosing and setting fire to his cell on two occasions. He denies suicidal ideation at present. However, he said he might have experienced hallucinations once. Does not appear psychotic, but is aggressive and resents authority.

The man's "resentment to authority" takes unusual turns. An incident report mentions that while on his way to religious services, he "broke formation, took a karate stance, hollered something in a foreign language and went after a sergeant, striking him a glancing blow on the left side of his jaw." The man later tells a psychiatrist, "I sort of flipped out. I guess I got a little mixed up." Two weeks after this interview the psychiatrist sees the inmate again and this time reports that "he claims that he is seeing things in his cell and would like to be transferred to another cell." The psychiatrist concludes that "this inmate is a manipulator and quite an anti-social personality who could act out at any time." The next day the inmate starts a fire in his cell, throws water into the hallway and spits at a fellow inmate when he is escorted out of his cell. He advertises that he "did this only to be moved to another cell area," given that he "was having problems with the inmate in the next cell." Thereafter he requests to be transferred to another prison, and later changes his decision because "I was given a job assignment where there are very few people working." A week later, however, he complains that officers and inmates "for some reason or other are trying to kill me."

Thereafter the man's deportment improves but his state of mind deteriorates. He writes a letter to the commissioner in which he tells him:

> I wish to inform you of a conspiracy going on in (this institution). This conspiracy is against me. . . . The officers are telling the inmates to try and commit sodomy on me. They are giving the inmates drugs and other forms of alcoholic brews to give me. I have written the superintendent about this matter but apparently he is also part of the conspiracy. . . . An officer was letting unauthorized and unofficial inmates come from one block or another offering

me drugs. . . . Sir, would you please review my records and have me transferred to another facility as soon as possible?

A week later the inmate threatens self-immolation and is placed in a psychiatric observation cell. Staff complain that he is "constantly screaming obscenities" and commit him to the hospital, from which he is discharged after six weeks with the diagnosis "schizophrenia, paranoid type, in remission."

After a period of quiescence, the inmate again expresses disgruntlement. In one incident he builds a fire, and in another incident he "threw a cup of water at an officer" and "attempted to get the other inmates on his gallery to start throwing objects at the officer." The inmate explains after the second incident that the officer has insisted that he return his supper dishes before he has finished his meal.

The inmate is transferred, and is recommitted to the hospital after assaulting correction officers "with no apparent provocation." He remains hospitalized for three months, and thereafter spends two years in the prison in which he records a great many disciplinary violations. These include unprovoked assaults on other inmates, attacks against officers, and charges such as:

Refused to attend class. Wanted to be locked in his cell so he could get out of school.

Talking aloud, totally incoherent and irrational.

Threatened an officer for standing on his spot.

Possible sexual assault on an inmate.

Refused to go to the adjustment committee meeting.

Refused to sit down in the movies when told.

Was under his bed with sheets and mattress pulled down around him so officers could not see him. Refused to come out.

Refused a strip frisk and made threats.

Refused to take medication. Threw it at an officer. Tried to hit the officer through the bars.

Had a fire in his cell and would not help put it out.

Refused to move from the special housing unit to the mental hygiene unit.

Under the bed and could not be seen for the count.

Spit in the face of a nurse and used abusive language.

Threw spaghetti and meatballs at me . . . gave me no warning . . . nothing was said between us prior to his throwing the food.

Began spitting on transportation officers forcing them to return to place him under sedation. It took a lieutenant, a sergeant and five correction officers to subdue him so the nurse could administer a shot. This medication did not seem to affect him as when the trip resumed he continued to spit at the transportation correction officers. At a stopover he was allowed to use toilet facilities, kicked a correction supervisor and had to be restrained by five officers. After arriving kicked a sergeant supervising his being frisked.

Put medication in his mouth but refused to open his mouth so the officer could see if he swallowed it.

Requested a bowl of soup and then complained that it was too full . . . spilled the soup on the floor and the officer.

When the sergeant approached cell told him to "get out of my face" and then spit in the face of the sergeant.

Set a blanket on fire in his cell which scorched the wall and the floor.

Failed to acknowledge the presence of an officer when he tried to wake him for the live count.

Refused orders to take a shower.

Was belligerent to the officer when getting his hair cut and would not let the officer take a picture of his changed appearance after getting his hair cut.

Treatened the officer in front of the companies, stating, "I'll punch your motherfucking head in and kick your ass all over the jail."

Stated to the officers, "I'm an inmate and demand the tobacco." Also, "What are you? A new fucking hack? I'll take those fucking glasses right off your motherfucking face." While being escorted, said, "Why don't you guys suck my fucking cock?" . . . (Later) refused other to strip for a frisk, told a lieutenant, "fuck you. I ain't taking off my clothes." Then turned, raised hands, shoved an officer up against the wall and kicked him in groin area. Then hit (another officer) in the left cheek.

Threw his food track and a number of articles out of his cell at an officer.

In the last incident, the inmate is assigned six months of segregation consecutive to accumulated previous segregation time for throwing food and cutlery at officers, demanding that they leave the vicinity of his cell and offering to kill them. Six days later he is recommitted to the hospital because he has been responding to paranoid delusions. He returns with the diagnosis "schizophrenia undifferentiated, chronic, in remission" and for the next seven months incurs no disciplinary infractions.

During five stormy years in confinement this man assaults a great many people, mostly custodial personnel, upon slight provocation. The man lives in an extreme and chronic state of disgruntlement. The most innocent demand can cause him to explode with demonstrative displeasure, and more substantial demands (such as being moved when he does not want to be moved) produce chain reactions in which he rages and struggles and kicks and spits at anyone within reach.

The man is extremely irritated by authority figures, and his recurrent response to those who irritate him is to angrily attack and threaten them and to struggle. The man also resists changes of his environment and his routines, and this includes demands that he take showers or present himself for mental health interviews. In this sense, the continuous segregation time the man earns meets some of his needs, in that it forces him to stay sequestered in his cell. Even in such settings, however, he reliably and frequently explodes in reaction to slight intrusions he finds unaccountably offensive.

### Fight Patterns (3)

*Cryptic Outbursts*

When people think of violence committed by disturbed persons they mostly think of explosions that occur "out of the blue," with no discernible motives, unrelated to the antecedents which we assume occasion violence. The description of such violence is apt, but tells us more about what the violence is *not* than what it is. To assess cryptic violence motivation would require that we have access to some of the concerns the disturbed person prefers to keep private or that he cannot communicate. If the person could enlighten us, moreover, his concerns would still make no sense, because we would find that they often include illogical inferences drawn from implausible premises.

The seemingly understandable outbursts of disturbed persons are actions that denote double failures, in that they mark junctures at which the pathology which is designed to help the person adapt to reality with which he cannot deal fails him as well, with the result that he is left feeling guilty, resentful, angry or panic-stricken. Many of the resulting acts, including outbursts (such as self-injuries or acts of arson) express such feelings, while others represent destructive outcomes of ill-fated delusions.

A career of this kind is that of a short, overweight young man who has participated in robbing a bus driver and his passengers. Most of the man's prison incidents involve fights with other inmates, but during long stretches of time he is hospitalized.

The man has mental health problems which become salient as soon as he is jailed, and his trial must be postponed for a year. The first psychiatrist who examines him must interview him in a straightjacket because he has assaulted another inmate who has taken one of his cigarettes without permission. A second psychiatrist has an equally difficult time because the inmate, whom he is trying to interview, is crying and drooling and stiff under the influence of medication. The psychiatrist concludes:

> It is my impression, even allowing for depression on the part of the defendant and side effects of medication, that he is a youth of limited intelligence, and that his intellectual capacity and function probably fall within lower reaches of the dull normal range.

Two weeks later another psychiatrist finds problems which transcend the effects of limited intelligence. He writes:

> So far so good. Now, however, the patient states what appear to be delusions of grandeur, specifically that he is Jesus Christ. . . . His purpose here on earth, he says, is to "forgive you for your sins. Everybody who prays is praying unto me." He points out the misty background to his Department of Correction photograph and states that this is proof of his identity. Later he says that every time he drinks alcohol "clouds become cloudy." On questioning he states that God does not speak to him directly but through the mouths of others. . . . On further questioning he states that God intends that he be released on these charges. . . . Despite repeated confrontations he seems to be persistent in his beliefs.

Later jail psychiatrists certify that the man is free of mental disorder and conclude that his principal problem is one of mental retardation. However, they also recommend that if the man is sentenced to prison, psychiatric help should be afforded him. The probation officer who prepares the presentence report writes that

> (The) defendant impressed as dull intellectually but possibly not positively retarded. "Limited" might be a better non-clinical word. . . . It is hard to picture this limited, friendly, slow, passive, eager-to-please defendant in an armed robbery. It is hard to fathom, furthermore, why anyone planning an armed robbery would enlist this ineffectual-seeming individual as a cohort since a successful robbery ought to be an efficient operation and this defendant does not impress as efficient, to say the least. In non-technical terms, if we may be allowed, he impresses as a somewhat "goofy," so to speak, "mama's boy" who finds some of the simplest points in conversation amusing, possibly inappropriately so.

The probation officer adds that "it is sometimes, in some cases, said that the criminal does not seem to fit the crime. This may perhaps be the case in the present offense with the defendant."

Despite the implication that the man is not a hardened criminal he is sentenced to prison. When he arrives in the prison he at once complains that he is "picked on" by other inmates and reports that he "hears voices telling him to kill himself." Intake staff write that he indicates that he is constantly harassed by other inmates and feels somewhat insecure. He also indicates that at times he has heard female voices suggesting that he commit suicide, but he indicates that he does not listen and claims he has no intention of committing suicide.

For a while the inmate's behavior appears slightly bizarre. On one occasion he gets up in the middle of a meal and traverses the prison, arriving at an exercise yard from which staff persuade him to return.

Two weeks later the inmate's problems transcend eccentricity. He sets his cell on fire "to get rid of garbage," and has to be removed from the conflagration by force. He insists on pacing his cell in the nude, masturbating and playing with excrement, smearing food on the walls, windows and the floor, and "placing things in his various orifices." When he is interviewed the inmate explains that he has "a generator in his body," and complains that there are "two women in his cell—one white and one black—both wanting sex with him."

The inmate is hospitalized on two successive occasions and is discharged suffering from "schizophrenia, disorganized, in remission." The "remission," however, is temporary and the inmate is transferred from the prison to a civil hospital, from which he is eventually released.

Two months after the man's departure from the civil hospital he is arrested for a bizarre offense in which he and a German shepherd dog attack a young female high school student and steal her purse. The offense is a serious one because the victim has been severely bitten and is badly traumatized by the incident. The man himself is less impressed than his victim, and a probation officer reports that

> he went on to admit guilt and express remorse, stating . . . "Tell him (the judge) I want to live down South. Can I have less time?" The defendant impressed as being sorry for his offense but is having less than the fullest appreciation of the seriousness of his actions and perhaps their consequences to the complainant and the seriousness of his own legal predicament. He impressed as a somewhat limited individual: "Tell the judge I ain't bad" he said on several occasions, sometimes smiling at what seemed inappropriate times.

After the man is arrested he is held in psychiatric hospitals until he is adjudged sane enough to be tried and is again sentenced to prison. The person preparing the presentence report writes that "the defendant's own statements to us indicate that he is not afraid of returning to jail and did not impress as being much bothered by the prospect. The defendant does not seem able to function, except marginally, at liberty."

Almost as soon as the man enters the prison he is sent to a hospital on an emergency commitment, and when he leaves the hospital he is assigned to a residential mental health program. At this point he is diagnosed as a chronic undifferentiated schizophrenic with borderline intellectual functioning, though there is some confusion about how psychotic the man is because when he is interviewed he proves "unable to respond to questions about hallucinations and delusions since he didn't seem to understand the terminology, and when asked whether he was hearing voices he said, 'yes, yours.' " The mental health staff member writes:

> It would appear that his almost complete inability to function intellectually makes him a poor candidate for survival in open prison population, and I can't off hand think of another program that would possibly be more appropriate for him to be in, so I guess we are left with no choice but to accept him into our program. Our goal will be to first of all help him be clean and neat and sanitary, to help him find his way around the prison, help him establish and follow programs, learn how to eat in the mess hall and eventually get him into some meaningful work . . . and hopefully be able to nurse him ever so gradually into population.

Even such minimal goals prove difficult to achieve, and the inmate is discharged within two months, accompanied by a discharge summary which notes that

> during his stay in the program he remained noncommunicative and mute. His only signs of life were in response to questions from correction officers and staff members, and he was also observed on several occasions to be masturbating openly, particularly in the presence of females. . . . He was given a shower on two occasions. (On a third occasion) corrections officers attempted to give him another shower and to clean his cell. During that time he assaulted and caused physical injury and subsequent hospitalization to three correction officers.

Subsequent incidents replicate the pattern referred to in this summary. On several occasions the inmate assaults officers who interfere with him, such as by insisting that he clean his cell. The inmate also continues to expose himself, particularly when female staff members are available as witnesses. In addition to periodically wrecking his cell and strewing garbage in the vicinity, the inmate starts an occasional fire, and as a result he spends most of his time in segregation. Here he receives occasional inspections from mental health staff, with whom the inmate refuses to communicate.

At the inception of the man's prison career he is a limited, victim prone, childlike individual with some psychotic symptoms. However, he soon blossoms into a full-fledged mental patient who lives in a fantasy world that heavily accentuates themes having to do with sex and other bodily functions. Unfortunately, the man has a tendency to translate his thoughts, such as they are, into action and as a result he masturbates, smears excrement on walls, sets fires and otherwise becomes difficult to manage, especially since any ministrations to which he is subjected make him explode with wounded rage.

The man's intellectual limitations compound the problems created by his disease, in that they further limit his ability to perceive and discriminate features of his environment and make it impossible for him to distinguish, for example, between helpful and aggressive acts. His limitations similarly make it difficult for the man to have residual awareness of the inappropriateness of steps he takes to satisfy his needs, such as when he importunes prepubescent girls or female correction officers. In other words, while the man's disease probably obliterates the lines between fantasy and reality, the primitiveness of his intellect reduces reality to the sort of world experienced by an infant, and the two problems converge so as to make it impossible for this man to function.

### Oscillating

One fact which complicates any effort to understand the link between pathology and maladaptation is that there are seriously disturbed persons who adjust differently in different settings, or react differently at different stages of their careers. Such persons can at times be said to *oscillate* between being disturbed and nondisturbed, and also oscillate between maladaptive and nonmaladaptive behavior.

The sharpness of transitions in some cases is such that it creates difficulties both for the person and the setting because it becomes impossible to define the person's problems and the responses appropriate to them. The behavioral inconsistency then becomes a pattern of maladaptation that is more salient than the detailed behavior it subsumes.

A case in point is that of an inmate who has served a long sentence for a predatory sex offense. His disciplinary record is dense during a two-year period in the middle of his sentence, and sparse before and after this period. The majority of disciplinary incidents appear eccentric. Some examples of incidents are "acting strangely, running back and forth from shower to shower saying someone stole his clothes," "having his cell door tied with a belt, acting quite disturbed," "refusing to be quiet, climbing on his cell bar," "obscene language to nurses," "aggravating black inmates, started fight," "yelling in bed for no reason," "stated that bed sheets fell into toilet and flooded his cell floor," "refused to take a bath upon being received," "urinated on floor in his room," "threw contents of tray in toilet," "shouting, demanding that light be left on at night," "started yelling for no reason," "spitting on wall," "plugged toilet with clothes," "refused to turn the light on in his cell," and so forth.

The inmate has served a previous prison sentence for an assaultive offense. He becomes involved in this offense as a member of a violence-prone Spanish-speaking juvenile gang, and he has a long record of other gang-related offenses. There are indications that the inmate is a respected senior gang delinquent, a charismatic figure who exercises a leadership role in his group. He has also had a record of fairly steady employment.

There is only one note that is discordant with the general impression of this man being a substantial figure of the juvenile underworld. In the detention facility the inmate smashes the contents of his cell, "wandered around the halls and claimed he had communicated with God, and further stated that he had been called back from the dead." The person who examines the inmate reports that

> he stated that the experience was real in his own mind, but he would not talk of it to anyone other than the examiner who became his confidant, because he could not prove his story and people would think he was fabricating.

During his first prison stay the man becomes involved in several altercations. In these he acts as a leader of inmates of his own ethnic group. In one report it is recorded that

> he was to be placed in segregation for a leveling off period. It is felt that he is trying to establish leadership among the Puerto Rican population and trying to tell other inmates what to do. He had been counseled and advised by the deputy superintendent on a number of occasions about his agitating activities and he has totally disregarded this advice. He is the type that just can't keep his mouth shut and keeps telling others of his ilk what to do, whether it is contrary to rules and regulations or not.

He is also described as "a chronic agitator with little or no respect for authority, race conscious, with a persecution complex." Aside from one incident in which the inmate becomes despondent because a female friend "had lost interest in him" there is no indication at this time of psychological difficulties, and the inmate's reputation is that of a disruptive figure who has recorded 150 infractions in a short prison stay.

About a year into the next prison sentence which the inmate earns there are indications of a marked change. The first indication is a report which records that the inmate has been observed sharpening a soda can and exclaims that "he wants to kill everyone." Shortly thereafter a doctor tries to commit the man to a hospital. The doctor writes:

he has been playing with feces but when observed said that everything was fine. A pint of ice cream that he had recently received was up-side-down next to the toilet bowl. When questioned about this he merely makes the statement that it had tipped over on him. . . . His cell is very disorderly, with everything strewn around, some feces mixed with ice cream on the floor. As soon as the cell is cleaned he messes it up again. . . . States that he wishes to serve out his full term and then sue the State of New York for half a million dollars for false imprisonment. Admits analyzing his feces to extract the paste in order to use this material to blot out images on some of his snapshots. When shown a photo of himself, states that the man was a marine and had died.

Interestingly this description of disturbed behavior does not satisfy a judge, with the result that the inmate is not committed at that time. He is committed shortly thereafter, however, after "playing with an imaginary rifle in the yard, shooting other inmates and officers from the wall. At the time he was dressed rather peculiarly, not wearing shoes and other garments."

The difficulty seems to be that the inmate is often described as undergoing "drastic personality change." After incidents such as the preceding he is interviewed by a psychiatrist and "appeared friendly, cooperative, clear, in good contact, and correctly oriented." The inmate is next reported in the dining room, throwing baked potatoes at other inmates, but in a subsequent interview seems level-headed and in possession of his faculties. There are referrals to mental health staff in which correction officers report extremely bizarre behavior, but the inmate is interviewed and classified as nonpsychotic. He cannot keep this up, however, and becomes so disturbed that concerns arise about his safety. He plays with electric outlets, refuses to eat, and lies covered in a sheet ranting and laughing. At such junctures he is committed.

He is no longer a substantial figure in the inmate world. He insists on preaching to nonreceptive audiences about his version of Muslim religion, and there is concern about his being teased and abused. A report from his work assignment indicates that "co-workers do not want to work with him for fear of his irrational behavior." On another occasion he "stole pictures from other inmates. These pictures were of the inmates' wives and girl-friends. He was also writing letters to girls of other inmates." A psychologist concludes,

a number of inmates now know him and have spoken to me about him. Many of these inmates are truly angry with him and as such I think that at this point we should release him to the population.

Psychotic episodes are resolved without the inmate being committed. One such instance finds him "in a catatonic state, lying on his bed, shaking, in a fetal position,'' but after substantial doses of medication ''his transitory psychotic disorder appears to have subsided. He was in excellent contact, was verbal, was pleasant and back to his old style of high verbal production, and the old con.''

A psychologist summarizes the situation as follows:

> we can see now a pattern for his behavior. He slips in and out of psychotic episodes with ease and with regularity. We can expect that this behavior will continue.

During one hospital stay a psychiatrist classifies the inmate as a dissimulator. Two months later the inmate is back in the hospital giving religious lectures that include delusional content and hallucinations. He also attacks fellow patients. When the inmate returns to prison he refuses to take medication and spends his time in observation cells after being referred by correction officers for walking around giving himself religious lectures and looking and smelling filthy.

Various experiments are tried to address the problem. One psychiatrist reports,

> regardless of everything, this examiner felt that the patient should be placed in a cell block and handled for at least some period of time in order to give him the opportunity to adjust to life situations in this facility. The patient was transferred during the day. The next day the patient was returned to the hospital area because the officers were not able to handle him in the block area.

Soon the inmate is back at the hospital threatening to kill his fellow patients and being restrained. Two months later he is released from the hospital. There is a note from the director of the institution which reads

> he impresses as being superficially cooperative with staff but capable of wide fluctuations in behavior and mood. His tendencies are usually to withdraw and avoid interactions with others. However, management problems have occurred on occasion in the form of acting out with other residents.

The inmate returns to prison, where psychiatrists interview him and find him friendly but overtalkative and preoccupied with religious ideas. He is shortly transferred back to the hospital where staff note that ''the inmate . . . presents typical symptomology of paranoid schizophrenia . . . is preoccupied with religion, the devil and satan . . . is irrational.'' In the hospital, patients again react adversely to the man's self-styled missionary work. Staff complains that the inmate usually has extreme difficulty keeping the lid on (as it were) his hostile, bitter thoughts towards staff and peers as well as delusional material in the area of religious pursuits. An open ward setting is the least likely environment for him to avoid the aggravation of such paranoid thinking. He would be far more capable of maintaining control in a cell setting where he can withdraw from continual contact with peers when he chooses. But he may also become active in a vocational or educational program once he is confident that he is in control of his feelings.

When the inmate returns to the cell environment which is recommended it does not seem to produce the predicted affect. He spends his time proclaiming loudly that "people are talking about me." After he is committed the hospital sends him back certifying that

> this patient, though showing improvement at the present time without the aid of medication, very likely will deteriorate when returned to prison and may require additional assistance from medication . . . (and) mental health workers who can recognize when he is decompensating and can recommend that medication be administered. In the meantime, attempts should be made to involve this inmate in programs.

The predicted oscillations occur: A counselor complains that

> he is constantly being transferred back to the hospital due to psychiatric disturbances disallowing any possible programming. . . . It seems he is being thrown from institution to institution because no responsibility appears to be taking place. He is presently at this facility because in the past he did less damage here than elsewhere.

For a while the inmate does well, takes his high school examination in Spanish, is reported to be an excellent worker, has no disciplinary problems, and appears to make good progress in therapy. But soon he is referred by the security staff because he has become "extremely belligerent without provocation and seemed to be completely out of control with his emotions." Another referral starts "the above inmate was referred by security due to his 'flaky behavior.' "

The next report originates in the hospital, where the inmate

> carries on an endless conversation with no one in particular, keeping most of the hospital patients awake. He is frequently flushing the toilet for no apparent reason. He at times is irrational and able to carry on an intelligent conversation, but at other times he becomes belligerent and expresses extreme hostility toward the nurses.

We are now past midway into the inmate's sentence and there are no disciplinary reports of consequence through the next five years. The inmate is now enrolled in college courses and in typing classes. Reports show him highly motivated and conscientious. He does a good deal of reading, has steady family contacts, and in interviews impresses everyone as rationally concerned with the pursuit of goals and as being a mature and hardworking inmate.

All of a sudden we have a report that the "resident was observed by the counselor this morning laying on the floor counting numbers in the air, talking incoherently." The inmate is committed to the hospital and is returned to the prison within a very short period. Soon there is another commitment reporting that the inmate

> has been very concerned about the way this institution is being run, and he is afraid another riot will break out. He doesn't believe in inmates having privileges in the institution. He also complains of someone trying to assassinate an inmate in the yard.

The inmate is next observed "throwing jars out of his cell, babbling incoherently." " complaining of glasses flying by his cell and otherwise in fairly serious condition." A series of commitments follow over the next two years. In one document the inmate is described as "threatening to kill himself by bumping his head into the cell wall." In another it is recorded that he "believes he is God and a Son of God. He came to earth to save mankind. He hears voices, but considers them normal."

Eighteen months before the inmate's discharge from prison, there is a progress report which notes "the inmate seems unable to adjust to institutional placement," and "due to psychiatric problems, the inmate is unable to maintain a program." However, the next report reads "in the last 14 months he has maintained a spotless record." The report also notes that the inmate is gainfully employed. Six months later it is recorded that there have been "no additional disciplinary reports since the last summary. He has continued in a positive manner getting along with staff and peers and is expected to continue in this positive manner." It is also reported that "the inmate was recently assigned to handicrafts and expresses his satisfaction with the program." The inmate at this time has been followed up by mental health staff and is on a steady regime of medication.

This long and redundant account covers a thirteen year period of continuous shuttling between prisons and hospitals. Disciplinary problems are mostly related to emotional problems which in turn are a result of illness. There are also periods when the inmate has his illness under control (mostly with the help of medication), where he is an impressive, rational, and socially adept person.

The man's adjustment problems range from a preliminary effort at self-insulation and self-neglect to a later stage of volatility, suspiciousness, fear, resentment and a lot of loud eccentric discourse. Possibilities of more serious disciplinary incidents come about when other inmates object to the subtance of the loud, eccentric discourse and when the inmate develops grudges against fellow patients that have to do with his religious delusions.

We have a prior prison stay in which the inmate is a serious disciplinary problem due to his self-appointed status as an ethnic gang leader. As this time he is regarded as a nuisance but also as an impressive and likeable person. He is aggressive only in a subcultural context, which includes the crime for which he has been convicted. If we ignore one episode of religious delusion in the jail, there is nothing to prepare us for what we encounter over the next thirteen years: We start with an impulsive sex-related offense irreconcilable with earlier behavior. We infer bizarre reactions in the jail because the man has been placed under special guard as a suicide risk. And one year into the prison stay the inmate shows a pattern he will follow for the remainder of his stay of periodically breaking down while he struggles as hard as he can to keep afloat. The disciplinary incidents reflect both the struggle and the failures of the struggle. There is a similar origin to the contrasts that perplex and confuse various staff members who see the inmate at one juncture or another: One day he is not only rational but meticulously dressed to the point of being prissy, and the next day finds him disheveled and rambling. It is a pitiful fight, and in the last year of the thirteen year confinement, it appears as though the man has won the battle with the help of medication. It is of course an open question whether he has won the war.

### Notes

1. Szasz 1961). See chapter 8, note 4.
2. In the Introduction to DSM (III) it is pointed out that "because DSM-III is generally atheoretical with regard to etiology, it attempts to describe comprehensively what the manifestations of the mental disorders are, and only rarely attempts to account for how the disturbances come about, unless the mechanism is included in the definition of the disorder. This approach can be said to be 'descriptive' in that the definitions of the disorders generally consist of descriptions of the clinical features of the disorders. The features are described at the lowest order of inference necessary to describe the characteristic features of the disorder. American Psychiatric Association (1980), p. 7 (chapter 6, note 1)
3. Howard and Scott, (1965), Intro., note 9.

# 11

# Distribution of Patterns

As noted, we reviewed 239 prison careers of chronic infractors who showed evidence of psychological difficulties, for whom we had enough data (behavior descriptions) to justify a review. The representativeness of this sample cannot be assumed, but caution is not required to conclude that all the inmates we surveyed had serious problems, at least in the prison.

We classified behavior by assigning one theme to each prison career. The categories we used most frequently were Maintaining Sanity (60 inmates) and Gratifying Impulses (57). Of the inmates whose behavior we placed in the first category, the largest subset (18 patterns) included both flight (self-insulating) and fight (impulse bursting-through) reactions. Of pure fight patterns the most frequent (15 out of 24) was what we called *cryptic outbursts*, meaning that relationships between external stimuli and aggressive responses would be difficult to specify, and one could have to class the inmate's aggressivity as reflecting bizarre or inaccessible motives. The finding is consistent with that of studies in psychiatric settings in which patient assaults are subjected to reviews,[1] and we infer that attention to the content of disturbed or delusional thinking could help to prevent violence. Another theme we encountered among disturbed inmates is that of Oscillating (N = 10), which means that there are contrasts over the person's career between *mental wellness* and *mental illness*, reducing the reliability of diagnoses at a given point in time.

Of impulsivity-related behavior, one third (19) proved subsumable under Games turned Sour, which is a compounded problem, because it suggests that a person's primitive approach to satisfying needs has misfired. Maladaptation is also compounded because the person at issue reacts with limited insight (egocentric self-pity and the externalizing of blame) to this discovery of failure. However, the pattern also points at a strategic juncture for intervention, in which the *game* the person impulsively plays have *turned sour*.

Other prevalent impulse-related patterns were *stress to aggression* (11) and *frustration-aggression* (10). In each case the link between stimulus situations (blocked goals or overstimulation) and responses (angry aggression or helpless aggression) is specifiable, a fact which could assist staff in addressing the person's problem.

The next most invoked pattern heading was that of Seeking Refuge, which we used for 52 patterns. The subcategory most frequently emerging under this heading was *earned rejection* (N = 13) which describes a sequence in which ineptness comes homes to roost, which in turn inspires flight. The second pattern was *stress avoidance* (N = 10), which reflects personal nonresilience. Also frequent (N = 8) was *sheep's clothing,* which depicts personal reactions that vary with setting, transforming the self-styled victim in a socially disadvantaged situation into a source of aggression when the power balance shifts.

Esteem-related patterns emerged for 37 inmates. The predominant theme (N = 11) was that of *advertising toughness,* followed by *countering aspersions* (N = 8). The first pattern features aggression as a demonstration of worth, and the second describes the propensity to react aggressively to perceived slights or affronts.

Pursing Autonomy was invoked for fewer (33) patterns, but two themes, Conditional Dependence and Rejecting Constraints, appear with frequency (N = 12 each). A theme which appears least frequently may be the most surprising. This theme (Defying Authority, N = 3) is the disposition most prison staff would expect to find with endemic frequency. The relative infrequency of our usage of the theme may mean that the behavior to which staff refer has more complex dynamics. It may also be the case that *defying authority* in pure form occurs among more routine violators than the problem inmates on whom we center attention.

Prevalent autonomy patterns are Conditional Dependence (N = 12) and Resisting Constraints (N = 12). The first pattern describes behavior ranging from anxious and demanding to surly rebellious, depending on responses the person receives to requests for attention, service and nurturance. Rejecting Constraints is impulsivity as well as autonomy-related, in that it describes difficulties in accepting curbs to unrestrained behavior as well as reactions to infringement on independence to which the person feels entitled.

## Pattern Relationships

Our goal in selecting the sample of 239 inmates was to pick persons whose careers reflect "extreme maladaptiveness." We wanted chronic prison offenders, but *particularly* offenders who had psychological or socio-psychological problems, including problems calling for mental health assistance. In reviewing the attributes of the sample, it appears that we accomplished our task. Our sample comprises 10 percent of the stratified cohort, leaving 90 percent of inmates we did not review. Of those in the sample, 30 percent have been hospitalized in the prison and 47 percent have received other mental health assistance; only 23 percent have received no mental health services. The corresponding proportions for the other 90 percent of the stratified cohort are 3 percent, 33 percent and 64 percent respectively, and the estimated figures for the prison population are 1.5 percent, 14.2 percent and 84.3 percent.

As for disciplinary infraction rates, the average for our sample was 10.6; that of the rest of the cohort was 6.8; the estimate rate for the population was 4.2. The infraction rate of our disturbed infractors (the sixty inmates classified as Maintaining Sanity) was 7.7. The rates for inmates in our other categories was 12.4, 11.9, 11.1 and 10.7 respectively. Even more impressive is the finding that 22.4 percent of our sample (compared to 3 percent of the population) consists of chronic infractors. The proportion is particularly high for impulsives (30.4 percent) and esteem defenders (35.1 percent). Autonomy seekers comprise a lower proportion of chronics (12.1 percent), as do the inmates with mental health problems (11.9 percent). Disturbed inmates, however, spend time in the prison hospital that makes them unavailable to infractions.

In this connection it is relevant that variation generally obtains for mental health status. Eighty percent of the Maintaining Sanity group had been hospitalized in prison during their criterion term; only 8 percent received no mental health assistance. Two other themes (refuge seeking and autonomy pursing) show mental health involvement: fifteen percent of the refuge seekers and 18 percent of autonomy pursuers had been hospitalized, and 64 percent in each category had received other mental-health assistance. Only the Esteem Enhancing pattern is associated with a low hospitalization rate (3 percent), though 57 percent of these inmates received other mental health services.

Our sample contains half (71 of 143) the hospitalized inmates in the population for whom records are available; two thirds (48) fall in the Maintaining Sanity category, and the rest are dispersed through the sample. The hospital patients in our sample, as we expected, have high infraction rates (6.4 compared to 2.5). They also have come to the system at an earlier age (19.7 compared to 23.7), have been first arrested earlier (at 17.3 compared to 20), have served more time (55 months compared to 43.8), and more frequently have prior prison records (47 percent prior prison, compared to 31 percent). Our group also contains more nonwhite patients (79 percent) than the residual other hospital group (63 percent).

Over one inmate out of five (22.7 percent) in our sample has a record of civil hospitalization; this proportion does not vary by themes. The figure for histories of forensic hospitalization is equivalent (22.3 percent) but the proportions vary: in the Maintaining Sanity group, half (47 percent) have histories of forensic hospitalization; the proportions in the other group range from 11.5 percent to 19 percent.

In other respects, the highlights of our classification-related profiles are the following:

(1) The Profile for Gratifying Impulses

The inmates classified as demonstrating impulsivity have by far the highest disciplinary violation rate (12.4) and show the highest assault rate in the prison (2.6). These inmates enter the system at the earliest age (at 17.5, compared to a population average of 20), have a relatively low average IQ (86.8) and the lowest proportion of high school graduates (11 percent).

(2) The Profile for Enhancing Esteem

The inmates classified as esteem defenders have the second highest prison infraction rate (11.9) and assault rate (2.2). The group is youngest at admission to prison (21), and the youngest of our groups; the inmates are also the youngest (15.4 years) at first arrest. These inmates show a low proportion of mental health problems (40 percent no service), and the lowest proportion of preprison employment (38 percent).

(3) The Profile for Pursuing Autonomy

This group is relatively old compared to the above (24.7 years at entry, commensurate with the general population), and at first arrest (17.4 years). The group also has a high proportion of men who have been imprisoned before (42 percent), and as a group serves long average sentences (44.7 months, compared to an estimated 31.1 months for the population). By contrast, the group shows a high proportion of preprison employment (73 percent), a low proportion of drug addicts (48.5 percent) and the highest intelligence level in our sample (85 percent IQs over 80).

(4) The Profile for Refuge Seeking

Inmates who are classified in this category are youngest at first arrest (15.4 years), are disproportionately white (50 percent) and include the highest proportion of drug addicts (75 percent). The group also contains a large number of inmates (16.9 percent) convicted of rape, murder, sodomy and assault.

(5) The Profile for Maintaining Sanity

Inmates classified in this group are the oldest men in our sample

(27.8 at prison entry), and serve the longest sentences (53.3 months). The group contains the highest proportion of nonwhite inmates (83 percent) and a high proportion of recidivists (45 percent with prior prison time). The group also contains the highest proportion of inmates with low measured intelligence (53 percent of inmates with IQs 80 and under) and a low proportion of addicts (44.1 percent). Eight of the 60 inmates (13.3 percent) serve sentences for murder.

The profiles contain differences we expected, and others we did not. Refuge seekers are least surprising, in that victim-prone inmates are often described as white inmates who are less sophisticated than the average inmate, and have a history of delinquency and addiction. On the other side of the ledger we find that our group contains a larger proportion of violent offenders that one would expect. The fact makes more sense once we recall that ours are not "pure" refuge seekers, but men who combine aggressivity (at least, in the prison) with refuge seeking.

The impulsivity profile is more plausible, in that it overrepresents aggressive, institutionalized men with limited roots in the community, who also have other deficits (such as low measured intelligence and lack of education). The esteem-related profile is similar, though the inmates are younger, have fewer mental health problems, show higher intelligence, and have less institutional experience.

The autonomy pattern comes as a surprise if we expect inmates classi-fied as autonomy-oriented to be youthful rebels. We find the group chron-ologically mature, prison-experienced, established in the community (high preprison employment), and serving long sentences. The group also con-tains low proportions of men with limited intelligence or a history of addiction. The inmates are not—as are the esteem-defending inmates— young toughs; they resemble older and more established denizens of the prison, whose violation records are low. However, we must recall that the issue for these inmates is not peer relations but staff relations, and it may be that they are "mainline" offenders who are less reconciled than equivalent offenders to the strictures of institutional life.

We have noted that inmates we have classified as disruptively Maintain-ing Sanity are different from other disturbed inmates, and are multiply disadvantaged, in that even allowing for the unreliability of intelligence measures among the disturbed, they demonstrate unusually high levels of cognitive deficits as well as emotional problems. These men also serve draconian sentences, and a large proportion of the men have checkered institutional careers, straddling the criminal justice and mental health systems. Though the disciplinary violation rate of disturbed disruptive inmates is the lowest in our sample, it contrasts with that of other inmate-patients. Moreover, the rate would be higher if we accounted for "time at risk" and allowed for reclassification of behavior by the prison as illness-related.

## Note

1. Such information can become available in those psychiatric settings in which staff make an effort to understand the antecedents of patient assaultiveness; see Quinsey (1977), Intro., note 22; also, St. Thomas Psychiatric Hospital, "A program for the management and prevention of disturbed behavior," *Hospital and Community Psychiatry,* 1976, *27,* 724–727. For a sampling of research studies of violent behavior in hospitals, see J. R. Lion and W. H. Reid, eds., *Assaults within Psychiatric Facilities.* New York: Grune and Stratton, 1983.

   A thought-provoking finding is that of V. L. Quinsey and G. W. Varney ("Characteristics of assaults and assaulters in a maximum security psychiatric unit," *Crime and Justice,* 1977, *5,* 212–220), which is based on a review of 198 patient assaults—mainly against staff. In most incidents, staff reported there was "no reason" for the assault. The patients, however, almost invariably cited what to them were compelling reasons, such as staff provocations (perceived abuse or teasing), orders to do something the patient didn't want to do, or staff refusals to honor patient requests.

# 12

# Success Stories

In tracing the careers of men in our cohort, we pointed out that almost irrespective of time spent in prison, the deportment of most inmates tends to improve over time. In other words, the prisoners' maladaptive behavior decreases; one also assumes the corollary, which is that their adaptive behavior increases.

This observation may strike some as counter-intuitive, both with respect to maladaptive behavior and prisons. With respect to maladaptiveness, it makes sense to think in terms of cumulative difficulties, in which first failure breeds failure, and then punitive responses cement the conduct they are meant to deter. As for prisons, the prevailing notion is that such settings are at best stultifying and at worst counter-rehabilitative, and that they function as "breeding grounds for crime."

Given that the picture is not as it is predicted by prevailing pessimistic postulates, one must explore countervailing and more heartening assumptions. Some have to do with the nature of man, and others with attributes of prison. The former must focus on resilience and maturation, on self-correction and growth; the latter must draw attention to nonpunitive features of the prison, such as ameliorative provisions and program opportunities.

In preceding chapters we have described types of maladaptive behavior in the prison, which we have illustrated with accounts drawn from relatively checkered inmate dossiers. We had expected these accounts to feature many downhill careers (that is, patterns of increasing maladaptiveness), but discovered that these patterns are rare, while the more encouraging sequence (of decreasing maladaptiveness) occurs with appreciable frequency.

### Causes of Improvement

What are some facts in the inmate histories that account for personal transmutations? Are there clues to the dynamics of change in careers that begin inauspiciously, but show constructive reform? To explore such questions we selected over fifty (out of our 240) case histories, in which cessation or diminution of maladaptiveness had occurred. We grouped these accounts in terms of the processes that we inferred might be at work in producing the changes we observed, and we will describe these themes under relevant process headings.

*Involvement*

According to the dictionary, the verb "involve" can mean "to engage as a participant:" and "to occupy (oneself) absorbingly; especially: to commit (oneself) emotionally." The first phrase describes what others must do to secure the impact denoted by the second and third phrase. In tandem, the phrases suggest a process whereby a person is invited to participate in activity which he or she finds enticing, which in turn produces emotional commitment to the goals of the activity.

Involving a person in adaptive behavior can serve to break a pattern of maladaptive acts by providing another option, given the "wrong" sort of involvement, or by creating meaning and purpose where it has not existed. Both of these paths are familiar to students of criminological literature because their counterparts are implied in theories that stress the regenerative value of "legitimate opportunity structures" or that prescribe commitment to prosocial norms as an antidote to delinquency.[1]

The dictionary definitions we have cited tell us that reform through involvement must be an active and not a passive process; the strategy of leading the horse to water does not in itself promote involvement, because involvement presupposes participation in *absorbing* activity. If we are concerned with promoting real involvement, we must provide tasks that entice rather than activities that fill time.[2] Our probabilities of success increase when the available activities intersect with the interests of the persons to be involved, which means that personal interests must be recognized and diagnosed by the task providers. Of course, "engagement" can mean self-engagement, which occurs when the involvement is not planned, that is, when a person is enticed by an enterprise he or she happens to run across, because it is routinely available.

In the prison, one arena in which involvement occurs is in educational programs, and another is in work assignments. In either case, an inmate discovers that what he is doing is enjoyable, meaningful, or engrossing, and that it is worthy of investment of his time and expenditure of his energy. The short-term benefit the inmate and the system derive is that of deinvestment of time and energy from maladaptive pursuits, to the extent to which this occurs. Longer term benefits also occur, but presuppose more substantial reorientations of investments and goals.[3]

Involvement is not necessarily a one-step process, nor need involvement entail immediate deinvestment in maladaptive pursuits. An example of a long-term mixed pattern is provided by a man who serves a long prison sentence for participating in two sadistic robberies. His disciplinary dossier is dense and variegated and contains reference to many fights and disturbances in which he is loud and threatening. The man also manufactures and carries contraband such as wine, and is involved in incidents of vandalism and in belligerent defiance of prison authority.

The last offense for which the man is convicted is a robbery in which the victims are gratuitously humiliated and threatened. This man does not impress probation officers. His attitudes and violence potential, however, are exoneratingly traced to a tragedy he experienced several years earlier. A probation officer writes that

> underlying the defendant's problems appears to be a deep sense of bitterness and hostility, in part owing to the unexpected deaths of his parents when he was 13 years old and the defendant's failure to accept or adjust to these circumstances. The defendant has expressed the attitude that life has unfairly dealt him "dirty" and that he intends to respond in kind; apparently unmindful or uncaring of the consequences either for himself or his victims.

The possibility of a link between hurt and anger is illustrated elsewhere in the man's presentence report, where the probation officer writes that

> the defendant is an only child (verified), although he convincingly gave the names and ages of a fictitious family of seven brothers and sisters who he claimed resided in various foster homes in Boston, Massachusetts. When the defendant was confronted as to the reason for the fabrication he became hostile and angry and stated that "everybody wants to have a family."

The man has been an inmate in a reformitory where he reportedly "became interested and participated in sewing and tailoring training, which he enjoyed." He does similarly well in his first prison work assignments. His counselor writes that "he is praised as being an excellent worker who does everything that is expected of him." He is requested on several occasions by mess hall correction officers who indicate that he is an exceptional worker in their operation. As to custodial adjustment, early reports complain that the inmate "will display frustration and a quick temper" though they also point out that in one fight he "assisted a correction officer in breaking up the altercation." Other staff characterize the inmate as "a very headstrong, demanding individual who has no concept of attempting to heed any constructive criticism that can be afforded him." The inmate is also discontinued from a work assignment because he is suspected of stealing glue, a fact which gains significance from his admission that he has extensively experimented with drugs in the community.

At this time the inmate enters a youth prison from which he is transferred with the notation that "he has a reputation for bulldozing and intimidating weak inmates," and he is assigned to a maximum-security institution. Here he at first does well, but eventually experiences problems. One report, for example, describes a disturbance in the prison yard, and notes that

> as the officer was assisting a sergeant who was assaulted you were seen by another officer as you attempted to kick the officer. As the second officer went to assist the first, you attempted to hit him with your fist. You then ran into a crowd of inmates. . . . By your actions you created a serious disturbance and participated in this disturbance.

The man receives a heavy penalty for the incident and is transferred to another prison. In this institution "he serves as a sheet shaker in the laundry and he likes this work, (stating) that he intends to seek this type of employment on the street." He is also described as participating constructively in extracurricular committee assignments and as demonstrating "a greatly improved record."

Later the inmate is apprehended carrying a homemade weapon and is transferred to another prison, where he is identified as a participant in extortion. This involvement leads to fights, and the inmate arms himself (again) and is placed in segregation, where he is described as "an arrogant, troublesome individual." Thereafter, however, he participates in vocational and academic training and in group therapy at the urging of the parole board. At this juncture staff write that "the inmate has been able to maintain a satisfactory rapport with both staff and peers (and) his custodial record has improved a great deal over the last six months." In light of this improvement the inmate is paroled, with a notation that he be assigned to "a residential drug program if possible."

This man participates both in the legitimate and illegitimate opportunity structures of the prison. These involvements to some extent are independent, and the man appears content in relatively simple, structured work assignments while he is also involved in drug trafficking and extortion in the inmate community. He does, however, make periodic efforts to impress staff and ends up achieving a dramatic turnabout in which he functions violation free and is involved in self-improvement pursuits.

Many of the man's prison violations are corollaries of his underworld activities, and others show ambivalence in his stance toward prison staff and other authority figures. One aspect of the ambivalence is that the man reacts against staff interference with his peer-related activities such as extortion and drug trafficking. The other aspect of the ambivalence is a paradoxical attachment to those who show him kindness and take an interest in him, which includes officers who supervise him at work. In this sense the man not only reacts against the loss of parental figures, which he has deeply felt, but unlike individuals who are more bitter, he seems able to accept prison staff as parental substitutes and to react positively toward them. This fact explains the contrasting characterizations of the man, some of which originate with staff members against whom he reacts with defiance while others are filed by staff who find that this man can be obedient, loyal, and hard working when he forms a dependent attachment.

The above inmate's pattern is not one of "pure" involvement. He gains satisfaction from completing simple tasks but also prizes benevolent supervisors, which means that the relationships that surround tasks may matter as much (or more) than the sense of accomplishment he derives from achieving a neatly shaken sheet or deft stitch.

*Support*

Where relationships boost morale and confidence, we think in terms of benefits derived from support. Support can undergird maladaptation (as in delinquent gangs). Where the wrong sort of support facilitates the wrong sort of conduct, some argue that change should occur if the polarity of this force can be reversed.[4] A similar argument applies where persons are hungry for support. This sort of situation is more complicated, however, because maladaptive behavior that is motivated by desire for support often revolves around counterproductive and therefore foredoomed efforts to establish links with others.

An example of the latter pattern is provided by an adolescent confined for burglarizing a home and destroying a car. There is a notation on this man's dossier which records that he has absconded from a juvenile home and tried to escape from a jail. Prison incidents include charges of disobeying orders, engaging in loud and unseemly conduct and fighting, and there is one charge of attempting escape. There is a period of four months without disciplinary violations, and no disciplinary incidents in the last months of the man's prison term.

The inmate enters the system at age sixteen after authorities have done a great deal of soul searching about what to do with him. His probation officer writes:

> He was referred to the school psychologist because he was "unable to cope with first grade work, very nervous, appeared afraid of admitting to be wrong, stubborn." The following year the school physician started him on mellaril which eliminated physical hyperactivity, but he was still seen as having difficulty in concentrating. . . . (Later) there was felt to be some decrease in his hyperactivity, but overall adjustment did not improve.

Teachers report that "the most outstanding feature of his difficulties in school was his continual clowning to get the attention of his peers." One teacher complains that

> he seems to be totally unable to stop talking. He will stand up in the middle of a class and do something quite distracting, for instance, tell a dirty joke, make an off-color remark to another classmate, etc. Today, in the middle of a lesson, he was playing with a leather bracelet. He unzipped his pants, put the bracelet almost inside and ran around the room saying, "what does this look like?" Since this is a mixed class, I believe this act was a definite offense to the girls in the class.

The inmate responds to the disciplinary reactions of a teacher by entering the man's office and having a bowel movement in his wastebasket. He similarly reacts to disciplinary efforts in the home by running away and wandering about the community. He then enlists a sidekick (age fifteen) and goes on a crime spree, estimating that he has perpetrated "about 55 burglaries." He also claims that he would welcome assignment to a camp for youthful offenders because "it will be better than staying (home). I hate it here." He changes his mind subsequently, however, and escapes from the institution, and this escape nets him an indeterminate sentence to prison.

In the prison the man gains visibility by escalating an incident in which he has been asked to pick up a piece of bread he has dropped on the floor. Though he is charged with "riot and disturbance" the incident ends with a confrontation that pits him against an officer and all of the other inmates in the mess hall. Most remaining incidents in this early term revolve around conflicts with other inmates, and have to do with a propensity to accumulate debts which the man cannot repay, requiring his placement in protection at his request. He is finally transferred and for a few months does well, but soon has renewed difficulties with peers which he resolves by drawing attention to himself. According to an incident report, the inmate had turned his bed up-side-down. His mattress was under the bed, the inmate under the mattress, when found by the officers. He had covered his body with red dye. He claims that inmates are trying to kill him and he wished to be placed in protective custody.

The inmate commits a burglary one month after being paroled from this first prison term. His first progress review describes "a disasterous adjustment," and points out that "the reports he receives are for fights, horseplay, disturbances, destruction of state property, refusing orders, refusing to accept programs and littering. His only defense for himself is I'm a criminal."

The inmate blames the parole board who he feels should have realized that "he was not ready to be released." In a more positive vein he "claims that he is a magician and . . . believes he could escape from any situation if he wished to." Staff conclude that the inmate "is a borderline psychotic case" and place him under a moderate regime of medication.

The man's self-proclaimed escape artistry proves a liability which nets him two months of segregation and six months loss of good time after he supplies toothed blades to fellow inmates to help them saw through cell bars of their windows. After this incident the inmate's violations are mainly confined to accusations that he engages in horseplay, fighting, refusing orders, and nonparticipation in programs. Such incidents are frequent, however, and earn the man a transfer to a tough prison, where he spends three months without a disciplinary incident, but signs himself into protective custody ten days before he is paroled.

The inmate is reimprisoned for a burglary which is noteworthy in that he has called the police, claiming credit as a helpful citizen. Later he escapes from a holding cell but instead of seeking freedom, "walked to the desk and said 'Hi' to the officers seated behind it." In prison, the man's first report records that he "appears to get along well with staff and peers" and "performs duties in an average manner." His second report describes his custodial adjustment as "outstanding" and points out that he is involved in college-level art study—is "an intelligent, interested student" who "accepts and completes assignments with minimal supervision." He has also become an active participant in a drug and alcohol counseling program.

The story has a happy ending, and one infers that its protagonist has undergone change, though he has also succeeded in a lifelong campaign to earn attention. The campaign starts at age six with a pathetic effort to obtain the esteem of peers by playing the clown, and the boy tries to capture a spark of love from his parents by running away, hoping that he will be missed. These efforts boomerang and make the boy an obnoxious figure to adults and an object of ridicule to peers. The boy reacts to whatever rejection he invites by resorting to fantasy, which results in his classification as mentally ill. He also builds a fantasy life, which consists of a one-person gang with whom he steals and drinks and patronizes amusement parks. Stealing sustains the boy's private world but also draws attention, and attention is probably the closest he can come to receiving affection.

In prison fellow inmates associate with the man only around the gambling table. But he is not very good at gambling, and he becomes involved in conflicts which he cannot handle. He discovers that clowning in the prison translates into disciplinary charges of horseplay, and results in conflicts with officers when they tell him to stop clowning and he disregards their instructions. He also discovers that escape fantasies are taken seriously in the prison. The situation improves in an adult prison where there is no audience for the man's performances and where the climate is one that demands sobriety. Concurrently the inmate has demonstrated an interest and an aptitude in art. He can now evolve a formula for gaining recognition which centers on conformity and achievement, and what he does also yields intrinsic satisfactions, making him less dependent on attention and approval from others.

A similar result is experienced by an inmate with a comparably checkered career, whose counselor reports:

> I have seen some of his art work, which is quite outstanding. He is quite an accomplished artist, has a lot of talent. . . . Since being incarcerated he has learned more skills in commercial art. . . . In art class the teacher has asked him to be her aide due to his advanced talent. . . . He has a lot of talent and can be easily worked with, especially with some positive reinforcement, encouragement and attention.

Both inmates are supported by civilian staff, who view their artistic output with admiration, which they freely and volubly express. In this way staff act the part of benevolent parental figures, and each inmate finds a niche as teacher's pet and as grateful counseling client.

### Attachment

Closely related to support is change through emotional bonds and obligations which compete with temptations and pressures that reinforce maladaptiveness. This process—of attachment—occurs among most offenders who "mature out" of offending. Gang delinquents, for example, graduate as they find mates and undertake responsibilities. Recidivism statistics also show that family links reduce return rates to crime.[5]

The difference between change through support and attachment lies in the effects of relationships. Support is nurturance, which is valued and builds confidence. Attachment comes with norms and obligations, which are prices one must pay to sustain a relationship. Attending to these norms and obligations means that a person cannot attend to other, conflicting norms. "Be dependable," for instance, competes with "act tough" or "be ostentatiously irresponsible."

Attachment not only goes hand in hand with support, but can also be combined with other processes, such as involvement. An example is provided by a man sentenced for a robbery in which the victim is shot and killed. In the last half of the man's career in prison there are no disciplinary incidents. The first half of the sentence, however, shows many problems, including a propensity to be caught stealing and fighting, threats against officers, involvement in disturbances and possession of contraband. The man is also often described as "argumentative."

This inmate's adult career begins at age seventeen with robberies and weapons charges, and he is identified as having acquired a .357 magnum which one of his crime partners uses in the offense for which he is imprisoned. At the time of this incident the man is on probation, "leading a nomadic existence without any stable home residence." The probation officer writes that "it should be strongly noted that when the defendant was questioned as to how he felt about his involvement in the present offense his response was one of smiling and laughter." Prison intake staff also describe the man as callous, and record that he "appears at times to attempt to bulldoze younger and weaker inmates." They send the man to a high-security prison, where he proves resistant to programming. A counselor writes that:

> The inmate states that he does not like the program of school at this facility. According to him the education program is slap at best and he is unable to learn. He says that when one leaves classrooms there are several other inmates that are looking for him and it makes it inordinately difficult for him.

The inmate also complains "that although he writes his family, they do not answer his letters." Subsequently his contacts with his family improve, and so does his prison adjustment. Initially teachers complain about his attendance, which is virtually nonexistent, and he is removed from work assignments because of "charges involving abuse of privileges, (being) out of place, abusive language and threats." Two months later the man has received a visit from his wife and son, his work supervisors are satisfied with his work and he reportedly makes progress in school. He also qualifies for an honors block program.

The man does so well that he is soon transferred to a lower security institution so that he can take college courses. Here his work reports range from good to excellent. His school performance is rated "satisfactory," but staff also complain that

> overall there has been a deterioration in this resident's attitude and behavioral adjustment since initially being received at this facility. It appeared at initial interview that he would be a model inmate and that his previous, poor disciplinary record was going to be left behind at (his last prison.) However, his disciplinary record to date does not indicate that he is maturing sufficiently enough to avoid disciplinary reports.

For eighteen months the situation remains relatively unchanged. The inmate receives many visits from his wife and child, does extremely well in his academic work, but sporadically commits disciplinary violations. He eventually receives a college degree and becomes involved in counseling. He also continues close contact with his wife, who eventually succeeds in changing the man's deportment in prison. In a progress report written six months after a dramatic change in the man's conduct, staff write:

> The inmate's biggest problem in this facility has always been his disciplinary record. While he is not regarded as highly assaultive he does become confrontative and consequently has subjected himself to numerous reports that could have easily been avoided. He had been counseled about this on many occasions. However, I think the point was finally driven home when his wife called the superintendent of the facility regarding the family reunion (conjugal visiting) program. She seemed very sincere and concerned about her husband. She stated to the superintendent and to this writer that if the inmate was going to continue to subject himself to disciplinary reports, thus curtailing his chances for a more positive program, then she did not see him as being worthwhile to wait for. Apparently the inmate got this message loud and clear. He was called out on an interview by the superintendent and this matter was discussed. After that there has been a marked improvement in his behavioral record.

This situation prevails for another two years, until the inmate is released. The change is extraordinary because early on, the man sees himself as tough and ready to deploy violence, and this self-image is symbolized by his fondness for weapons, including large caliber handguns. The self-image also makes the man indifferent to the impact he has on victims, who are drawn from a pool of individuals who are not his associates and are not tough, and who own commodities that he (or his associates) want and therefore feel entitled to. The view that "to the tough belong the spoils" also accounts for the involvement of this inmate in stealing from others in the prison. The man's self-conception as "tough" also colors his interactions with staff, with whom he insists on being dealt with on a level of equity, which means that his word is as good as any staff member's in an altercation.

There are two chinks in this man's armor, however. One is an intense thirst for education and a propensity for becoming interested and involved in work assignments. This propensity provides the prison system with a strong incentive or reward for use in modifying the man's behavior. It also takes the man into a social setting containing others who are similarly oriented, and separates him from his antisocial group of peers. The second chink in the man's armour is his close attachment to his family who are also concerned about modifying his behavior, and not above using the continuation of the relationship as a lever to inspire compliance. In this connection the inmate undergoes a crisis, and after the wife's seminal intervention a counselor even complains that "the inmate has apparently broken up with his wife." However, faced with the realization that he must choose between the world of tough manliness and that of middle-class responsibility, the inmate successfully opts for the later.

*Detachment*

To the extent to which maladaptiveness responds to attributes of settings in which the person does not function, a change of scenery can often be regenerative. One reason for this fact is that the particular stimuli that promote a person's maladaptive behavior may be less available in his new environment, which provides him with new options. As example, prison administrators contend—and our data verify—that young inmates often improve their deportment when transferred to a prison with an older population.[6] Entering an age-heterogeneous environment that "detaches" because it reduces peer pressure permits increased relaxation and tempers anxiety. The more mature environment also offers fewer occasions for conflict, and it provides diminished opportunity to play to inmate audiences.

Where a transfer between settings works, this does not mean that setting-attributes have been to blame for the person's maladaptiveness. Since the entire relationship between person and setting has been changed, the person's propensities to maladaptiveness are as much affected as the environment in which they are displayed.

This point is exemplified by the career of a youth imprisoned for a burglary and for participating in a mugging. In prison this man participates in a great many fights, but he ends his prison sentence with six months that are free of violations, and this period coincides with a transfer from a youth institution to a maximum-security prison.

The inmate has been in structured settings of various kinds since the age of four, and his probation officer notes that

> he has continued to experience rejection on the part of his family, who presently won't even allow him to reside within their home. He was in fact living in an automobile at the time he committed the present offenses.

The probation staff suggests that the man be placed in an in-patient treatment program for addicts, but he is instead committed to prison. He is first assigned to a low-security facility which is structured around a cottage system. His removal from this setting is soon requested. The prison reports that

> He has been moved to several different cottages because of a confrontational and outspoken self presentation with peers and staff and because at each new location the possessions of others soon disappear after his arrival. As a consequence the inmate has been involved in fighting episodes which threaten the security of the facility. At this point in time the inmate is no longer deemed an appropriate placement in a minimum security facility. His behavior and other needs require a more structured setting.

This summary represents the conclusions of a number of cottage officers. One officer writes:

> The above inmate is in my cottage for the second time. Both times he has been nothing but trouble. A short time after arriving in the cottage things start to disappear. The cottage becomes very noisy. He is the type of inmate who cannot get along with anyone. In the short time that he has been here he has only enemies in the cottage—no friends. . . . I have been informed today that he is stealing in the cottage. Also I have been told today that he has been provoking another inmate all day, and that tonight's fight is the result.

Another officer writes,

> it has been brought to my attention by two inmates that this inmate has been stealing various and sundry items from them (e.g. soap, shampoo, deodorant) and selling these items to other inmates. . . . An inmate stated that he found the inmate in his unattended room on several occasions, whereupon items would turn up missing . . . Since the inmate has a lengthy history of thefts within other cottages and because of the extant potential for a physical confrontation between the inmate and the inmates from whom the inmate has reportedly stolen, I strongly urge that the inmate be removed from this cottage forthwith or perhaps be removed from this facility.

The man is transferred to a secure youth prison after losing six months of good time for fighting. In the second institution he continues to be involved in fights, but these conflicts are of a different order, in that the inmate now generates ethnic confrontations. He rejects drug therapy "because he has serious racial prejudice and therapy groups are mainly ethnic black and Puerto Rican" and also leaves school "due to peer pressures" after making substantial progress.

The inmate undergoes "grief shock" when he learns that his younger sister has committed suicide. At the same time he is accorded a heavy penalty (90 days of segregation and 180 days loss of good time) because he has assaulted another inmate with a chair. He is transferred to a third youth prison, but keeps being segregated for involvements in fights, which reduces the time he spends in the classroom. At this juncture, in response to strong recommendations from the youth prison administration, the inmate is transferred to a maximum-security prison with an older population, where he spends over six months without a single disciplinary incident.

This man has spent most of his life in institutions, but has not been acculturated to norms of cohabitation. He is a source of conflicts with both sophisticated and unsophisticated peers. When he is placed with a relatively vulnerable group he engages in underhanded predatory behavior or clumsily seeks attention and thus incurs universal emnity. In a more sophisticated group he expects to be victimized and engages in preemptive strikes and then lives in fear. The type of setting with which this young man can finally cope combines structure and an older population, so that issues of pecking order and of outgrouping and ingrouping and peer rivalries do not arise, and program involvement becomes the only show in town.

### Respite

One way in which settings can differ is in terms of amounts of stimulation they offer. Stimulation levels matter particularly to persons who react adversely to boredom (low stimulation) or to confusion (high stimulation.) Where a person moves from a setting in which the stimulation levels are higher or lower than he or she can handle, he or she should experience relief; reductions in maladaptive behavior can consequently be expected if the person has reacted with aggression or irritability to stimulus overload or underload. This is the type of change that is reported, for example, with students who are removed from classrooms which overwhelm or under-challenge them.

Persons settle down in low-stimulation settings because they relax or regroup in such settings. A reduced level of stimulation is particularly relaxing when a person tends to overrespond—when a great many stimuli are viewed as demands to which the person feels obligated to react.

A case in point is that of a thirty-two year-old man with a weight problem who serves a short sentence for forcibly stealing money from a senior citizen. The victim is a eighty-seven year-old lady who sits in a bank with savings she has withdrawn. The man wrestles the lady for her money and leaves the bank pursued by customers who capture him.

The man's disciplinary record is dense and checkered, and contains a litany of profanity he uses in refusing to follow orders. One incident description reads:

> You were told by the officer to wear socks when you went to breakfast. At the time you had shoes on but were wearing no socks. There had previously been noted a problem with foot odor. You told the officer that you had no socks. Your room was checked and three new pairs of socks were found. You went to breakfast wearing just shoes and no socks on your feet. You were then ordered to wear socks to attend the noon meal, you again refused, this time stating that your new socks didn't fit you. At the adjustment committee meeting the adjustment committee members had you go to your room and get the new socks. When you returned they looked at them and it appeared apparent to all committee members that if you put them on they would fit you. You were asked to try them on before the committee and you refused, stating that even if they did fit you were refusing to wear them, for you felt it was just a continuing effort on the part of the staff to harass you, and you wanted no part of any aspect of this program any longer.

The file starts with a document pertaining to a previous offense in which the man has threatened two ladies with a knife, requesting permission to commit a flagrantly indecent act. The man again tries to escape, but is wrestled into submission by the police. The police and others opine that the man's behavior at this time is bizarre, and he is committed to a hospital for a psychiatric examination. The probation officer writes that "it goes without saying that the individual is a highly disturbed, emotionally unstable, antisocial and dangerous individual." The man's history shows that he has been admitted to medical institutions at age nine, suffering from "childhood schizophrenia." He is later diagnosed as having graduated to "schizophrenia, paranoid-type, severe." As an adult the man has been found incompetent to stand trial and on another occasion is admitted to a prison hospital from a detention facility. The presentence report concludes that "he appears to be in need of a highly structured, secure treatment modality where he can receive the necessary assistance in coping with his various emotional problems." This prescription is intended to fit the prison.

At prison intake, a counselor broaches the possibility of an academic program, which the man rejects, stating, "school is for kids." Test scores show the inmate classifiable "within the borderline range of mental functioning."

Two months later the inmate has been sent to a special program. Though a psychiatrist classifies him as "without mental illness," he has medicated him for insomnia. Program staff find the men resistant. They record that

> he has had at least two writeups since his program began, one of which consists of verbally threatening an officer. On occasions where he has been confronted in therapy he becomes very nasty and aggressive. . . . However, in recent weeks, in fairness to the inmate, he has begun to relax more and at least speak civilly to other group members and staff.

Three months thereafter optimism has faded, and we read that the inmate

> has acquired six misbehavior reports for refusing orders, abusive language and harassment. This man apparently feels his masculinity is threatened if he backs down in a situation. Thus he has difficulty relating to officers, staff, and inmates and will not retreat even if he knows he is wrong. When not in an angered state he can function in a fairly reasonable manner. However, it appears that when he feels challenged he throws all caution to the wind and impulsively acts.

The staff conclude that the inmate's "preoccupation with 'being a man' may be reflective of low self esteem and self doubt." Three months later, staff expand on their observation and describe the inmate as follows:

> He has a very heavy fixation on the validity of his masculinity and will exhibit anger whenever this is challenged. Unfortunately he also feels that his ability to make his own decisions, be they right or wrong, is part of that masculine expression. As a result when he was recently offered the opportunity to attend school he refused and chose to follow disciplinary-type procedures to prevent his attendance. After several attempts to talk with this man and allow him to get by his false pride it was decided that his need for therapy outweighted his need for education at present, and he was reverted back to a shop program.

Five months later the unit staff continue to bewail the man's "preoccupation with his masculinity," as a result of which "he feels that he will be less manly if he concedes his errors or changes his mind" and "will stubbornly refuse any help, although he acknowledges his need for help." Staff add:

> In all, he has accumulated sixteen reports to this date. The bulk of these refer to his refusal to meet program activities such as school, therapy, or work. Also, behavior such as harassment, refusing order, threats, and verbal abuse have

been reported. In interviews both prior to and after these incidents he is able to generate acceptable alternative behaviors, but chooses to act out in a manner that pleases him regardless of the consequence.

In another document staff point out that the prison strikes the man as preferable to the outside world. They write that

the inmate appears very resigned to institutional life and has spoken on the positive aspects of institutional life on several occasions. The outlook of this inmate is quite sad in that he feels that the basic needs met by institutional life offers this as a better lifestyle than perhaps that which he is forced to live in on the street. With this rather low opinion of himself and poor outlook for the future he almost appears resigned to illegal activities until his eventual arrest and return to a facility-type setting.

The staff conclude that

one cannot help but suspect that he is depressed as a result of these prospects and sees little if any motivation towards change. This overall outlook reflects this man's very low self esteem and poor self image. It is this attitude that likely causes him to receive occasional misbehavior reports for very minor incidents which he is fully capable of avoiding. There are times when he feels that others may see this feeling in him. It is suspected that these are the times when he acts out very irrational decision-making type of behavior.

In the following few months there are fewer misbehavior reports, and the man's relationship with correctional staff and peers are noted as having improved. However, shortly thereafter occurs the incident with the socks, which appears to have been sparked by the fact that the inmate's peers had complained to correction officers about "foot odors while they were sitting by him in the mess hall, eating." The incident shows the inmate digging in, claiming that he has no socks or that socks do not fit him, taking a conscientious objector stance because he makes the assumption that any compromise or retreat is inconceivable.

As a result of such sequences we find the inmate in disciplinary segregation settings where he is invariably described as "quiet, polite, and cooperative," and as "relaxed and content." Not only is he observed to socialize with other segregated inmates and to participate in recreation with obvious enjoyment, but officers record that "he has admirably refused to involve himself in the various shouting matches and other disruptive behavior that has occurred in this special housing unit recently." When the inmate emerges from segregation, however, he renews his "passive resistance to authority figures which has become more aggressive, in the form of threats." Only when he returns to confinement status, observation reports record that he "adjusts well to the mundane routine and appears very content."

Staff point out that whenever the inmate is confined to his cell, "it has been noted that he generally has adjusted quite well." Segregation unit officers report that

> he presents no custodial problems and is cooperative and friendly to special housing-unit staff. The inmate also tends to sing and talk to himself in his cell, but the latter behavior on inspection seems to be his way of "thinking out loud."

Generally speaking the policy of the institution has become to leave the inmate on unemployed status in his cell, and as a result the last few months of his stay pass without incident.

It is clear that if and when the inmate does not feel challenged or tested and is left alone few problems arise, but when he is instructed to do something or not to do something there is a risk that he can see himself having to prove his worth, in which instances he digs in his heels and becomes stubbornly wedded to his predefined stand. When custodial moves have to be escalated this makes the man feel doubly impotent and angry, which causes him to scold and threaten staff. All ends well, however: The ultimate custodial gambit is that of punitive segregation, which is a setting in which the man no longer feels over-tested and over-challenged, and he is therefore at peace.

*Sanctuary*

One implication of the *need hierarchy* described by the psychologist Maslow is that safety concerns can monopolize attention, and thus keep "higher" goals (esteem or social needs) from being experienced.[7] The process does not distinguish between justified and unjustified safety concerns, nor could it do so, because (1) when the danger persons feel is great, they cannot afford to play odds in assessing threats, (2) imagined threats feel just as real as actual danger, and (3) once afraid, persons become attuned—and often oversensitive—to danger cues.

Just as the unsafeness of environments is to varying degrees in the eyes of the beholder, so is their safety. When we speak of "sanctuaries" we thus speak of settings which are subjectively reassuring, or that feel safer than other settings. A sanctuary must offer physical security, but it also must contain a relaxed, assured atmosphere and an absence of constraints and pressures that fearful persons can regard as malevolently hostile.

Another attribute of some sanctuaries are involvements that distract or deflect the fear-inspired person from obsessive discomfort.

In New York prisons, "victim-prone" inmates are recognized as a special class, and settings have been designed to respond to the needs of this group. The concern of those who run such settings is humane but also reintegrative, in the sense that inmates are expected to graduate from the settings into the prison population at large.[8] Change implications arise because inmates who have reacted maladaptively to fear can be expected to behave differently when they feel reassured and able to abandon reactions (preemptive strikes, self-insulation and so forth) that respond to perceived danger.

An example is provided by one of our mature inmates. This man has robbed a gas station and claims that he "doesn't know why" because he was "under the influence of drugs and alcohol." The man lists many drugs to which he is addicted and he confesses that he is an alcoholic. He becomes involved in conflicts with correction officers and inmates, as well as violations of the prison sanitary code.

The man has spent two years in the armed forces. He has been discharged for a psychiatric disability, and the probation officer who prepares his presentence report writes that:

> During our interview the defendant appeared transfixed as he rambled on about everyone trying to "screw" him. With his psychological disorders and his extensive drug abuse and with his wildly exaggerated stories, (the inmate) presented the profile of a man trying desperately to convince this writer that he is completely insane and does not deserve to be in jail but rather undergoing treatment. . . . He did impress this writer as suffering from one or several mental disorders. It would be difficult to explain otherwise why he would rob a gas station unmasked where everyone could identify him. . . . He stated over and over in several different ways that everyone was out to get him.

In the prison the inmate signs himself into protection claiming that other inmates have made sexual overtures to him and have subjected him to extortion attempts. He is sent to a second prison where he is seen by a psychiatrist, who writes:

> He tells many stories of the many people he is suing. . . . He also spoke of planning to sue the State Corrections Department, officers and whomever else he says "he can get." He has intentions of suing various psychiatrists he has seen while in the correctional system and is literally looking around for people to sue. He stated he has not been out of special housing during the eight months he has been incarcerated. When I suggested he could possibly enter into a program at this facility he said he could not because he has enemies. . . . What we have here is a very paranoid man who suffers from classical delusions of persecution. . . . He is paranoid and refuses to leave the special housing unit

because he is fearful and won't encounter enemies. . . . He will be followed up, and his paranoid state monitored.

Later it develops that the man does have real enemies whom he has good reason to fear, though he also has imaginary enemies, including the military and various agencies of government, and mental health professionals with whom he has dealt. The man eventually agrees, however, to be placed in a protective program, where he does well. Staff write:

> Since his arrival here very little inappropriate behavior has been observed. The structure of the environment appears to offer the safety and support as well as activity stimulation needed by him. He has been emotionally stable and has not been threatening legal action. He has utilized appropriate channels for suggesting administrative changes which would be helpful in enhancing the effectiveness of our program. He has demonstrated personal initiative in solving problems, and has been patient and delayed gratification. It may be questionable (however) if he can continue with his positive behavior when released.

The man's difficulties are a summation of objective and subjective factors. The man is a disturbed individual who is sensitive to imaginary conspiracies in which he is either a victim or a participant. Narcotics use also influences the man's incapacity to distinguish between reality and fantasy, as illustrated by the fact that he holds up a business establishment in which he has been employed, which makes his arrest virtually certain. Thereafter, the man turns state's evidence against his codefendant, which is where reality is added to fantasy because the codefendant arrives in the prison, spreads the news that the man is "a rat," and seeks to do him harm. This creates a fateful confluence because when this man, who suffers from residues of paranoid schizophrenia, senses danger, he evolves conspiracy schemes to "explain" and counter the threat.

Matters are not improved by the fact that the man becomes aware of the skeptical reactions he evokes in some prison staff members, who thus qualify for inclusion as protagonists in his conspiracy scheme.

The problems get even worse when the man is segregated and has little to do beyond embroidering his conspiracies, but as a corollary the problem is solved through assignment to a program which is safe and supportive and offers opportunities for activity and constructive participation. In this program the man feels reassured, his attention is constructively occupied and his symptoms subside.

*Asylum*

One problem prisons share with community settings is that they need conditions short of hospitalization under which disturbed persons can lead some semblance of a normal life. This means settings in which tolerance for deviance must be high, but not high enough to reinforce eccentricity. Such settings must also assist persons with chores of daily living, and encourage involvement in activities that transcend self-management. Beyond these attributes, such environments must provide medical and psychological services to help disturbed persons control their symptoms, which includes occasional transfers into more structured (hospital or quasi-hospital) settings when the need for more comprehensive ministrations arises.

To the extent to which asylums exist, it is often possible to reduce a person's functional handicaps to the point where a semblance of normalcy can be achieved, which means that the person can engage in as much adaptive behavior as we can expect from a person with continuing symptoms of pathology.

New York prisons offer asylum arrangements, and a number of disturbed inmates have benefitted from them. One such inmate is a man serving ten years in prison for injuring police officers trying to take him to a hospital for a psychiatric commitment. The man's disciplinary record is inconsistent in that it contains periods with disciplinary incidents and periods without incidents. The offense categories are also mixed. The man is repeatedly written up for being unclean and refusing to take showers and otherwise to take care of himself. He is also written up for refusing to do things such as go to school and go to work, and he is occasionally charged with being disruptive, destroying and throwing objects, and once for flooding his cell. There are also fights, and one or two instances of bootleg wine making.

As a boy the inmate is arrested for bringing a gun and ammunition to his junior high school. He also belongs to "a neogang" and participates in a robbery for which he serves a prison term. He enters the army where he earns an honorable discharge, but also spends five months in the stockade for stealing from his peers. A turning point in the man's life occurs when a brother of whom he is fond is shot to death by police officers. "during a dispute at a welfare center." Shortly thereafter the man becomes convinced that people are trying to kill him and has to be hospitalized. Hospitalization does not work, however, and the man's wife complains that "he heard voices, listened at the walls, armed himself with a hammer, broke her nose and twice stabbed her with scissors and a spear." The man is evicted by his wife and moves in with his mother, who has him committed to the hospital twice within a three-month period. The mother reports at this time that

> (her son's) behavior had become increasingly bizarre. Fearful that others meant to kill him he refused to leave the home, using neighborhood boys to run errands for him and began sending mail orders for the purchase of weapons.

One morning the man goes on a binge of breaking glasses and accuses his family of being "in it together," whereupon his mother telephones the police "hoping that they could remove him to a mental hospital." An emergency service van arrives and officers find the man "at the top of the stairs leading to the second floor, brandishing a hunting knife." After hours of attempting to reason with the man police call reinforcements who throw canisters of tear gas from an adjoining roof, and the man jumps out of a window and engages the police in a running battle which leaves several officers injured. Thereafter he spends one year in a hospital from which he is discharged as fit to stand trial, tried and convicted. The presentence report records that the man is

> depressed, suspicious, and often close mouthed and covertly hostile and resentful . . . describes probation and parole as "too much of a strain" and says that he prefers to "do my time" so that thereafter he would owe no one anything and do as he pleases. He does not offer insanity as a defense for his offense. . . . He implies that he was justified, inasmuch as he was in danger from "certain people out to harm me" and "felt like resisting them."

The man is taken at his word, and receives an indeterminate sentence with a maximum term of fifteen years. Shortly after he arrives in prison correction officers report that he "never participates in any activities nor speaks to anyone. He sometimes paces the floor speaking to himself. He was heard recently asking another inmate to cut his throat." The man explains that "you can't mingle with everybody" and describes his behavior as an attempt to "formulate my thoughts and see if they seem logical." He also explains that he couldn't care less if people observe his soliloquies.

At this time the man engages in repeated eccentric behavior for which he is written up and also brought to the attention of mental health staff. Mental health staff find the inmate dirty, disheveled and unshaven but willing to answer questions because "he said that if he didn't answer them the white man would put the law onto him again and he might even be killed." The man also expresses reservations about his own ethnic group who, he asserts, are "causing me to be in a place like this." The interviewer concludes that the man needs hospitalization, but a month elapses during which he "hears voices telling him not to trust anyone" and engages in conversations with "white and black specters in his cell." There is also an incident in which the man "appeared as if he were going to throw a cup of human excrement at the officers who were feeding the supper meal on the special housing unit." He is instructed to move to a cell with a plastic front, but refuses. He takes a stand with "both fists clenched, with the point of a pen protruding out of each," challenging the officers to come and get him, which they do, first dousing him with "one small blast of tear gas.'' The inmate reports that he feels great though he "claimed his penis had shrunk,'' and the next day he is transferred to the hospital where he remains for six months.

For the next eighteen months the inmate marginally survives in the prison. He refuses mental health assistance. He does not wash. He talks about "sonic noises" that control him, "insists on being the last in line, and wants no one behind him in the food line,'' "sits at the table very dirty about himself and stares at the other inmates who are afraid to sit and eat with him'' and "goes through garbage, especially cans that people have spit in.'' Hospitalization occurs after the inmate throws a food tray at an officer, shouting "feed this to the panthers,'' punches a second officer in the shoulder and hits another officer in the face, which leads to a wrestling match. Unsurprisingly the man reacts with extreme "free floating anxiety'' and "delusions persecutory in nature'' and is sent to the prison hospital, where he remains for one year.

As a patient the man is involved in incidents in which he is attacked by other inmates, or he assaults inmates for "no apparent reason.'' He also attacks a brother who has come to visit him. He is returned to the prison with a notation that "there is acting out potential in relation to a paranoid decompensation during which time, if the patient feels he is being attacked, he may become violent.''

The inmate thereafter manages the prison for about two years with only sporadic incidents of disorderly conduct, but continues to have emotional problems as evidenced by a note he writes to his brother instructing him to kill somebody who is sending the inmate hostile messages in hallucinations. Prison authorities inform the brother that there are "psychiatrists available to help" but that the inmate "does not feel that he needs this help.'' Several months later the man's mother visits him, whereupon "he became very disturbed, got up, and assaulted a correction officer who was standing nearby without any provocation.'' The inmate is committed to the hospital for two months. Six months later another commitment is considered but it is cancelled after "the inmate showed some improvement in his mental condition and agreed to cooperate with a treatment plan.'' The inmate also complains about machines implanted in his head and reports

> that the men controlling the machines started to disturb him more once they saw he was not going to the hospital. He said they caused his bones to pain. They were able to break bones in his body. They caused the other inmates to be hostile toward him and can incite them to attack him.

The man is at this point committed to the hospital and subsequently assigned to a residential mental health program. In school he becomes a "good student" and experiences no disciplinary problems except for an occasion in which he refused to go to school. He manages to control most of his symptoms, though it is reported that "occasionally he talks about 'machines' controlling people. This is a delusional process he regresses to in times of depression or boredom." The inmate is even released to population, where he manages under mental health supervision, alternately enrolled in a prevocational program and unemployed, with only two minor disciplinary violations in his last year in prison.

This man has continuing problems but does surprisingly well considering that his delusional system centers around the assumption that people, including people in police uniforms, manifest intentions to kill him. The man's success in part derives from the indulgence of officers who permit him to stay in his cell quietly hallucinating and let him take evasive measures to protect himself, provided these do not include attacking officers and other inmates. The man's most prevalent difficulty arises from his phobia in relation to showers which includes simulating a shower when he cannot evade it altogether.

The inmate is permitted to partially control his psychiatric treatment, including his hospital commitments. He is permitted to modulate his exposure to perceived danger and he survives a decade of imprisonment oscillating along a continuum that ranges from mild apprehension to panics which require hospitalization, but which ultimately dissipate under an indulgent regime.

*Reassessment*

One fact which makes maladaptive behavior fascinating is that it frequently continues despite evidence that it does not "work" or that it achieves results that are counterproductive. This fact tells us that superficial change strategies—such as reasoning with the maladaptive person and giving him advice—are unlikely to work, since they merely tell the person what is (or should be) obvious to him.

It does not follow, however, that insight is impotent as a tool for change. History is redolent with reforms that are based upon reevaluation, and most people's lives, including those of most critics of insight-related approaches, contain turning points in which reassessment has led to change.

The conclusion to be drawn is not that insight-based change is unachievable, but that it is difficult, and that it must be targeted at critical junctures in the lives of clients, such as when they are susceptible to change because of guilt and extreme discomfort. Even this requisite does not suffice, however, because insights include self-critiques which are unflattering and frequently painful. Insight-related approaches must thus include techniques for attacking, circumventing or working through expected defensive reactions.

Prisons have not been havens for insight-centered interventions and are even less so now because of prevailing doubts about the value of rehabilitation. Some residues of the insight-related approach persist, however, in the shape of therapeutic communities which rely on inmate peer groups with catalytic staff as their modality of choice.[9] New York prisons have several such communities which are sometimes invoked for maladaptive inmates, occasionally with successful results.

One of the persons who has benefitted from this strategy is a man imprisoned for shoplifting and for selling drugs to a police officer. Early on in prison he is involved in an assault, but subsequent offenses are mostly minor transgressions such as "refused orders to lock in, demanding to be given his medication," "did not have his ID card in his possession," "created a disturbance at the commissary," "absent for a tutoring session," "smoking in a restricted area," "had commissary supplies evidently bought with stamps," "lied to an officer about contraband being held," "violates 'strict bed rest' order," "playing radio without headphones," and so forth. No violations occur during the last six months of the man's sentence.

In the assaultive incident in which the man is involved the charge reads:

> You refused to leave (the hospital) stating to the officer, "I'm not going back to my cell until I receive a phone call." However, you complied and accompanied the officer along the tunnel back to your housing unit. Suddenly and without warning you ran to the officer and grabbed him around the neck from behind. As the officer attempted to restrain you and protect himself you struck him in the stomach and kicked him in the groin. At that point other officers intervened and you were escorted to the SHU where you remained approximately for half an hour, at which time you were escorted to the hospital. As this operation was progressing you suddenly kicked an officer's right leg, thus causing the officer to fall down the stairs. . . . You were placed under special watch.

This incident earns the inmate a heavy penalty, but before it is assigned the custody staff request that a psychiatrist examine the inmate because "he is experiencing anxiety and disorientation." The psychiatrist reports that the inmate is suffering from "an anxiety reaction, situational." A month later the inmate is committed to the prison hospital from another prison. Psychiatrists report that the inmate

> was admitted to the psychiatric service on the same day of his transfer to this prison. . . . During the first three days of admission, attempts at interviews with the resident were unsuccessful as he looked lost, confused and bewildered. The

delusional picture alternated between marked withdrawal and periods of agitation where he would become hostile, impulsive and demanding. During these periods of agitation he would scream and yell and would almost continuously bang his fists and feet and sometimes his head against his room's metal door. . . . He continues to be confused and incoherent, and the clinical picture has remained essentially the same as above. If anything, he has decompensated further and has become a danger to himself. . . . Yesterday he ripped up his bedsheets making long strips, causing the staff to take precautionary steps regarding his suicide attempt. (The inmate) also said to the writer that he "cannot take prison any longer" and that "sooner or later something would happen."

From the hospital the inmate is sent to a therapeutic community. Here, at first, the inmate "states emphatically he doesn't want to be in the program," and staff write that "he seems to carry the proverbial 'chip on his shoulder,' and this attitude will probably make his adjustment to prison difficult." Later they write about the inmate:

He has made a rather erratic adjustment to the Program. He gives every indication that he considers himself above and beyond those who are his fellow residents. He has been confronted about this by his peers who perceive this at various times. Moreover, he is quite immature and has a problem properly handling authority. He feels that within this environment he can consider himself an exception to the rules and procedures. This is a former drug user who led a vicarious hedonistic life on the street, void of any responsibility. In addition, his family, particularly his parents, appear to have shielded him when he got himself into trouble. He admits that this has probably not helped him learn from his past experiences. What this man needs most is to learn some responsibility and acceptance of authority.

Staff's point about parental protectiveness is illustrated at this stage of the man's career by a set of letters from his father to various officials, in which he demands that his son be transferred closer to home. One of the man's disciplinary reports also describes an arrangement he has made with his parents to send packages which (due to his disciplinary status) he cannot receive, to a second inmate for transmittal.

Staff conclude that the inmate "appears to be conveniently continuing his dependence upon his parents" and imply that the inmate refuses to accept dictates of authority and strictures of confinement because he considers himself a prodigal son in exile. They complain that the inmate

has demonstrated continued disciplinary problems. He has had three misbehavior reports in the past sixty days for contraband, lying and violating bed rest restrictions. His participation in therapy has been minimal and he has preoccupied himself in putting forth an image of "an old experienced convict." His lack of experience, attitude and immaturity all betray the validity of this image to both staff and peers. He therefore maintains very few associates and keeps a low profile in the community. . . . He goes on at great length about his own personal discomforts, has been extremely indifferent to the therapy and has on occasion fallen asleep during the sessions.

A traumatic experience, however, unfreezes the inmate's stance, and staff are able to report that:

Several weeks ago he became the center of the community's attention and was confronted very heavily about having involved himself in some homosexual activity. . . . Finally he admitted, be it superficially, that he had been involved in such activity. . . . During this process he became much more relaxed, surprisingly, in the community setting and was able to deal at least in one group session in a more positive fashion. He somehow feels that he has been short-changed in life and perhaps deserves his just reward. This outlook serves as a justification for all of his immature and acting out behaviors. He was able at least to acknowledge and perhaps absorb some of this in a recent group session, and has been functioning somewhat better since that time.

The breakthrough has lasting effects, although for a while there is ''some reversion.'' During this period, for example, the inmate

quickly points out faults in others but cannot accept reciprocal feedback. He appears to envision himself as quite different in a superior sense from other inmates. He functions satisfactorily in his work assignment, but still appears to seek out and maintain a small group of associates, generally weaker community members.

Soon change becomes more substantial, and staff report that the inmate ''has been successful at eliminating a great deal of the immature behavior noted in previous reports'' and ''a great deal of his facade of being a 'tough guy' has been dropped and a rather likeable well mannered gentleman remains in place.'' Six months later the inmate continues to do well and even receives a commendation for ''applying first aid and promptly transporting to the clinic an inmate who attempted suicide,'' and he is credited with successfully tutoring inmates enrolled in a vocational training program. The inmate is also approved for work release, and is eventually assigned to the institution his parents have continuously requested for him.

Several observations are highlighted by those who have become involved with this man. The first impression has to do with a symbiotic relationship the man has with his family, who offer him favored treatment and unconditional protection which the man then expects elsewhere. He, therefore, (in the words of a counselor), ''impresses as being the type of person who expects the rewards of life without paying the required price.'' It is also observed that the man's family keeps him from becoming self-reliant, effective and self-confident, so that, as one staff member puts it, "his failures in school, business and crime, together with his dependency on his parents to get him out of trouble only reinforce a poor immature self-concept." Another set of observations has to do with the man's coping style and his mental health, which vary over time. The first stage of the progression is one in which the man falls aparts, traumatized by the contrast between his permissive upbringing and the impersonality and strictures of the prison.

It may not be an accident, for instance, that the man explodes and attacks correction offices after he has been told that he cannot hold a telephone conversation with his parents. Having exploded, the grim reaction to his actions makes him anxious. But when the man makes his anxiety obvious, he discovers that this does not impress prison officials (including a psychiatrist), nor does it mitigate his disciplinary disposition. Almost on the day of his transfer to a maximum-security prison, the man becomes traumatized and extremely depressed, and he manifests his despair by screaming and helplessly pounding on a cell door and threatening to kill himself. Even these extreme reactions, however, do not change his fate, beyond the fact that they earn him a four-week stay in the prison hospital, a discharge diagnosis of dysthymic disorder and the label "antisocial personality."

The man's departure from the hospital and his advent in the therapeutic community mark the onset of another stage of his reaction to the prison, in which he makes it obvious that he expects and deserves favored and individualized treatment, and that he does not feel that productivity or expenditure of energy can be expected from him. He also expresses disdain for the peasants who surround him and shows that he regards prison authorities as individuals to whom he can lie and whose rules he can defy or circumvent to advance his interests. In this enterprise the man still enjoys the backing of his parents, who have embarked on a letter campaign designed to extricate him from his prison assignment and to bring him within commuting distance, which is the same strategy they have deployed to end his military career after six months (with a "hardship" discharge) so that he can rejoin the parents who ostensibly feel inconvenienced by his absence.

The strategy this time fails, and the man is left at the mercy of the prison and the therapeutic community, but this in and of itself does not unfreeze his stance, and it is not until he is caught redhanded in a homosexual encounter that the stage is set for the man's maturation, which marks the last phase of his prison career. This transformation is a success story for the therapeutic community because it is doubtful that any change could have occurred in the abscence of combined confrontation and support, which defines the therapeutic community process.

What seemingly occurs is that the man for the first time is forced to examine his outlook and his approach to life and the reactions of others to his spoiled-child expectations. He is confronted with the nature and consequence of a destructive dependency on parental support which has kept him from being his own man and has made it unnecessary and therefore undesirable to face responsibility, particularly in his role in the community. Subsequent instances in which the man exercises responsibility (such as in his tutorial capacity) suggest that he has indeed been freed and made more autonomous in the prison—at least in the short run. This paradox must be placed in perspective by our recognizing that the liberating impact is not merely due to impersonal limits set by the institution (which show the man at prison intake that the world is no longer unconditionally responsive to his needs), but it requires interventions which force the man to examine his assumptions and to explore alternative approaches to life.

*Deterrence*

The dictionary defines "to deter" as "to turn aside, discourage, or prevent from acting (as by fear)." None of the examples we could review suggest that undesired behavior can be routinely deterred in this sense. We see offenders whose maladaptiveness has continued unabated in the face of frequent, and often predictably painful repercussions.

In the cases in which deterrence works, it appears to exercise an unfreezing, sobering effect, which causes the person to think twice in situations in which he might otherwise proceed to act. Dispositions may be unaffected—the person may be just as impulsive, or feel just as wounded or indignant—but he does not translate motives into acts as casually as before. The impact is short-run, but new habits may become ingrained if they bring rewards and satisfactions.[10]

In prisons, deterrence is exercised by the parole board. The board may keep the person imprisoned because of his misbehavior, and they may promise (at least by implication) that improved deportment will lead to freedom.

Among inmates with whom this intervention has worked is a twenty-one-year-old man, 5'4" tall, who serves a four-year sentence for robbing a token booth in a subway system. The inmate proves extremely troublesome to the prison, except for the last six months of his sentence in which no disciplinary infractions are listed. Many incidents are recorded that involve escalating confrontations with correction officers which invariably begin with refusals to obey instructions. There are also a number of fights with other inmates.

The man has been involved in incidents in the community which read like his prison violations. On one occasion he is convicted for an offense in which he "used boisterous and obscene language causing a crowd to collect, and then resisted arrest." In another incident the man is apprehended by the transit police when "observed kicking the glass out of a subway car."

In his last offense the man walks up to an attendant at a token booth, "pointed black revolver and said 'be cool or I'll blow your stomach off.' " In retrospect, the man "states that had he been in his right mind, he would never have committed the offense, as he was always afraid of doing something big." He is also overheard .by a police officer "discussing feigning insanity and drug abuse in order to mitigate the seriousness of the offense." In the jail, staff report that the man feels sorry for himself because his mother has not visited him, and "he doesn't think she cares."

In the prison, typical incidents start with casual violations followed by angry reactions to the prospect of sanctions. In one incident, for example, the man throws trash in front of his cell and when he is escorted to the disciplinary committee, "stopped about three-quarters of the way down the gallery, squared off with me (the officer) raised his hand in a fighting stance, then stated 'back off me. You better cut me some slack.' " In another incident the man leaves the area where he is supposed to be after having taken a shower, and when he is instructed to lock in his cell offers to take a swing at officers, jumps into his cell, produces a string of obscenities, and ends up spitting at an officer. Three hours later he throws a tantrum in his cell, banging furniture with his shoe, and finally plugs his toilet and sink and floods a prison gallery.

In one incident the man is caught out of place, is asked for his identification card which he does not have, runs away and is chased all over the institution by officers, who obviously become increasingly annoyed. In another incident the man approaches an officer who is packing the belongings of a fellow inmate and wants to know what is going on. When he is told to remove himself he not only refuses but delivers a string of expletives and is chased through half the facility after having refused to lock in. On another occasion he is ordered to leave an exercise yard and declines because he feels that his time is not up. When he receives a Notice of Report he threatens the officer, three hours later throws a cup of liquid through his cell bars at one officer and subsequently threatens to throw something at another officer, which he proceeds to do.

Needless to say the inmate serves an inordinate amount of time in segregation settings for such incidents. And while he is generating a reputation as a troublesome person with staff he simultaneously evidences a comparable capacity to initiate and sustain conflicts with peers. It is the latter involvement which finally comes to a head and forces the inmate to seek assistance, testifying that:

> I am being threatened by the majority of inmates here and quite a few times I have been confronted in life and death situations. The inmates here are attempting to work me into a punk "faggot" and it's gotten so that I am afraid to step out of my cell.

The inmate requests a transfer to another prison to escape from the situation. Meanwhile he receives a sound rebuff from the parole board who note that "you have incurred some 50 disciplinary reports, several for assaultive behavior" and also point to the man's "minimum participation" in programs. All of this appears to exercise a sobering effect: In his last six months in prison the man not only does not receive a single disciplinary report but makes what is described as "satisfactory progress in a vocational training assignment."

This inmate appears to feel that he has a reputation to uphold based on demonstrations of autonomy with staff and a willingness to face enemies among peers, but simultaneously he has a low threshold for coping with the adversities that result when staff and inmates react to being challenged in this way. It appears that when this man feels threatened, he loses control and rants and raves, though his preferred strategy is flight. This unfortunately simply delays the game by one move because at the next juncture, he is cornered and rants and raves to express his displeasure. The inmate invariably is left feeling impotent and angry, and this self-defeating pattern seems to be redundant and interminable. Somehow, however, the seriousness of consequences in terms of time served are impressed on the man, and the unfreezing trauma produces at least temporary reformation.

The point is, of course, that the man acts tough but is not really tough. He talks tough when pointing a gun at a subway attendant, but looks less tough when sitting in jail bemoaning the absence of his mother; he also finds it easy to hurl obscenities at guards until the behavior affects his parole. The man has a thin facade which will not stay in place over the long haul, and it is probably this fact which makes deterrence ultimately effective.

*Relaxation*

Even strongly felt concerns can dissipate, facades can be dropped, and compensatory behavior can be discontinued. However, such changes often cannot be traced to experiences that occasion them, nor can specific influences be credited for transmutations.

The common denominator in such change is that the concerns that impel the person to maladaptive behavior are no longer operative, so that the person becomes freed to behave in non-maladaptive ways. Typically, extreme defenses the person uses against stimuli that threaten him have been dropped or *relaxed*, and he can then afford to face life with greater equanimity.

An example of the pattern is a young man who spends over ten years in prison for killing a seventeen-year-old girl with a butcher knife. The man's prison violations are concentrated in a two-year period early in his sentence, and mainly consist of fights with fellow inmates and altercations with staff. There is a period of four years in which the man commits no violations, and there are also no infractions recorded (except for one very minor incident) in the last year and a half of his prison term.

The man's victim is a fellow employee to whom he is attracted, who steadfastly resists his advances. The crime is described as "seemingly the overt explosion of long simmering feelings of self depreciation, lack of masculinity and sexual inadequacy." According to counselors attached to the high school which the inmate attends, he is

> highly insecure and highly sensitive to remarks by others concerning his physical appearance. (The inmate) was so sensitive about his appearance that he refused to take a swimming class because of the necessity of disrobing. When psychiatrically examined he was described as "obviously paranoidal," with feelings that everyone, including teachers and friends, hated and rejected him because he was ugly.

In reviewing his offense the inmate describes himself as "temporarily insane" and "concluded that the deceased was a 'witch' who cast an evil spell on him so that his mind 'busted.' " He also speculates "that the deceased really loved him," but confesses that he "was jealous because she had a boyfriend." He also explains that he would like to "find a girlfriend, since he had never had one and had never experienced sexual intercourse."

At prison reception the inmate is seen by a psychiatrist, who writes:

> He is a rather hostile type, and tried to give the examiner a hard time. He made such remarks as that the undersigned as well as his fellow Americans are all murderers, having taken over the lands of the Indians, killing them when they attempted to defend their property, etc. If looks could kill, the undersigned would probably not be writing this. . . . The inmate projects his own hostility and then sees this hostility that he projects as coming from others to him. . . . He is very definitely dangerous.

The inmate is first assigned to a maximum-security prison, where he is soon referred to another psychiatrist. This psychiatrist describes him as follows:

He presents an appearance literally begging for help. "People keep staring at me. They talk about me and gesture. Eventually they drive me crazy. Pressure is building up in me more and more. I am afraid for my life. It is like a conspiracy." Who is involved? "Everybody in prison." Why are they doing this? "I don't know. This I would like to know from you. I asked already the priest but he couldn't answer this question." Are you sure they do it with intent? "Conceivably so. 50 to 50." The inmate appeared obviously concerned and frightened. . . . Diagnosis: paranoid psychosis.

One and a half years after this juncture, the inmate's propensity to become involved in conflicts dissipates. He is assigned to a low-security institution, in which he spends the remainder of his sentence. After spending three years in this institution, the inmate is able to report:

I have had but one minor disciplinary report in the last five years. During my long incarceration I obtained my high school equivalency diploma, earned certificates in barbering and woodwork, attended one-on-one psychotherapy for 18 months, attended six months of group therapy and have maintained close relations with my parents, sister, and brother-in-law, who visit me regularly during my confinement.

Before he is released the inmate receives additional therapy and completes other vocational training programs.

This man's difficulties span his adolescence and very early adulthood. During these years he has deeply felt doubts about his own worth and efficacy and is extremely sensitive to negative assessments by others and to the experience of being slighted or rejected. This hypersensitivity is so extreme that it at times takes the form of paranoid delusions and possibly psychotic states. It also involves considerable self-pity.

The inmate reacts by attacking those who slight him, and makes himself unpopular because he is obnoxious, which confirms his unfavorable opinion of himself. His counterattacks range from confrontative verbal hostility to physical explosions, including at the extreme the crime for which he is sent to prison. The prison experience, however, is a success story in that a combination of maturation, low-pressure and structured settings, psychotherapeutic assistance and possibly even weekly visits from a friendly Jehovah's Witness extending over several years ameliorate the man's sensitivity to negative assessments and affronts, and his explosions of outrage and anger when he feels hurt.

*Maturation*

In our review of maladaptive career patterns our principal finding is that misbehavior diminishes over time, and that age and maturation appear to account for the trend. The two variables (age and maturation) are admittedly intertwined. One reason maladaptiveness (such as crime, violence, and prison misbehavior) peaks at early ages is that developmental change continues beyond adolescence, and development means that one expands one's roster of prosocial and adaptive skills.

Given the pervasiveness of age effects, no single explanation is liable to account for them. It is also true that persons can achieve tangible increments of sobriety and equally tangible decrements of playfulness at varying ages and to varying degrees. The move in question is one from childhood to adulthood. It can be described in terms of contrasts between antecedent childlike, nonserious, ebullient and irresponsible behavior and consequent adult, serious and responsible behavior. This does not imply abruptness, however, in that maturation denotes *gradual* change, change that results from cumulative impingements and pyschological growth.

An example of seeming maturation is the career of a young man who enters the system for committing a mugging and a narcotics violation while on probation for two other offenses. The most frequent type of incident in which the man becomes involved in the prison has to do with combinations of being out of place, loitering, lying and carrying contraband or stealing. There are also instances in which the man threatens officers and one serious incident in which he is caught holding a cache of marijuana.

In one of his offenses the man has twenty-six envelopes of heroin he insists he has found just before he is arrested. In the man's second offense he has sold heroin to an undercover police officer, but he explains that he is helping a narcotics dealer who is his close friend. Probation officers conclude that the man is "somewhat slow" and refer him to a psychiatric clinic which reports that he has "a full scale IQ of 67, which falls in the borderline defective range of intelligence on the Wechsler tables." The clinic notes that the man's "self esteem altogether is so chaotically organized and primitively underdeveloped that his condition constitutes an unstructured psychosis." The probation officer reports that the man is indifferent to his fate, "seems unable to appreciate the seriousness of his action" and impresses as "street-wise."

When the man enters prison the reception unit staff describe his "custodial adjustment" as "atrocious." They report that "he received five misbehavior reports, which were for horseplay, having a fishline, two reports for throwing water and another report for horseplaying." The man is sent to a secure prison, where he alleges he has enemies, but he "feels no need for protective custody screening at this time." He also "demonstrates a complete reversal in behavior," in that his disciplinary record becomes violation free and his teachers report that he "tries hard to learn." Work supervisors, on the other hand, describe the man as doing "average to below average" work, and indicate that he is "a bit slow, but functions," and "gets along well with others."

Given the man's (relatively speaking) good performance in prison, staff conclude that he is "a suitable candidate for a lower level of security" and assign him to a camp setting. Here he repeatedly refuses work assignments and is found in possession of "a red balloon filled with a leafy substance" which to no one's surprise is identified as marijuana. The man subsequently contends that "he was set up by one of his roommates" and enlists a fellow inmate who perjures himself on his behalf.

Two months later the inmate is paroled, but within twelve days is identified as the perpetrator of an incident in which a handbag is stolen from a lady by a mugger who "displayed a knife and pointed it at her." The offense makes the inmate eligible for sentencing as a predicate felon, and he returns to prison, where he does well in a work assignment, expresses interest in furthering his education, receives no disciplinary reports and is described as "quiet and reserved in appearance and manner."

When a probation officer describes the man at early prison entry as "streetwise," he depicts the way the man thinks of himself. The characterization is correct in so far as it denotes heavy involvement in drug usage and drug trafficking and other minor criminal activities, and involvement with a substantial network of congenial acquaintances with compatible interests. Such is the life this man leads in the community, and such is the life he leads in the prison when the opportunity affords. The man is not "streetwise," however, if the term denotes sophistication, efficacy or expertise in negotiating the contingencies that arise in the pursuit of underworld activities. He is caught redhanded selling drugs, presents explanations that are transparently implausible, sells more drugs within days after receiving probation. He similarly essays three different (and equally noncredible) versions of an alibi for a prison offense, a strategy which at best is not taken seriously.

Such behavior reflects limited perceptiveness of social reality, such as the reactions of authorities to the man's wildly improbable concoctions and his assessment of risks he can reasonably take when the police and probation or parole authorities have reason to take an interest in his activities. Another implication, of course, is that there is no veracity when one is "streetwise" even if there is zero benefit to mendacity. In other words, one does not admit that one has done something even where the evidence is overwhelming.

None of this, however, makes the man a hopeless cause, in that none of it is seriously intended. The man appears to know when the game changes and the time for playfulness, prevarication and wishful thinking is over. He thus pleads guilty to his last offense, does not persevere in his subcultural games, responds to the best of his ability in vocational and educational settings and demonstrates sobriety when he finds himself in prison shortly after he has been released. The evidence cautiously suggests that the man's unambiguous induction into the mainline prison world has not only traumatized him sufficiently to ensure improved deportment but may have expedited his progression from slap-happy adolescence to relatively mature adulthood.

## Notes

1. The first of these two implications is drawn by Cloward and Ohlin; the second is implicit in the work of Hirschi and his colleagues. (See R. Cloward and L. E. Ohlin, *Delinquency and Opportunity: A theory of Delinquent Gangs*. Glencoe, Ill.: Free Press, 1960; T. Hirschi, *Causes of Delinquency*. Berkeley: University of California Press, 1969).

2. The 1972 "Work of America" Task Force wrote that "work has been used as a form of rehabilitation for centuries—but not always successfully. Apparently, many failures occur because meaningless work has been prescribed. Its very uselessness has lowered the self-esteem of the mental patient, welfare recipient, prisoner, or physically handicapped person. Instead of being the means by which self-confidence was improved, inadequate work struck a further blow at the pride and self-respect of the person who needed help. . . . Work may be the best therapy possible for juvenile delinquents, mental patients, prisoners, drug addicts, and alcoholics but unless job satisfaction is made possible as a part of such therapy, work will only compound their difficulties" (Special Task Force to the Secretary of Health, Education and Welfare, *Work in America*. Cambridge, Massachusetts: MIT Press, 1973, p. 90).

3. Irwin (1970), chapter 6, note 6 discusses self-betterment by inmates as a mode of prison adjustment, and he refers to it as "gleaning." Most studies of attitudes toward incarceration have reported that the prime interest of inmates is in program-related activities (See Toch, 1977, chapter 8, note 3; also, D. Glaser, *The Effectiveness of a Prison and Parole System*. Indianapolis, Indiana: Bobbs-Merrill, 1964).

4. See, for example, H. H. Vorrath and L. K. Brendthro, *Positive Peer Culture*. Chicago: Aldine, 1974.

5. R. Ericson and D. Moberg, *The Rehabilitation of Parolees*. Minneapolis: Minneapolis Rehabilitation Center, 1967; V. O'Leary and D. Glaser, "The assessment of risk in parole decision making," in D. West, ed., *The Future of Parole*. London: Duckworth, 1972.

6. The strategy of using prison environments that contain older inmates to modulate the problems of younger inmates must be pursued with caution, since

large numbers of young inmates interfere with the prison adjustment of their
elders (Toch, 1977, chapter 8, note 6).
7. Maslow (1954), chapter 7, note 1.
8. In some cases, this goal can be accomplished if an inmate's anxiety gets
   reduced through the passage of time, but the most plausible way of reintegrating
   vulnerable inmates into the inmate population is to enhance their repertoire of
   coping skills (Toch, 1975, Intro., note 20).
9. H. Toch, ed., *Therapeutic Communities in Corrections*. New York: Praeger,
   1980.
10. A. Bandura, *Social Learning Theory*. Englewood Cliffs, N.J.: Prentice-Hall,
    1977.

# Part III

# What Have We Learned?

# 13

# Conclusions

Studies of lives over time tell us more than reviews of lives in cross-section. If we compare individuals to each other, we may learn that some are more resilient and competent than others, but if we view the same persons over time, we discover that some grow and mature, whereas others do not. In this sense, some evolving personal histories encourage an optimistic view of development, and others document a pessimistic view, which asserts "once a bum, always a bum."

Longitudinal views of good copers often tend to be misleading because they adjudge nonchange favorably, and deplore change. As Jack Block has noted,

> The connotations of words indicating absence of change are generally positive, viz., consistency, stability, constancy, continuity, congruence. The connotations of change are often pejorative, viz., inconsistency, instability, inconstancy, discontinuity, incongruence. The Puritan value of solidity appears to have affected our language so that an unchanging character carries the aura of moral and mental soundness, while a transmogrified person is suspect. Connotatively neutral labels to identify continuity and change are most difficult to find, suggesting that an implicit value orientation may have influenced the cast of prior developmental research.[1]

Allport similarly complains that psychology is biased toward static views of development, except when psychologists (or any of us) engage in retrospection. He writes:

> When we ask ourselves about our own course of growth such problems as the following come to mind: the nature of our inborn dispositions, the impress of culture and environment upon us, our emerging self-consciousness, our conscience, our gradually evolving style of expression, our experiences of choice and freedom, our handling of conflicts and anxieties, and finally the formation of our maturer values, interests, and aims.[2]

Among the careers we have reviewed, change is generally to be welcomed, and lack of change deplored. This is so because the behavior our subjects engage in is frequently undesirable, both from society's perspective, and—should our subjects take the long view—from their own. We intersect with young but "matured" offenders at a juncture at which change for the worse is rare and room for improvement overwhelming.

Such facts account for the strange paradox that in a study such as ours, of nightmarishly depressing careers, two firm conclusions stand out as established: The major trend we describe is maturation, and, second, where chronicity of maladaptation occurs, there is patterning and consistency which permits problem definition and (hopefully) regenerative efforts.

## Maturation

The maturation potential of maladaptive behavior has been implicit in a substantial body of data which shows that maladaption (other than mental illness) achieves high rates early, and decays over time. The most extreme patterns of maladaptation (quantitatively speaking) are those which have their inception at the earliest ages, and manifest chronicity while they last. This trend is so consistent that the *age variable* has become the most reliable predictor of measures related to crime and delinquency, and youth (twenty-four or below) virtually delimits behavior (disruptiveness) that is of concern to us.[3]

Before we consider this pattern, which is the modal maladaptive career, we must note some exceptions to the sequence which prove instructive because of the contrast they offer. The most contrasting example is that of the "downhill" career, such as that of alcoholics, in which maladaptation starts late and gets worse as it evolves. The maladaptation is not a sudden creation, however. Typically, the alcoholic invests years in sporadic or dedicated drinking, but combines such behavior with a more conventional career. The onset of maladaptation occurs as drinking bouts encroach on the person's main career, and interfere with vocational success and/or family life. Failure in these areas creates stress and poses threats to the person's self-esteem, which invites steady alcoholism as an ameliorative response. This response in turn exacerbates disability, until a juncture is reached where the maladaptive behavior (full-time intoxication) interferes with the person's self-care and ultimately endangers his or her survival.

Such cycles contrast with maturation in that they produce decrements of skills and capacities, and make recovery increasingly difficult. The point is not that alcoholics are older while the maladaptive individuals we describe are mostly young, but that the pattern typified by the alcoholic is cumulative. The cumulation is partly a function of age (at least, in the sense that the career-segment that remains is shorter, but more saliently a product of failure which breeds loss of self-confidence as well as decrements in coping skills and capacities. Even more dramatically the behavior has direct disabling consequences; these promote physical and psychological decay, making recovery problematic.

Subpopulations can be expected to vary in the admixtures of career patterns they include. Groups in which the age range is large, such as the group of urban homeless, include a melange ranging from dead-end alcoholics to young incipient schizophrenics. Hospital patients are a similarly varied group, ranging from young and chronic psychotics to old and senile patients. Predominantly young adult populations such as prison inmates, however, are apt to contain less variation and to overrepresent uphill careers, which offer more promising prognoses.

Our data suggest an interaction between age and adaptational effects. Prison misbehavior is a manifestation of youth; it peaks during early phases of imprisonment, but it mostly does so for younger inmates, and particularly so for younger inmates who serve long terms in prison. Young inmates maladapt more frequently, but improve with experience in the prison. The longer the imprisonment, the greater the improvement (except for seriously disturbed inmates and "chronics"), but the greater, also, the inmate's age. This does not mean that age accounts for change, but neither does prison exposure. The older the inmate, and the longer the exposure, the greater the improvement.

The result is heartening, but not easy to explain. One option is to think of maladaptiveness as a talent or skill: Just as other genius peaks (in mathematics, say, or music), so may a refined penchant for rambunctiousness or knavery. Precocious entropy is another explanatory formula: it posits that as vital juices (such as testosterone levels that undergird aggressivity) ebb, so does the behavior they energize.[4]

Other explanations have to do with aspects of maturation or development. One such view is that of Wilson and Herrnstein, who write about crime that

> The opinions of adult peers will, in most cases, further diminish the attractions of crime by inculcating internalized prohibitions against it. For that reason, as well as for purely developmental changes in how people view right and wrong, the typical person passing into adulthood shifts from the egocentric and hedonistic focus of childhood to more abstract and principled guidelines to action. Meanwhile, time horizons extend further into the future; the averae adult delays gratification more readily than the average child or adolescent. If for no other reasons, with stronger internal constraints against wrongdoing and a greater weight on delayed consequences of behavior, the average adult should more often choose noncrime than those less "mature" in these respects.[5]

Wilson and Herrnstein also provide room for decay of misconduct over time. With respect to offenders who "mature out" at more advanced ages, Wilson and Herrnstein write:

> But they (the offenders) too slow down eventually, perhaps as the drives cool off, or the prohibitions or community ties finally sink in, or the time horizons finally stretch out, or the increasingly severe penalties of the criminal justice system for recidivists finally make crime insufficiently rewarding. Or, failing all that, simply the diminishing capacities of later life make crime too dangerous or unlikely to succeed, especially where there are younger and stronger criminal competitors, or victims who will not be cowed.[6]

The developmental view of change leaves scope for the role of environment, but the score is limited. In the above quote "the opinions of adult peers" to which Wilson and Herrnstein refer is a commodity that is sometimes available, and sometimes not. This fact explains, for instance, that offenders who have been transferred from youth to adult facilities undergo improvements of behavior. The advent of a favorable environment may speed up maturation, but that of an inhospitable environment may retard it.

A more differentiated picture is provided by Jack Block, who talks of change that varies with the maturity level of the person who undergoes change. With respect to "impulse-ridden" persons, for example, Block implies that deterrence should work as an incentive:

> At this time, the individual views his social world as a more or less illogical jungle. Impulse control generally is lacking. However, one's actions for pleasure may also, without rationale, receive harsh punishments. The teachable child at this ego level may, as a matter of repeated contiguities and the simple pragmatism of reinforcement, learn to contain certain of his desires, not because they are bad—indeed, the idea of badness does not exist—but in order to avoid the anticipated retribution. "Better control myself, otherwise someone will hurt me" is the control paradigm at this stage.[7]

Block's definition of "impulse-ridden" persons resembles ours and derives from a classification (by J. Loevinger) of stages of personality development.[8] The next stage in Loevinger's taxonomy is the "opportunistic" stage, which revolves around egocentric exploitation. The inception of change in this stage, according to Block, has to do with exploitive games, and how these are won or lost:

> Personal pleasure and personal advantage are the aims; expedience is the way. Alas, manipulation cannot always be successful—instead of controlling his environment, the individual at this stage may find his environment threatening to control him. The exploiter of others is, in a fundamental way, also dependent

upon those he exploits. In many interactions, it is a matter of interpretation, doubt, or taste as to which party dominates; certainly, the dominance relations often shift in an on-going relationship. Confronted with the possibility that his actions for advantage may have adverse consequences, the opportunistic individual may choose to prevent the chance of loss by foregoing the chance of gain. He will not pick up on an opportunistic opportunity and will thus appear, self-controlled, not because of high considerations of morality, but rather for reasons of situational expedience. "Better control myself, otherwise someone will dominate me" is the control paradigm of this stage.[9]

Block's view suggests that environments can affect even those who are low in maturity, but implies that the effects are of necessity limited, because they are not internalized. In other words, the behavior of the immature can be externally controlled, but it does not (in Block's terms) become *self*-controlled. More hopeful implications emerge from our review of prison "success stories" (chapter 12), which show inmates enticed or sidetracked from immature pursuits. The difference may lie in the imperfect correspondence of childhood stages to the adult patterns that approximate them. The infant's view of reality can thus be wholly chaotic or impulse-ridden, but corresponding adult perspectives have a richer, more eclectic mix. It may also be that extrinsic experiences such as those Block alludes to (punishments, powershifts, and so forth) are not the only spurs to change among adults. The changes we have talked about seem to illustrate Bandura's point that

> incentives are not the only, nor necessarily the best, means of cultivating interest . . . involvement in activities through goal setting can build intrinsic interest. Proximal subgoals serving valued aspirations are well suited for enlisting the sustained involvement in activities that builds competencies, self-efficacy, and interest where they are lacking.[10]

Finally, change potential may vary with degree of maladaptation. All maladaptive persons fail to learn from experience, but many may be able to learn, and others (the chronics) do not—at least, they do not do so unaided. A spontaneously developed capacity for learning from experience helps explain our skewed curves and enables us to think of decreased maladaptiveness as coping.

### Adaptation

Past studies have noted that constructive change takes place in prisoners over time, and such changes have been attributed to "anticipation of release." Our curves, and some of our other findings (such as the lack of the impact we have noted of parole date assignments) do not support this view. Inmate misbehavior peaks after a preliminary interval, and diminishes gradually over time. Aging (maturation) plays a role; the remaining variance has to do with what the dictionary defines as "adaptation." Adaptation means "adjustment to environmental conditions"; it means "modification of an organism . . . that makes it more fit for existence under the conditions of its environment".

The environment, in our case, is the prison. Adaptation means learning not to run into trouble as one negotiates life in the prison. At first glance, this task looks very difficult. The literature accentuates obstacles one is apt to encounter and implies that prison poses excrutiating challenges to one's identity and self-esteem.[11]

It comes as a surprise, therefore, to note that most prisoners serve fairly trouble-free terms, in the sense that they violate few rules and receive few formal and aversive dispositions. One assumes that these inmates accomodate far-from-ideal conditions by leading compromise existences in which they achieve compromise goals, operating within available constraints. The incarceration experience of these men may be at minimum unpleasant, but proves no more overwhelming to them than other constraining situations they have encountered in their lives.

The fact that this picture of compromise does not describe the experience of maladaptive inmates is not a result of imprisonment (which is a constant), but of the way these inmates react to prison once they have passed the point of "orientation," which is the phase of appraisal. Two key attributes of the maladaptive inmates' reactions are particularly relevant: first, the inmates do not appraise constraints as parameters within which one most operate (which is the problem to be solved), but seek to ignore, evade or defy constraints; and second, such behavior increases constraints because it invites unwelcome reactions, thereby exacerbating the situation with which these persons are unable to deal.

Given the possibility of *ad infinitum* escalation, the peak of the misbehavior curve is the low point of the inmate's career and the dilemma from which he must escape. Because the inmate is confined, this dilemma is exacerbated, because escape, truancy, drug use, vagrancy and other means of physically evading the dilemma are foreclosed.

Inmates do not escape, nor do they undergo marked conversions or reform. They do not become resilient, flexible, competent, or achieve insight, perspective and self-knowledge. Adaptation (unlike maladaptation) is incremental. It consists of hit-or-miss, trial-and-error migrations. Settings are tried for size, and some challenges, temptations and pressures prove more manageable than others. The system helps by transferring maladapters for "fresh starts," and by essaying special, low-pressure experiences in extreme cases. Elsewhere, accidental confluences occur, such as where inmates find punitive settings tolerable, or encounter activities or staff members or peers they find congenial or helpful.

The process is unselfconscious and it is serendipitous, but once we see it and know it, we can in theory use it. What we have to do is to attend to regenerative consequences where they accrue, to experiences that improve personal functioning. This point has been made by Bandura, who describes unplanned experiences as "chance encounters." Bandura argues:

> Some chance encounters touch people only lightly, others leave more lasting effects, and still others branch people into new trajectories of life. Psychology cannot foretell the occurrence of particular fortuitous intersects, however sophisticated its knowledge of human behavior. The unforeseeability and branching power of fortuitous influences makes the specific course of lives neither easily predictable nor easily socially engineerable. Fortuity of influence does not mean that behavior is undetermined. The unforeseeability of determinants and the determination of actions, by whatever events happen to occur, are separate matters. Fortuitous influences may be unforeseeable, but having occurred, they enter as evident factors in causal chains, in the same way as prearranged ones do. A science of psychology does not have much to say about the occurrence of fortuitous intersects, except that personal proclivities, the settings in which one moves, and the kinds of people who populate those settings make some types of intersects more probable than others. However, psychology can provide the basis for predicting the nature, scope, and strength of the impact these encounters will have on human lives.[12]

## Locating Silver Linings

The slightest and most modest respites can serve as cues to what may be possible. In a workshop of mental health and corrections staff, for example, a group reviewed a case they described as follows:

> Our group got what is now a 23 year old inmate, who was incarcerated since he was 17, and prior to that was a youthful offender. He came into the system as a result of an armed robbery; also, an outside charge for arson, for setting fire to an adjacent cell with somebody in it, about a year after he was in the system. . . . His primary problem is extreme acting out. . . . He is a real winner at this. He seems to have outlasted the system and he's still going. . . . He has eight pages of disciplinary actions on his Superintendent's card—threats, self-mutilation by cutting, swallowing, hanging himself. He swallowed pens, toothpaste tubes, bed springs . . . and these appear to be an expression of rage at the system. He hates the system, particularly whenever any kind of disciplinary action occurs—when he's not getting what he wants. His most extreme acts have occurred as a result of discipline.[13]

Are there no ways of breaking this sort of cycle? Our group asked whether the cycle had in fact been broken—however briefly—before it escalated to new lows. The group searched for redeeming clues, and it reported that:

> He (the inmate) has had a couple of good experiences, or initial experiences that were positive, with female therapists and female nurses or some kind of female therapeutic staff. Typically, what he does soon after, is he gets sexually attracted and makes some kind of statement about that. He gets in a love-hate kind of situation. The staff becomes very nervous and pulls away the therapist, and he gets another rejection.
>
> One thing we find is he's rejected a lot. He obviously also rejects by his actions, by the extreme anger that he's acting out. But clearly, attempts at making some kind of positive involvement with him fail each time because he's just too much for anybody that tries to deal with him.
>
> One of the interesting things we found is that when he's doing well—which he has done especially when he's been working—he starts working, he starts relaxing, he doesn't act out as much, and he starts getting depressed.
>
> In these short periods of time he's depressed he has sleep problems, sees a psychiatrist and gets some kind of anti-depressant medication. He continues to do okay for a while under the medication, and then something happens. He immediately starts fighting the system again and then he loses his job—he's off and running again in a very aggressive, angry manner.
>
> From what we can see, he has done okay for periods up to maybe three or four months at various times in five or six years. The interesting thing is that when he is doing well he's not getting any attention from anybody. There are no reports. One other thing that was pretty obvious is that there's not much of anything anybody can say about him in a positive way. And so one of the things that we're considering is that if it's possible to treat this kind of person effectively, you'd probably have to get the most patient person in the world; beyond that, somebody who would put a lot of effort into encouraging whatever positive features this person has, if in fact he has any. He obviously has escalated his behavior, his impulsive, demanding, attention-seeking behavior to such a degree he's outlasted everybody. He's won, except that he's destroyed himself or is in the process of destroying himself.

The comments of one clinician proved particularly hopeful, because they defused impressions on record that made the inmate appear uniformly unpopular:

> It takes a great deal of patience to work with him. A good deal of hard lining, a good deal of letting him know respect and that sort of thing. As long as we have a case manager, somebody who can stop in once or twice a week to say "how ya doing"—that's all it took—he was fine. He does these little antics. Like he wrote the President and told him he was going to rub him out. . . . So that means the Secret Service has to come and visit him every 3 months. So he assures himself of a visitor. I don't find him a particularly offensive guy to deal with, I really don't.

If we profit from such observations we can accelerate the process of adaptation, which otherwise consists of inchoate gains and fits and starts. It is only when viewed in averaged fashion as a cumulative deescalation of conflict, tempering of emotions or diminution of impasse situations that trends can be defined. The result of trends is an accommodation of person-to-environment, which in retrospect seems mildly surprising and takes the form of entries such as "this person had a horrendous performance record, but has been involved in no incidents over the past six months." No explanation can be offered, and the dynamics of change are unascertainable by observers or the person himself.

The changes we encounter can be described as the diminution or discontinuance of the sort of patterns we have reviewed. The person has learned to control temper, to accept adversity, to tolerate infringements, accept instructions, live and let live. He postures less blatantly, accommodates more, becomes less demanding, feels less affronted. He is calmer, more serious, less afraid, more confident. Maturation and compromise have converged to achieve more congruence between demands and responses, challenges and the meeting of challenges.

No doubt much such change is superficial, evanescent and transient. To make it less tenuous, interventions are needed which create self-awareness that can lead to self-management. In the absence of such cognitively centered experiences, the best we can hope for is that some of the adaptive change we see can survive new (or familiar) challenges in settings to which the person returns after he leaves the prison.

### Chronic Maladaptation

The problem of chronic maladapters is more serious and leaves less leeway, but some facts we have discussed give us hope. Chronic maladapters engage in frequent, redundant misbehavior. They create many problems, but they show patterned consistency. This does not mean that they do the same things over and over, but that they do different things for the same, or similar, reasons.

We can predict chronicity (as we have shown). We can also, however distinguish chronics from each other, defining the problem to be addressed in individual cases. Chronics can be disaggregated into subsets of individuals who manifest similar patterns of conduct. This not only helps us to make sense of what chronics do, but provides homogeneous target groups that can be logistically separated. Such separation is a prelude to sensible management and reform, and differs from the current "maxi-maxi setting" strategy which creates heterogeneous enclaves of persons who prove unmanageable elsewhere.

Consistency, of course, may be enhanced by the beholder. The mind seeks closure, and human messiness (variety of behavior) offends. But behavior is seldom messy on all levels. Conduct is a product of personality, which gives it direction and a measure of unity. Where surface (phenotypic) variety exists, personologists (such as Allport) tells us to look deeper.[14] When we do so, we often find genotypic consistency, which means that subsurface motives underlie disparate surface concerns. Our review has shown that, except for extremely disturbed chronics, many consistencies in maladaptation are phenotypically available even where we find more consistency by digging deeper. This makes pattern-analytic thinking more accessible to observers of conduct, including those such as the person himself and his peers, whose insight is most needed and critical if change is to occur.

Conceptual availability is a necessary but of course woefully insufficient granter of insight. The adaptation literature points out that bad copers invariably deny their problems, which means that they hold external environments (or fate) responsible for their misadventures. Another way of describing this propensity is to speak of "defenses," of indignant reactions to information about oneself that make the person resistant to change, inflexible and rigid in outlook and demeanor.

Much change literature has to do with ways of dealing with defenses. The prevailing wisdom is that defenses should never be attacked head-on, but that they must be surfaced and highlighted and discussed. Another way of saying this is that resistances to change must be "worked through."[15] This means that we must make it easy—if possible, inviting— for the person to face and examine his defenses, and to rehearse their discontinuance. It also means that there are two patterns at issue in change—one of defenses, and the other of the behavior the defenses defend and of the motives that underlie it. In both cases, we must understand the pattern, the person himself must understand the pattern, and the person must learn to abandon it.

### Expanding Our Perspective of Disruptive Behavior

Maladaptive behavior of the kind we have reviewed is invariably disruptive, in the sense that it is seen as causing problems by those who govern the person's environment. We have implied, however, that disruptiveness cannot be equated with maladaptation, even if it is persistent. In theory, a person can *elect* to disrupt his environment, can do so competently and with the utmost consideration for his fellows, can accept penalties as a price worth paying, and can improve his skill at disruptiveness with accumulated experience. When a person behaves in this way his keepers can confront him with equanimity and subject him to sanctions. The game (cops-and-robbers) can be played as an adult game, with professionalism and dignity.

The games we have been concerned with have not been played with professionalism or dignity. They have been played poorly, in unsportsmanlike ways, by persons driven to them, who lose without profit or grace. This is so because the persons we have looked at have not been "disruptive" but "disruptive-plus," with the "plus" making their behavior maladaptive.

This "plus" (or perhaps minus) is difficult to define, except as a deviation from standards of mental health or competence. But a deviation in this sense must not be equated with membership in a deviant group. To be unwell is not to be ill: the former invites rest and the latter, medication or surgery. Qualitatively deviant behavior calls for special measures and radical responses which are inappropriately targetted at deviations from norms: mediocre students may not need remediation, and couples need not file for divorce when their honeymoons (figuratively speaking) are over.

Nonmental health (or mental nonhealth) is different in degree from mental illness or mental disorder; the former includes the latter, but covers a wider range. Our concern has been with the full gamut of nonmental health, and we see value in being sensitive to deficits in personal competence where they recur. We simultaneously see risks (and few benefits beyond reducing the unemployment rate of mental health personnel) in needlessly pathologizing personal deficits.

The problem is that maladaptiveness "this side" of pathology is an unsung and untended category, which poses sticky definitional problems and makes it difficult to match clients with services. The matching problem becomes obvious when persons are shuttled between service deliverers who (justifiably) feel that these persons do not fit their definition of who is an appropriate client. It is also exemplified by the generic outcasts one finds in storage depots or holding pens (such as the homeless) and by the need to mainstream deviants even where this exacerbates their maladaptation and strains the hospitality of settings (such as, classrooms) designed for more adequate copers.

To pathologize a problem at such junctures becomes an understandable response, particularly where pathology-related services, such as psychiatric clinics, are the only service show in town. Moreover, other obvious avenues of defining the person as "special" to get him off the streets or out of the hair of settings he contaminates usually involve stigmatizing him as a behavior problem. This option strikes service workers and other observers as inhumane, though some clients—given their druthers—prefer to be seen as *bad* rather than as *mad*, and find the label less injurious to their self-esteem.[16]

If the person becomes more tangibly disruptive, or disruptive for a sufficiently long time, the options begin to change. The person gradually acquires membership in the category of "disruptive person," which gives him a definite identity. Once the person is defined as a behavior problem, it makes pathology specialists reluctant to deal with him. Though staff do have a set of (behavior control) options for dealing with disruptive persons, they sense that these options do not *fit* the maladaptive client. Even while they are disciplining or punishing the person, they know at some level that what they do is inappropriate and does not address the real problem.

In fact, those who discipline discover that "the problem" they are addressing can be exacerbated through disciplinary sanctions. Vernon Fox makes this point about maladaptation in prison when he writes that

> the individual offender who builds up a series of misconduct reports within the prison is a seriously disturbed individual with complex mental dynamics. . . . Yet for this complex individual, the pattern of custodial routine is an original demand for compliance, and subsequent deprivation and punishment reinforce the original demand, which intensifies the problems by imposing more pressures upon already existing pressures without providing any solution to the original problem.[17]

The response becomes more sophisticated when staff live with ambiguity and complexity by taking an eclectic approach to it. Hybrid categories such as *special education* are created to accommodate multiproblem persons, and offer the potential of multimodal services that can address different deficits (behavioral, emotional, educational) of persons who combine presenting problems to varying degrees. The fly in this ointment is that some attributes are more preemptory than others. Options become foreclosed, for example, as delinquency, truancy and scholastic failure remove the person from the setting and deprive him of its multiple services.

Behavior preempts, and maladaptive behavior does so by inviting punitive responses; it takes persons out of circulation and makes them unavailable for scrutiny. The system's attention, and its response, are drawn to the act rather than to the person who commits it. Due process demands this approach because otherwise we could adjudge the person guilty because he has a pattern of transgressing, rather than because of evidence relating to his transgression. We also risk penalizing the person for past behavior (or worse, for past propensities) for which he has already been punished or exonerated.

The stance makes legalistic sense, but forecloses a promising avenue for addressing maladaptiveness. An example is that of police officers who amass citizen complaints or who become involved in conflicts on the street. Due process demands that each incident in which such an officer becomes involved is separately assessed, with careful inattention to other incidents in which the officer has been involved. This result is fair in terms of disciplinary processing, but creates blindness to the evidence that could help us understand the officer. It means that we must disregard a specifiable pattern of maladaptation where it exists, even if we could (hypothetically) address the pattern, save the officer's career, avoid grief to future beneficiaries of the officer's attentions, and save the police costly law suits and public relations debacles.

Police departments attest to the fact that the problem, as delineated, is real.[18] Fortunately there is a solution that addresses the problem, which leaves due process inviolate but responds to the officer as well as to his behavior.

### Behavior Control and Self-Control

The formula which permits us to address the problem officer's problem creates a two-tier system. It presumes that (1) the culpability oriented disciplinary process can run its course until it results in a finding and disposition; (2) once this juncture is reached, the disciplinary process can be supplemented by a second process, which asks different questions, with different goals in mind; (3) the officer who is targeted by the first process becomes a participant in the second process; (4) unlike the first process the second process is concerned with understanding why the officer does what he does, and with helping him to behave differently if he elects to behave differently; (5) while the first process centers on the last incident with which the officer has been charged, the second process is concerned with reviewing a number of incidents in which the officer has been involved, searching for patterning and consistency in these incidents; (6) the first process is public and risk-laden, while the second is private and has no adverse repercussions; (7) the second process (unlike the first) is concerned with the officer's future behavior and makes provision for reviews and feedback sessions.

The strategy has been deployed with no need for professional involvement other than at its inception.[19] This was the case because the approach relied on a peer review panel of patrolmen, many of who were problem officers who had themselves been *reformed* by the process. Despite (or because) of this staffing pattern, the experiment showed success, with marked diminution of problem arrests and conflicts with citizens.[20]

The reason for alluding to this experience (to which we shall return) is to point up the fact that nonmental health problems can be addressed by expanding the behavior control process rather than by expanding the domain of pathology-related services. There are advantages to the first procedure compared to the latter: (1) the client's role is a more dignified one, in that the person becomes a *student* of his behavior rather than a *patient*; (2) the experience of non-professionals who observe behavior in its context becomes invoked, and such persons gain an opportunity to think about behavior they observe, to understand it better, and to expand their involvement; (3) the process makes disciplining less mindless, and gives those who must run the process new options to address problems they feel they are not addressing through punishment of behavior. According to Vernon Fox, they "must be prepared to understand human behavior, rather than trying to judge the amount of pressure necessary to keep a man in line."[21]

### The Role of Mental Health Experts

The option, paradoxically, opens new roles for mental health professionals, who often feel that they operate in circumscribed ghettoes. A survey in federal prisons, for example, found that psychologists reported that "they were not being allowed to participate enough in the correctional process," while "administrators/managers requested (from psychologists) more involvement in the overall correctional process through consultation, staff training, and general program development."[22] Clinicians on occasion train nonprofessional colleagues, but the way they do so (through abnormal psychology lectures, listings of "symptoms" or "cues to mental illness") presupposes that answers to motivational questions exist in consumable form.

With respect to maladaptation, the clinician does not have ready-made diagnoses or prescriptions he can disseminate. The clinician's role as trainer must therefore be more modest, but it can also be more exciting. One way of defining this role is as follows:

> As a trainer, the psychologist has the job of preparing prison staff to solve human relations and mental health problems they encounter at work. This function may be exercised if the psychologist is familiar with the gamut of on-the-job problems that arise in the institution, taps the ingenuity of staff members in working out innovative solutions, and designs learning experiences that are dramatic, realistic, and compatible with relevant theory and data. This is a stiff prescription, but it does not pose impossible tasks. . . . It entails tapping the problem-solving skills of other staff members, which engenders mutual respect and colleagueship. It finally means devising nonclassroom learning experiences, including role-playing, the use of critical incidents, and the deployment of

supervised inmate-staff confrontations. Good training may also involve trainees in institutional research exercises that sharpen their information-gathering skills and correct for stereotypes of other staff members and inmates. Such exercises may include some that are clinically relevant, such as interviewing inmates who are under stress or participants in violent confrontations.[23]

This definition of training borders on what is called consultation, though the latter presupposes a continuing relationship and some sort of collaborative (team) activity:

Where the therapist cannot treat, he or she can often help exercise the function indirectly by helping other staff (or the inmate's peers) to diagnose and address inmate problems. The psychologist may do so by working with a given staff member of peer group, by linking staff groups, and by experimenting, where possible, with "teaming" of the sort that is popular, in theory at least, in hospital settings. A team member is not a ghetto resident, nor an authority figure, nor a person who "does his thing" under different auspices in reshaped groups. A team is a functional unit designed to address the unique problems posed by a client. The membership includes whatever persons (psychiatrist, chaplain, fellow-inmates, etc.) seem to be serving the interest of the client. Ideally the team also includes the client, who must not be an object dissected in absentia in a democratic version of a case conference.[24]

A third role for mental health experts is a catalytic role, and it has to do with facilitating self-diagnosis among maladaptive persons. It is this role (which we shall describe in more detail later) that requires the most self-effacement of professionals, because the client becomes his own clinician. Albert Bandura refers to this process in the following terms:

Habitual patterns of behavior become so routinized that people often act without much awareness of what they are doing. If they observe their behavior and the circumstances under which it occurs, they begin to notice recurrent patterns. By analyzing regularities in the co-variation between situations and their thoughts and actions, people can identify the psychologically significant features of their social environment that serve as instigators for them. For those who know how to alter their behavior, the self-insights so gained can set in motion a process of corrective change.

Efforts to unravel the causes of behavior traditionally rely upon incomplete and hazy reconstructions of past events. Systematic self-observation provides a self-diagnostic device for gaining a better sense of what conditions lead one to behave in certain ways. Diagnostic self-monitoring need not be confined simply to observing natural occurrences. Significant determinants can be identified more effectively through personal experimentation. By systematically varying things in their daily lives and recording the accompanying personal changes, people can discover how those factors influence their psychological functioning and sense of well-being. . . . A science of self can be partly based on systematic self-study.[25]

In our last chapter we turn to a consideration of how this can occur in the prison.

## Notes

1. J. Block, *Lives through Time*. Berkeley, Cal.: Bancroft Books, 1971, p. 12.
2. G. W. Allport, *Becoming: Basic Considerations for a Psychology of Personality*. New Haven: Yale University Press, 1955, p. 23.
3. Wilson and Herrnstein note that "criminal behavior depends as much or more on age than on any other demographic characteristic—sex, social status, race, family configuration, etc.—yet examined by criminologists." (Wilson and Herrnstein, chapter 2, note 3, p. 126).
4. K. E. Moyer, *Violence and Aggression: A Physiological Perspective*. New York: Paragon House, 1987.
5. Wilson and Herrnstein, chapter 2, note 3, p. 147.
6. Ibid.
7. J. Block, note 1, supra, p. 149.
8. J. Loevinger, "The meaning and measurement of ego development", *American Psychologist*, 1966, *21*, 195–206. For a more general discussion of consistency in personality development, see J. Loevinger and E. Knoll, "Personality: Stages, traits and self," *Annual Review of Psychology*, 1983, 34, 195–222.
9. J. Block, note 1, supra, pp. 249–250.
10. A. Bandura, *Social Foundations of Thought and Action: A Social Cognitive Theory*. Englewood Cliffs, N.J.: Prentice Hall, 1986, p. 248.
11. Sykes, Intro., note 12, Goffman, Intro., note 13.
12. Bandura, note 10, supra, p. 33.
13. H. Toch, *Coping with Noncoping Convicts*. Address to the Bellevue Forensic Psychiatry Fiftieth Anniversary Symposium, November 5, 1983. The transcribed text derives from a Workshop on the Disturbed Disruptive Inmate for the New York State Department of Correctional Services underwritten by the National Institute of Corrections, Federal Bureau of Prisons.
14. G. W. Allport, *Pattern and Growth in Personality*. New York: Holt, Rinehart and Winston, 1961, pp. 363–364. See also, H. Toch, "True to you, darling, in my fashion: The notion of contingent consistency," in A. Campbell and J. J. Gibbs, eds., *Violent Transactions: The Limits of Personality*. London: Basil Blackwell, 1986.
15. K. Lewin, "Group decision and social change," in T. M. Newcomb and E. L. Hartley et. al., eds., *Readings in Social Psychology*. New York: Holt and Company, 1947. The same point, of course, is made by Sigmund Freud. See, for example, S. Freud, *Therapy and Techniques*, New York: Collier Books, 1963.
16. Irwin, chapter 6, note 6, pp. 46ff.
17. Fox, Intro., note, 10. p. 326.
18. The New York City Police Department is currently in litigation with its union over the issue of whether patterns of complaints against officers that have been adjudicated (including unsustained complaints) can be used to locate officers with behavior problems.
19. H. Toch, J. D. Grant and R. Galvin, *Agents of Change: A Study in Police Reform*. Cambridge, Ma.: Schenkman, 1975.

20. J. D. Grant, J. Grant and H. Toch, "Police-citizen conflicts and the decision to arrest," in V. J. Konecni and E. E. Ebbeson, eds., *The Criminal Justice System: A social-psychological Analysis*. San Francisco: Freeman, 1982.
21. Sykes, Intro., note 12, p. 326.
22. R. Powitzky, "Reflections of a prison psychologist," *Quarterly Journal of Corrections*, 1978, *2*, 7–12, p. 9.
23. H. Toch, "The psychological treatment of imprisoned offenders," in J. R. Hays, T. K. Roberts and K. S. Solway, *Violence and the Violent Individual*. New York: Spectrum (SP), 1981, pp. 339–340.
24. Toch, note 23, supra, p. 340.
25. Bandura, note 10, supra, p. 338.

# 14

# Building Coping Competence

Responses to maladaptive behavior can have all sorts of goals, but the most directly relevant objective is that of seeking to enhance the person's coping competence, which means trying to increase the appropriateness and sophistication of his or her behavior in everyday situations.[1]

It is axiomatic that promoting growth experiences in people must begin "where they are at." Such modest beginnings may require removing persons from situations with which they cannot cope and placing them in less demanding environments which pose fewer challenges to their coping skills. The next task is to create a set of graduated demands each person *can* meet, until a hypothetical level of difficulty is reached beyond which development cannot take place. This endpoint is one we should rarely achieve, however, because it requires that we take the position that there is no further room for personal development. Criteria we can instead employ have to do with assessing when a person's level of functioning has become congruent with a given set of demands (say, a special classroom or a sheltered workshop), which suggests that the person can now face a more complex set of demands (such as a regular classroom with a resource room or a halfway house) with some chance of survival or mastery. Such decisions are judgment calls that must be calculated to provide maximum challenge with minimal risk to enhance the person's chances of success and reduce his or her chances of failures as much as possible.[2]

Other components of a graduated strategy have to do with resources and influences that can be brought into play to help the person to evolve new competencies. The aim here must be to promote discontinuance of dysfunctional behavior and to add to the person's repertoire of coping skills. These undertakings are separable, but attempting the first task without addressing the second invites the person ultimately to regress, because recidivism is often the only alternative to resourcelessness.

The danger of such consequences of not evolving new coping strategies is worth underlining because it not only applies to the prevailing approaches we have discussed (the disciplinary and mental health approaches), but it also holds for the deployment of our proposed intervention (self-study) as a self-sufficient strategy.

Mental health approaches are concerned with removing disabling symptoms of emotional disturbance.[3] This strategy works where dysfunctions fit the model of being (1) the result of manifested symptoms superimposed on "normal" behavior which (2) can be dealt with independent of quotidian environmental demands. This would mean that the removal of symptoms allows the unfolding of behaviors that have been superceded by the symptoms, and that the emerging "normal" conduct is sufficiently resilient so that new challenges do not invite resurgent symptoms or new symptoms. These conditions, however, are rarely met, and relapses are frequent where ostensibly recovered patients are still nonresilient and mental health systems do not offer gradations of challenging and supportive environments with the necessary rehabilitative services. A standard egregious arrangement is one that "mainlines" hospital patients into the streets on a sink-or-swim basis, with a lifeline consisting of uninviting outpatient services, such as medication. Another vacuum has to do with the unavailability of waystations between the street and the hospital for those who suffer from incipient difficulties.

The exclusivity of the concern with removing dysfunctional behavior (as opposed to a parallel concern with enhancing coping competence) is even more characteristic of disciplinary strategies, which explicitly seek to discourage undesired conduct. The disciplinary approach invokes painful or unpleasant experiences to communicate to a person that his or her behavior is unwelcome to other persons in the community. The assumption is deterrent, but a secondary benefit of the approach is that it isolates maladaptive persons to reduce the impact of their behavior on other persons by exiling or sequestering them.

With regard to the prison, Vernon Fox has complained that "in the majority of adult penal institutions in the United States, psychological and social treatment ceases when the rules are violated, and the offenders are placed in solitary confinement or in other punishment status." Fox points out that there is a "dilemma" in a policy of "withdrawing treatment facilities from those who, by their very behavior, have demonstrated that they need treatment most."[4]

Behavior control may, of course, in some instances constructively affect conduct. But we have recorded many instances in which this strategy has not worked, or has proved counterproductive. In such instances it would not be unreasonable to attempt a different strategy, which combines self-examination with the rehearsal of more effective approaches to life situations, including those one can test in the prison. We assume that the offender can become a participant in this self-reform strategy, and that maladaptive person's intelligence and resolve can be harnessed in the service of change. This participatory component may strike some as a naive approach to take with persons who have behavior problems, but Bandura has pointed out that

> according to the basic tenet of cognitive therapy, to alter how people behave one must alter how they think. To endow thought with causal efficacy need not imply a unidirectional cognitive determinism. Although thought enters into the determination of action, obviously action is not governed solely by thought. Nor is faulty thought necessarily best modified by talk alone.
>
> There is a common misconception that the modality of treatment must match the modality of dysfunction: Behavioral dysfunctions presumably require an action-oriented treatment; emotional distress requires an emotive-oriented treatment; and faulty thinking requires a cognitively oriented treatment. In fact, powerful experiences can effect changes in all modalities of functioning—motor, cognitive, and affective. . . . In short, the strength of influences rather than the modality in which they are conveyed is more likely to determine the scope of change.[5]

In arguing that our approach can create such change experiences, we start by assuming that understanding behavior patterns in the way we have described them is a process that can be shared with chronic maladaptors, if one can convince them to engage in systematic self-study.[6] We assume that the best vehicle to promote self-study is to create a special setting—a group of the offender's peers with whom he can share perceptions of his own behavior—with the goal of helping the offender to control his behavior.

Participation in self-study is possible and useful where the offender

- has important experiences to offer the participant group,
- where his experience is an asset rather than a liability,
- where improvements benefit both the person and the setting.[7]
- where the person is motivated to concentrate on his problem,
- where increased understanding is possible, and
- where the person's self-image is enhanced rather than degraded by self-analysis.

The self-study process presupposes that a person who has experienced a problem can bring "local wisdom" to bear that can contribute to the resolution of the problem. But how do we get a serious troublemaker to engage in the trouble's solution?

There are two related initiation problems that must be addressed. One is how to obtain the involvement of the offender in a process that he may find at once unfamiliar, threatening and demanding. We cannot assume, of course, that one can succeed in every instance, but offering the person an experience which makes him an object of interest and concern provides a plausible approach to the issue of motivation. In self-analysis, the subject, one's own behavior, is of consuming interest. It also helps that a person discovers to his surprise that he is not defined as a target for the punitive or controlling action of others, but as providing content from which he and his peers can learn.

A later incentive to participation emerges if and when the program candidate becomes aware of his own contribution to the difficulties he has encountered. This process is illustrated by John Lochman of Duke University, who has designed a group-centered program for violently disruptive students. Lochman notes that such youngsters often know that their losses of temper are liabilities. In case the point escapes them, Lochman reinforces it by appealing to their own cherished values: "We tell the boys that if another kid gets them so mad they blow up, then the kid is controlling them," said Dr. Lochman. "We tell them they can win by not getting mad."[8]

A contingent incentive can be mobilized when the person, however tentatively, considers the prospect that he can expand his repertoire of response options by participating in the program. This element is illustrated by the Duke University program's emphasis on social skills training:

> "We tell the boys that this is a group that will teach them how to better handle situations that get them frustrated or angry." Dr. Lochman said." We give them new ways to respond: instead of getting angry, for instance, they can try to come back at a kid in a playful way. . . . One large problem for these children is that they can't think of a friendly response that preserves their own dignity and self-image."[9]

The other initiation problem is how to create a group culture for obtaining understanding through mutual trust and sharing. This calls for starting small and building a nucleus of committed participants with peer leadership potential. Once such a culture nucleus is established, initial peer leadership becomes less essential, and the enterprise can gain respectability, or at least acceptance.

The beauty of the pattern-analysis procedure is that it not only groups people in terms of their coping problems but provides criteria for assessing their regenerative behavior, which makes it an adaptable screening-in device for developing a nucleus culture. A pool of potential participants can be identified over whatever nominating strategy is compatible with the institution's needs. The actual selection of group members, as a first step to their participation in the program (let us call it a self-management study center), is easily controlled by the program's staff, while the performance of the candidate in shared reviews of their own behavior is both a screening-in or acculturation process and a screening-out or rejection process for those who are ultimately deemed not able to contribute to culture buildup.

### Antecedents of the Proposed Approach

1. *Use of Inmates and Staff.* Twenty-five years ago, two of the authors of this book ran a pair of companion NIMH-sponsored studies that grew out of a 1963 national conference.[10]

   The first of these studies, the Offender New Careers Project, was intended to train prison inmates as paraprofessionals who would work, after their release on parole, with California state correctional agencies.[11] The second project included offenders and ex-offenders as individual and group interviewers in a study of recidivistic violence.[12]

   The idea of using ex-offenders to work with correctional staff to bring about change in prison programs was a chancy one at best, and with a change in the external political climate it became close to impossible. Fortunately, the emergence of Economic Opportunity Act programs allowed ex-offenders to move to the national scene into reform efforts that tried to create new roles for the poor in public service careers. The new careers movement of the late sixties and seventies offered not only offenders but also other persons screened out of legitimate participation in society an opportunity to make meaningful contributions to the solution of problems with which they had firsthand experience.[13]

   Our recidivistic violence study provided another kind of role. The offenders who participated in this study made splendid coresearchers, working in partnership with persons who brought more respectable academic credentials, but less experience, to the problem.[14] In fact, several of our nonprofessional colleagues in this research could have qualified as subjects for the study.

   It is particularly out of this latter experience which included a concern with patterns of prison violence, that we concluded that pattern analysis is a safe and sane approach to self-study: safe because it is relatively nonthreatening to the inmate, sane because it does not threaten the institution with reorganizations of its operation.

2. *The Peer Review Model.* Following our study of violence, we moved to the applied problem of trying to reduce violence between police officers and citizens in a large urban community.[15] We worked with problem police officers, men who had been involved in unusually high numbers of confrontations with citizens, and we set them the task of developing

approaches to the reduction of violent incidents involving the police and citizens. The officers developed the police peer review process to which we have referred (chapter 13), which became a part of the police department's ongoing operation. It may be worthwhile to describe this process here, for it forms the groundwork for the prison operation we shall outline below:

In its original form, the review panel consisted of the following stages:

(1) *The necessity for the panel is documented.* Typically, the process would be initiated when an officer reaches a threshold number of incidents on an up-to-date inventory of violent involvements. The number used would not be the number of raw incidents, but a refined index in which the active role of the subject had been established. It would exclude situations in which unwilling participation had been secured. It would include instances in which another officer had filed a report despite the subject's active role in bringing violence about.

Other ways of mobilizing the review panel would include requests by supervisors or by the subjects themselves. In such cases, however, the record would have to bear out the man's eligibility by showing a substantial number of recent involvements.

(2) *A preparatory investigation for the interview is conducted.* Data relating to the subject's performance on the street is obtained from available secondary sources. This includes interviews with supervisors, reports by peers and all information on record. The investigation culminates in a "study group" where panelists formulate hypotheses and draft questions that streamline the panel session.

(3) Then comes the interview itself, which can be subdivided into three stages:

(a) *Key incidents are chronologically explored,* including not only actions taken by all persons involved in the incident, but also their perceptions, assumptions, feelings and motives.

(b) *The summation of these data in the form of common denominators and patterns* is undertaken primarily by the subject, with participation by the panelists. An effort is made to test the plausibility and relevance of the hypothesized patterns by extrapolating them into other involvements.

(c) *The discussion of the pattern* occurs last and includes tracing its contribution to violence. This stage features the exploration of alternative approaches that might be conducive to more constructive solutions.[16]

Note that the inception of our group for problem officers required a complete reversal of the subcultural position that, like offenders, each officer must do his own time. The officers in our study themselves developed the idea for the Peer Review Panel, designed the procedures, identified the problem participants, and conducted the panels. They also drafted proposals for programs concerned with landlord/tenant disputes, domestic discord, communications, and training and assisted in their implementation, again demonstrating that individuals who had been designated as problem persons can develop creative and effective solutions to problems of which they had been a part.

3. *Social Learning.* During the time we were concerned with the resocialization of inmates—in fact, before the inmate studies were begun—we had begun collaborating with Maxwell Jones, a British psychiatrist who had been working with maladapted people in settings that he described as therapeutic communities, in which patients and staff jointly addressed problems of living together as a way of developing increased personal and social competence.[17]

Social learning of the sort discussed by Jones centers on constructive feedback about a person's maladaptive behavior (particularly maladaptive behavior that causes problems in his relationships with others) which provides "live" learning content for social learning (therapeutic) groups. It is a short step from this view to envisage a group that does not center on day-to-day feedback relating to single instances of behavior, but on the reviews of *patterns* of maladaptive behavior which can be deduced from a series of incidents in which the person has created difficulties both for himself and for others.

4. *Self-management and Perceived Control.* A pattern-analytic self-study approach has other benefits, some of which have been demonstrated in an emerging multidisciplinary field of study concerned with issues of choice and perceived control. A summary of the research implications of this work states:

> It is now known that control and choice, however they are operationalized, almost invariably have good effects. Moreover, this has been shown to be the case for a wide variety of situations and manipulations. For example, both people and animals are happier, healthier, more active, solve problems better, and feel less stress when they are given choice and control. . . . We are hard pressed to think of another area of psychology that has provided so many potential benefits for mankind in so short a time. The psychology of control and power has implications for cardiovascular functioning, retardation, IQ performance, job satisfaction, learning ability, child-rearing practices, therapy, pyschopathology, poverty, and the lives of the elderly as well as the lives of college students.[18]

Studies of dependent populations other than offenders have been summarized by Ellen Langer as follows:

> I have been struck by the apparent relationship between the individuals' involvement in whatever task we placed before them and the degree to which they seemed to improve both psychologically and physically. The process of mindful involvement is control. And control in this form is consistently potent.[19]

Langer makes a clear distinction between the outcome of a decision (shared or not) and involvement in the process of decision making. There may well be a positive impact (e.g., a successful self-management strategy) derived from a specific decision process (e.g., an incident pattern analysis) but, whether or not this outcome occurs, there is likely to be enhanced self-esteem from the person's involvement in the (mindful decision making) process itself.

Langer cites many ingenious studies and experiments to show that these are independent consequences. Both can and should contribute to the development of self-management skills.

## A Self-Management Study Center

The goal of a self-management study center would be the creation of a fostering and supportive climate, in an appropriate setting, for the shared self-study, decision making, and understanding necessary for the development of self-management skills.

What do we have a right to expect from such a center? *First,* chronic maladapters should develop an understanding of and a strategy for managing their own patterns of conduct. *Second,* the participants should increase their general social coping competence, including reading, writing, and thinking skills. *Third,* there should be improvement in the participants' self-image. Not only should participants become more competent, they should also *feel* more competent. Feelings of competence can be expected to reduce anxieties, depression, and defensiveness, and allow more freedom to think, understand and grow. *Fourth,* beyond the profit derived by individual participants, we can expect contributions to the development of our knowledge about maladaptation as pattern analytic schemes are updated and expanded and as management strategies are developed for different kinds of incident patterns and for different kinds of settings. Three kinds of knowledge should evolve: institution-specific understandings and specific how-tos (local wisdom); contributions to general concepts and theories concerning the nature of prison incidents and their management (very much including, but not limited to self-management); and contributions to the psychology of social behavior in general.

A central theme of a self-management center would be the interaction of local wisdom (experience) with general (academic) knowledge. Resource documents, reports, articles and books, as well as diaries, files, and chronological accounts of experience could be maintained. General knowledge could be fed into the study of incident patterns, as it is appropriate, and into studies of incident-prone settings.[20] At the same time, local knowledge could be used to modify and develop social science principles and theories. This process could enhance a natural (and needed) interaction between the information derived from the institutional setting and that available elsewhere, including in other institutional settings. Further, such cross-fertilization would fit with current philosophy of science approaches to the nature of reality and the limits of theory in specific (local) behavior prediction and control.[21]

Concern with the specific situation (local wisdom) is the essence of action research or participatory research efforts.[22] There is a temptation among participation researchers to define their work as a separate paradigm from established "objective" research.[23] However, a case can and should be made for a mutually enhancing relationship between locally applied and general knowledge. In our case, this point not only holds for the information to be obtained about maladaptive behavior, but for the knowledge developed concerning the establishment and expansion of the self-management approach.

### Operation of the Self-management Program

The inmates at issue could be selected by disciplinary hearing officers or other custody staff,[24] though nominations could originate elsewhere, such as through statistical reviews of incident patterns. Program participation *must be voluntary* on the part of the inmate,[25] but it might involve suspension of disciplinary penalties as an incentive.

The groups of inmates in the program could be staffed by two-person teams consisting of a mental health staff member and a corrections officer. At later stages, inmates drawn from among program graduates could become third members of the staff team, but full participation in center activities would be required from each inmate member throughout the program.

The program would be carried out in small groups, not to exceed eight members, including staff. These groups could initially focus on reviews (such as ours) of prison disciplinary incidents, in an effort to define individual patterns of maladaptive inmate involvements. The review could then be expanded to include incidents that are not fully described in documents such as warden's cards, in order to enhance the pool of data available to the groups. Pattern analysis would be followed by the design and rehearsal of alternative approaches to social encounters, and by periodic review and reevaluation of behavioral approaches over a period of months.[26]

As we now think of the sequence, there would be eight steps in which the inmates could engage in order to become full participants in the program:

(1) nomination, volunteering, and selection
(2) orientation, group formation and preparation
(3) preliminary pattern analysis for each of the three to five inmate participants in the group
(4) role and reverse role-playing of representative incidents by and with each participant
(5) development of an incident prevention strategy for and by each offender
(6) setting of an early (10 days?) reconvening date to verify application of the behavior strategy in regular prison settings
(7) reconvening for a quality control session (within three months?) to review performance and to provide feedback
(8) development of an extended strategy and a quality control procedure for each participant.

Upon completion of step 5 (the development of an incident prevention strategy), the offender would become a probationary center participant. He would then sign a contract with his group specifying his and the group's commitments for the operation of the strategy he has planned. The importance of this step has been highlighted as follows by Bandura:

> When the enactive part of the treatment is implemented only verbally, corrective courses of action are structured for persons to pursue, but they are left to their own devices to carry them out. It is one thing to prescribe corrective action; it is another thing to get people to carry it out, especially when it involves onerous or threatening aspects. The successes achieved will depend on a number of factors: the extent to which individuals are provided with the cognitive and social skills and the self-beliefs of efficacy required to perform effectively, judicious selection and structuring of performance tasks to disconfirm misbeliefs and to expand competencies, incentives to put behavioral prescriptions into practice, and social supports for personal change. . . . Conditions conducive to personal change are more reliably achieved by enlisting the aid of significant others in the treatment. In fact, when enactive modes of treatment are well developed, nonprofessionals can serve as well or better than professionals in guiding mastery experiences that promote rapid change.[27]

Graduation to probationary status would symbolize a key move in the offender's participation, commitment and ownership in the program, because it would put the person on record as intending to fulfill his behavioral contract with the support of his group. This would be a strong indication that both the person's commitment and the integrity of the culture are plausible. It would also supply a shared set of activities for the group members, because the task of monitoring behavior would provide both the participant and the group members with a means for the quality control of their enterprise.

The specific commitments that are undertaken could be as simple as exercises for reducing acute anxiety, or as complicated as the development of a special self-help group for inmates with comparable incident patterns. The rehearsed behavior could include self-control routines, actions which the person derives from role playing and shared thinking of the group about just what sets him off when. These self-management responses to incident cues could be a "time out" session, a memorized talk to oneself (counting to ten or its equivalent), contacting a previously identified supportive other, working out, counseling, sharing with peer-inmate counselors, involvement in program development or conflict negotiation of mediation, AA-type procedures such as apologizing and seeking a fresh start in one or more relationships, scheduled and/or emergent encounters, including conflict situations. The behavior at issue *must* be tasks the offender understands and in which he is willing to engage as part of his own self-management.

Two kinds of quality control must be undertaken. One concerns the offender's strategy—what does he say he will do, by what time, and does he get it done? The other concerns the center's development, operation and effectiveness. While the latter would require some external observation, a major part of both kinds of quality control could be conducted as team projects by the center's participants.

When any participant moves beyond step 5, he would be expected to engage in other activities of the center, to share in its housekeeping, social structure, and educational activities. There could be a twenty-four-hour-a-day routine of study and the maintenance of living space, including a daily living-learning session for handling interpersonal (staff and staff/inmate) issues.

The center should have its own (reasonably isolated) living and work quarters. Although the availability of bed space is always an institution problem, it is important that there be some potential for expanding center space as the self-study culture expands. The center could start with, say, ten beds (enough for two study groups) which would be filled in one week through the initial selection process. The ten could be expanded to twenty over the next three weeks.

If the program is to function as a living unit, expansion beyond twenty beds or so is undesirable. However, a cadre of inmates drawn from one unit could help to form a second unit, which in turn could be expanded to twenty. The center could thus end up serving forty inmates, with further expansion depending on the strength and effectiveness of the culture developed in the center.

Each participant must have a full day's schedule built into his self-management strategy. Commitments would include, but would not be limited to, participation in his own group and in teams concerned with the operation of the living unit and the center (such as concern with the infiltration of gangs or cliques in the center, victim-predator relationships, the use of educational resources, housekeeping organization and operation).

A typical day in the self-management center for a participant who has reached stage 5 (that is, who has developed his own incident-prevention strategy) might look like this:

6:00 A.M.– 8:00 A.M.   Housekeeping and breakfast
8:00 A.M.–10:00 A.M.   Reading/writing tutorial
10:00 A.M.–12:00 P.M.   Serve as a member of a pattern-analysis team considering a new potential center participant
12:00 P.M.– 1:00 P.M.   Lunch
1:00 P.M.– 4:00 P.M.   Work with a project team developing a scenario for a TV tape showing the operation of the center
4:00 P.M.– 6:00 P.M.   Recreation
6:00 P.M.– 7:00 P.M.   Dinner
7:00 P.M.– 9:00 P.M.   Living/learning session (group discussion of interpersonal problems within the living unit)
9:00 P.M.–10:00 P.M.   Reading and homework

We have noted in chapter 12 that educational experiences can play an important role in reversing chronic patterns of maladaptation. Education—the improvement of reading and writing skills and related knowledge—could be enhanced through tutorial support. Although professional education resources should be available, the self-development cause is best advanced when inmates work with peer (inmate) tutors. There may well be confined professional educators who could merge these roles.

### Organizational Development Issues

Inherent in the center's operation would be the development of resources for its own modification and expansion. The incident pattern analyses done in this study offer an initial group of protocols, provide a classification scheme, and contribute coder experiences in the sharing of perceptions which could assist the staff who serve as founders for such a center.[28]

Once started, however, the center must become an integrated component of the prison organization rather than an "innovation ghetto" because even success can breed suspicion, distrust and competitiveness.

A central survival theme of the center could be "positive, helpful participation," which is the converse of maladaptive behavior. The approach used with inmates can be expanded to the center's relations with the rest of the institution, and particularly with staff who are concerned with behavior-control problems; but eagerness to work with one's host institution must not negate the first priority for an effective center. An initial climate of trust and commitment must be established before the center can have any real effectiveness to demonstrate and before it is entitled to expand. Though organizational understanding and support must be established before a center can begin operating at all, officials cannot allow—in the name of helpfulness to the host institution—the premature "dumping" of notorious problem cases into the center before an effective self-management climate is developed. Early and consistent mutual understanding is needed to allow the development and maintenance of a helping relationship between the center, the institution and the system, while at the same time protecting the center's precariously evolving nucleus culture.

Finally, it is possible to think of a self-management center contributing to the development of an informal resource network involving other self-study and participatory research programs. The availability of computer communication makes such exchanges easier on a day-to-day basis, and the knowledge that one is not alone provides feedback and support that helps to build program commitment.

### Behavior Self-Management as a Modality

The approach we have delineated illustrates a modality of change which differs from other approaches in that (1) it involves the maladaptive person as participant rather than as *client;* (2) it does not require a definition of the person's problem (such as substance abuse, mental illness or learning disability) to define the service he or she receives, (3) it provides for gradations of environment in which to *test* developing competence; (4) it mobilizes teams of staff members, including staff primarily concerned with behavioral and mental health problems; (5) it relies on group process and group thinking to buttress staff influence, and (6) it accomodates tailor-made interventions to address individual patterns of maladaptation.

One advantage of the approach is that it circumvents organizational interface problems in service delivery networks which are detrimental to those who fall in definitional penumbras and became members in residual or "garbage pail" categories. An example of such a category is special education, which inherits a melange of behavioral problems by default, despite efforts to define the problem area (learning disability) to which programming is in theory addressed.[29]

In other areas we find that definitions of problems evolve to accommodate available services, rather than vice versa. "Homeless persons" thus become "emotionally disturbed homeless persons" as psychiatric out-reach efforts evolve, and to the extent to which they do. Similarly:

Children considered emotionally disturbed in Delaware or Utah, where that handicap is liberally defined, could find themselves instantly "cured" by moving to Mississippi or Arkansas, where the definitions are more narrow.[30]

In the prison, epidemiological estimates of mental illness can vary with the availability of mental health services,[31] though we assume that the latter would be measured responses to estimates of the prevalence of pathology. The fact may seem to reflect cynicism, but does not, in that definitional lines, except at extremes, are actually arbitrary. Moreover, generosity of definition need not translate into appropriateness of re-sponse, particularly when services remain narrow-gauged, while clients suffer from wide ranges of problems and deficits. This fact matters for maladaptive persons, who almost invariably are multi-problem clients.

We have noted that maladaptive persons not only *have* diverse problems, but *constitute* diverse problems in their environments. The disruptive impact of maladaptiveness ranges from mildly annoying (as with indivi-duals who clutter up landscapes or follow vagrant lifestyles) through very serious affronts to the community, including assaultiveness and predation.

We have mentioned that such disruptive effects of personal maladapta-tion frequently preempt attention. They foreclose the examination of the dynamics of maladaptive behavior, and prevent responses that can address these dynamics. Where responses do occur, combined helping-punishing strategies are frequently deployed—such as counseling with disciplinary action—or the person can find himself shuttled between junctures at which services are rendered and those at which punishment is inflicted.

The problem of choice of responses is compounded by the fact that deficit-related service delivery seemingly adjudges the person not respon-sible for conduct that is a "product" of some disabilities, whereas punish-ment credits the person with sometimes implausible exercise of volition. Service delivery can also be adjudged to reflect empathy, and punitive responses can be seen as expressions of vengeance. The choice of re-sponse can thus be deemed discriminatory if apparently comparable be-havior is differently reacted to. This enhances the plausibility of such charges as that of an angry newspaper reader who writes that

for too long, black men and women who engaged in deviant behavior because of emotional and mental handicaps have been perceived to be bad, not mad. Whites, on the other hand, under similar circumstances, were apt to be consid-ered mad, not bad.[32]

Substituting the concept of "maladaptive" behavior for the bad/mad, responsible/irresponsible dichotomy reduces the need to undersell either the impact or the motive of conduct. Responses to maladaptive behavior such as those we have suggested attend to behavior impact, and can include custody staff (or their equivalents) as members of treatment teams. Punitive dispositions will at times be suspended, but this fact does not carry exculpatory implications, because, first, addressing motivational (why?) questions means that we must implicitly consider the impact of the behavior (what? questions) which is to be explained; second, self-studying conduct is impossible without considering its dysfunctional results, including damage done to others, and finally, critical reviews are no less uncomfortable (and sometimes more uncomfortable) than the pay-as-you-go complacency of being punished.

What may matter most, however, is that regenerative enterprises can interdict more personal disruptiveness than punitive approaches. Whereas punishment responds to past harm, it need offer no respite—other than through temporary incapacitation—from future reoffending. Personal reform, however, interrupts maladaptive careers and can thus prevent much harm to the community over long stretches of time.

## Notes

1. Johnson (Intro., note 3) refers to this goal as "facilitating mature coping." By "mature coping" among prisoners Johnson means

   (1) Dealing directly with one's problems, using the resources legitimately at one's disposal; (2) refusing to employ deceit or violence (other than in self defense); and (3) building mutual and supportive relationships with others. Inmates who cope maturely come to grips with problems in prison living, and they do so without violating the rights of others to be safe in their person and in their property. More generally, they treat others, staff and inmates alike, as fellow human beings who are possessed of dignity and worth. (pp. 4–5)

2. G. W. Fairweather et. al., *Community Life for the Mentally Ill: An Alternative to Institutional Care*. Chicago: Aldine Publishing Company, 1969.

3. There are some mental health experts who do not share this conventional view. Thomas Szasz (1961), chapter 8, note 5) comes closest to outlining a maladaption-centered intervention when he writes that he favors

   abolishing the categories of ill and healthy behavior, and the prerequisite of mental sickness for so-called psychotherapy. This implies candid recognition that we "treat" people by psychoanalysis or psychotherapy not because they are "sick" but rather because: (1) They desire this type of assistance; (2) They have problems in living for which they seek mastery through understanding of the kinds of games which they, and those around them, have been in the habit of playing; and (3) We want and are able to participate in their "education" because this is our professional role. (p. 255)

4. Fox, Intro., note 10, p. 321. Zamble, Porporino and Kalotay (Intro., note 1) have observed that:

> It is a paradox that penal institutions usually have fairly detailed and explicit rules specifying prohibited behaviors with the consequences of their occurrence, but there are no specifications or lists of prosocial behaviors to be encouraged. If the goal of changing behavior is to be taken seriously, the system must formulate a list of desirable behaviors which inmates ought to acquire. For example, inmates should be taught to plan their time and to anticipate the future. One way they could do this to formulate plans for use of their term in prison, normally with help from their C.O.'s they could be rewarded both for formulating the plan and for meeting its objectives (pp. 141–142).

5. Bandura, chapter 13, note 10, p. 519.
6. This attribute constitutes an advantage when one compares a behavior-career-based typology to one that is derived from responses to a personality inventory, such as the MMPI. The results of psychometrically derived typologies can be communicated to persons thus classified, but the rationale for arriving at classifications cannot be shared and internalized by subjects. Interestingly, however, there are similarities and close parallels between some of the patterns we have outlined in this book and those derived from MMPI item clusters. (See E. I. Megargee and M. J. Bohn, *Classifying Criminal Offenders: A New System based on the MMPI*. Beverly Hills: Sage, 1979.)
7. With respect to behavior modification in the prison, for example, an authoritative monograph points out that:

> Persons using behavior modification procedures have been particularly criticized for their attempts to deal with rebellious and nonconformist behavior of inmates in penal institutions. Because the behavioral professional is often in the position of assisting in the management of prisoners whose antagonism to authority and rebelliousness have been the catalyst for conflict within the institution, the distinctions among his multiple functions of therapy, management, and rehabilitation can become blurred, and his allegiance confused.

> Behavior modification programs are intended to give prisoners the opportunity to learn behavior that will give them a chance to lead more successful lives in the world to which they will return, to enjoy some sense of achievement, and to understand and control their own behavior better.

> Behavior modification should not be used in an attempt to facilitate institutionalization of the inmate or to make him adjust to inhumane living conditions. Further, no therapist should accept requests for treatment that take the form "make him 'behave,'" when the intent of the request is to make the person conform to oppressive conditions.

These quotes derive from B. S. Brown, L. A. Wienckowski and S. S. Stolz, *Behavior Modification: Perspective on a Current Issue*. Washington, D.C.: Department of Health, Education and Welfare, NIMH, 1975, pp. 16–17.

8. D. Goleman, "The bully: New research depicts a paranoid, lifelong loser," *New York Times*, April 7, 1987. The same syllogism that is referred to by Lozman appealed to the police groups we have mentioned (Grant et. al., chapter 14, note 20): The groups were taken by the notion that any suspect could control a reactive officer's response by challenging him, thereby motivating the officer to "control" the suspect.

9. *Ibidem.* Differences in level of participation among behavior management strategies may have to do with the degree to which the alternative responses to be rehearsed are "discovered" by the subject, or evolve out of group deliberation, or are introduced by an expert change agent.

10. C. Spencer, ed., *Experiment in Culture Expansion.* Proceedings of Conference on "The use of products of a social problem in coping with the problem." Sacramento, Ca.: Department of Corrections, 1963.

11. J. D. Grant, "From 'living learning' to 'learning to live': An extension of social therapy," In H. Toch, ed., *Therapeutic Communities in Corrections.* New York: Praeger, 1980.

12. Toch, chapter 6, note 3.

13. A. Pearl and F. Riessman, *New Careers for the Poor: The Nonprofessional in Human Service*, New York: Free Press, 1965.

14. H. Toch, "The convict as researcher," *Transaction*, 1967, *9*, 71–75.

15. Toch, Grant, and Galvin, chapter 13, note 20.

16. Ibid., pp. 246–247.

17. M. Jones. *The Therapeutic Community: A New Treatment Method in Psychiatry.* New York: Basic Books, 1953.

18. L. C. Pearlmuter & R. A. Monty. *Choice and Perceived Control.* Hillsdale, N.J.: Erlbaum, 1979, pp. 367–368.

19. E. J. Langer, *The Psychology of Control.* Beverly Hills: Sage, 1983, p. 293.

20. We have suggested elsewhere that the type of research that could directly contribute to reducing prison violence would be a strategy in which "hot spots" and low-violence prison subenvironments are studied with the concerned assistance of staff and inmates who live or work in such settings. (See H. Toch, "Social climate and prison violence," *Federal Probation*, 1978, *42*, 21–25.

21. P. T. Manicas & P. F. Secord, "Implications for psychology of the new philosophy of science," *American Psychologist*, 1983, *38*, 399–413.

22. K. Lewin, "Action research and minority problems" (1946), in K. Lewin, *Resolving Social Conflicts: Selected Papers in Group Dynamics.* New York: Harper and Row, 1948.

23. P. Reason & J. Rowan, eds. *Human Inquiry: A Sourcebook of New Paradigm Research.* New York: Wiley, 1981.

24. Who does the screening of clients into a program of this kind is strategically and conceptually critical. Front line staff (custodial officers or teachers) make ideal nominators of candidates because such staff are in the best position to observe behavior and to identify maladapters who have problems that could be addressed. Persons allotted the responsibility of dispensing disciplinary sanctions are the best sources of referrals because they are in the position of discriminating individuals for whom sanctions are or are not inappropriate. It is also critical that such staff consider the behavior self-management option as supplementary to existing behavior management options, and as a tool that they themselves (as opposed to some bureaucratic entity) can invoke.

    By the same token, the staff members of any program must have flexibility in selecting their candidates from a pool of nominees, so that they can assess the risks to be taken and the appropriateness of their modality to the behavior pattern of their clients. (Risk taking must be especially minimized during the first phases of the program, before its culture is established, but at later junctures risk taking must be rewarded, or staff would tend to "play it safe."

25. Early experiments using behavior modification for dealing with disciplinary problems invited condemnation by insisting that involuntary assignment of clients was not only appropriate but necessary. A founding father of the least popular experiment (whose name was START) maintained that "the basic argument for involuntariness arises from the original idea of such a program"; an expert testifying on behalf of the program complained that "a voluntary program could be expected to be used by those prisoners who find themselves distressed by their situation, not by those who are causing extreme distress to others but are little inconvenienced themselves" (A. F. Scheckenbach, "Behavior modification and adult offenders" [1974] in I. Jacks and S. G. Cox, eds., *Psychological Approaches to Crime and its Correction*. Chicago: Nelson Hall, 1984, p. 468. See note 3 supra.

26. The same sort of sequence has been envisaged in the program design (not implemented) of Special Handling Units established to deal with recalcitrant inmates in Canada. The presumption in the design was that each inmate "would examine his problems with his classification officer, his case manager and possibly with other inmates as identified by the case management team." Based on such problem reviews, the inmate would evolve an individual program plan (IPP) to "evaluate his own progress whilst staff measure his development." Inmates would deal with their problems "through dyads, group settings and individual counseling sessions." They would belong to seven-member groups and participate in activities "to provide opportunities . . . to demonstrate meaningful behavioral change." Provision was made for "regular reviews, carried out every thirty days" (K. McReynolds and J. Vantour, "Inmates in Special Handling Units," Undated unpublished manuscript *cit.* in M. Jackson, *Prisoners of Isolation: Solitary Confinement in Canada*. Toronto: University of Toronto press, 1983, pp. 152–153).

Another Canadian report (Zamble, Porporino, and Kalotay, (Intro., note 1) suggests interventions for inmates who have coping problems that "would include training in ways of analyzing problem situations, formulating effective strategies for changing problems, and evaluating possible responses" (pp. 144–145).

27. Bandura, chapter 13, note 10, p. 520.

28. It goes without saying that the staff cadre must internalize the program's design and insist on having the required facilities and support. Jackson (note 24, supra) illustrates this fact by describing the operation of Special Handling Units, which degenerated into segregation settings because the content of programs was never instituted.

29. C. Connell and L. Mitgang, "Special education has its own problems," (Associated Press), Albany *Times Union*, October 26, 1987.

30. Ibid.

31. M. McCarthy, "Mentally ill and mentally retarded offenders in corrections: A report of a national survey," in *Source Book on the Mentally Disordered Offender*. Washington: National Institute of Corrections, 1985.

32. A. Green, "Reader's Forum," Albany *Times Union*, October 25, 1987.

# Index

Adaptation, 253–55; definition of, 254; explantions of, 251; literature, 258; prevalence of, 254; prison's criterion of, 177; process, xiv–xv. *See also* Adjustment Maladaptation

Adjustment: patterns of, 21, 26; compound problems of, 54. *See also* Adaptation; Coping; Maladaptation

Age: adjustment to prison by, 21, 242, 251; and chronic disruptive behavior, 32; improvement as result of, 242–44, 250–53; and infraction rates, 16–18; and maladaptive behavior, 250–53; as predictor of crime, 250; and prison behavior, 19–20, 22, 46

Aggression: esteem and, 116–19; frustration turn to, 90–94, 107n4; gratifying impulses and, 88–99, 107n4; paranoid, 183–89; predatory, 88–90, 107n4; stress turn to, 94–99. *See also* Violence

Allport, G. W., 249

Asylum arrangement and inmates' improvement, 228–32

Attachment leading to improvement of behavior, 217–20

Autonomy. *see* Pursuing autonomy

**Bandura, Albert,** 253, 255, 263, 268, 275

Behavior, xiii, xvii, adaptive and maladaptive, xv; age and, 19–20, 22, 32; control and self-control, 261–262; deviant, 259; disturbed-disruptive, 50–53; hospitalized inmates, 40–44; illogical patterns of, xx–xxii; impulsive, as destructive, 85–106; inconsistent, 197–203; infractions and, xvii, 15–22; modification in prison, 281n7, 283nn25, 26; as outcome of personality, 258; of outpatients, 43;

preempts, 260; self-management as a modality of, 278–80, 282n9; staff assessment of, xiii–xiv; study's reliance on, xiii; symptomatic, 51, 53. *See also* Career; Change; Maladaptive behavior

Block, Jack, 249, 252–53

Career: of chronic mental patients, 177; criminal, 39; definition of, 8; disciplinary, of patients, 53–54; jailing as a, 102; maladaptive, 250–53; prison, xi, 8–12, 205; shortened, 174; studies, 8; typology, 23–33, 35nn14, 16, 251

Causes of inmates' improvement, 211–44

Change, 249–50, 252; insight as a tool for, 232–37; instigating. 268, learning and, 20, 253; literature, 258; in maladaptive behavior, 211–44; and maturity, 242, 252; patterns of, in disciplinary rates, 20–21; potential, 252–53; in self-image, 219–20; self-management as a modality of, 278–80; of settings and improvement, 220, 226, 227. *See also* Improvement of inmates

Chronic maladaptors: as a problem for their environment, 279; self-management program for, 274–77; self-study process for, 266–73

Classification of maladaptation: applying the, 77–84; data for the, 204–9; goals of the, 73; nature of the, 70–73; outline of the, 73–77. *See also* Taxonomy

Clemmer, Donald, xii, xxviin6, 34n6

Cohen, Albert, 110

Coping: building competence for, 266–280; and cognition, 153; decreased maladaptiveness as, 253; definitions of, xv, xxviin9, 253; vs. fight-flight, 178–83;

285